THE FUTURE OF

EUROPEAN SECURITY

RESEARCH SERIES / NUMBER 84

THE FUTURE
OF
EUROPEAN SECURITY

Beverly Crawford, Editor

Center for German and European Studies
University of California at Berkeley

Stephen Van Evera, "The Domestic Sources of Peace and War in the New Europe," is adapted from Stephen Van Evera, "Primed for Peace: Europe After the Cold War," *International Security* 15, 3 (Winter 1990/91): 7–57. Used by permission of the publisher, MIT Press Journals.

Library of Congress Cataloging-in-Publication Data

The Future of European security / Beverly Crawford, editor.
    p. cm. — (Research series ; no. 84)
    Includes index.
    ISBN 0-87725-184-3 : $23.50
    1. Europe—National security. I. Crawford, Beverly. II. Series:
Research series (University of California, Berkeley. International and
Area Studies) ; no. 84.
UA646.F87 1992
355'. 03304—dc20   92-6706
                                                  CIP

CONTENTS

ACKNOWLEDGMENTS

This book has been written as a collective effort involving the contributions of many people and organizations. I would especially like to acknowledge the Friedrich Ebert Foundation and the director of its Washington office, Dieter Dettke; the MacArthur Foundation; and the University of California Center for German and European Studies and its director, Richard Buxbaum. Dean Albert Fishlow of International and Area Studies at UC Berkeley offered encouragement and support for this project from its very beginning, and I am especially grateful to him.

John Leslie not only provided valuable research assistance, but also read and offered critical comments and insightful suggestions on all of the chapters. I would also like to thank S. J. Fifer, Syd Mintzer, Susan Overdorf, and Jackie Stevens for their research assistance and for often going the extra mile to help complete this project. Thanks also to Peter Katzenstein for helpful comments and suggestions.

Working with a talented and committed group of people to bring the book to completion has been a great pleasure to me. Peggy Nelson's unflagging assistance in launching the project was invaluable. Shelagh Eldon went beyond the call of duty to manage the manuscript preparation. Bojana Ristich expertly guided the editorial and production process and prepared the index. Jackie Stevens provided valuable editorial assistance. Stephen Pitcher typeset the manuscript and always provided general good cheer. Gail Cook not only gave valuable assistance in the initial stages of the project, but also designed the book's cover.

B. C.

NOTES ON CONTRIBUTORS

BEVERLY CRAWFORD is Lecturer in the Political Economy of Industrial Societies Program, University of California at Berkeley.

EMANUEL ADLER is Professor of International Relations at the Hebrew University of Jerusalem.

ALEXEI B. ARBATOV is Professor and Head of Disarmament Studies, Institute of World Economy and International Relations, Moscow.

VALERIE BUNCE is Professor of Government at Cornell University.

DIETER DETTKE is Executive Director of the Friedrich Ebert Foundation, Washington, D.C.

BARRY EICHENGREEN is Professor of Economics at the University of California at Berkeley.

JOST HALFMANN is Professor of Sociology at the University of Osnabrück.

STEPHEN D. KRASNER is Graham H. Stuart Professor of International Relations at Stanford University.

RICHARD ROSECRANCE is Professor of Political Science at the University of California at Los Angeles.

PETER W. SCHULZE is Senior Research Fellow at the Friedrich Ebert Foundation, London.

JANE M. O. SHARP is Senior Research Fellow at King's College and at the Institute for Public Policy Research, London.

IVAN G. TYULIN is Vice Rector of the State Institute of International Relations, Moscow.

STEPHEN VAN EVERA is Assistant Professor of Political Science at the Massachusetts Institute of Technology.

STEVE WEBER is Assistant Professor of Political Science at the University of California at Berkeley.

CAUSES OF WAR AND THE FUTURE OF PEACE IN THE NEW EUROPE

Beverly Crawford

In 1989 Europe's postwar security system was history. Even before the revolutions in Eastern Europe, the dissolution of the Warsaw Pact, and the unification of Germany, the waning of the cold war in the last half of the 1980s had left Europe with the task of constructing a new security order. By the close of 1991, the civil war in Yugoslavia and the dramatic death of the Soviet Union had transformed Europe from the center of a seemingly stable bipolar world of cohesive sovereign states under two "superpowers" to a region where territorial boundaries and political and ideological identities were dissolving. Moreover, the very existence of the nation-state as the provider of security in many places was in question.

Contested and disappearing boundaries are a potent source of insecurity in international relations and the single most important threat to peace in Europe today. This volume explores how boundary and identity changes on the European continent affect the odds of war and peace there. The contributions analyze the responses to boundary transformation and disappearance and suggest a set of institutional responses to preserve the peace.

The transformation of Europe offers new fuel for the enduring scholarly debate on the causes of war and the prospects for peace in international relations. Our beliefs about the causes of war and peace and our uncertainty about those causes shape the kinds of security arrangements we prefer. Differing perceptions of the security threat in the new Europe are at the root of social and political debates over desired security arrangements and defense expenditures. Indeed the policy relevance of these issues cannot be overstated: faulty security arrangements that give rise to false expectations can exacerbate old conflicts triggering more terrible disputes than would otherwise have arisen.

Given the importance of the links between beliefs about security and institutions needed to provide it, this chapter does three things. It begins by defining the scope of our concern with European security issues. It then turns to an assessment of the conditions in Europe that increase or decrease the odds of peace from each of three theoretical perspectives on international relations. Two of the theories focus on international conditions: the structural realist view sees international economic competition, international economic crisis (such as a worldwide depression), and unstable power balances among states as causes of insecurity in Europe; liberal theories predict that international processes like economic interdependence can mitigate interstate violence. The third perspective focuses on domestic conditions and predicts that the rise of liberal political identities in Eastern Europe and the former Soviet Union will create a foundation for peaceful state behavior. The concluding section examines the role of existing and emerging multilateral European security institutions and how they are linked to these alternative arguments about the future of European security. Finally, it will lay out some criteria by which progress in securing the peace in Europe can be recognized.

DEFINING THE SCOPE OF EUROPEAN SECURITY ISSUES

Because security is an essentially contested concept,[1] the scope of this project requires definition. The essays here are concerned primarily with the phenomenon of war and with the threat, use, and control of military force, both within the expanded area that we call "Europe"—including the nations of Central Europe, Eastern Europe, and the states that were formerly part of the Soviet Union.[2] European security means a set of both global and regional conditions that reduce the odds of a European war or European involvement in international war.

There will, of course, be objections to this narrow definition of security. Military power is not the only means by which security can be assured. Security is threatened in ways that are more indirect and not easily countered by military force.[3] Indeed military force itself can be the most potent threat to security. Uncertainty over boundaries and borders leads analysts and policy makers alike to view many cross-border challenges and risks as security threats. Peter Schulze's essay here, for example, argues that the European security agenda should be opened to include ecological and social issues as well as economic and human rights problems.

Most of these essays, however, base their analyses on more traditional security definitions. As Robert Art has persuasively argued, although military power guarantees neither survival nor prosperity, it is almost always the essential ingredient for both.[4] And although nontraditional security threats may indeed arise, the threat and use of force are at the heart of the security issue in international relations. Although the threat of environmental degradation and challenges posed by trans-boundary social problems— e.g., migration and drug traffic—impinge upon our "security," they are unlikely to lead to interstate violence in Europe.[5] The contributions here focus on those issues likely to lead to war.

VULNERABILITIES AND THREATS

Following this admittedly narrow definition of security, then, let us define the scope of issues which might lead to interstate violence in Europe by making a distinction between vulnerabilities and threats.[6] The source of vulnerability can be found in one's *capabilities* in relation to the capabilities of others; the source of threats can be found in one's *intentions* toward others. In order to reduce relative vulnerabilities, states must implement policies that expand their own military and industrial power, reduce the military and industrial power of others, and reduce their dependence on others. In order to reduce threats, states attempt to affect the intentions of others; traditional means include the negotiation of treaties like arms control or trade agreements.

This distinction is crucial for our efforts to forge a link between theories about the causes of war and policy prescriptions for peace. Those who focus on international causes disagree about the relative weight of vulnerabilities and threats. As we shall see below, struc-

tural realists tend to focus on vulnerability and vulnerability reduction as the central security concern in Europe; they believe that
states will enhance their capabilities to reduce vulnerabilities, and
that they are constantly in the process of measuring the capabilities
of others; indeed war boils down to a dispute about the measurement of vulnerabilities. They further argue that states care more
about relative than absolute gains of interaction because the state
which gains more will be the more powerful. Peace is thus best
preserved by balancing power among states or clarifying unequal
power relationships.

Liberals, in contrast, look to a set of processes and institutions
that shape intentions to reduce the threat of war, despite a potential
lack of clarity abut power positions or vast differences in power.
For example, the United States is a much more powerful state than
Mexico or Canada, but the processes and institutions structuring
the relationships among them reduce the threat of war.

Finally, those who examine the domestic causes of war and
peace also look to the sources of threat rather than vulnerability.
They argue that the nature of states and societies will determine
the intensity of military threat. Peace can be preserved by international measures to shape societies in ways that foster and preserve
peaceful intentions, no matter what the power balance among states
might be. The European region in the post–cold war, post-Communist world offers the student of international relations a new set of
conditions for determining the roles of vulnerability and threat or
capabilities and intentions in setting the odds of international war
and peace.

DISSOLVING AND CONTESTED BOUNDARIES

Despite the traditional framework within which we analyze
security in this volume, the European region as a "laboratory" for
the study of the causes of war and peace suggests a shift in conditions underpinning traditional security studies: the territorial, ideological, and issue boundaries which both guarded and threatened
national security are changing.[7] This has important consequences
for the security function of the state. The responsibility to society
for countering military threats to national security has been lodged

in the state; most studies of "security" take the "state" and its ability to protect its territorial borders as the central focus of analysis.

The triumph of the sovereignty norm among European states in the late nineteenth century led to an important condition for the state's protection of its territory. As the rules of diplomacy shifted from great power primacy to the juridical equality of all states, great and small, European states came to accept some limits on maximizing their power, particularly through the instrument of force. Respect for territorial boundaries provided a means by which threats of interstate violence could be minimized, even between states whose ultimate goals conflicted or whose power capabilities were vastly unequal.

The cold war overlaid these territorial boundaries with stiff ideological boundaries dividing Europe into two ideological camps. These ideological boundaries shaped political identities within the two camps and defined each camp's perception of threat. Ironically, although inherently unstable and bound to disintegrate, these boundaries protected security in Europe: they provided certainty about the sources of threat and permitted states to take clear measures to prevent vulnerability. Such certainty no longer exists.

Not only have these ideological boundaries disappeared, but in Europe's post-Communist region, territorial boundaries are also contested. Furthermore, as the EC moves toward economic and political union, territorial boundaries in the West have become increasingly permeable. The consequence is the most important challenge to state sovereignty since the nineteenth century. A challenge to state sovereignty is a challenge to a state's ability to provide national security. Several essays in this volume examine two kinds of boundary changes posing such a challenge: international economic interdependence and internal political confrontations over a state's legitimacy.

Forces of international economic interdependence challenge state sovereignty by virtue of the fact that transnational actors *ignore* boundaries, international institutions *usurp* traditional economic functions of the state, and the globalization of production and exchange provides an environment in which other states *control* resources required for one state's security. Barry Eichengreen looks carefully at some of the effects of European economic integration on state sovereignty. He argues that each of the attributes of sovereignty—the right to determine economic policies, regulate what crosses borders, and issue and control the supply of money—have been or will be renounced to some extent in Western Europe. The transfer of these rights to the EC reduces the sovereignty of member states, thus reducing their ability to provide security to their societies. Therefore West European states will also seek security arrangements at the Community level. If the forces of international economic interdependence tend to reduce the capabilities of the state to provide security, then we may see the emergence of multilateral institutions as the chief guardians of "national" security and the disappearance of the institution of "neutrality" in Europe. Peter Schulze looks at this issue of a "European defense identity" in depth.

The second challenge to sovereignty, internal political confrontation, is illustrated by the Yugoslav civil war. Rigid cold war ideological boundaries provided the illusion of state sovereignty over divided nations, and those states were able to keep domestic peace. The Yugoslav civil war shows that with the removal of the ideological boundaries, states formerly under Soviet domination may now be challenged by internal forces seeking "national" self-defense for separate ethnic groups. Clearly this challenge undermines the state's ability to define national security and protect society from war.

The fate of the former Soviet republics may point to a similar weakening of sovereignty. Except for Armenia, Georgia, and the Baltic states, divided nations lived within territory administered by "states" that were actually created by the Soviet Communist Party to keep a lid on both nationalist upheaval and Islamic fundamentalism. With the removal of Communist Party domination, the region may be beset with domestic struggles over the control of sovereign rights. The odds that these struggles will spill over into the international arena will be highest when persecuted minorities have strong bonds to other nation-states. Bulgaria, Albania, and Hungary all have populations within Yugoslav territory. Similarly, the former Soviet Union leaves substantial national minorities outside their homelands. Strife-torn states are vulnerable to foreign intervention, thus increasing the chances that civil wars will lead to international violence.

In sum, economic forces appear to be challenging the sovereign state's ability to provide security in Western Europe, leading many political elites to seek a "European defense identity" and multilateral means to protect "national security." In addition, the political challenges to sovereignty from below in the East increase the possibility of war in Europe, calling for a multilateral solution to security problems. As we shall see below, however, multilateral solutions may not be possible without common liberal definitions of political identity throughout Europe. Although both international economic and domestic political forces challenge our concept of "national security," their impact on European security will be asessed differently, depending on the theoretical perspective of the analyst.

THREE THEORIES OF WAR AND PEACE IN EUROPE

As noted, three broad schools of thought dominate the debate about the odds of interstate violence in Europe and the institutions necessary to prevent it. The first is the structural realist view, which takes the most radical stance by ignoring the weakening of sovereignty. This view sees the causes of war and peace arising from the distribution of state power in an anarchic international system. An alternative, liberal perspective focuses less on anarchy and power and more on processes and institutions emerging at the international level to attenuate power relationships, promote common interests, and lead to peace. A third perspective sees the causes of both war and peace arising from *domestic* forces which nurture peaceful international behavior or push toward violent interstate conflict.

STRUCTURAL REALISM AND THE THREAT OF WAR

The essence of the structural realist perspective is that the international system is anarchic. States—the unit and focus of analysis—must amass power in order to protect their societies and survive. International anarchy produces a "self-help" system in which there is no central authority over states to ensure peace among them and collective security is difficult if not impossible to achieve. Wars occur because there is nothing to prevent them.[8] It is the distribution of power among states in an anarchic system which is the best predictor of peaceful or violent conflict.

Students of international relations debate the stability of bipolar versus multipolar international systems, but prominent scholars point to the international system which emerged after World War II as evidence that a bipolar distribution of power is the more peaceful.[9] John Mearsheimer used this argument to predict that with the retreat of the United States from Europe and the decline of Soviet power, Europe would again become part of a multipolar system in which the odds of war would increase.[10]

The argument can be stated in the following way: If war is a dispute over the measurement of power among states, power positions are most clear in the immediate aftermath of war; thus it is when the guns fall silent that there is the most certainty about power positions. And that certainty brings peace to the environment.[11] In a multipolar system, however, this clarity disappears as power positions shift among many states. Under the Concert of Europe after 1815, for example, clarity was assured for a period after the Napoleonic Wars but disintegrated after 1870 as Prussia increased its power position at the expense of Britain and France.

Under a bipolar distribution of international power (like the one Europe experienced after World War II), the relative equality of power between the two great powers and the relative disparity of power between each of them and other states in their respective systems meant that they had only to look to one another as a source of threat to their security. Clarity was thus relatively easy to achieve. Bipolar stability was bolstered by nuclear deterrence, and the clarity that bipolarity and mutual deterrence offered made arms control agreements easier to reach.[12] Smaller states, anchored in alliances with the two superpowers, were protected from conflicts with each other and from the rival alliance.

In multipolar systems, power positions are less clear and uncertainty is high about the source of the next conflict. Furthermore, a multipolar distribution of power has many more potential conflict situations than a bipolar one. For example, small states are not protected from one another; nor are they protected from larger ones. Therefore, arms racing increases, and alliances shift and overlap as relative power calculations change, further increasing uncertainty.

Interwar Europe provides a good illustration. Some small states joined together in the Little Entente and overlapped in the Balkan Pact. Germany and the Soviet Union signed the Treaty of Rapallo and the Molotov-Ribbentrop Pact, and smaller states tried to sign pacts with both Eastern and Western great powers in order to prevent conflict among the latter from spilling over onto their territories. The Locarno Treaties attempted to recreate the Concert of Europe and the League of Nations attempted to institute a collective security system in Europe; these overlapping arrangements, however, though they did not cause World War II, did nothing to prevent it.[13]

These kinds of shifting, ad hoc alliances may discourage any one state from seeking hegemony in Europe, but they breed instability because they foster suspicion, encourage double-crossing, and prevent the building of regional consensus. Structural realists thus argue that we can expect more conflict in a multipolar than in a bipolar Europe.

Central Europe's Response to the New Multipolarity. The age of bipolarity in Europe ended with the cold war. Jane Sharp's contribution to this volume describes the effects of the end of bipolarity on military relationships in Central Europe. Her evidence suggests that the onset of multipolarity will have destabilizing consequences. Structural realist theory would predict that bipolarity's end should trigger a scramble for various overlapping alliances and bilateral treaties to counter uncertainties and risks and to provide protection and assurances against domination by stronger powers. Sharp argues that in the aftermath of the cold war, Central European states immediately feared German economic and cultural absorption; these fears were exacerbated when Germany broke from a common EC policy and unilaterally moved to recognize Slovenia and Croatia as Yugoslavia broke into civil war in summer 1991. These smaller countries were also beset by uncertainties about their fate in the shadow of a dying Soviet Union.

What was the response? By the end of 1991, cooperation among Central European states to counter these risks was minimal—although evident in their intention to hold jointly to the Conventional Forces in Europe (CFE) treaty. Many political elites in Central Europe had hoped that the Conference on Security and Cooperation in Europe (CSCE) would become a pan-European security institution that would bring East Europeans into "Europe." But the initial lack of a CSCE response to Soviet military action in the Baltics and the Yugoslav crisis did not inspire confidence in that emerging institution.

Poland, Hungary, and Czechoslovakia requested membership in NATO. Ivan Tyulin's essay in this volume, written from what had been a Soviet perspective, views this prospect as a double-edged sword. On the one hand, he argues that NATO should offer security guarantees to the emerging democracies, but on the other he warns that it must unambiguously renounce the extension of its military activities to the East so as not to provide fuel for conservative forces in Russia and in the former Soviet military who might use the renewed Western threat to increase their domestic political power.

Could NATO be the institution to secure the peace in Europe? Could it accept new members from the East and counteract the emergence of the overlapping and unstable arrangements that Sharp describes? As 1992 opened, NATO was in the midst of an identity crisis, and its members were initially reluctant to extend territorial guarantees further eastward at the same time that they were thinning out their forces on the former front line and beginning to create a multinational rapid reaction corps to deal with new uncertainties and risks that might arise outside the defense area. At its summit meeting in Rome in late 1991, the most its leaders could do was to urge the creation of a new council enabling former Warsaw Pact countries and the Baltic states to consult with NATO.[14]

Central Europeans also approached the West European Union (WEU), hoping that association would bring them closer to EC membership. But these hopes, too, were dimmed. Poland joined Hungary, Czechoslovakia, Italy, Austria, and Yugoslavia in the "Hexagonale" to balance German economic power in Central Europe.* Sharp's

---

*Multipolar systems also encourage the increasing "Finlandization" of states. This situation might be temporarily stable, but it will not resolve security problems arising from domestic conflicts which spill over borders, territorial disputes, or conflicts between divided nationalities. The Finlandization of Eastern Europe would inhibit the mobilization of coalitions to deter an aggressor there and deal with crises in other parts of the world. By late 1991, none of the Central European states appeared to be moving in this direction, however. This can in part be explained by their desire to eventually join the European Community.

essay describes how these countries have begun to conclude overlapping bilateral agreements with individual former Soviet republics, with one another, and with France, Britain, and Germany. Her findings are remarkably consistent with the structural realist prediction and do not auger well for peace in Europe.

Economic Sources of Instability in a Multipolar Europe. Above I argued that international economic interdependence undermines state sovereignty and thereby challenges the concept of national security. Structural realists address this problem by pointing to the issue of relative gains and new vulnerabilities under multipolarity. The relative gains problem and new vulnerabilities emerge when others control one's vital markets and when shaky states lose the ability to establish and enforce stable property rights. Realists argue that states react to economic interdependence and the challenge to sovereignty in ways that deplete security.

Under the bipolar distribution of power, economic interdependence between the two military blocs was low, while economic interdependence among Western allies grew. As Barry Eichengreen reminds us, this was a direct result of America's containment policy. "Economic containment," a national security approach to U.S. foreign economic policy, became a central component of this strategy.[15] There was an implicit assumption behind this policy that international economic interdependence between rivals would undermine state sovereignty and national security.

The approach was two-pronged. First, relations with other industrial democracies were guided by liberal economic ideology, policies of economic "openness," and American leadership. A leader was needed to manage the interdependent system and bear a disproportionate share of the costs to maintain openness, whether to provide markets to stimulate exports or be a lender of last resort.[16] Open markets in democratic societies would nurture economic growth, vitiate internal Communist movements, and build a bulwark against Soviet expansion. Economic interdependence among industrial democracies, under the hegemonic leadership of the U.S. "pole" in the bipolar system, would lead to absolute gains for all allies—a requirement for unified strength to counter the Soviet threat.

Second, there would be an explicit denial of trade with the Soviet Union. Because the Soviet economy was geared to drive the

Soviet military machine and because Western exports to the Soviets would simply satisfy their thirst for power, East-West trade was thought to lead to the West's vulnerability. Economic interdependence with the adversary would lead to his gain and increase the vulnerability of the West. American leaders, then, formulated policies to increase the benefits of *absolute* gains from trade resulting from high interdependence among Western democracies and reduce the costs of any *relative* gains the Soviets might achieve in economic interaction with the West.

The end of bipolarity and the decline of U.S. hegemony have changed those calculations as relative gains come to matter in interdependent economic relationships among Western states and between states in the western and eastern parts of Europe. Two central foreign economic policy questions have emerged in the aftermath of the cold war: how will the fruits of economic interaction be divided, and who will gain more from the relationship? Answers to these questions are not immediately apparent; the relative and slow decline of U.S. economic power, the rapid rise of Japan, the sprint toward an integrated West European economy, and the development of markets in the former Soviet republics make calculations about changing economic power positions increasingly difficult, breeding mistrust and suspicion.[17]

Relative gains from interdependent economic relationships matter for national security for two reasons. The first is the increasing importance of industrial strength to military power. A superior economy can be rapidly converted into a stronger war machine. No modern state has been able to maintain a first-rate military capability with a declining industrial base. Economic power, in turn, depends on technological excellence. And technological strength developed in commercial competition can quickly be adapted to bolster military capabilities to counter potential new threats. Therefore, states who are more innovative are both more competitive in the international economy and can more readily achieve military superiority.

Second, just as states have come to rely increasingly on industrial strength and commercial technology for military power, the factors of production have become increasingly mobile: corporations can easily move their bases of operation to lower-cost production areas; technology and information diffuse almost instantly across national boundaries; raw materials are rapidly transported to production sites thousands of miles away. Thus military power has increasingly come to rely on goods and services allocated by global commercial markets. Not only will the market increasingly allocate goods necessary for national security, but also those goods cannot necessarily be confined to home markets which states can control. Market forces create a specialization of production such that different firms around the globe occupy niches in the markets which supply the defense industrial base of any particular nation. Vernon and Kapstein argue that market forces will push most countries to rely on foreign technologies in order to maintain defense capabilities.[18]

An inability to control the global markets supplying goods to the defense industrial base can make a home state vulnerable in two ways. First is the vulnerability of dependence. Theodore Moran argues that if the sources of supply to a state's defense industrial base are concentrated in too few hands, one state's national security becomes increasingly dependent on others. As the state's dependence upon resources outside its borders increases, its ability to act autonomously is threatened and its capacity to channel resources to its military through authoritative allocation is diminished.[19]

Michael Borrus and John Zysman make a second argument about the effects of globalization, claiming that it does not necessarily lead to the specialization of production based on efficiency criteria.[20] If disparities of wealth and/or technological prowess pose new threats, states are likely to use national capacities to exercise power in their economic relationships. States in intense competition with one another will seek to manipulate markets to control the resources of others, increasing the possibility that they will clash directly in economic competition. Conflicts over economic issues can thus break out among interdependent states in a multipolar world. If national strength in the global economy is the basis of political power, trade frictions can be interpreted as security threats.

In this context, Eichengreen discusses some of the motivations for European integration and the potential security threats that may result from economic unity. To free themselves from dependence on the United States and revitalize their economic power, European nations saw the need to shed "excessive regulation," which created barriers to innovation. Economic integration was a means by which deregulation could occur and a technological base could be created to assure regional autonomy and independent action in an anarchic world. The threat is that with increasing economic and political integration, Europe may emerge as a power bloc in a multipolar world. Jointly exercised economic power and influence may be increasingly used to counter economic threats. Because trade and security issues are tightly linked, trade conflicts will reduce incentives to cooperate on security issues.

Ironically, in addition to increased incentives for all actors to control markets to their own advantage, another source of insecurity under conditions of economic interdependence in a multipolar world is the loss of market control by some states. This is often overlooked by structural realists. It is the result of shifting and contested boundaries between states and markets and has an important impact on states' vulnerabilities. Realists have argued that the very basis for growing international interdependence has been the consolidation of state sovereignty in the international system.[21] This is because states with interdependent economies have been able to establish stable property rights; in fact, states have been the only actors capable of doing so. Stable property rights are essential for the growth of international interdependence: "without secure property rights, market activities would be constrained because of uncertainty about the possessor's right to sell the commodity and the threat to achieve transfers through force and coercion rather than voluntary exchange."[22] States whose economies have become competitive, interdependent, and strong have established stable property rights on the basis of market rational economic behavior.

The rapid changes in state power and legitimacy in the East at the end of the cold war, however, have triggered massive insecurity over the regulation and control of property rights, leading to increased vulnerability for trading partners. For example, the threat of a powerful Soviet Union cutting off energy supplies to the West in order to harm Western economies or manipulate Western politics under the bipolar system has now virtually disappeared. But the disintegration of the Soviet state and the inability of new authorities to establish stable property rights made the West and Eastern Europe vulnerable to energy supply cutoffs. Ninety percent of all

"Soviet" oil was produced in Russia, and the former Soviet Union was the world's biggest oil producer. In late 1991 Russia announced a ban on oil exports. The reasons for the cutoff were clearly not tied to the threats the West had perceived throughout the cold war period. The ban simply reflected declining production capability and was part of an internal struggle within Russia between the state and private actors over the control of exports.[23] The ban illustrates the West's new potential vulnerability to a supply cutoff despite the disappearance of the cold war threat.

Further signs of multipolar instability appeared in economic relations. Those states who were heavy arms exporters found it difficult to convert their industries to civilian production with the threat of high unemployment looming. They thus continued to export weapons to dangerous Third World states. For example, Hungary sold weapons to Croatia, fueling the Yugoslav civil war. In addition, uncertainty over control of economic forces and the disintegration of the Soviet state began to force thousands of Soviet scientists trained in building nuclear and chemical weapons to sell their expertise to states like North Korea or Iraq.[24]

Stephen Krasner's essay here assesses some of the issues affecting Europe's economic security in this new global environment. He argues that in a multipolar system, economic security will be a function of the size of a state's economy, the degree to which its markets are developed, and the stability of its political institutions. Even large West European states with highly developed markets and the smaller states with robust political institutions will be vulnerable to economic collapse in an international economy devoid of hegemonic leadership. Nonetheless, since the onset of American hegemonic decline, they have generally been able to absorb external shocks to their economies and "their economic security has not yet been jeopardized by the loss of American power and leadership." Furthermore, because their economies are locked together, they are unlikely to be targets of economic pressure or market control from each other.

Again, it is the Central European states that will be most vulnerable to both economic shocks and external pressure. They are more dependent on their trading partners than their partners are on them; in particular, Germany will be in a position to exercise considerable economic leverage over them. However, even if Germany were to try to exercise malevolent economic leverage, it would likely be countered by the United States and Russia or other large former Soviet republics.

Realism and the Role of International Institutions in Creating Peace. Krasner thus recognizes new vulnerabilities which face European states with the demise of bipolarity, and he takes a stark realist position when he recommends balance of power solutions to Central Europe's potential security problems. Nonetheless, like Alexei Arbatov and others in this volume, he believes that there is a rational basis for states as self-interested actors to create institutions that can foster cooperation and keep the peace in a multipolar Europe. Hardcore realists (like John Mearsheimer) have argued that under international anarchy and a multipolar distribution of power, where relative gains matter more than absolute gains, states have little incentive to trust others in cooperative regimes when it comes to their own survival; they would rather go it alone.[25] More to the realist point, they will join alliances to balance the power of their adversaries or potential adversaries, but they will not institutionalize security arrangements with potential opponents. From the hard realist perspective, if institutions joining opponents are built, they will be weak and ineffective.[26] Witness the record of the League of Nations and even the United Nations. We can therefore expect institutions that join, for example, Hungary and Romania, Bulgaria and Turkey, Ukraine and Moldavia, or Armenia and Azerbaijan to be weak indeed.

Krasner's article represents a "softer" realist perspective that recognizes a role for security institutions (as opposed to alliances) under anarchy.[27] These institutions do not have to transform states' interests to make them peace-loving rather than security-seeking; they simply have to establish the incentive for self-interested states to cooperate in the pursuit of peace by assuring them that others will do the same. Indeed the institution of the international treaty has served this function for centuries.[28] Institutions can provide the necessary transparency and information to reduce the suspicions associated with multipolarity; they can raise the costs of defection, and they can link issues in ways that lead to agreement.[29] It is from this perspective that Krasner suggests, for example, that if Germany is a potential threat to Eastern Europe, Germany's membership in the EC and in liberal multilateral trade regimes will mitigate that threat. Indeed for Krasner, institutions are more important to Europe's economic security than power balances. Arbatov focuses on the necessity for new arms control regimes which will institutional- ize and thus stabilize the military balance of power between the states of the former Soviet Union, Europe, and the United States.

LIBERAL VIEWS OF THE PROSPECTS FOR EUROPEAN PEACE: INTERNATIONAL PROCESSES AND INSTITUTIONS

Liberal theories depart from this "soft" realist perspective by looking to processes among states and international institutions which shape the definition of self-interest in ways that can reduce threats and thus lead to peace, despite the distribution of power in an anarchic international system. Some of these processes that have been discussed extensively in the literature are complex learning, "cognitive evolution," elite socialization, or movement toward re- straint, obligation, and empathy in states' behavior as they recog- nize their interdependencies.[30]

Institutions can be created which codify this redefinition of interests in ways that reduce threats and reinforce the processes that can attenuate the effects of anarchy, mute a concern with relative gains and power positions, and lead to peace. Within this approach, the system has an effect on states' *interests*—a deeper effect than on behavior. If the approach is correct, it is powerful because interna- tional processes can transform bad states into good ones—that is, overcome second image causes of war.

One way to understand how processes might overwhelm power as an explanatory factor in the debate over the sources of war and peace in Europe is to look at the changing definition of security in European societies and among political elites during the last stage of the cold war. With the placement of Pershing missiles in Europe, fierce debates over new definitions of security began to cast doubt on NATO's original organization and purpose and the role that nuclear weapons played in Europe. Many argued that traditional concepts of security were too narrow, lending to an overly military interpretation of the requirements for peace. The cold war concept of security meant "containing" an inherent aggressor and deterring any incentive it might have to invade Western Europe. It was a unilateral notion of security which prescribed one-sided efforts to maintain or restore superiority in the balance of forces.

In the early 1980s a movement began to replace this military notion of security with the idea of *common security*. In 1982 the Independent Commission on Disarmament and Security Issues (the Palme Commission) published a report entitled *Common Security*, which argued that in a nuclear age, the old notion of security was no longer possible or feasible. It suggested that with the survival of all countries at stake, a reduction of tensions and mutual efforts toward security were essential in Europe. Security could not be achieved through national defense efforts; nor could it be achieved through opposing alliances. The idea of common security implied the reduction of military forces throughout Europe. The idea was a powerful one which influenced both mass publics and political elites alike.[31] It was mirrored in and given more power by Mikhail Gorbachev's "New Thinking," which let go of the idea that there was an inherent conflict between socialism and capitalism and argued that cooperation between the Soviet Union and the West was the surest way to security.[32]

How were these new definitions of security, emerging in the Soviet Union and among significant West European elites in the 1980s, diffused and reinforced? I mention only a few of the ways here: the Helsinki process which codified sovereignty; nonintervention and human rights norms; the Stockholm Agreement of 1986, in which measures to reduce surprise attack in Europe were codified; confidence-building measures embedded in arms-control agreements like the INF and the CFE treaties; NATO's move toward less aggressive force postures; the decision to delay modernization of the Lance missile; and unprecedented Soviet troop withdrawals from Europe.

Through this process of redefining security, European states with ideologically opposed regimes began to change the frame of reference by which they planned for their own security; increasingly intentions began to matter and affect how states managed their capabilities; absolute gains through arms control agreements became important; the reduction of threats had an important impact on perceptions of vulnerability.

The process singled out for discussion in this volume is that of international economic interdependence. From the liberal perspective, economic interdependence not only creates vulnerabilities by changing the economic capabilities of states (as structural realists have argued), but it also affects intentions by reducing threats among interdependent states. The more threats are reduced, the more absolute (rather than relative) gains matter. The more absolute gains matter, the more peace is produced.

There are three ways in which interdependence can reduce military threats. First, economic interdependence among advanced industrial states can enhance security directly by reducing incentives to use force in settling disputes.[33] Richard Rosecrance elaborates on this argument in his essay here and argues that because all advanced industrial nations have stakes in each others' economies, none can afford to threaten the others militarily. This means that the likelihood of a "Fortress Europe" and trade wars among industrial powers is low.

Second, because the terms of interdependence may favor one nation over another, interdependence can spark new conflicts not possible among states who remain aloof from one another. But to reduce such conflicts, states have institutionalized their interdependencies in international regimes. The rules and procedures of the regimes enforce the norm of reciprocity and ensure a convergence of expectations which can lead to compromise. Mediated through international regimes, interdependence reduces threats to national security from economic partners by reducing their incentives to translate power into military threats. This was the argument for increasing economic interdependence with the Soviet Union in the early days of detente. It is an argument supported by Western Europe's evolution from bloody balance of power politics to the halting but relatively peaceful regional integration of the European Community.

A third argument focuses on the trend toward the globalization of production and exchange. As structural realists argue, globalization increases competition among states for wealth and power. But at the same time, it shifts economic priorities in ways that can reduce traditional threats to national security. How is this possible? Heightened economic competition among states emerges under conditions of globalization as they search for ways to ensure that innovative activity takes place on their territory and not on someone else's. Because an open international economy and the institutions that bolster it foster global production and exchange, if national firms are not competitive internationally, the societies in which they are based will grow poorer as capital moves elsewhere in search of efficient production. To enhance their own power, states seek to ensure that wealth-generating production stays within their territory.

There is a growing debate about the sources of national competitiveness in the international economy, but most analysts agree that nations which have a skilled workforce and are capable of rapid technological innovation to adapt to new market opportunities and make production more efficient in all sectors will be the most competitive internationally. Technological advance is crucial to a state's successful participation in an interdependent international economy.

As a consequence, there has been an important shift in economic priorities among industrialized nations. The foundation of a state's economic strength and ability to compete internationally is no longer sought in the promotion of heavy industries, which depend on relatively simple technology and a large unskilled labor force. It is sought instead in knowledge-based production which relies on a cadre of highly trained engineers and a smaller, technologically sophisticated production workforce in all sectors of the economy. Factor endowments such as raw materials and cheap labor are less important in creating competitive advantage and determining the total cost of production than the ability to absorb new technologies.[34]

This shift in economic priorities can enhance national security by reducing threats in a way not previously discussed in the interdependence literature. In the past, incentives to engage in military aggression often derived from opportunities to extract wealth from others in the form of land, raw materials, or industrial capability. Nowadays, more territory may not add to economic power, but innovative technology certainly will.[35] High-technology industries would be of little use to a conqueror without the expertise to exploit them, or without the cooperation of the local population. With some important and notable exceptions, territorial aggression for economic gain is increasingly less frequent.[36]

Alexei Arbatov's essay here argues that this process will determine the future relationships among the states of the former Soviet Union. These economic relationships will be the basis for cooperation in defense, political, and social issues; indeed based on economic interdependence among these countries, Arbatov sees a relatively peaceful transition in the wake of the demise of the central Soviet state.

Economic interdependence is not the only process which acts on intentions to reduce threats. For example, Emanuel Adler here discusses how processes of negotiation, bargaining, and institution-building among political elites can socialize political actors and create bonds which reduce incentives to engage in violent conflict. Nonetheless, for Adler—and for other contributors discussed in the following section—the original causes of international security and insecurity lie within domestic politics and society. It is thus to this domestic level of analysis that the discussion now turns.

DOMESTIC SOURCES OF WAR AND PEACE

International relations theorists generally agree that there is insufficient evidence to determine whether the particular distribution of power in the state system is a decisive force for war or peace. The process of interdependence can lead to war if state actors believe that it increases their vulnerabilities more than it reduces their threats. Furthermore, many claim that whether a particular distribution of power or a particular set of international processes leads to peace or war is highly dependent on the individual characteristics of the states and societies in the system, on their policies and preferences; it is these individual characteristics which determine whether relations will be peaceful or violent.

From this perspective, it is how societies define their political identity that provides the central explanation for war and peace. How this identity is worked out in the domestic arena will determine how political elites view their role in the international order. Some states can define their identities in ways that lead political elites to overturn the international order by secession, irredentism, or aggression; others can define their identities in ways that lead elites to cooperate with others to maintain international order. States whose political identity is contested invite intervention from opposing forces who want to shape that identity.

Cold war boundaries clearly defined political identity in each camp on the basis of opposing political ideologies and in ways that closed off all interaction with the adversary, thereby contributing to a peaceful if not cooperative environment. Neither camp was particularly tolerant of the other's ideological identity; nonetheless, both respected the boundaries that kept them from conflict.

Now the definition of political identity, particularly in former Communist countries, is up for grabs. Some argue that Germany's new sovereignty will permit a new definition of political identity that may be more aggressive. In some areas like Yugoslavia and the former Soviet Union, political identity is contested by violent means; in other areas it is not clear whether political identity will be formed along ethnic, territorial, or ideological lines.[37] The essays in this volume that pitch their analysis at the domestic level implicitly argue that both *whether* a political identity emerges in the wake of disappearing ideological boundaries and the *content* of that identity will determine the odds of war and peace in Europe. As 1992 opened, the contest for political identity could best be characterized as a struggle between "ethnic" dominance and "liberal ideological" dominance over populations within (often disputed) territorial boundaries.[38] The assumption that undergirds the bulk of the essays here is that liberal ideology must be victorious in that contest for peace to be assured. Liberal ideology will be the basis for the creation of political institutions that create channels of legitimate action in which the losers of political battles accept the political authority of the winners.

Liberal ideology creates a commitment to means rather than ends of political debate and thus creates a commitment to a legitimate political process rather than to specific individual leaders. Liberalism rationalizes society by introducing contractual relations; procedural rules; individual rights; civil liberties; pluralism; secular society; social, political, and religious tolerance; and the fragmentation of political power. Liberals want social and ethnic integration in single civil societies.

"Ethnics," on the other hand, espouse values of collective exclusivity. They oppose diversity, and political identity is based not on a commitment to impersonal processes but on separate and bounded cultural characteristics defined in opposition to the "other." Ethnic identity coalesces around race, religion, language, or a combination of these factors in opposition to other races, religions, or languages. Ethnic definitions of political identity do not accept minority rights within the political arena they wish to define and do not accept the legitimacy of opposing groups in power. They will therefore engage in violent conflict to achieve their own ends of political power or engage in territorial aggression to reclaim land populated by their ethnic kinsmen.

Liberals will be more likely to insist on adherence to procedural rules for settlements of conflicts between divided nationalities and among themselves. Liberals in different states can, as Adler suggests, form a "we" feeling that can provide the basis for an international community and a sense of moral solidarity. The very basis of ethnic identity, however, precludes the creation of this "we" feeling or a moral community, and when irredentist claims are at stake, it will be difficult for states with rival ethnic identities to agree on what constitutes an acceptable international order.

According to this logic, the chances of war increase when different ethnic groups compete for political dominance over territory, when ethnics compete with liberals for political power, and when liberalism as the ideological definer of political identity is defeated. The chances of peace increase when liberalism triumphs because liberals can more easily agree on a common set of procedures to resolve disputes, a set of common values, and compatible policy preferences. We shall now turn to an assessment of these arguments and their power to explain recent events in the European political arena.

Contested Identities. Before the revolutions of 1989, Communist ideology defined the identities of Yugoslavia and the Soviet Union. Its death in these multi-ethnic states has meant the emergence of a struggle over the content of political identity within a given territorial space. In Yugoslavia in the period since Tito's death in 1980, the power of the central government has eroded; Communist political elites in the republics seized as much political control as they could, using ideological definitions of political identity to repress "other" ethnic groups in their regions. The demise of Communist ideology meant that ethnic identities would compete, and that it would be difficult for liberal ideology to define the region's political identity.

Slovenia and Croatia were historically the wealthiest republics, earning most of Yugoslavia's hard currency. A common "western" tradition meant that there was little animosity between these two regions. But Serbia, a poorer southern region, with a less educated population and a tradition of ethnic solidarity, sought more federal control in order to transfer wealth from the northern region to the south, leading to increasing tension between Serbia and the other two regions.[39] Serbian nationalist ideology called for both a "greater Serbia" and a Serb-dominated Yugoslavia.

Serbia initially opposed liberal reforms at the federal level in the wake of the 1989 revolutions throughout Eastern Europe, leading Slovenia and Croatia to seek independence, both to escape the financial burden of membership in the federation and to pursue democratic and market-oriented reforms. While Slovenia, which lacked a significant Serbian minority, quickly obtained de facto independence, Croatia, with a well-armed Serbian minority, struggled with Serbia for both independence and territory. Serbian officials claimed that they would not fight Croatian independence as long as Croatia would redraw its boundaries to bring all Serbs under one government. This would reduce Croatia to 60 percent of its size, a proposal Croatian officials would not consider.[40] The dominant Croatian Democratic Union (HDZ) espoused increasingly nationalist sentiments with clear statements of anti-Serbian racism.

Political identity in Yugoslavia is violently contested, and the battle for identity has been transformed into a battle over rival ethnic definitions of identity within contested territory. In addition, all conflicting political elites push toward increasingly virulent ethnic identities, which conveniently distract populations from economic crisis. It is clear that the central state can no longer protect the security of society. The fear is that contested identities within territories invite international intervention, increasing the odds of widening the war. Clearly the Yugoslav case supports the hypothesis that contested identities increase the odds of violent conflict.

The Yugoslav crisis, however, does not support the case that these kinds of conflicts are likely to spread as a result of wider territorial claims or foreign intervention. As 1992 opened, it became certain that no other East European countries would use their national militaries to intervene in the crisis. As Jane Sharp's essay suggests, the armies of Eastern Europe are not equipped to engage in external conflict. With the exception of Bulgaria and Romania, they have all taken steps to reduce their ground forces; even Bulgaria and Romania are prepared to mount only a conventional defense, and growing equipment and maintenance problems are likely to make any defense ineffective.

Unlike the pre-1914 situation in Europe, no animosities in West European states can be inflamed by a breakup in the Balkans. In 1914 Croatia and Slovenia were drawing away from Austria and the West, not toward it like they are in 1992. Nonetheless, as Stephen Van Evera points out here, West European countries have proven that they are sensitive to pressures from ethnic groups from particular regions in forming their policies. Germany is home to 700,000 ethnic Croats, and 200,000 of these are voting citizens. They were highly active in lobbying the Bonn government to recognize Croatia and were decisive in shaping the German government's tilt toward recognizing Croatia, even when other EC members pushed for continued support of the central Yugoslav state.[41]

As a more immediate source of conflict, we can expect a "demonstration effect," in which ethnic groups throughout Europe and the former Soviet Union are encouraged in their separatist tendencies. And ethnic separatism can become a potent force to unite populations against governments who fail to provide for economic welfare.

Of course the next arena in which the drama of contested identities will be played out is the former Soviet Union. Van Evera notes that "the newly freed states now find themselves thrown together with no preexisting agreements on their rights and responsibilities toward each other, or on the rules of the game that should govern their interactions." Assuming that ethnic rather than liberal principles come to dominate political identity and recognizing that many borders in the region lack legitimacy, Van Evera argues that bitter national conflicts can break out, made more dangerous by the intermingled distribution of the peoples of the region.

It is not clear to what extent the identity battle in the former Soviet Union will be between divergent ethnic identities. In Ukraine, regions heavily populated by Russian minorities voted for Ukrainian independence along with the Ukrainian population, indicating more liberal tendencies uniting different ethnic groups and a preference among those groups for national independence over ethnic dominance. Ethnic Poles in Lithuania supported Lithuanian independence along with ethnic Lithuanians because they felt they shared a set of religious and anti-Communist values. On the other hand,

Russians and Ukrainians in Moldavia protested independence for that republic, fearing that an independent Moldavia would not respect minority rights. Moreover, the Turkic-speaking Gagauz minority declared its ethnic independence within the Moldavian state.[42]

The Defeat of Liberalism and the Rise of Aggressive States. Contested identities can raise the odds of violence within states; the emergence of decisively nonliberal identities can lead to states' aggressive behavior, particularly if the content of that identity justifies expansionism and militarism. Below I shall discuss the prospects for liberalism's triumph in Eastern Europe and the former Soviet Union; here I shall briefly look at the possibility of the emergence of aggressive states. In this volume, this question focuses on Germany.

Looking at the history of European wars in the twentieth century, three contributors to in this volume examine the potential for Germany to emerge again as an aggressor. Stephen Van Evera argues that the dramatic transformation of German society since 1945 has removed such a possibility. Social leveling and the firm establishment of democratic institutions have dissipated the hyper-nationalism and militarism that led to previous German aggression, and the nuclear revolution has made available to Germany weapons of absolute security if it faces a serious threat.

Dieter Dettke underscores the importance of Germany's membership in Western multilateral institutions. Firmly tied to the EC, Germany signals its commitment to international cooperation based on liberal principles. By tracing the historical evolution of German foreign policy, Jost Halfmann and I show how this commitment—though imposed by Germany's security dependence on the United States—took root among the political elite across the political spectrum and continued after that dependence waned. The historical evidence also suggests that Germany's commitment to Western institutions and its historic interest in drawing closer to the East will shape its diplomatic position in ways that will lead it to support multilateral security institutions that include both Eastern and Western Europe as well as Russia. Furthermore, we argue that contrary to becoming an aggressor state, the fragmentation of the German party system and the lack of a sense of "mission" in the world combined with the entrenched commitment to multilateralism, will lead Germany to refrain from acquiring the capabilities that would enable it to become a global military power. Others dispute this argument by suggesting that Germany is simply using multilateral means and the appearance of striving for consensus within the Western community to pursue a purposive strategy of domination.[43]

Although each of these contributions seems to lay to rest the problem of German aggression in Western Europe, they all overlook the issue discussed at the outset of this essay—i.e., the disappearance of firm boundaries has created a source of insecurity within Western Europe which has been expressed in rising xenophobia, violence against immigrants, and the growing strength of right-wing nationalist parties.

For example, the EC Commission calculates that by the year 2000 Arab countries will have 100 million people more than they may be able to accommodate in Arab countries, and that the answer will be migration to the EC. There are now over 4 million Muslims in France and 60 million directly across the Mediterranean in North Africa. Fear of immigrants has led to a defection of working class voters from the French Socialist and Communist parties to the far-right National Front. These workers complain of job and wage competition from North African immigrants, who account for 20–30 percent of the population in urban industrial areas. Indeed conservative parties in France have also lost supporters to the National Front. In Germany the beating and killing of refugees has raised international concern.[44]

Liberal Identity as a Condition for Peaceful Behavior. In this volume Van Evera and Adler make prescriptive arguments about the importance of liberal definitions of political identity within states as a condition for European peace. Although they disagree on the proper institutional embodiment of security cooperation in Europe, they agree that cooperation will be more robust among like-minded liberal states. Van Evera emphasizes that the adoption of market economic policies in the East will prevent beggar-thy-neighbor practices that lead to trade wars. He further makes a persuasive argument about the transparency of liberal institutions: open political discourse can provide an important critical and evaluative function for public policy. Liberal institutions and the autonomy of civil society from the state help avoid debased public discourse, political demagoguery, and the domination of propaganda purveyed by the government or private special interests.

Using the example of Western Europe, Adler argues that a community of like-minded democracies can develop a "security community" because each can demonstrate its respect for the rule of law and human rights in its relations with others, and democratic mechanisms of peaceful conflict-resolution can be used in relations with others. Political identity shaped by liberal ideology will create values which are shared and trusted by other liberal states, and common identities can emerge which form the basis for community.

This is less possible when democracies face states whose political identities are not liberal. In that case, democracies may be compelled to resort to force because the states with whom they interact will not respect more peaceful liberal principles. Moreover, a security community is probably not possible among states whose basis for political identity is ethnic-territorial because there is no common ideology to unite them. If each bases its identity on separateness, there will be little basis for mutual trust and common values.

Valerie Bunce's essay here points out that Communist ideology was also unable to create a solid basis for cooperation among states. CMEA and Warsaw Pact cooperation proved to be hollow, and as the Soviet Union withdrew, these institutions disintegrated, leaving isolated East European states in competition. Unlike the West, the Soviet bloc was fragmented, not integrated.

Liberal ideology, in contrast, *can* create the basis for cooperation. If Adler is correct, liberal democratic states have "solved" the security problem for Western Europe because they have created a security community. In addition, common values unite Europe and the United States in this broader security framework. Thus there is no cause to worry about the Atlantic partnership. If a community of like-minded liberal states can lead to peace, then the real focus of our concern for European security should be former Communist states' "transition to democracy."

Ken Jowitt provides two caveats to this scenario. First, he cautions that the "Leninist legacy" will continue to shape political identity in Eastern Europe, and that the transition to democracy is far from certain.[45] He argues that forty years of Leninism created a "ghetto political culture" in which society is deeply suspicious of government and people are distrustful of one another. Because rumor is the chief mode of discourse, Van Evera's requirement of evaluative political discourse is difficult, if not impossible. And the socioeconomic division of labor—in which the workplace doubled as the marketplace, often growing its own food and functioning as the focus of social life—enforced social isolation and prevented the creation of civil society.

Second, even if the Leninist legacy is overcome, liberalism may not take hold in the East (no matter how much the West pushes in this direction), and it may be even be weakened in the West in the new post–cold war, post-Communist, and post-Soviet environment. Jowitt argues that because it is incomplete and always contested, liberalism will generate challengers;[46] its focus on individualism, materialism, achievement, rationality, and impersonalism leaves out community, security, and heroism—all essential ingredients of political identity. Moreover, history has demonstrated that it has not been easy to sustain a liberal capitalist democratic constitution.

Valerie Bunce, however, presents convincing evidence that the Leninist legacy, as well as ethnic definitions of political identity, have been attenuated if not eliminated in many areas, and that liberal values are coming to dominate political life in much of Eastern Europe. She argues that the revolutions of 1989 were the culmination of a redistribution of power from state to society which began in the 1950s and that governments in Hungary, Czechoslovakia, and Poland, established according to liberal principles, are both stable and peace-loving. Indeed domestic institutions show signs of being able to manage both economic difficulties and ethnic disputes. Furthermore, she argues, among East European states there are increased political ties and signs of successful adjudication of cross-border ethnic disputes.

POLICIES AND INSTITUTIONS TO SECURE THE PEACE

Structural realists would disagree with the wider implications of Bunce's analysis for European security. They would argue that bipolarity repressed rather than erased underlying historical disputes, which will now reemerge. They would further argue that the rising importance of both global industrial production and relative over absolute gains from trade mean that trade frictions will increasingly be interpreted as security threats; Soviet collapse further means a loss of market control in the East that threatens economic crisis.

The overwhelming majority of the authors in this volume, however, argue that much progress has occurred in Europe in the years since 1945, and policy makers can now build on growing interdependence and the triumph of liberalism to secure the peace. Even realists admit that although vulnerabilities persist, states will make commitments to multilateral security institutions to reduce threats.

It is important to note that the bipolar balance of power in Europe did not create a stable peace. Both NATO and the Warsaw Pact, as military alliances, were institutional responses to a failed collective security experiment in the United Nations and were created in the aftermath of World War II. NATO had its origins in the failed aspirations of "internationalist" architects of the post–World War II global order. These postwar planners—whose beliefs in the causes of war arose from the painful experience of two wars that caught fire in Europe and spread throughout the world—had hoped to create a global collective security system in the new UN organization. Collective security, they believed, with its slogan of "One for all and all for one" would deter aggression wherever it occurred if all states promised to unite against the aggressor. Grounded in the belief that alliances contributed to war because they aroused suspicion and pulled many states into disputes among a few, collective security meant that all nations would automatically become allies in the case of an act of aggression.

This hope for a global collective security system was dashed, however, with the onset of the cold war. Superpower conflict and veto power in the UN security council created gridlock on security matters. Hopes for global collective security and a cooperative system among neighbors were dissolved into two rigid alliances in Europe, NATO and the Warsaw Pact, each of which tried to protect itself by maximizing its own power and military might. For forty years, the nuclear stalemate in Europe both prevented war and stopped either side from imposing its will on the other. But this nuclear standoff came at great cost and had no guarantee of success. U.S. extended nuclear deterrence and NATO's nuclear doctrine raised the real threat of nuclear war. The threat that war could be caused by miscalculation was higher than the threat of Soviet aggression. The 1980s in Europe looked more like 1914 than 1939. If deterrence had broken down, Europe would have been destroyed.

Indeed the cold war persisted for forty-five years because of the inability of World War II's winners to agree upon a security structure for Europe. The substitute for agreement was political and military stalemate that was stable as long as power positions remained fixed, but it was never a satisfactory way to preserve the peace. Under the peculiar logic of the cold war the prospect of disintegration and chaos in the Soviet Union represented a welcome scenario to many. It is an ironic twist of history that as the region is being integrated into Europe, turmoil and chaos in the former Soviet region can no longer be cheered but are now seen as a security threat.

Taken together, the essays in this volume argue that with the dissolution of the Warsaw Pact, the dramatic reduction of armaments (especially nuclear weapons) throughout Europe, and the dissolution of the Soviet empire, the world is faced with two central challenges. First, in Europe new sources of conflict are emerging that result from uncertainty over boundaries. Second, an agreement on an all-European security structure is both possible and necessary for the first time in forty-five years. Our essays suggest that agreement must establish new boundaries, not necessarily based on the requirement of preserving the traditional territorial functions and sovereignty boundaries of the nation-state. Such agreement must be based on a redefined notion of security which evolved during the cold war as a result of nuclear technology and a changing meaning of sovereignty. It must take into account new vulnerabilities and threats. Finally, it must institutionalize security commitments with potential opponents, not against them.

What are the most appropriate institutional arrangements to secure peace in Europe? Here the authors disagree. All of the essays in this volume suggest that the central factor affecting the stability of new European security arrangements will be the course of reform in former Communist regimes and that stability will vary with the robustness of liberalism in the East. They disagree, however, on which institutions would be the most appropriate to nurture liberal tendencies, especially in the East. While many argue that NATO should be scrapped, others suggest that it is the most appropriate institution upon which to build Europe's security future. While some argue that the CSCE is the most appropriate European security institution, others suggest that it is too large to be an effective instrument of peace. While some claim that Europe should develop its own security identity, others claim that peace will not be stable without U.S. participation. Let us turn now to these debates.

THE CASE FOR PRESERVING NATO

Under U.S. leadership, NATO members were protected from both the Soviet threat and one another. Defense budgets could be initially low, and West European states were free to pursue economic and social goals. There are three arguments for the preservation of NATO. First, Russia is likely to come back as a great power. If it revitalizes its economy, it will not only continue as a nuclear power, but also will have built the economic basis for renewed global influence. Also, the project of institutionalizing a liberal political identity may fail. If structural realists are correct, a weakly defended Europe would be open to future Russian domination.

Second, NATO must be preserved because out-of-area threats are likely to increase. Potential instabilities in the Persian Gulf, for example, can become a military threat to Europe. Even if such conflicts are contained, European energy resources become vulnerable, and conflict in the Middle East can quickly become an economic threat to Europe. NATO is the most appropriate institution to reduce vulnerabilities.

Finally, it can be argued that U.S. nuclear guarantees within a revived NATO must continue because without them, a non-nuclear Germany would face a nuclear Russia. If the project of liberalization is successful, this is not a cause for alarm. But if it is not, such an imbalance would push Germany to acquire nuclear weapons, greatly increasing the security threat within Europe. Indeed it is widely argued that NATO must be preserved in order to harness German power and prevent Germany from acquiring weapons of mass destruction.

Countering these claims, both Schulze and Arbatov suggest that while NATO might be an interim solution to Europe's security problems, the European continent's peaceful evolution depends on transcending the cold war requirement for military alliances. If NATO persists as a military alliance, including the United States and excluding the East European states, it is likely to face problems of internal friction among its members and new kinds of instabilities in Eastern Europe. For one thing, there will be renewed disputes between the United States and Europe as the European allies gain an increasingly prominent voice in West European defense matters and as U.S. willingness and ability to pay for Europe's defense continues to decline. Such frictions were evident before the cold war order crumbled. Differing European and American interests in NATO were patched over in the past because of U.S. dominance in the alliance. But as the United States retrenches, these differences may become irreconcilable, and Western Europe may establish a defense "fortress."* As Barry Eichengreen suggests, U.S.-European disputes on trade issues may exacerbate these conflicts.

Steve Weber, however, argues here that the solution to these problems is to revamp NATO in such a way that it is both an alliance and a security community. By security community, he means that states recognize that to enhance their interdependence, they must settle disputes peacefully and promise not to use force against one another. To do this they must create institutions which embody liberal principles of transparency, information-sharing, and confidence-building. And they must establish a set of liberal dispute-settlement procedures. Weber argues that because we do not know whether the structural realists or the liberals are correct in their predictions about the causes of war and peace in the new Europe, NATO must become an institution that can counter different kinds of threats. Furthermore, he does not believe that liberal states will

---

*For example, the United States was increasingly excluded from the European defense market even before the old order collapsed. In 1988 European governments began to collaborate on military research and open more of their annual procurement of defense equipment to bids from each other's companies. West Germany, Italy, Britain, and Spain agreed to build a European fighter plane without participation from the United States. The establishment of a French-German Defense Council, the coordination of a European naval presence in the Persian Gulf, and the adoption in October 1987 of a European platform on security in anticipation of NATO's task redefinition all pointed to a reduced role for the United States. The German-French decision to expand its common military cooperation in 1991 provided further evidence for a more distanced role for the United States.

"naturally" cooperate. Therefore, security institutions need to be created which can both meet external threats and counter internal threats "from a member of the group itself which chooses to betray its friends and use force against them." NATO, he argues, is suited to both purposes.

Weber also believes that NATO is well suited to steer the East European liberalization effort. Although individual states can influence change in the East by persuasion, the West needs to enforce a more rigorous strategy of conditionality and linkage. Only NATO can coordinate linkage among Western states, offering certain types of aid to Eastern Europe. Only NATO's supra-sovereign alliance structure can coordinate Western conditionality on economic aid for reduced East European military expenditures or weapons exports and avoid bargaining for better terms by East European actors.

Weber's essay raises the issue of Western intervention in the East to steer the course of change. Intervention normally violates the principles of self-determination and national sovereignty, and it is self-determination and sovereignty that Central and East European countries have finally gained. Conditionality and issue linkage are common and accepted forms of intervention. But Weber's NATO as an alliance may be called on to intervene with military force in civil wars or other disputes in the struggling East. Under what conditions could such intervention be considered legitimate? Under what conditions would West Europeans be willing to sacrifice the lives of their young men in a conflict in Eastern Europe or the former Soviet Union?

THE CASE FOR COLLECTIVE SECURITY

The alternative argument is that an alliance is a relic of the balance of power system of the past and is not suitable as the basis for a new European security community. For a new security system to be stable—that is, conducive to adjusting conflicting interests through diplomacy—it must be accepted as legitimate by all the major players. History suggests that peace settlements based on compromise are far more durable than those imposed on the losing side by the victors. It follows then that the creation of a new, truly European architecture is the central pillar of any strategy that seeks to integrate the East into Europe.

According to this logic, Europe's peace depends on the transition from alliances to collective security arrangements built on new concepts of common security which link human rights with territorial guarantees and provide a forum for further arms reductions in Europe.[47] Adler's "pluralistic security community" in Western Europe might provide a model. Security problems are minimal in Western Europe, even without U.S. protection: common democratic values inhibit the use of force, the ideologies of democratic nations do not conflict, and it would be difficult for a European democracy to legitimate an act of war against another democracy. Entrenched democracies help protect minorities against human rights abuses. Although many abuses still persist, they are unlikely to lead to wider conflict in a stable democratic international order. In a pluralistic security community, defense expenditures can be low. Western Europe has a highly developed human rights regime. Economic growth, stability, and integration managed by the EC help prevent economic competition from spilling over into military conflict. The CSCE is the most likely forum for the creation of a pluralistic security community for all of Europe. Promoting human rights, it played a vital role in encouraging the emergence of civil society in Eastern Europe, particularly in Czechoslovakia. It has also provided a framework for negotiations on conventional arms reductions in Europe.

But collective security arrangements, too, raise the issue of intervention. To what extent should the right of self-determination for minorities be recognized? Should international institutions intervene in domestic conflicts to protect minority rights? Intervention within collective security arrangements will be more legitimate than intervention by an outside force, and the possibility must be considered in the construction of a collective security system.

OVERLAPPING INSTITUTIONS

An alternative to one or the other type of institution would be the creation of overlapping security institutions which nurture the forces discussed throughout this volume that "produce" security and mitigate the forces that "deplete" it. Steve Weber's vision of NATO, for example, could provide for the external and internal defense of a group of European states to guard against the multiple sources of threat found in a multipolar world. Together with a revived WEU, it could guard against arms buildups (which are likely to occur under multipolarity) by continuing to provide a forum for arms control negotiations. Moreover, NATO could deter potential agressor states and prevent the spread of conflict caused by contested identities in multi-ethnic states. The CSCE could serve as a dispute settlement mechanism in such contests, and it could establish and institutionalize liberal democratic norms protecting human rights and liberal principles of conflict-resolution. To mitigate economic crisis as a source of conflict, aid to Eastern Europe could be carried out by NATO or the European Community. Political conditionality attached to such aid could serve as a force for further liberalization in the East. Commitment to all of these institutions and the division of labor among them will bolster cooperation in Europe and between the "new" Europe and the United States, mitigating trade conflicts as a security threat. This cooperation will permit diversity in European political culture but nurture economic interdependence among liberal and liberalizing states, further reducing incentives for violent conflict.

There are two objections to the suggestion for a division of labor in providing for an institutional solution to Europe's security requirements. First, the structural realists can argue that it is a signal of multipolarity's instability. Recall that in the interwar period, states entered into overlapping and sometimes clashing security arrangements in order to guard against multiple and uncertain threats. The arrangements did nothing to prevent the outbreak of World War II. Because structural realists see multipolarity as a cause of war, overlapping institutions are viewed as a manifestation of that cause rather than a solution to it. Although the arrangements suggested here are different in their institutional structures and processes, they may still dissipate one another's energies.

Second, alliances, collective security organizations, and institutions which promote "common security" may all embody mutually exclusive notions of security. Can an alliance like NATO—which is organized to maintain a balance of power and confront an enemy militarily—perform alternative functions and peacefully coexist with a collective security system in which all European states act together to renounce the use of force in their dealings with each other, create dispute-settlement mechanisms, and maintain a common military force that would intervene to oppose an aggressor or still a conflict? An alliance among some members of a collective security system would only rouse suspicion among the others. We saw this throughout the cold war: institutions created to balance power separated blocs in a way that stifled the development of institutions to protect "common security."

Nonetheless, given the shifting, contested, and disappearing boundaries in Europe, a set of overlapping arrangements to create a temporary set of issue and ideological boundaries is the best interim alternative. Security institutions are hypotheses about the causes of war; multiple arrangements can be tested and repaired to bring about the most robust security environment. For example, if the European Community's efforts in Yugoslavia were unsuccessful, it was not because the EC was incapable of providing for conflict-resolution. It simply may mean that the EC needs to devise a new set of instruments to perform this task, or the task might be better handled by another organization.

According to the logic of overlapping institutions, those that mitigate the most potent causes of war in Europe will survive and those based on misplaced beliefs about war's causes will disappear. Security arrangements that leave out key players and key issues will have little enforcement capability, and those that include too many players will suffer from high information costs, problems of reaching agreement, and lack of control, rendering these arrangements ineffective. Those which constrain too much will disintegrate, and those that do not constrain enough will be irrelevant. Presumably these institutions would fall by the wayside, while more effective institutions gain credibility.

It is essential to recognize that a firm foundation for progress in European security has been achieved in the years since the end of World War II. There is little evidence that Europe has returned to 1914 or 1939 or that conditions in Europe are pushing in either of these directions. Now is the time to build institutions on the progress that has been achieved. Actions taken in the next few years will do much to determine the shape of the European security order for the next several decades.

NOTES

Thanks to Kenneth Waltz and Albert Fishlow for comments on a previous draft of this chapter.

1. Barry Buzan, *People, States, and Fear*, 2d ed. (Boulder, Co.: Lynne Reiner, 1991), p. 7.

2. See Stephen M. Walt, "The Renaissance of Security Studies," *International Studies Quarterly* 35, 2 (June 1991): 211–39, and Joseph S. Nye and Sean Lynn-Jones, "International Security Studies: A Report of a Conference on the State of the Field," *International Security* 12, 4: 5–27.

3. See, for example, arguments by Richard Ullman, "Redefining Security," *International Security* 8, (Summer 1983): 129–53; Jessica Mathews, "Redefining Security," *Foreign Affairs* 68, 2 (Spring 1989): 162–77; and Lester Brown, *World without Borders* (New York: Random House, 1972).

4. "To What Ends Military Power," *International Security* 4, 1 (Spring 1980): 4–35.

5. Walt makes this point in "The Renaissance of Security Studies" (note 2 above), p. 213. It might actually be useful to consider these non-traditional problems as risks and challenges rather than threats; indeed military interests in the United States have attempted to couch drug problems in terms of military threats in order to enhance their role in the aftermath of the cold war. For an excellent argument against translating environmental degradation into a national security threat see Daniel Deudney, "The Case against Linking Environmental Degradation and National Security," *Millennium: Journal of International Studies* 19, 3 (Winter 1990): 461–76.

6. Buzan (note 1 above), pp. 112–16.

7. See Ken Jowitt, "A World without Leninism," unpublished manuscript.

8. Kenneth N. Waltz, *Man, the State, and War* (New York: Columbia University Press, 1959), p. 232.

9. See Kenneth Waltz, "The Stability of a Bipolar World," *Daedalus* 93 (Summer 1964): 881–909, and Karl W. Deutsch, "Multipolar Power Systems and International Stability," *World Politics* 16, 2 (April 1964): 390–406.

10. John J. Mearsheimer, "Back to the Future: Instability in Europe after the Cold War," *International Security* 15, 1 (Summer 1990): 5–56.

11. This is the argument Geoffrey Blainey makes in his excellent book, *The Causes of War*, 3d ed. (New York: Free Press, 1988).

12. Collective goods literature supports this claim with its demonstration that agreements are more stable in small groups than in large ones. See Mancur Olson, *The Logic of Collective Action* (Cambridge, Mass.: Harvard University Press, 1965).

13. The best discussion of alliances in this period can be found in Stephen M. Walt, *The Origins of Alliances* (Ithaca: Cornell University Press, 1987).

14. Alan Cowell, "Bush Challenges Partners in NATO over Role of U.S.," *New York Times*, 8 November 1991, p. A4. The United States had argued for East European membership in NATO in order to enhance NATO's security role at the expense of competing arrangements which would exclude or downplay U.S. participation. France, in a transparent effort to reduce American influence in European security issues, blocked the idea, arguing that the expansion of NATO would duplicate the role of the CSCE.

15. See Michael Mastanduno, "Strategies of Economic Containment: United States Trade Relations with the Soviet Union," *World Politics* 37, 3 (July 1985): 503–31.

16. Charles Kindleberger, *The World in Depression* (Berkeley: University of California Press, 1973).

17. The end of the cold war brings dire warnings from Western commentators about the rise of Japanese economic power. For example, Karel von Wolferen writes: "Japan's power is unprecedented. It has been created through the consolidation of an intricate informal system of control over economic and political life, to a point where there is no line of true demarcation between public and private sectors. This means that large, well-connected companies *cannot* go bankrupt. So foreign companies, no matter how much they increase their efficiency, can ultimately never compete with Japanese firms. . . . The U.S. cannot afford to wait for another Pearl Harbor to wake up" ("An Economic Pearl Harbor?" *New York Times*, 2 December 1991, p. A15).

18. Raymond Vernon and Ethan B. Kapstein, "National Needs, Global Resources," *Daedalus* 120, 4 (Fall 1991): 19.

19. Theodore Moran, "The Globalization of America's Defense Industries," *International Security* 15, 1 (Summer 1990): 82.

20. Michael Borrus and John Zysman, "The Highest Stakes: Industrial Competitiveness and National Security," in Michael Borrus, Wayne Sandholz, Jay Stowsky, Steven Vogel, and John Zysman, *The Highest Stakes: Technology, Economy, and Security Policy* (New York: Oxford University Press—forthcoming).

21. See, for example, Janice Thomson and Stephen Krasner, "Global Transactions and the Consolidation of Sovereignty," in *International Politics*, 3d ed., eds. Robert Art and Robert Jervis (New York: Harper Collins, 1992), pp. 310–30.

22. *Ibid.*

23. Matthew L. Wald, "Russians Ban Some Oil Exports," *New York Times*, 16 November 1991, p. 17.

24. See Eric Schmitt, "U.S. Worries about Spread of Arms from Soviet Sales," *New York Times*, 16 November 1991, p. 5.

25. See John Mearsheimer's reply to Robert Keohane and Stanley Hoffman in "Correspondence," *International Organization* 15, 2 (Fall 1990): 196–99. See also Joseph M. Grieco, "Anarchy and the Limits of Cooperation: A Realist Critique of the Newest Liberal Institutionalism," *International Organization* 42, 3 (Summer 1988): 488.

26. See Daniel Deudney and G. John Ikenberry, "Soviet Reform and the End of the Cold War: Explaining Large-Scale Historical Change," *Review of International Studies*17 (1991): 225–50.

27. At the risk of proliferating labels, I use the term "softer realist" to distinguish the rational/behavioral view of institutions in international relations from the more process-oriented, liberal view discussed below. See Robert O. Keohane "International Institutions: Two Approaches," *International Studies Quarterly* 32, 4 (December 1988): 379–96, and Alexander Wendt, "Anarchy Is What States Make of It: The Social Construction of Power Politics," *International Organization*—forthcoming.

28. This has been the historical function of treaties in international law. See Joseph M. Sweeney, Covey T. Oliver, and Noyes E. Leech, *The International Legal System* (Mineola, N.Y.: The Foundation Press, 1981), pp. 951–1038.

29. A good discussion on the role of institutions from this perspective can be found in Charles A. Kupchan and Clifford A. Kupchan, "Concerts, Collective Security, and the Future of Europe," *International Security* 16, 1 (Summer 1991): 130–33.

30. See, for example, Joseph Nye, "Nuclear Learning and U.S.-Soviet Security Regimes," *International Organization* 41 (Summer 1987): 371–402; Robert Jervis, "Realism, Game Theory, and Cooperation," *World Politics* 40 (April 1988): 340–44; Emanuel Adler, "Cognitive Evolution: A Dynamic Approach for the Study of International Relations and Their Progress," in *Progress in Post-War International Relations*, ed. Emanuel Adler and Beverly Crawford (New York: Columbia University Press), pp. 43–88; G. John Ikenberry and Charles Kupchan, "Socialization and Hegemonic Power," *International Organization* 44, 3 (Summer 1990); and Beverly Crawford, "Toward a Theory of Progress in International Relations," in Adler and Crawford, eds., pp. 438–68.

31. For a detailed discussion about how these ideas shaped new NATO policies and strategies and how they bolstered the legitimacy of the CSCE, see Beverly Crawford, "Creating a New Europe: Challenges and Opportunities," pp. 6–13; Ferenc Mislivetz, "Redefining the Boundaries of the Possible: European Integration from Eastern and Western Perspectives, pp. 84–101; and Michael R. Lucas, "The Conference on Security and Cooperation in Europe and the Future of U.S. Foreign Policy," pp. 45–83—all in *New Europe Asserts Itself*, ed. Beverly Crawford and Peter W. Schulze (Berkeley: International and Area Studies, 1990).

32. Mikhail Gorbachev, *Perestroika: New Thinking for Our Country and the World* (New York: Harper and Row, 1987).

33. This is the argument of Robert Keohane and Joseph Nye in *Power and Interdependence* (Boston: Little Brown, 1977), pp. 27–29.

34. For a detailed discussion of this argument, see W. Michael Blumenthal, "The World Economy and Technological Change," *Foreign Affairs* 67, 1 (January 1988): 529–50.

35. Richard H. Ullman, *Securing Europe* (Princeton: Princeton University Press, 1991), goes even further in this argument. He cites modern weaponry, the

substitutability of resources (except petroleum), the demographic changes which reduce the value of farmland, and other factors affecting the declining value of territory (see pp. 23–27).

36. Most of the wars of our time have not resulted from conflicts over territory, raw materials, or colonies—the Gulf War of 1991 notwithstanding. In fact, most of the political violence which has inflamed the world in the postwar period has resulted from conflicts within states and societies. More often than not, they have been struggles within new states about their national identity or over who will govern them. See Timothy J. McKeown, "The Limitations of 'Structural' Theories of Commercial Policy," *International Organization* 40, 1 (Winter 1986): 53.

37. See Ken Jowitt, "The Leninist Legacy," unpublished manuscript, 1990.

38. This argument draws heavily on two important essays: Adam Michnik, "Notes from the Revolution," *New York Times Magazine*, 11 March 1990, and Ken Jowitt, "A World without Leninism" (note 7 above).

39. A good history of ethnic and political animosities in Yugoslavia can be found in J. F. Brown, *Eastern Europe and Communist Rule* (Durham: Duke University Press, 1988), pp. 337–70. See also Dennison Rusinow, "Yugoslavia: Balkan Breakup?" *Foreign Policy* 83 (Summer 1991): 143–59.

40. See "Yugoslavia Appears Ready for Attempt to Restore Peace," *Christian Science Monitor* 4 September 1991, p. 1; "Europeans Arrive in Yugoslavia to Promote Peace Plan," *New York Times*, 2 September 1991, p. 3; "Yugoslavs Joust at Peace Meeting," *New York Times*, 8 September 1991, p. 9; and "Quiet, But No Peace," *Economist* 320 (28 September 1991): 55.

41. See Stephen Kinzer, "Slovenia and Croatia Get Bonn's Nod," *New York Times*, 24 December 1991, p. 3.

42. See Stephen Kinzer, "Atom Plant's Staff Clings to Pleasant Life in Lithuania," and Brenda Fowler, "In Moldavia, Claim of Independence Incites Protests," *New York Times*, 2 September 1991, p. 6.

43. They point to Germany's unilateral recognition of Slovenia and Croatia in spite of the caution urged by President George Bush and Secretary General Javier Perez de Cuellar of the United Nations. See Stephen Kinzer, "Germany Jostles Post-Soviet Europe," *New York Times*, 27 December 1991, p. A6.

44. The number of attacks on foreigners increased tenfold from the end of 1990 to the end of 1991, to 2,368. See "Big Rise in Attacks on Foreigners," *Financial Times*, 17 January 1992, p. 2.

45. Ken Jowitt, "The Leninist Legacy" (note 38), pp. 6–10.

46. See Ken Jowitt, "The Leninist Extinction," unpublished manuscript, pp. 26–39.

47. On the potential for collective security in Europe, see Kupchan and Kupchan (note 29 above), pp. 114–61.

THE FUTURE OF NATO IN A CHANGING EUROPE

Ivan G. Tyulin

"NATO's future" is one of the most challenging and widely discussed topics in contemporary European politics. NATO was established as a counterbalance to the Warsaw Pact. Having lost its initial raison d'être, will NATO persevere in the post–cold war era? If so, in what guise, and carrying whose mantle? Are there genuine threats to the security of the Western alliance or perceptions of threats that will themselves guide NATO's future shape? This chapter will survey the portrayal of European security issues within foreign policy institutions in the United States, Western Europe, Eastern Europe, and the Soviet Union. Their understandings of the role of NATO in Europe's newly redrawn geopolitical map depend on factors ranging from predictions about the survival of old military infrastructures to newly emerging inter-European collective institutions. Thus this chapter will consider the far-ranging yet interconnected shifts in power and perceptions of power.

For a long period to come Europe will organize its political, economic, and military affairs as one large "multi-institutional" society. The collective components of European politics—including the CSCE, EC, NATO, West European Union (WEU), and Council of Europe—will continue to serve many of their current functions, while some will be redistributed among other newly emerging transnational institutions during this "transition period." It appears likely that NATO in particular will perform the following functions.

Undoubtedly, NATO will retain its traditional role as security guarantor for its members. Indeed it may even expand its defense umbrella to cover the "new democracies" in Eastern and Central Europe. While decreasing its efforts to coordinate its members' positions on numerous aspects of European political issues, NATO will likely play a greater role in developing arms control policies. Lately NATO members have stressed the need to "renationalize" security policies. Such a move toward nations formulating their own security agendas is likely to weaken any face-offs between the old blocs and thus should prove stabilizing.

In light of the rapid disintegration and collapse of former collective structures in the East—that is, the Warsaw Pact and COMECON—no one doubts that NATO will play an extremely important role in coordinating arms control policy and ensuring the cohesion of the European-American partnership. In fact, given the variety and overlapping functions of the new multinational political, economic, and military institutions in Europe, NATO's only unique contribution will be its incorporation of U.S. interests and aid. The EC, WEU, Group of 24, and the European Bank for Reconstruction and Development all coordinate Europe's political-economic activities.

NATO's potential to support democratic reforms in Eastern Europe will be limited as well. The role is being progressively taken over by the Council of Europe. Similarly, NATO's ability to prevent the balkanization of Southern Europe will also be limited. This task should be addressed by the institutionalization of interdependence and the cooperation of nations on regional and subregional levels, not a central authority attempting to throttle conflicts.

Even NATO's leading role in arms control may decline. One should not discount the prospect of conventional arms negotiations between blocs shifting toward a pan-European approach. Such a prospect is outlined by the Paris Charter for a New Europe for the period after the Helsinki meeting in spring 1992. In this new framework at least part of the coordination of the West's approach to arms control could be undertaken by the EC, especially when it becomes a consolidated political union in the 1990s. It has already been established that the WEU will increase its participation in European security matters. The CSCE also currently contains a precedent for the EC to relegate the NATO caucus to the "second tier" of negotiation processes (as happened in the prepatory stage of the Paris CSCE summit in November 1990).

NATO's new agenda may include the assumption of more nonmilitary tasks—in particular those of an economic character. This remains hypothetical since any actual attempts at such tasks have been virtually nonexistent. As Pierre Hassner has noted,

The existence of NATO's "third dimension," i.e., its Economic Commission, was always an illusion. An attempt to cope with the economic problems arising between the Community and the U.S. within the NATO framework or to coordinate the policy toward the Third World through the "globalization" of the alliance was always challenged by the Europeans. The latter tend to pursue their own policies and by now at least, they sense that the achievement of agreements and coordination of actions with Washington must not be done within the organization where the U.S.A. prevails because of its inevitable strategic domination.[1]

NATO is likely to remain an important player in European politics, although the particular functions it will maintain are unclear since other European institutions may appropriate them. This fact underlies the need to examine the broader political-economic character of today's Europe to better understand which of the possibilities will most likely be realized in the near as well as more distant future.

The spectrum of prognoses for NATO's future is remarkably wide. If we looked strictly at the European political order, we would say that NATO's role in Europe's future was negligible. European security experts are more divided. The eminent German specialist Egon Bahr, in an interview with the Soviet newspaper *Izvestiia* stated the following:

> The moment of an apparent NATO triumph [will] become the beginning of its end. This is because NATO has no other "doctor." The menace that existed for decades has vanished. NATO is doomed to become futile in the near future. The NATO men have not realized this so far, they do not want to face that, they seek a new threat, but this effort is ridiculous.[2]

At the same time, a French expert from the IFRI notes that France, which traditionally has been suspicious of bloc structures in Europe, seems to be recovering from its former allergy toward NATO. Analyzing the evolution of the North Atlantic alliance, Frédéric Bozo writes:

> This country is ready for contemporary changes, which were forecast by the de Gaulle policy. Just because NATO will be

increasingly like that model, France must participate in the design of the alliance's new appearance.[3]

This forecast is to some extent being borne out by current events. In March 1991 France made the symbolic decision to rejoin the NATO Committee for Military Planning, an activity it had abandoned in 1966. Nowadays France is ready to participate in discussions of purely military questions. The main item on the agenda of this committee is the rating of existing risks. French representatives, however, have declared that they would not participate in the next round of work, which would be an elaboration of policy based on the assessment of risks. In Parisian diplomatic circles there are rumors that France may join with its allies in the subordination of its military to the Integrated Military Command of NATO.

Thus in various countries and within different political institutions there are different and even contradictory attitudes toward NATO. One of the central projects must be an understanding of the potential framework for consensus among participants in the current discussion.

This essay primarily reviews the main tendencies in the international discussion of NATO's future. In this context, the circle of major participants should be enlarged to embrace indirect parties, including the nations of Eastern Europe and the former USSR. Their attitudes toward NATO reforms must be taken into account in order to grasp the common effort to surmount a divided Europe and ensure a "new unity" of the Helsinki process partners. Before we move to this discussion, one further remark is in order. We are in the midst of a transition period of tremendous proportions, in the course of which the political architecture of an entire continent will gradually take shape. What works during this transition period may not necessarily remain in place later.

One of the factors that cause uncertainties about NATO's future is the position of the United States. Certainly there are disagreements among Europeans, sometimes quite substantial. Yet NATO's usefulness and its need to exist are not under discussion by West Europeans, nor will they be in the foreseeable future. Rather, Europeans discuss how NATO should change to accommodate a changing Europe.

The most difficult and divisive question for NATO is how it should participate in conflicts beyond the geographical area of its current member nations. Great Britain shares with the United States the idea of conferring to the alliance a leading role in promoting global peace, which implies the possibility of sending troops to regions far from the European continent. France and Spain, however, strongly oppose any NATO interference in non-European conflicts. They refer to the text of the North Atlantic Treaty, which limits the objectives of the alliance to the defense of Europe.

Serious disagreements remain as to the nature of European and transatlantic military activities. Lately these have become evident in competing visions of the structure and functions of the WEU. There are two main views of what the WEU should do. One of them reflects the position of France and Germany. They would like the WEU to be a bridge between the EC's Political Union (soon to be established) and NATO. France and Germany wish to establish organic links between the future Political Union and the WEU. This predisposes the European Council to be the organization that makes decisions about common security policies and for these guidelines to serve as "directives for cooperation" for the WEU. The goal, then, is the integration of the administrative bodies of the WEU and the EC and the assembly of multinational forces by the West European nations.

This conception is challenged by the UK. The control of foreign policy and security policy, formerly under the control of the "United States of Europe," is perceived by the English as presenting a risk to their security. British Foreign Secretary Douglas Hurd said that London rejects a merging of the WEU and EC. According to this view, the WEU will play an auxiliary role to NATO, and NATO will continue to assume the major responsibility for defending the "Old Continent."

Tensions among West European nations are far more substantial today than previously during tough bloc confrontations. The thirty-sixth session of the WEU Assembly, which met in December 1990, discussed the introduction of European rapid response forces to various regions of the Third World in case of conflicts "threatening the European interests." The session also considered the WEU political role in dealing not just with Iraq, but other areas of the Middle East as well. WEU support of French Foreign Minister

Roland Dumas's proposals reflected the revival of the autonomous European Defense Community projects. The meeting also reflected new possibilities for European self-confidence—that sense of self-determination that came into being as bloc confrontation in Europe diminished. The broadening dialogue of the WEU with the states of the former USSR and the WEU's newly established contacts with Central and East European nations document this phenomenon. The activation of the WEU alongside plans for a new political union of EC members poses a serious challenge to NATO's plans to consolidate its political and military functions.

France's negative attitude toward political functions for the alliance is at first sight one of the more confusing problems of NATO's transformation. It has, however, a certain coherence. The logic of France's ambivalence is reflected in Bozo's remarks:

> The alliance must . . . return to its original mission—to ensure the defense of its members and exclude other political objectives. This means NATO will have to admit a certain "remilitarization" of its role. On the other hand, France needs the "politicization" process. The CSCE and the European Community must become the respective fora of political security in Europe.[4]

A new consensus regarding the role of NATO in Europe will be difficult to achieve, and the stances of today's participants in various negotiations will change over time. The negotiations currently assume that the purpose of NATO is to offset military power in the East and counter new risks associated with the turmoil in Eastern Europe. The emerging consensus on European security will focus on European economic development, as well as look to expanding the geographical area of NATO's responsibility.

Ironically it is not the countries of Western Europe, but the new democracies in the East which are anxious to expand NATO functions. Since summer 1990, former Soviet allies in the Warsaw Pact have stressed the need to create a European system of collective security based upon the CSCE. To a large extent these aspirations simply mask the Central European countries' goal of abandoning the Warsaw Pact. According to the 1955 treaty, mutual aid provisions must cease when a system of collective security in Europe is established.

During 1990 interest in a strong NATO also increased in Central European nations. At first the interest was prompted by German reunification, which occurred within the framework of the North Atlantic alliance. Since early 1991 this tendency had been increasing because of the growing uncertainty over developments in the USSR.

Beginning in January 1991, after the developments in the Baltic states, Czech President Vaclav Havel, without rejecting the idea of collective security in Europe, named NATO as its master instrument. The actions of at least three European countries—Czechoslovakia, Poland, and Hungary—were directed toward exploring contacts with NATO, even to the point of joining it. Today it is NATO that is restraining these aspirations. Answering a question on the possibility of admitting Eastern European countries into NATO, Belgian Minister for Foreign Affairs Mark Eyskens has stated his position bluntly: "They know that in the near future it is impossible." In an interview with *Libre Belgique*, he notes:

> During the last visit of Czech Foreign Minister Jiri Dienstbier I told him that we want good relations with the Soviet Union and cannot assume the position which would be regarded by the Kremlin as provocative. That is why I suggested that he choose a European way of guaranteeing security, instead of counting on NATO. Economic association with the EC, associative forms of cooperation with the WEU, possibly with certain guarantees—here I believe is the direction to follow.

Taking into account all the benefits and costs associated with the foreign policies germinating in Eastern Europe, one can make a good argument not only for preserving NATO's role in Europe, but also enhancing it beyond its current scope. The current instability in East Europe suggests the need for NATO to continue its presence throughout the continent. A possible compromise, to accommodate the French objections, might be the signing of bilateral agreements between NATO and East European states, as well as NATO's partial involvement in a wider variety of European political and economic problems.

NATO's new character in the near future will depend on the behavior of the former Soviet states. Though the USSR did not participate directly in decisions about NATO's plans, NATO members need to take some account of Eastern concerns when it comes to the most important decisions for two reasons. First, the new political thinking and the democratic revolutions in Eastern Europe have made possible a gradual formation of a nonconfrontational model of European security. These transformations require a shift from NATO proceeding unilaterally to making bilateral or parallel decisions.

Second, the internal development of the former Soviet states remains one of the less predictable aspects of European social change, capable of influencing it positively or negatively. Beginning in the middle of 1990, foreign policy issues began to play an increasingly larger role in debates between conservative and reformist forces in the USSR. In such a situation, political developments in Europe, superficially independent of what the East does, can seriously influence the disposition of political conflicts within the former USSR. The question of NATO's future in Europe is one of the most obvious sources of such tensions.

Apparently this potential is already well understood in the West. NATO decisions throughout 1990 and into 1991 have helped on several occasions to ameliorate potentially harmful foreign policy discussions in the USSR. Among the important NATO decisions in this respect was the London Declaration of the NATO Council, adopted at the summit of July 1990. Eduard Shevardnadze emphasized the following:

1) The NATO countries' declaration of the need to increase the political component of the alliance.

2) The declaration that the NATO countries have no aggressive intentions, that they adhere to the peaceful settlement of disputes and will never resort to the first use of force.

3) Proposals to establish formal contacts between NATO and Warsaw Pact countries, including diplomatic as well as military relations.

4) Unilateral measures, including force reductions downgrading the level of military readiness, and a reduction in the number of maneuvers.

5) A declaration renouncing the idea of an "advanced defense" and reviewing the current concept of a "flexible response" in light of the diminishing role of nuclear armaments in Europe.

6) The declaration of the intention to reduce the number of nuclear weapons in Europe and to modify their potential uses.

7) The acceptance of new institutions being established within the CSCE.[5]

For a more precise understanding of the correlation of the changes within the former USSR with changes in NATO it is necessary to consider two tendencies: first, the acceptance in political circles in the former USSR of the evolving role of NATO in the ongoing changes in Europe; and second, the increasing activism in conservative circles, which tend to regard any changes in Europe as a major defeat for what was the USSR.

In Soviet intellectual circles the changes in Europe have led to a serious reconsideration of NATO responsibilities in the near future. The traditional Soviet view focused on disbanding the blocs and introducing a system of collective security in Europe. That approach remained purely propagandistic for a long while, insofar as the former Soviet leadership was quite comfortable with the bloc system. Nevertheless, this conception influenced thinking about foreign affairs during the era of *perestroika*.

As early as 1988, first among experts and then within the political establishment, another thesis emerged that entertained the notion of a transformation of alliances rather than their complete disbanding.[6] The idea of turning the blocs into military-political entities instead of simply military organizations has played an important role in changing the general attitude toward NATO. It conceded that a positive role for NATO in Europe was possible and paved the road for contacts and cooperation between the two blocs.

During 1989 and for most of 1990 experts focused on two problems. First, basic guidelines for the reform of the blocs—and in particular for the politicization of the Warsaw Pact—were developed;[7] second, the possibility of establishing permanent interaction between the alliances was discussed.[8] These forecasts were based on the assumption that NATO and the Warsaw Pact would undergo parallel transformations, as reflected in the resolutions of the Political Consulting Committee of the Warsaw Pact in June 1990.

By 1990 it had become increasingly evident that the disintegration of the Warsaw Pact was accelerating. The previous spring the pact's political and military apparatuses were purely paper organizations. In that context experts formulated the thesis that NATO's fate was by no means bound to that of the Warsaw Pact. Moreover, in this new context the USSR itself was interested in preserving NATO as an institution that could ensure some restraint over a unified Germany.[9]

S. Blagovolin has noted that there has been a lot of speculation on the part of the "right wing," couched as blame for the West for aspiring to preserve NATO while the Warsaw treaty was ceasing to exist and concluding that the result was a dangerous military imbalance in Europe. With a frightening ease the right in the USSR ignored profound changes that are under way in NATO—among them a rejection of the very concept of a foe in the East, a revision of "front-lines" strategy, and a reduction of military forces and budgets that has begun in literally every NATO country. It must be noted that according to U.S. forecasts, military expenditures will be cut by approximately one-third (compared with 1985), and the number of troops will be reduced by 25 percent. There are also considerable modifications in the structures of military forces in NATO countries—including their reorientation from preparing for military confrontation with the USSR to a focus on preparing for military confrontation at the regional level. Such modifications obviously required a different military ideology in the USSR. Finally, we have witnessed a substantial reduction of the American military presence in Europe.

Currently NATO is the only security structure on the continent. It would be rather strange if its members abandoned it before any adequate new structure emerged to take its place. For the former Eastern bloc itself a desire for stability is especially strong, and cooperation with NATO is instrumental to guaranteeing its own security.

Alongside the prognoses of the experts in the USSR, a more ideological camp offered its suggestions for Soviet foreign policy. Specifically, the leadership of the Communist Party in Russia and the parliamentary group Soyuz (union), which demanded the dismissal of Shevardnadze, have been the most active partisans frequently and vehemently criticizing the European policy of the USSR, beginning in the last months of 1990. These criticisms consisted of denunciations of the collapse of the Warsaw Pact, and warnings about the role of NATO in the new Europe. The North Atlantic Treaty was regarded in these circles as a force potentially antagonistic to the USSR. The critics of the anti-Iraqi position of the USSR in the Gulf crisis portrayed a similar scenario: the military triumph of the United States would heighten the security risks along the southern Soviet borders.

The criticisms of Shevardnadze's foreign policy on the part of conservatives and neo-conservatives in the Soyuz group were not shared by most professional foreign policy analysts in the Soviet Union. As shown above, intellectually this group long ago overcame past mistrust of the United States and NATO. It did not see serious threats to national security coming from the West. In any case, judging from the evolving internal discussions in the former USSR, it appeared the East would compensate for the effective collapse of the Warsaw Pact by emitting clear signals encouraging a changing role for NATO in Europe, one that decreases the military "density" of the alliance as well as the nonexpansion of its area of responsibility to the East.

Despite the apparently ongoing strengthening of the political position of NATO in Europe and the fact that in the near future the alliance will remain one of the most important organizations in a multi-institutional Europe, its status further down the road remains cloudy. One can say with certainty that in the transition period NATO will retain its duties as a defensive instrument. However, this will be accompanied by a revision of previous military doctrine, due to the absence of any confrontation with the Warsaw Pact. NATO will coordinate stances between Western Europe and the United States, as well as exercise some control over German military forces. (The latter will have been integrated into the NATO structure during this peaceful period.) Much more difficult are the questions of the alliance's broadening political role in Europe, the extension of NATO's domain of responsibility, and the policies of integrating Eastern Europe's new democracies into NATO structures.

It is necessary to understand that in a more distant future NATO may gradually cease to perform many of its major functions. Democratization and "marketization" in the former USSR, the formation of a Western Political Union (and the attraction of the countries of EFTA and Eastern Europe toward this), and a more active involvement of the states of the former USSR in the system of European and global interdependence (on the basis of the integration model of security, following the practice of the EC) will lead to NATO's weakening if not disbanding. In the context of the widespread integration of other European transnational organizations, NATO will simply lose its legitimacy among the European citizenry.

The above projection corresponds roughly to that of Hassner, who believes that "The blocs will survive. While their significance will diminish, the EC, CSCE, and UN will gain more political weight and play important roles."[10] This does not mean that NATO is doomed to progressively wither away. One can easily anticipate several variants of interaction between NATO and the former USSR, and between such structures as NATO and the CSCE to coordinate the positions of interested parties in European as well as non-European problems.

NOTES

1. Pierre Hassner, "NATO and the Warsaw Treaty: The Beginning of the End?" *USA: Economics, Politics, Ideology* 8 (1990): 31.

2. *Izvestiia*, 2 August 1990.

3. Frédéric Bozo, "France and NATO: Towards a New Union," *Défence Nationale*, January 1991, p. 13.

4. *Ibid.*

5. *Izvestiia*, 7 June 1990.

6. A. Rassadin, "Military Integration in Western Europe: Prospects and Possible Consequences," *MEMO* 2 (1989).

7. See, for example, A. Kokoshin, "Contours of Changes," *USA: Economics, Politics, Ideology* 2 (1990): 31–33; M. Bezrukov and A. Kortunov, "The WT Reform is Needed," *USA* 3 (1990): 30–35; P. Bayev, "Beyond the 'Atlanticism,'" *New Times* 27 (1990): 18–19.

8. See for example, V. Baranovsky, "Optimal Model for Bloc Interaction," *USA* 3 (1990): 36–39; V. Mazing, "To Guarantee the Freedom of Choice," *USA* 3 (1990): 41; Y. Davydov, "Towards a New European Order," *USA* 3 (1990): 45.

9. See for example, V. Baranovsky, "Europe: Formation of a New International Political System," *MEMO* 9 (1990): 15; A. Kokoshin, "Europe We Need," *International Moscow News* 11 (1990); S. Blagovlin, "WT: Farewell to Arms," *Moscow News*, 3 March 1990; L. Gladkov, "Requiem for the Treaty," *New Times* 9 (1991): 23; A. Zagorsky, "We Are in the 'Big' Europe," *International Affairs* 6 (1991).

10. Hassner, p. 32.

SECURITY OPTIONS FOR CENTRAL EUROPE
IN THE 1990s

Jane M. O. Sharp

This chapter reviews the security policy options for Poland, Hungary, and Czechoslovakia in the post–cold war era. All three countries have had to struggle with multiple transitions in addition to changes in their political-military relationship with the USSR. These have included transitions from central economic planning to reliance on market forces; from backward, often primitively agrarian, economies to modern industrial competition with the West; from Communist Party domination to multi-party democracy; from the straitjacket of COMECON trading rules to the confusion of the world market; from regional relationships dictated by Moscow to new international relationships in which they can pursue their own national interest. Each has assumed that economic power would be far more important than military power in the coming decades and has made membership in the European Community (EC) its primary foreign policy goal.

Nevertheless, civil war in Yugoslavia, as well as the breakup of the USSR into its constituent republics, suggests that traditional security threats could continue to drive foreign and defense policy in the new Europe through the 1990s. Thus in addition to decisions about with whom to associate economically and politically, these three former Warsaw Treaty Organization (WTO) countries have also had to decide whether and with whom to align militarily. All three already belong to the Conference on Security and Cooperation in Europe (CSCE), which many hoped in the late 1980s would replace NATO and the WTO as a collective security system for all Europeans. But the Conflict Prevention Center (CPC) established by the CSCE summit in November 1990 proved less than adequate to to deal with Soviet military action against the Baltics in January 1991, the waves of refugees that poured out of Albania and Romania, or the crisis that erupted in Yugoslavia in summer 1991. If the CSCE did not inspire confidence or provide reassurance in the short term, what was to be done "until the doctor came"—i.e., how was security to be achieved in the new, increasingly uncertain mutlipolar Europe through the 1990s?

States formulate defense and foreign policies based on historical experiences of whom they can or cannot trust as friends and allies and on assessments of external threats. This chapter begins by outlining the short-term choices facing the three states of Central Europe, then reviews in more detail each state's threat assessment and likely security policies in the coming decades. In the early 1990s there appeared to be four sets of options. The first was to opt out of association with others and become militarily neutral; the second was to seek some kind of links with existing Western alliances (the Western European Union [WEU] or NATO); the third was to form a new Central European alliance with each other; and the fourth was to establish new bilateral links with a strong regional protector.

THE NEUTRALITY OPTION

For many years Finlandization—implying Soviet *droit de regard* over a state's foreign and defense policy—was a pejorative term employed by U.S. conservatives critical of West Europeans they considered overly sympathetic to the USSR and its Warsaw Treaty allies. During the early Gorbachev years, however, Finlandization, or some other form of neutrality became a laudable goal to which former non-Soviet WTO states might aspire, the relative freedom of Finland being beyond the wildest dreams of most WTO countries dominated by the USSR. Of the three Central European states, Hungary was the most interested in neutrality in the 1980s. One Hungarian analyst, Attila Agh, proposed a five-stage transition from WTO membership to eventual neutrality. The first three stages of the process were based on differentiated memberships in NATO.*

*Lord Carrington used to refer to countries not fully integrated into NATO as "allies à la carte."

Stage I was the Scandinavians-in-NATO model, in which Hungary would forbid Soviet nuclear installations and stationed Soviet forces. Stage II would adopt the Greek model by scaling down participation in WTO activities, training and exercises, etc. Stage III was the French model, in which Hungary would leave the integrated military command of WTO, while remaining party to the Warsaw Treaty. In Stage IV, the Finnish model, Hungary would move out of the legal alliance framework and negotiate a bilateral defense arrangement with the USSR. Finally, in Stage V Hungary would achieve true neutrality on the Austrian model—or better yet the Irish model (since Ireland combined neutrality with membership in the EC).[1]

By early 1991, however, Hungary, like its Central European neighbors, had given up the idea of neutrality in favor of some form of security guarantees from stronger powers in the region.

JOINING A WESTERN ALLIANCE?

It was clear in the early 1990s that none of the non-Soviet WTO countries felt threatened by NATO. On the contrary, they saw NATO as a more important element of stability in Europe than did most Western countries, whose elites wondered, absent the Soviet threat, if NATO had become an anachronism. The absorption of East Germany into NATO was difficult for the Soviet leadership to swallow in 1990, and NATO spokesmen emphasized to other would-be aspirants that they would not risk provoking the USSR by extending the alliance any further eastwards. Nevertheless, all three Central European governments went to Brussels asking for some kind of security guarantee short of membership, and all were initially rebuffed. In early October 1991, however, facing a disintegrating USSR to the east and the war in Yugoslavia to the south, Central European leaders at their second trilateral summit in Cracow renewed their calls for membership in NATO as the only means of reassurance in an increasingly unstable Europe.[2]

Meanwhile, within NATO opinion varied about what kind of reassurance to offer the former WTO members; the debate was reflected in ever more conciliatory communiques. In July 1990 came a statement to the effect that members of the WTO were no longer considered adversaries, and in June 1991, a statement in Copenhagen entitled "Partnership with the Countries of East and Central Europe." By October sympathy to the Central European need for reassurance inside the NATO bureaucracy was growing, particularly in the office of the secretary general. Indeed offering more reassurance to the East was one issue on which NATO Secretary General Manfred Woerner and German Foreign Minister Hans-Dietrich Genscher were in accord. James Baker also subscribed to this view, as it brought the United States closer to the action in Europe after being on the sidelines throughout the Yugoslav crisis. Baker and Genscher used the first anniversary of German unification to issue a statement calling for a new relationship between NATO and the former non-Soviet WTO countries that sought to bring the new democracies in the East under the NATO umbrella. The proposal (endorsed by the North Atlantic Council meeting in Rome in December 1991) included regular meetings, military and civilian exchanges, joint action on conversion of military industries, disaster relief, and refugee settlement.[3]

Parallel to their overtures to NATO, the Central Europeans also approached the nine-state WEU, which was more attractive than NATO on two counts. The 1948 Brussels Treaty (on which the WEU is based) offers a firmer security guarantee than does the 1949 North Atlantic Treaty. At the same time, because the WEU has no assigned forces, Central European membership in WEU was considered less provocative to Moscow than membership in NATO, an alliance widely perceived as adversarial to the USSR until the summer of 1990. In the debate as to whether and how a European defense entity ought to be established, the Central Europeans tended to line up with those who wanted the WEU to be unambiguously associated with the EC, since joining the EC would then automatically mean joining the WEU. By October 1991, however, the door to the EC seemed to be closing rather than opening, and the Central Europeans appeared to accord higher priority to joining NATO than being admitted to the EC.

Proponents argued that no restructuring was necessary to join NATO, whereas radical restructuring of all three economies would be necessary before they could approach EC membership. Opponents of expanding NATO membership argued that the armed forces of the Central European countries were well below NATO standards, but other NATO members fielded either no armed forces (Iceland) or very few (Luxembourg). Another argument against widening NATO was that consensus would become difficult with more members and that NATO could soon become as unmanageable as the CSCE. But this would not necessarily be the case if widening stopped with the three Central Europeans. One short-term solution might be to widen NATO with the three Central European countries who are looking for military reassurance and to widen the EC with the five EFTA countries who would be net contributors to EC coffers and want to maintain their neutral status. To admit the wealthy EFTA countries to the EC ahead of the Central Europeans would generate enormous resentment unless some compensation was offered to the latter.[4] NATO membership could serve as the reassurance umbrella under which Poland, Hungary, and Czechoslovakia could restructure their economies up to EC standards.

A CENTRAL EUROPEAN OPTION?

The interest of Central European states in joining existing Western alliances assumed, or implied, the continuation of a bipolar world in which NATO balances the potential threat (now more politely called risk) of the post-Soviet states. But the states of the region were also mindful in the early 1990s that Europe could return to a truly multipolar system, especially if the United States were to revert to isolationism and leave the West Europeans to provide for their own defense. In this case, the Central Europeans would need to cooperate with each other at many levels, including the military level.

History suggests that it would not be prudent for the Central European states to put too much faith in guarantees from the West. In the 1920s and 1930s the main sources of instability in Central Europe were territorial disputes (often with reference to the borders of Poland) and German expansionism, which led to the incorporation and dismemberment of Austria and Czechoslovakia and so to World War II. The states of the region sought security through three kinds of alliances, characterized by Samuel P. Huntington as clubs, condominiums, and sandwiches.[5] Smaller East European states clubbed together to protect themselves against threats from larger states. Czechoslovakia, Yugoslavia, and Romania formed the Little Entente. The Balkan Pact involved Turkey, Greece, Romania, and Yugoslavia. The big powers—Germany and the Soviet Union— joined together in condominium arrangements like the Treaty of Rapallo (in which the USSR helped Germany evade the restrictions of Versailles) and the 1950 Molotov-Ribbentrop Pact that sealed the fate of Poland and the Baltic states for the next fifty years. Smaller powers anxious to contain German power formed sandwich alliances between East and West: the Little Entente powers with France, for example, and an alliance between Poland and France.

The Locarno Treaties were an effort to recreate the Concert of Europe, which had kept the peace after the Napoleonic wars that ended in 1815.[6] They included the Rhineland Pact, in which Italy and Britain guaranteed the Franco-German border. A pair of agreements (between France and Poland and between France and Czechoslovakia) stipulated that if Germany rejected arbitration, these countries would assist each other. Finally, Germany joined the League of Nations. Neither the USSR nor the United States were parties to the Locarno Treaties, which left a bitter legacy in Eastern Europe, as they guaranteed only the western border of Germany against change, but left the Germans free to move eastwards.[7]

Not surprisingly, the fear of another Locarno—i.e., another set of asymmetrical security guarantees—was on the minds of Poles and Czechs in the early 1990s. If Germany did not follow the rules after the Congress of Vienna, after the Treaty of Versailles, and after the Locarno Treaties, the smaller European powers were understandably nervous about what guarantees there would be in the 1990s and beyond. The apprehension was not about German military power, but rather about political, economic, and cultural absorption. Might a united Germany, faced with a disintegrating Soviet Union and an East European vacuum, be tempted to absorb the region in a new Deutsche mark zone—essentially a Greater Germany? These fears erupted again during the summer of 1991, when Germany tended to move unilaterally toward recognition of Slovenia and Croatia rather than act in concert with its partners in the EC.

CENTRAL EUROPEAN COOPERATION IN THE 1990S

In contrast to the turbulence in the Balkans, developments in Central Europe for the first two years after the breaching of the Berlin Wall were relatively calm. Poland, Hungary, and Czechoslovakia tamed or turned their Communists out of office without violence; the new democratic leaders showed admirable tolerance for their political adversaries, conducted free elections for the first time in half a century, and showed considerable skill in managing industrial unrest under the most adverse economic conditions.

Despite their history of rivalry and anatagonism, the three countries also strove to cooperate with each other. One example was a series of meetings during 1990 in which the WTO group of states allocated ceilings for the five categories of treaty-limited equipment at the CFE talks. Although several states wanted higher ceilings than had initially been set, Czechoslovakia was willing to lower its allocations, donating part of its assigned quota to others. An important test of the region's potential for cooperation will be how the different countries share information under the compliance regime of the CFE treaty.

An important landmark in Central European cooperation was the meeting of foreign and defense ministers of Poland, Hungary, and Czechoslovakia in Zakopane, Poland, in October 1990. Soviet ministers were specifically excluded from this gathering because, as Polish Deputy Defense Minister Bronislaw Komoronski noted,

> The Soviet Union has not been able to make sufficient progress on the path of democracy. Moreover, its army has always played a pre-eminent role among the allies, and that is exactly why we are not inviting its representatives.[8]

While these sentiments were understandable from Central European perspectives, they were resented in Moscow and flew in the face of other statements from Warsaw, Budapest, and Prague to the effect that Moscow must not be marginalized in the debate about new security arrangements.

Another important regional gathering was a summit meeting of the presidents of Poland (Lech Walesa) and Czechoslovakia (Vaclav Havel) and the prime minister of Hungary (Josef Antall) at Visegrad on the Hungarian-Slovak border on 15 February 1991.

Visegrad was chosen because in 1335 the kings of Bohemia, Hungary, and Poland met there to establish political and economic cooperation among the three kingdoms. The 1991 meeting was a deliberate attempt to move away from competition for Western favors toward trilateral cooperation for membership in Western institutions. The Visegrad Declaration, which had been drafted by the three foreign ministers in January in Budapest, pledged cooperation on security issues as well as in political, economic, humanitarian, and ecological matters.

The signatories sought four major goals: restoration of independence, freedom, and democracy; the dismantling of the economic and spiritual structures of totalitarianism; the building of parliamentary democracy with respect for human rights and fundamental freedoms; and total integration into the European political, economic, security, and legislative order. The three countries failed, however, to agree on a free trade zone, while Poland failed to persuade Hungary and Czechoslovakia to liberalize travel across state borders. Nor were several transnational environmental problems resolved; for example, differences remained between Hungary and Slovakia over a proposed dam on the Danube River. To cope with these and similar problems the three countries established a number of commissions and working groups and scheduled another summit meeting in Cracow in early October 1991.[9]

During early 1991, when it was clear that the WTO and COMECON were to end, senior Soviet spokesmen expressed tolerance for new Central European regional groupings on political, economic, and ecological issues, but were uniformly critical of any new associations dealing with military security that did not include the USSR.[10] Tass criticized the Visegrad Declaration, claiming that in establishing a new regional grouping that included aspects of military security and in seeking closer ties to NATO, the three Central European powers had ignored the interests of the Soviet Union.[11] Romania and Bulgaria also expressed concern after the Visegrad summit since neither was included. Clearly there was a danger that marginalizing the Soviet Union and the Balkans in the debate on new security structures could lead to a Versailles complex and strengthen conservative elements in Moscow, Sofia, and Bucharest.

BILATERAL LINKS WITH A REGIONAL HEGEMON?

In addition to the alliance structure, each WTO state was tied to the USSR in a bilateral defense treaty that gave Moscow a droit de regard over all aspects of defense planning, training, and procurement. Thus all three Central European states suffered a common legacy of Soviet domination in their military affairs: maldeployed forces oriented to Soviet rather than national interests; dependency on Soviet equipment; an officer corps, trained in Moscow, which in many instances felt residual loyalty to the USSR; and a desire to shift to Western equipment and training that was hampered by fiscal constraints and Western reluctance to supply equipment free or at low cost.

By mid-1991, all three powers were beginning to overcome these problems. Democratic governments had regained national command over their armed forces, although not all changes instituted were universally popular in the region. In almost all states, troops were redeployed to serve national interests—for example, away from borders with friendly Western or neutral states to borders with potentially troublesome Soviet or Balkan neighbors. All three governments passed legislation forbidding the use of their armed forces against their own populations, but at the same time established emergency powers to be used in crises. The regaining of sovereignty also involved new uniforms and patriotic emblems; unfortunately in some instances old heroes were resurrected, which risked provoking neighboring states. Political officers loyal to the USSR were replaced by national educational officers or chaplains or both. Training schemes were organized in Western countries, but it was hard to abruptly halt programs in Moscow as long as the national armies were using Soviet equipment. In April 1991, for example, some three hundred Hungarian officers were still attending military academies in Moscow, and only a handful had begun training schemes in the West. Czechoslovakia and Hungary replaced military ministers of defense with civilians. Poland appointed an admiral but with two civilian deputies. All three Central European countries reinstated officers dismissed under the old Soviet-dominated system, some posthumously.

None of the Central Europeans wanted to be under Soviet control again, but even after the breakup of the USSR into its constituent republics, the Europeans recognized the need for a continuing security relationship with the post-Soviet states, if only because of geopolitics. Although much weakened in all the indices of power (political, military, and economic), Russia alone will continue to cast a long shadow over the region. Thus even before the August 1991 coup, the Europeans sought new treaty arrangements with individual Soviet republics, just as they began to establish a new network of bilateral relationships with each other and with key Western countries.

Once the WTO had collapsed in 1991, the Soviet Union wanted to renegotiate its additional network of bilateral treaties with its former allies. Before the August 1991 coup these ran into serious difficulties over what became known as the Kvitsinsky Doctrine (after Deputy Foreign Minister Yulii Kvitsinsky)—Soviet insistence on a clause that forbade either party to join an alliance prejudicial to the other. In March 1991 the USSR and Romania signed an agreement containing such a clause, to which the Central Europeans objected on the grounds that all CSCE countries had explicitly acknowledged their right to join or not join any alliance of their choice.[12] After the coup and the political demise of Kvitsinsky, the new foreign minister, Boris Pankin, explicitly renounced the Kvitsinsky Doctrine, and all three Central European countries initialed new bilateral agreements with Moscow in October 1991.[13]

But all three countries were also looking to negotiate bilateral treaties with key Western countries in NATO; all wanted a relationship with Germany; Poland also sought treaties with France and the UK, and Czechoslovakia with France.

POLAND

Poland was the last of the three Central European states to hold genuinely free elections, in the late 1980s and early 1990s, but it scored well in the conditions conducive to democracy, especially in the makings of a civil society and the legitimacy of its new government. The Solidarity movement pioneered grass-roots political opposition in East Central Europe, but the Communist Party was also blessed with many enlightened reformers, so Poland was always the most democratic of the non-Soviet WTO countries in the postwar period. The move from one-party rule to multiparty elections was gradual, via round table discussions between government and opposition, but Poland's Solidarity-led government enjoyed as much public confidence as any in the region in 1989–90, permitting its ministers to take the boldest steps toward economic reform.[14]

ASSESSING THE THREAT TO POLISH SECURITY

In a *Paris Match* poll taken in 1983, Poles rated France, Hungary, and the United States as "best friends," and the USSR, GDR, and Czechoslovakia "worst enemies." Then as now, neither the people nor the government saw a military threat coming from NATO countries. In assessing threats to their national security, Poles have always felt squeezed between a Russian rock and a German hard place. Polish leaders especially resent the fact that it took German chancellor Helmut Kohl until November 1990 to codify the Oder-Neisse line as the German-Polish border. When President George Bush called for the complete withdrawal of Soviet troops from Poland in July 1989, for example, there was some embarrassment in Warsaw, where the government still saw Soviet troops as an important guarantor of Poland's border with Germany. After November 1990, however, Poles no longer had any incentive to host Soviet troops and wanted to negotiate complete withdrawals.

THE USSR-POLISH NEGOTIATIONS ON SOVIET TROOP WITHDRAWALS

During 1990–91 negotiations to remove Soviet troops proved difficult since the Soviet general staff argued that the USSR's Northern Group of Forces in Poland served the specific military mission of protecting communication links between the USSR and the Western Group of Forces in East Germany.* Thus as long as Soviet troops were stationed in Germany, they would be required in Poland—i.e., until the end of 1994, when President Gorbachev and Chancellor Kohl agreed that Soviet troops would leave Germany.[15]

---

*Soviet troops were not employed to suppress political dissidents in Poland as they were in the GDR (1953), Czechoslovakia (1968), or Hungary (1956). Nor were they used to impose martial law in 1981. In that instance the crucial factor was Soviet political control over Polish forces.

Negotiations became especially heated after Soviet military action against Baltic citizens in January 1991, when Poland turned back a troop train from Germany. In an extraordinary address at the third round of talks in Moscow, Viktor Dubinin, commander in chief of the Northern Group, complained that Poland was humiliating "a great power such as the Soviet Union" and treating Soviet troops like occupation forces or prisoners of war, wanting to ship them home in sealed cars, disarmed and with no military equipment.[16] Polish authorities recognized Soviet difficulties in finding housing for troops and their families in the Soviet Union, but worried that Moscow's tougher attitude stemmed from a desire to maintain troops in the vicinity of Lithuania, noting that tanks withdrawn from the Western Group of Forces in Germany were being redeployed to the Baltic states.[17] An agreement was reached in April 1991 that 10,000 troops would leave Poland in 1991 and all would leave by the end of 1993.[18]

POLAND'S NEW DEFENSE PRIORITIES

In February 1990—i.e., before the collapse of the WTO—Poland announced a new set of defense priorities.[19] These explicitly asserted national as opposed to alliance responsibilities and defensive as opposed to offensive capabilities. Poles would no longer train forces to attack Denmark, for example, as required by Soviet coalition doctrine. The new policy announced that heavy tank forces would give way to air defense, anti-tank, and forces to counter amphibious landings. One hundred thousand men were to be cut, but the remaining forces were to be modernized as unrest from the USSR could spill over Poland's borders. Ten percent of Polish manpower was transferred from the Western border (with Germany) to the border with the USSR, generating complaints from Moscow about exercises on the USSR's borders.[20] Poland also began to diversify its arms supplies as Soviet arms priced in hard currency were no longer cost effective. Political officers were replaced by education officers and more chaplains, service time was shortened, and where possible, conscripts were allowed to serve near their homes.

POLAND'S REGIONAL POLICY AFTER THE WTO

Despite its often difficult relationship with the USSR, Polish anxiety about the strength of a united Germany and its bad experience with Western security guarantees in the 1920s and 1930s made Poland less anxious to abolish the WTO than either Hungary or Czechoslovakia. After the WTO collapsed in early 1991, Poland, more than its neighbors, felt a security vacuum in Europe, as few Poles were reassured by the CSCE. The government in Warsaw continued to search for ways to strengthen the CSCE but also sought closer ties with NATO and the WEU, as well as bilateral arrangements not only with former WTO allies, but also with France, Britain, and Germany.[21] In May 1991, Poland also joined the Pentagonale countries (Hungary, Czechoslovakia, Italy, Austria, and Yugoslavia) to make a Hexagonale, the primary purpose of which appeared to be to balance German economic power in Central Europe.[22]

Agreements were also sought with individual Soviet republics. These were relatively easy to conclude with Latvia, Russia, and the Ukraine, but more difficult with Belorussia and especially difficult with Lithuania. Two actions by newly independent Lithuania troubled Poland: the exoneration and rehabilitation of Lithuanian Nazis, and the dissolution of several regional government councils largely staffed by ethnic Poles.[23] In response, in mid-September 1991 Polish Foreign Minister, Krzysztof Skubiszewski postponed a scheduled visit to Vilnius until new legislation could be drafted protecting the rights of national minorities. The Polish government argued, for example, that Poles living in Lithuania should be granted Lithuanian citizenship by right and not on the basis of a loyalty declaration that Vilnius was demanding.[24]

CZECHOSLOVAKIA

In Czechoslovakia, unlike in Poland and Hungary, there were few reform elements in the Communist Party in the 1980s. The late 1989 reform government, apart from Prime Minister Marian Calfa, was primarily made up from the coalition of reformers known as Civic Forum led by Vaclav Havel. The government consolidated its legitimacy in a landslide victory in the 1990 elections. There were few protests about the pace and direction of reform, though there was some clamoring for a separate Slovak state.[25] Through 1990, however, the new government did not appear as sure of its mandate as the government in Poland and was not willing to apply the same degree of economic shock treatment.[26] On the other hand, Czechoslovakia emerged from its decades of Communist mismanagement without a serious debt problem and seemed a better credit risk for potential donors in the West than Poland or Hungary.* Czechoslovakia had also experienced pluralistic democracy before World War II and a legal system that even under Communist rule retained its basically Western orientation.[27]

With respect to defense policy, in common with Hungary and Poland, the Communist government that remained in office through 1989 followed Gorbachev's December 1988 example of unilateral cuts and restructuring toward a more defensive posture and doctrine.[28] In September 1990 Defense Minister Miroslav Vacek told Manfred Woerner that Czech forces would no longer participate in WTO exercises and that troops were being redeployed away from the Western border with Germany to the eastern border with the Soviet Union. Czechoslovakia also made arrangements for regular bilateral military contacts and training schemes in France and the UK.[29]

During the 1980s, relative to other non-Soviet WTO states, Czech troops were well armed and equipped and could afford to save funds in the early 1990s by foregoing the purchase of new equipment.[30] In October 1990, when the WTO met to allocate equiment allowed the group under the CFE treaty, Czechoslovakia was more willing than other states in the region to take a smaller share.[31]

WILL CZECHOSLOVAKIA CONTINUE TO EXPORT ARMS?

The Havel government was deeply embarrassed that a Czech product, Semtex explosive, was widely used by international terrorist organizations.[32] In January 1990 Foreign Minister Jiri Dienstbier declared that Czechoslovakia would no longer export arms.[33] But this proved difficult to put into practice as much military equipment was already in the export pipeline. Since 1975 Czech

*In fact, during 1990–91 Hungary received the lion's share of all Western investment in the East.

arms exports had accounted for 47 percent of foreign trade, and in 1990 officials planned to cut arms production by 25 percent by 1993. This would have affected over 100 enterprises employing almost 200,000 people. In Slovakia, tank factories that used to produce T-72s for export to Africa and the Middle East tried to diversify with increased production of bulldozers and agricultural machinery.[34] But the conversion program became controversial when workers were laid off. The Slovak National Party, which called for independence from Prague, campaigned in the 1990 elections on a platform that called for continued weapons production as one of the region's best earners of hard currency. In January 1991, Slovak prime minister Vladimir Meciar announced that Slovakia would defy the Prague-imposed ban on arms production and export and would resume the production and export of heavy weaponry.[35] In April 1991, however, Meciar and seven of his ministers were dismissed from office by the Slovak parliament. Jan Carnogursky, the new prime minister, a former deputy to Meciar, was also committed to independence for Slovakia, but more sympathetic to the arms conversion process.

This was a difficult task, however, since it was not only fear of unemployment but also the fact that the old arms exporting bureaucracy remained intact that undermined the prospects of Czechoslovakia's renouncing its former role as a heavy arms exporter. In spring 1991, for example, the state arms agency, Omnipol, continued to function with much the same management as under the former regime, with each of the seven departments still run by former Communist Party officials. Moreover, the director general of the Hlavni Technicka Sprava (Main Technical Administration) of the federal ministry of trade was Stanislav Kozeny, until December 1990 Omnipol's representative in the commercial sector of the Czech embassy in Baghdad. In March 1991, Libya was still Czechoslovakia's most important arms importer, with several hundred Czech military experts working at the tank and aircraft depots in Garja and Sebha.[36]

In spring 1991 there was confusion about precisely what had been in the export pipeline before the CFE agreement was signed. In February 1991, Czech delegates reported to the CFE Joint Consultative Group in Vienna some 5,000 fewer pieces of Treaty Limited Equipment (TLE) than they had reported in November 1990, claiming the unreported items were exempt from treaty limits (under

Article 3) since they were "awaiting export."[37] Under Article 8, however, a state cannot reduce its destruction requirements unless compensated by adjustments by another party in its group of states.[38] The United States and Israel complained to the Czech government about arms exports to Syria and Libya, but Foreign Trade Minister Jozef Baksay said sales would go ahead unless Western aid was forthcoming to convert Slovak arms enterprises or compensate for the hard currency that would otherwise be lost. The United States was in no position to criticize the Czech sales, having launched its own new arms sales program to the Middle East in early June 1991 with promises of F-15 fighter aircraft to Israel, as well as tanks, APCs, and attack helicopters to Bahrain and the United Arab Emirates.[39]

CZECHOSLOVAKIA'S REGIONAL POLICY

In developing Czechoslovakia's foreign policy, Vaclav Havel has tried to ameliorate the traditional rivalries of the region. In common with the other non-Soviet WTO countries, Havel saw no military threat from NATO and the West and shared Polish concern not to isolate the USSR in the new arrangements for Europe.[40] During 1990 Czechoslovakia was thus at the forefront of the effort to reform rather than abolish the WTO. At the June 1990 WTO summit meeting in Moscow, for example, Havel persuaded Prime Minister Antall of Hungary not to leave the WTO until serious efforts to reform the alliance had been tried.

Czechoslovakia was initially the most optimistic of the Central European states about the potential for the CSCE to take over the former security functions of NATO and the WTO. After the unrest in the Baltics and the Gulf War in early 1991, however, Havel and Dienstbier showed more interest in NATO as security guarantor for the region. As Dienstbier put it in March 1991, "We would hope if attacked to be treated at least as well as Kuwait has been."[41]

HUNGARY

If Poland was the pioneer of political reform in Central Europe in the 1980s, Hungary was the boldest economic reformer in the two decades before the revolutions of 1989. Despite the relative openness of the Hungarian economy, however, and the encouragements offered to private enterprise, Hungary still suffered heavy debt problems and slow growth rates through the 1980s. One difficulty seemed to be that the reforms that helped Hungarian enterprises trade with the West made trade with CMEA countries more difficult. Decentralized Hungary was thus often at a disadvantage when negotiating with larger CMEA ministries under central control.[42]

After the elections in spring 1990 Hungarian officials emphasized their relative advantage over Poland and Czechoslovakia in factors attractive to Western investors: telecommunications, banking, administrative efficiency, decentralization, free capital, and profit repatriation.[43] Foreign investment increased considerably with substantial credit from Japan, joint ventures with Western automobile manufacturers, and a doubling of income from tourism.[44] In August 1990 Hungary reported a $200 million surplus that officials suggested marked the end of doubts about the country's solvency and the beginning of economic recovery.[45] By mid-1991, however, Hungary was suffering from the collapse of COMECON trade with the USSR and the difficulties of entering EC markets.[46] One of the few commodities that met Western standards in the early 1990s was agricultural produce, but without at least associate membership in the EC, Hungary could not overcome the high tariffs imposed by the Common Agricultural Policy.[47] A combination of the collapsed Soviet economy and EC protectionism forced Hungary to seek out other markets, and in 1991 the Ikarus bus company managed to stave off bankruptcy with the sale of 2,000 buses to Iran that were initially ordered and built for the Soviet market.[48]

HUNGARY'S DEFENSE POLICY

Like Poland and Czechoslovakia, Hungary saw no military threat from NATO and announced substantial cuts in defense spending and deployed forces after the December 1988 speech by Gorbachev to the United Nations. During the cold war years, Hungary was not a front-line state with respect to a potential NATO-WTO confrontation, but Soviet war plans assigned Hungary two missions against NATO. The first was an attack on southern Bavaria through neutral Austria. The second, against Italy, required transit of troops through Yugoslavia. As early as June 1989, more than a year before the collapse of the WTO integrated military command, the Communist government of Hungary announced that it would restructure its forces away from the borders with Austria and Yugoslavia to the border with Romania.[49] Hungary also moved to improve relations with Romania after the overthrow of Nicolae Ceausescu in December 1989. The two governments explored a number of confidence-building measures during 1990 and in early 1991 negotiated the first bilateral "open skies" agreement allowing aerial surveillance of each other's territory.

During 1985–90, the Hungarian defense budget decreased steadily in accordance with Mikhail Gorbachev's policy of unilateral cuts. Once the WTO collapsed, however, and Hungary struggled to establish a national defense policy, the military argued that restructuring and modernizing would require budget increases, or at least less drastic cuts. Lack of funds hindered the modernization of Hungarian forces, but in the short term the military hoped to acquire surplus equipment that had belonged to the East German army (NVA) and was in the custody of the Bundeswehr since German unification. For the longer term—i.e., after 1995—the defense ministry hoped it would be able to re-equip Hungarian forces from Western sources.

In October 1990, the Hungarian National Assembly amended the 1976 National Defense Law by 328:1, with 3 abstentions. The main changes were cuts in manpower from 106,000 in January 1990 to 75,000 by the end of 1991; a reduction in service time from 24 to 18 months (for university graduates, 12 months); the possibility of alternative service for conscientious objectors; an increase in military pay; reduction in Soviet training of officers; and the possibility of moving from a conscript to a professional military.

Meanwhile, in late 1990 the Ministry of Foreign Trade sold 24,000 Kalashnikov rifles to Croatia. The sale triggered angry reactions not only from Serbia, but also from Moscow and Bucharest, with reminders that fifty years ago Hungary had broken a treaty with Yugoslavia to join Hitler's invasion of that country; then Croatians had helped to kill over 700,000 Serbs, Jews, and gypsies.[50] The initial Hungarian response was to deny the sales had occurred, followed by an embarrassing series of retractions and admissions from senior officials.[51] Apparently, of the five ministries that should have been consulted, two had not been, including the one responsible for national security.[52]

HUNGARY'S REGIONAL POLICY

The post-Communist government in Hungary differed from those of Poland and Czechoslovakia in being consistently and unambiguously negative about continued membership in the WTO. Hungarian analysts also tended to be impatient with the concept of a security vacuum in the wake of the WTO collapse and dismissive of Polish anxieties about German unification.[53] Hungarian military officers complained that the WTO served only Soviet interests and hampered rather than helped the defense of Hungary by structuring forces for an attack on Yugoslavia, with whom Hungary enjoyed relatively good relations, rather than to defend against Romania, the long-time adversary. At a meeting of WTO defense ministers in June 1990, Hungarian defense minister Lajos Fur said that Hungary wanted to negotiate its withdrawal from the pact rather than leave abruptly and unilaterally, that the WTO should be integrated into a new all-European security system, and that all elements of the WTO that violated member states' sovereignty should be abolished, such as supranational command of WTO forces.[54]

By early 1991, however, like its Central European neighbors, Hungary had given up the goal of neutrality in favor of a search for membership in Western institutions. Overtures for membership in NATO were firmly rebuffed through 1990 and most of 1991 by Manfred Woerner and by individual NATO governments, but Hungary continued to hope for a series of bilateral agreements and understandings (even if these fell short of firm security guarantees) with key Western countries. France was considered too close to Romania, and Britain deemed unlikely to enter into formal bilateral agreements with any of the former WTO allies. But Hungary has enjoyed good relations with Germany since the 1940s and grew especially close to the Kohl government during 1989, when, over the objections from the Communist regimes still in power in Prague and East Berlin, Hungary opened its borders allowing East German refugees free passage to the West.[55]

IRREDENTISM AND CONCERN ABOUT HUNGARIAN MINORITIES

Hungary's concern for its ethnic minorities in neighboring states sometimes smacks of irredentism. A *Times-Mirror* poll published in early October showed that a larger porportion of the Hungarian population than any other in Europe (68 percent) believed that "there are parts of neighbouring countries that belong to us."[56] There are understandable historical reasons for this, as the 1920 Treaty of Trianon ceded almost 70 percent of Hungarian territory and 60 percent of its population to Czechoslovakia, Romania, and Yugoslavia.[57] Thus in summer 1991, Serbia was alarmed not only by Hungarian arms sales to Croatia, but also by Prime Minister Antall's statement that should frontiers be redrawn in the aftermath of the conflict in Yugoslavia, Serbia could not automatically retain the Hungarian-speaking province of Vojvodina.[58] This statement troubled not only Serbia, but also several foreign ministries in Western Europe.

CONCLUSION

An assumption at the beginning of this chapter was that the prime foreign policy goal of all three Central European states is membership in the EC, but that this was unlikely to happen before the end of the decade. There has been little attempt by the EC countries to renounce protectionist policies and open up markets. Moves to end the cold war have been impressive, with radical unilateral disarmament measures by the great powers (if not by the pretentious smaller nuclear ones), but these have not been accompanied by generous assistance to support the peace. There has been little Western investment in the East. Post-Communist leaders deplored the discrepancy between the huge Western investments in fighting the old WTO threat and the paltry investment in securing peace and democracy now that the WTO has collapsed.

Another assumption was that all three states hoped that the CSCE would become a reassuring system of collective security with its own peace-keeping forces and enforceable standards of rights for minorities. Given the abysmal showing of CSCE institutions in resolving the crisis in Yugoslavia, this too is clearly a long way off, although the crisis certainly concentrated minds on the problems of minority rights and intervention forces.

Of the four short-term options to survive the transitional 1990s, the three Central European countries clearly preferred unambiguous membership in NATO over neutrality, or a Central European concert, or reliance on bilateral agreements with regional hegemons. With EC membership negotiations moving at a snail's pace, all three believed that NATO membership would provide the most reassuring climate in which to rebuild their economies and develop pluralistic democratic institutions. Ironically, much as the Central European states welcomed the cuts in nuclear weapons announced by Presidents Bush and Gorbachev in September and October 1991, NATO's minimum nuclear guarantee may have become more important in the wake of the dissolution of the Soviet Union and the prospect of three or four more post-Soviet states with their own nuclear arsenals.

In 1991 the NATO bureaucracy was more sympathetic to this notion of widening alliance membership than were the NATO capitals, however. Except for Washington and Bonn, NATO governments were even cooler toward the idea of widening the membership of NATO than they were to the widening of the EC. On the right wing of the political spectrum the argument was that NATO should be kept small and cohesive in the face of instability in the East; on the left, that NATO itself was an anachronism more appropriate to the cold war.

The greatest danger is that NATO and the EC will continue to thwart Central European aspirations for firm security guarantees and open markets. With no such help the three states would feel increasingly isolated, impoverished, and vulnerable, and could turn to either Germany or Russia for reassurance, or squabble among themselves. If NATO cannot offer full membership, it should at least offer planning and training on a bilateral basis to avoid the renationalization of defense policies in the region.

NOTES

1. For the Agh proposals, see Vlad Sobell, "Austria, Hungary and the Question of Neutrality," RAD Background Report 156, 24 August 1989; see also Lászlo

Valki and Alex Carlile,"Looking Forward to a Secure Life without the Warsaw Pact," *The European*, 13–15 July 1990.

2. "East Europeans Seek Direct NATO Role," *International Herald Tribune*, 7 October 1991.

3. "U.S.-German Call for Closer NATO Ties to East," *Financial Times*, 5 October 1991; Martin Walker, "Links to NATO for Eastern Europe," *Guardian*, 4 October 1991.

4. See Ian Davidson, "The Only Club Worth Joining," *Financial Times*, 7 October 1991.

5. Samuel P. Huntington, "Democratization and Security in Eastern Europe," in *Uncertain Futures: Eastern Europe and Democracy*, ed. Peter Volten (New York: Institute for East-West Security Studies, 1990), pp. 44–49; for the concepts of balancing and bandwagoning in alliance formation, see Stephen Walt, *The Origins of Alliances* (Ithaca: Cornell University Press, 1987).

6. On the advantages of concert diplomacy for the new Europe, see Charles and Clifford Kupchan, "Concerts, Collective Security, and the Future of Europe," *International Security* 16, 1 (Summer 1991): 114–61.

7. Michael Mandelbaum, *The Fate of Nations* (Cambridge: Cambridge University Press, 1988), pp. 86–91.

8. Cited by *Izvestiia*, 21 September 1990.

9. Nick Thorpe, "Central Europeans Huddle Together Against the Cold," *Observer*, 6 October 1991.

10. Interview with Eduard Shevardnadze in Moscow, 12 April 1991. See also V. Marushkin, "From Love to Hatred," *Krasnaya Zvezda*, 5 February 1991; in FBIS-SOV-91-031, 14 February 1991.

11. Tass, 19 February 1991; cited in *Report on Eastern Europe* 29 (1 March 1991): 43.

12. Ian Traynor, "Former Clients Fight Moscow's Buffer Zone Scheme," *Guardian*, 2 May 1991.

13. Summary of World Broadcasts, "Soviet-Hungary Treaty Ready for Signing," SWB SU/1189 A2/1, 28 September 1991; "Prague to Initial Pact with Moscow," *International Herald Tribune*, 1 October 1991; Susan Grenberg, "Pankin Back with Pact for Prague," *Guardian*, 1 October 1991.

14. Jeffrey Sachs and David Lipton, "Poland's Economic Reforms," *Foreign Affairs* 69, 3: 47–66.

15. Agreement on Soviet troop withdrawals from Germany, 16 July 1990, in Zheleznovodsk.

16. Dubinin's remarks were reprinted in the official Polish daily *Rzeczpospolitica*, no. 14 (17 January 1991): 7, and in *Gazeta Wyborcza*, 16 January 1991. See also "Doubt on Moscow's Pullout of Troops," *The Times*, 17 January 1991; "Moscow Is Stalling on Troop Pullout, Poland Says," *International Herald Tribune*, January 1991; Mary Battiata, "Soviet Army and Poland Stalled over Withdrawal," *Internaitonal Herald Tribune*, 22 January 1991.

17. "Tanks Sent to Baltics," *The Times*, 22 January 1991.

18. "Poland Details Soviet Troop Pullout," *International Herald Tribune*, 5 April 1991.

19. M. Sadykiewicz and Douglas Clarke, "The New Polish Defense Doctrine: A Further Step towards Sovereignty," *Report on Eastern Europe* 1, 18 (4 May 1990): 20–23; "The Defense Doctrine of the Republic of Poland," *Monitor Polski*, February 1990.

20. Christopher Bellamy, "Polish Forces Look West as They Shift East," *Independent*, 12 December 1990.

21. Hella Pick, "Britain Placates Poles with Pact," *Guardian*, 25 April 1991; Leslie Colitt, "Warsaw and Bonn Agree on Goodwill Treaty," *Financial Times*, 3 May 1991; Stephen Kinzer, "Germans and Poles Pledge Mutual Help," *New York Times*, 18 June 1991.

22. Laura Silber, *Financial Times*, 17 May 1991.

23. On the exoneration of Lithuanian Nazis, see A. M. Rosenthal, "Lithuania and the Facists: The World Awaits a Sign," *International Herald Tribune*, 11 September 1991; "Lithuanians Ask Israelis to Help," *International Herald Tribune*, 12 September 1991.

24. Gillian Tett, "Minorities Offer Acid Test of Lithuanian Democracy," *Financial Times*, 10 September 1991; "Poles Protest in Vilnius as Ethnic Tensions Rise," *International Herald Tribune*, 11 September 1991; Edward Lucas, "Lithuanian Dispute with Poles Worsens," *Independent*, 16 September 1991

25. Steven Greenhouse, "Hyping the Hyphen in Czecho-Slovakia," *International Herald Tribune*, 29 March 1990; "Plaque to Fascist Unnerves Slovaks," *New York Times*, 22 July 1990; John Lloyd, "Slovak Separatist Issue Stays Unresolved," *Financial Times*, 13 August 1990.

26. President Havel seems more reticent to undertake drastic economic reform than Minister of Finance Vaclav Klaus would prefer. See John Lloyd: "Prague Reformer Fends off Havel Attempt to Sack Him," *Financial Times*, 21 June 1990, and "Conflicting Czech Voices Threaten to Slow Drive for Swift Economic Change," *Financial Times*, 12 June 1990; Jennie Mills, "Czechoslovakia Overhauls Legal Framework," *Financial Times*, 9 August 1990.

27. Mills (note 26).

28. Prague Domestic Radio, FBIS-EE, 30 January 1989.

29. *International Defense Review*, October 1990, p. 1094.

30. See interview of Lt. Gen. Josef Vincenz, First Deputy Chief of the General Staff, with Jan Oberman, in *Report on Eastern Europe* 1, 29 (20 July 1990): 14–17.

31. For details on intra-WTO allocations at the CFE negotiations, see Jane M. O. Sharp, *The Negotiations on Conventional Armed Forces in Europe* (Oxford University Press—forthcoming).

32. Sarah Helm and John Voos, "Czechs Sold 1,000 Tons of Semtex to Libya," *Independent*, 28 March 1990; Edward Prague, "Czech Forces May Have Sent Libya Extra Semtex," *Independent*, 6 April 1990.

33. As reported in the *New York Times*, 25 January 1990.

34. Nick Thorpe, "Prague Bids a Costly Farewell to Arms," *Observer*, 28 October 1990.

35. Leslie Colitt, "Slovakia Will Defy Prague's Arms Export Ban to Protect Defence Jobs," *Financial Times*, 10 January 1991; and "Arms and the Man in Slovakia," *Financial Times*, 22 January 1991.

36. *Eastern Europe Newsletter* 5, 5 (4 March 1991): 8.

37. Steve Lilly Weber and Randall Forsberg, "Czechs Exclude 5,500 Weapons from CFE Limits," Vienna Fax, 8 May 1991.

38. Article 8, paragraph 8, Treaty on Conventional Armed Forces in Europe.

39. Unsigned editorial, "Mr. Bush Waffles on Mideast Arms," *New York Times*, 31 May 1991; Eric Schmitt, "Cheney Says U.S. Plans New Arms Sales to the Mideast," *New York Times*, 5 June 1991.

40. See Vaclav Havel's speech to the U.S. Congress, February 1990, reprinted in *NATO Review*, no. 2 (1991).

41. *The Economist*, 30 March 1991.

42. Karen Dawisha, *Eastern Europe, Gorbachev and Reform: The Great Challenge*, 2d ed. (Cambridge: Cambridge University Press, 1990), p. 176.

43. John Lloyd, "The Kick in the Capitalist Cocktail," *Financial Times*, 15 August 1990.

44. Kevin Done, "GM in Joint Venture to Produce Cars and Engines in Hungary," *Financial Times*, 15 January 1990; Robert Thompson and John Griffiths, "Suzuki's Hungary Venture May Lead Investment Wave," *Financial Times*, 10 January 1990.

45. Nicholas Denton: "Hungary Agrees $200 Million Credit Deal with Japan," *Financial Times*, 7 August 1990, and "Glimmer of Economic Recovery in Budapest," *Financial Times*, 9 August 1990.

46. Nicholas Denton, "Hungary Goes West with a New Urgency," *Financial Times*, 2 May 1991.

47. Anthony Robinson and Leyla Boulton, "High Hopes Give Way to Empty Shelves," *Financial Times*, 2 April 1991.

48. Peter Maas, "New Markets and New Hope in Hungary," *International Herald Tribune*, 29 May 1991.

49. Douglas L. Clarke, "The Romanian Threat to Hungary," RAD Background Report, Radio Free Europe Research, 27 July 1989.

50. Stevan Tosic, "Serbs and Croats," *The Economist*, 8 June 1991, p. 6.

51. Judith Pataki, "Relations with Yugoslavia Troubled by Weapons Sale," *Reports from Eastern Europe* 2, 8 (22 February 1991): 15–19.

52. Interview in Budapest, April 1991.

53. On the concept of a security vacuum in Europe, see Laszlo Valki, "Eastern and Central Europe in the New Security System," in *Towards a New European Security Order*, ed. Bo Huldt and Gunilla Herolf (Stockholm: Swedish Institute of International Affairs, 1991), pp. 228–37.

54. Albert Reisch, "Hungary to Leave Military Arm of Warsaw Pact," *Report on Eastern Europe*, 29 June 1990.

55. On the secret negotiations between Helmut Kohl and Miklos Nemeth in August 1989, see Leigh Bruce, "Hungarian Tells of Meeting with Kohl on Opening Border," *International Herald Tribune*, 24 September 1990.

56. *Times-Mirror* poll, "Fearful States of Mind," *The Guardian*, 4 October 1991; see also Neal Ascherson, *The Independent*, 6 October 1991.

57. Jozsef Galanti, "Trianon and the Protection of Minorities," Budapest KJC 1989; cited by Laszlo Valki in October 1991 paper at IISS conference, Wilton Park.

58. *Nepszabadsag*, 9 July 1991.

ECONOMIC INTEGRATION AND EUROPEAN SECURITY

Barry Eichengreen

INTRODUCTION

In contrast to the attention they lavish on international economic relations, economists rarely deal with international security affairs. Notwithstanding Richard Cooper's (1986) dictum that economic policy is foreign policy, specialists concerned with recent trends in European economic integration—the 1992 program and its most dramatic manifestation, monetary unification—have not pursued the implications of economic change for the European Community's (EC) security arrangements. That is the task upon which I shall attempt to make a start here.

In the following section I shall review the salient features of the 1992 program, highlighting aspects particularly relevant to Europe's international security. Then I shall approach the issue from the other direction, analyzing aspects of Europe's security relations as they relate to the process of economic integration. These complementary perspectives suggest that the member nations of the EC are engaged in a pair of simultaneous games, one over the conduct of economic affairs, the other over the structuring of security arrangements. The section which follows will therefore describe an analytical framework, adapted from the literature on game theory, which can be used to draw out the implications of the fact that strategic interaction exists in both domains, and the framework will be applied to the problem of economic-security interaction. The final section will summarize the implications of this analysis for policy.

ECONOMIC INTEGRATION

To speak of national security presumes that there is something called the nation-state to be defended. The 1992 program, as its participants have belatedly discovered, fundamentally challenges traditional European conceptions of what is meant by the sovereign state. Three of the most basic rights of a sovereign state are (1) to regulate what crosses its borders, (2) to determine its economic policies, and (3) to issue and regulate the supply of its national money. The 1992 program challenges each of these rights and consequently promises to transform what is meant in Europe by national sovereignty.

The right to regulate what crosses their borders will be renounced by the members of the EC if the 1992 program goes according to plan. There will no more exist barriers to the movement of goods between European countries than there exist barriers to the movement of goods between California and other U.S. states. EC members will not have the right to tax goods imported from other European countries at different rates than they tax goods produced at home. The domestic taxes any one European country will be able to levy will have to be harmonized with the taxes levied by other EC members. This is because the 1992 program will also remove barriers to the movement of capital and labor within the Community. Workers will be able to cross the Community's existing national borders without a passport, and they will be able to work throughout the Community without having to obtain a permit. This new situation will fundamentally transform European labor markets. In fact, the new situation already obtains in European capital markets. Over the last year all significant controls on capital movements within Europe have been removed. Already individual European nations have essentially renounced the right to regulate what crosses their borders.

The right to determine economic policies will be very significantly compromised by 1992. Social and regulatory policies will have to be harmonized. Unemployment or health benefits significantly more generous than those provided elsewhere in the Community will attract foreign workers to a jurisdiction like metal shavings to a magnet. Regulations designed to enhance workplace safety, if they raise production costs, will provoke the exodus of manufacturing firms. None of this is to imply that unemployment assistance, national health systems, or safety regulations will be casualties of the 1992 program—only that their provision will have to be coordinated at the Community level. The sovereignty of individual nations over their provision will be severely limited.

It is in the design and implementation of macroeconomic policy that the new constraints are likely to bind most severely. Individual European countries will have little leeway to pursue tax policies that are significantly different from those of their European neighbors. Any EC member state attempting to tax labor income at rates significantly in excess of those applied by its neighbors will be threatened by an exodus of footloose labor to lower tax rate jurisdictions, forcing it to reduce its tax rates to more conventional levels. Equally, individual EC member states will retain relatively little ability to borrow to finance budget deficits. Borrowing today means that there will be more debt to be serviced tomorrow, implying higher taxes down the road. Realizing that no one EC state will be able to raise taxes in the future significantly above those of its neighbors (since if it tries, footloose factors of production will flee), investors will not buy the additional government bonds that the deficit-ridden government attempts to issue. No one government will be able to borrow more than its neighbors.* This, in combination with the need for similar levels of taxation, implies that individual European governments will have relatively little control over the level of government spending. Government budgets will have to converge across European nations much as they have done across American states.†

---

*Eichengreen (1990) and Goldstein and Woglom (1991) provide evidence that U.S. state and municipal governments are quickly rationed out of financial markets when they attempt to borrow more than is consistent with their capacity to tax in an environment of high factor mobility.

†The point should not be overdrawn. Eichengreen (1990) compares the variability of tax rates across U.S. states and European countries, finding that the coefficient of variation of tax rates is about half as large across U.S. census regions as across EC member nations. This confirms only that European tax rates will have to become more equal, not that they will be equalized. For reasons of culture and relocation costs, factors of production will never be perfectly mobile (as they are not in the United States), leaving some scope for tax independence. Jurisdictions can compensate their residents for different levels of taxation through the provision of different packages of services, so long as those services benefit only those

Tax rates and borrowing requirements will have to be coordinated among EC member states to prevent destructive tax competition in which countries try to undercut the levels of taxation of their neighbors in order to attract footloose enterprises. The same goes for industrial subsidies: the more mobile are productive factors, the greater the incentive for local governments to offer subsidies and concessions to lure them into locating in their jurisdiction—a fact of which Japanese automobile companies establishing plants in the United States are not unaware. The greater the subsidy competition, the higher the cost to taxpayers and the less the benefit to domestic residents of having production take place locally. The solution is to coordinate and regulate the provision of subsidies. Indeed the EC possesses a commission in Brussels whose responsibility it is to identify excessive government subsidies to industry and to ensure that they are not just eliminated but repaid, although the scope of its powers remains a matter of dispute. For all these reasons, then, as a consequence of the 1992 program individual European states will find themselves with significant new constraints on their ability to determine their own economic policies.

If ongoing discussions of currency unification proceed according to plan, the right to issue national money in the quantity a nation chooses will be renounced, perhaps as early as 1997. A European Central Bank, the "EuroFed," will be established, perhaps in Frankfurt. Existing national central banks will be transformed into mere branch offices of the new central banking institution. The EuroFed will issue a new national currency. Existing national currencies will be converted into this new European bank note before being abolished once and for all. The EuroFed will be run by a council comprised of one representative of each participating nation and several members at large. Decisions will be by strict majority vote. National governments will have no right to issue bank notes of their own or even to attempt to influence the monetary policy decisions of the EuroFed. Thus as a consequence of the process of economic and monetary integration, individual European nations will have renounced the third traditional right of a sovereign state.

---

who pay the taxes. Under these circumstances, individuals will sort themselves across jurisdictions, clustering with others possessing similar preferences for public goods (see Tiebout 1956).

It is impossible to understand why Europe is undergoing this revolutionary transformation without considering security motivations. The European Economic Community (EEC) was established after World War II, on Europe's impetus but with American encouragement, to deal with security threats. Economic integration, it was argued, would enhance European interdependence in healthful ways. Nations that traded and invested in one another were unlikely to go to war. The more Germany and France needed one another economically, the less likely they were to come to blows. The European Coal and Steel Community, the Common Market's first significant achievement, was designed to ensure that no European nation would be denied the coal and steel viewed as esssential to its national security, and specifically to reassure France that it would retain access to German coal supplies. The restoration of prosperity, which depended on successful reconstruction of intra-European trade, was seen as necessary to repel the Communist threat from the East.*

Similarly, the 1992 program cannot be understood in isolation from security concerns. The 1970s and 1980s were decades of high unemployment and low productivity growth in Europe, the age of "Eurosclerosis." Europe was seen as lagging behind the more vibrant U.S. economy and hence as growing more and more dependent for its own security on America's military might. Revitalizing the European economy was seen as necessary for restoring the continent's security autonomy.

Eurosclerosis, according to the dominant diagnosis, was a symptom of excessive regulation. Governments had thrown up barriers to innovation and initiative, stifling economic growth. The economies of Europe needed to be deregulated. Given the precedent of the immediate post-World War II decades, when economic integration had provided the lever for reinvigorating the European economy, renewed steps toward integration represented a logical way of stimulating deregulation. Highly regulated jurisdictions would be forced to conform to the pattern established by their more laissez-faire counterparts or would find themselves unable to attract and retain mobile factors of production.

---

*See Wightman (1956) for an introduction to the European Coal and Steel Community and other early achievements of the EEC.

Integration, moreover, was seen as delivering a variety of ancillary benefits. Many important technologies of the late twentieth century exhibit economies of scale and scope.* They can be adequately exploited only when the size of the market permits. The internal market in Europe was long balkanized by trade and regulatory barriers. For Europe to regain its economic and political power, the market needed to be unified and thereby rendered comparable to the North American Free Trade Area and Japan's prospective "East Asian Co-Prosperity Zone." Intra-European trade was to be the engine of growth. Stable exchange rates within Europe were a natural corollary of the desire to promote internal trade, and currency unification—the only credible way to guarantee that devaluation would be avoided—was seen as a natural corollary of exchange rate stability.

If security concerns provide, at least obliquely, a significant part of the impetus for the 1992 program, the accelerated pace of economic integration in Europe also poses potential security threats. An obvious illustration of this statement is the specter of Fortress Europe and the strains it will place on the Community's relations with its American and Japanese trading partners. Completion of the internal market naturally implies erection of a common external tariff. France can hardly tax American computers at one rate and Germany at another; if they try, American computers will be exported to the low-tax country and trans-shipped to the high-tax one. A common external tariff is inevitable. The question is whether it will be set at high or low levels. If it is set high, American enthusiasm for European unification will certainly wane.

The danger that Europe's common external tariff will be set at prohibitive levels is heightened by the dislocations that will inevitably accompany completion of the internal market. The 1992 program will involve large-scale rationalization and relocation of European industry. There is no explanation based on technology or tastes for the fact that Europe possesses many more automobile companies than the United States (to cite but one illustrative industry example). These exist only because national producers receive preferential treatment in their home markets. Once internal barriers to the sale of autos in Europe are eliminated, a shakeout will ensue;

---

*Caballero and Lyons (1990) is the most widely cited study finding evidence of significantly increasing returns to scale in European industry.

only the strongest producers will survive. Inevitably this painful process will intensify the pressure to minimize competition from abroad (read "Japanese cars") that otherwise would exacerbate the difficulties of this adjustment. Hence the likelihood that Europe will generalize the most restrictive EC members' quotas on Japanese cars, rather than the most liberal ones.* The trend is already evident in semiconductors, where the EC has followed the United States by engineering trade arrangements requiring Japanese producers to limit price reductions in periods of excess supply.

The danger of Fortress Europe is reinforced by German unification. By applying new strains to the European Monetary System (EMS) and throwing a wrench in the process of monetary unification, the economic implications of German unification will surely heighten protectionist pressure in Europe. Rehabilitating Germany's eastern *lander* will require substantial amounts of investment. As German investment rises relative to German savings, German interest rates will march upward. Higher German interest rates help to equilibrate the market in two ways. First, they encourage saving and discourage investment in the least productive projects. Second, high German interest rates will draw capital to Germany from other countries. Unfortunately, both mechanisms will aggravate economic difficulties elsewhere in Europe. As France, Britain, and other members of the EC export financial capital to Germany and import from Germany its higher interest rates, investment in their own economies will suffer. The problem will be exacerbated by the tendency for the high interest rates caused by Germany's investment surge to strengthen the Deutsche mark (DM). High interest rates caused by an excess of investment over saving should drag up the German currency in the early 1990s much as analogous imbalances dragged up the U.S. dollar in the early 1980s.† The difference between the

---

*Negotiations with the Japanese, ongoing at the time of writing, suggest that the Community's highly restrictive quotas on Japanese cars will be phased out very slowly at best. It seems unlikely that they will be significantly reduced before the end of the century, raising fears that promises to phase them out at that time will be renegotiated before the deadline is reached.

†For such an increase in spending to drive up the exchange rate, tight money is also required, as in the United States in the 1980s. See Hooper and Mann (1989) or Goulder and Eichengreen (1991) for discussion and for a reconstruction of U.S. experience. Of course, it does not stretch credulity to imagine that the German authorities will continue to insist on a relatively tight monetary policy.

two situations, of course, is that other European currencies are now tightly tied to the DM. With the removal of capital controls, exchange rate realignment is now much more difficult than before.* Given this inability to realign, the franc and pound will rise along with the DM, pricing French and British producers out of international markets. As in the United States in the early 1980s, the result will be howls of pain from domestic producers and the intensification of protectionist pressure.

Moreover, with Germany forced to finance the reconstruction of its eastern lander and the EC having to help finance the modernization of the economies of Eastern Europe, there is less money to compensate regions whose industries decline as a result of 1992, and less money to retrain unemployed workers. Fortress Europe becomes correspondingly more likely.

Economic and political turmoil in Eastern Europe and the Soviet Union poses an equally disturbing threat. Hard economic times and political strife raise the specter of large-scale migration from Europe's East to the more prosperous West. The nations of the EC, already undergoing the difficult structural adjustments associated with economic integration, can hardly be expected to welcome this flood of immigrants. Europe will have to adopt a common external policy toward immigration; otherwise, immigrants will enter through the country with the most liberal policy and quickly move on to others. For the reasons just described, there is good reason to expect that the Community will adopt tough rather than lenient policies on immigration. That is likely to antagonize the governments of Eastern Europe and to suggest an obvious analogy to the treatment of imports of foreign goods.

EUROPEAN SECURITY

The specter of Fortress Europe—a Community unified internally but suffering from strained relations with the United States, Japan, and the Soviet Union—suggests that Europe will become

---

*Capital controls increased the cost of speculative attacks and gave monetary policy-makers a modicum of insulation. Now, however, as soon as there is the slightest hint that governments are contemplating a realignment, speculators will dump the currency likely to be devalued, forcing its depreciation. If policy-mak-

increasingly self-reliant for its security needs. Its American ally will no longer be willing to contribute to the continent's defense if U.S. exporters find their goods shut out of European markets. Evidence that defense spending diverts resources from alternative uses contributing more directly to the growth of productivity, combined with the ongoing need to cut U.S. public spending on nonessential programs, will undermine the American public's sympathy for sharing the burden of European security. Thus for economic reasons, not merely for diplomatic and political ones, NATO as we know it may not survive far into the twenty-first century.

As this recognition dawns on European politicians, national security arguments for protecting strategic industries will acquire new life. The kind of arguments that gained currency in the United States during the Gulf War will become fashionable in Europe. The EC, it will be argued, needs its own semiconductor and aircraft industries because it cannot afford to rely on Japan or the United States for components essential to its military capability. This argument, in my view, is fallacious. Increasingly self-reliant is not the same as self-reliant. Europe need not aspire to economic or military self-sufficiency. Economic and diplomatic cooperation with the United States and Japan can continue. For Europe, just as for the United States and Japan, economic self-sufficiency in high technology as in most other kinds of goods comes at high cost. Policies creating trade frictions increase the likelihood that those costs will ultimately be incurred.

What form will Europe's new defense arrangements take? It seems logical that the continent's new defense architecture will grow out of political arrangements designed to manage the process of economic integration. Economic integration, I have argued, creates difficult policy problems with far-reaching political repercussions. How to handle immigration, how to set the common external tariff, how to structure the EuroFed are all fundamentally political problems, like defense. The 1992 program has provided much of the impetus for the new political union treaty now being negotiated between the twelve members of the Community. The Germans in particular have made clear that they regard monetary and political

---

ers are truly committed to stabilizing the exchange rate, they cannot now afford to let the market think that they are willing to contemplate devaluation.

union as inseparable. France seems inclined to go along. Jacques Delors, President of the European Commission, has urged that defense be written into the political union treaty. In January 1991 France and Germany proposed that the Western European Union (WEU) defense grouping should eventually become the vehicle for an EC security policy.

It is inevitable that Germany will play a larger role in Europe's security relations than it has for the last forty years. In part Germany's prominence will reflect the growing weight of its economy, a trend that will only be accentuated by German unification. In part growing Germany influence can be forecast on historical grounds. Just as the fears and memories of a bellicose Germany that encouraged the Allies to dismantle its economy after World War II—a misguided policy that ultimately contributed to the partition of the country—have receded sufficiently that by 1990 they posed no obstacle to reunification, with the passage of time those fears and memories will become less likely to prevent the reestablishment of a German standing army or an integral role for Germany in Europe's security affairs.

Ultimately, however, Germany's prominence in Europe's new security system is a corollary of the 1992 program itself. Other European countries see monetary unification as an integral element of the integration process, for they wish to recapture from Germany at least some control over European monetary policy. The Bundesbank now essentially controls the monetary rudder for all of Europe. When Germany pursues a restrictive monetary policy, other European countries, unwilling to allow their currencies to depreciate against the DM, are forced to follow suit. With the establishment of the EuroFed, the other members of the Community will essentially obtain a vote on the board of the Bundesbank. The question this raises, of course, is what is in it for Germany. Germany presently controls its own monetary destiny. Given its traditional phobia about inflation, it is hard to see why it should willingly delegate even partial control over its monetary fate to its more inflation-inclined European neighbors. The obvious explanation is that monetary unification is part of a larger bargain. Germany has decided to sacrifice a modicum of inflation insurance in return for increased say over Europe's security arrangements. Reunified Germany's border would be the first to be breached by either tanks or immigrants from Eastern Europe, the Balkans, and Russia. From this perspective it is not surprising that Germany is willing to contemplate a trade of economic for security influence.

A FRAMEWORK FOR ANALYZING ECONOMIC-SECURITY INTERACTIONS

Our parallel discussions of economic integration and European security suggest that the countries of the EC should be thought of as engaged simultaneously in a pair of strategic games, one over the conduct of economic affairs, the other over the structuring and financing of security arrangements. The simultaneity of these two games should be evident to the participants themselves. In this section I shall introduce an analytical framework that can be used to assess the implications for policy of this situation.

The issue is what ramifications the simultaneity of strategic interaction in the two domains has for the likelihood of cooperation. In both the economic and security domains cooperation is advantageous. In the economic sphere there are benefits from coordinating tax rates and limiting industrial subsidies to prevent destructive competition in which countries undercut their neighbors in order to attract footloose enterprises. There are advantages to both Europe and North America of maintaining open trade between the two continents. In the security sphere there are advantages to coordinating financial and physical contributions to the continent's collective security.

At the same time there are strong incentives in both domains for countries to defect from cooperative arrangements. Even if all jurisdictions are better off when none offers subsidies and tax concessions to lure business away from other areas, each government retains the incentive to reneg on its agreement to refrain so long as it believes that it will escape retaliation. Similarly, even if all countries are better off when they jointly shoulder the burden of collective security, each one retains an incentive to shirk insofar as it bears the full costs of its own financial and physical contribution but the returns in terms of collective security accrue to its allies as well as to itself.* So long as it anticipates that other countries

*This application is the basis for the classic article on the free-rider problem by Olson and Zeckhauser (1966).

will continue to contribute to the Community's collective security, it has an incentive to contribute less than it would if the cooperative solution could be enforced.

Each of these dilemmas is nothing more, of course, than an example of the free-rider problem that leads to the underprovision of all commodities with public good characteristics. It is precisely analogous to the dilemma facing members of a cartel that reap monopoly rents when they jointly restrict output but nonetheless have the incentive to violate their agreement and increase production if they think that they can avoid detection and retaliation. What is distinctive about the present situation is that two such games involving the same players are underway simultaneously.

This is a problem to which specialists in industrial organization have devoted some attention under the guise of multimarket oligopoly. The question they address is whether firms that compete with one another in a number of distinct geographical markets or in the provision of a number of differentiated products are better able to cooperate. The traditional answer, according to economists like Edwards (1955), is that a multiplicity of contacts is conducive to cooperation. Since firms that cheat can be punished with retaliation in all markets, they are likely to be deterred from behaving noncooperatively in any one of them. The problem with this argument, as Bernheim and Whinston (1990) note, is that agents, recognizing that they will be punished in all markets, will revert to noncooperative behavior in all markets should they decide to reneg. Multimarket contact, in other words, increases the returns to reneging along with the potential costs. In general, there is no obvious presumption that multimarket contact or, in our application, the existence of simultaneous games in the economic and security domains increases or reduces the likelihood of cooperation.

More purchase on the problem requires a specific model. In Alt and Eichengreen (1989), we follow Bernheim and Whinston in considering infinitely repeated, full-information games. We assume that at every point in time the strategies selected comprise a Nash equilibrium. Since there may be multiple Nash equilibria, we restrict our attention to those which are subgame perfect.* We further

---

*In a Nash equilibrium, no player has an incentive to alter its strategy, given the strategies of its rivals. A subgame perfect Nash equilibrium to a repeated game is one in which strategies form a Nash equilibrium in every subset of repetitions.

narrow the range of alternatives by focusing on optimal collusive Nash equilibria.* We focus on the optimal collusive Nash equilibrium identified by Abreu (1988): governments adopt the simple strategy of retaliating against deviations by their foreign counterparts with the most severe punishments feasible.[†]

With these assumptions, Bernheim and Whinston provide an irrelevance result showing that when the two simultaneous games are identical in every respect, whether or not the same players are involved in both is irrelevant to the prospects for cooperation. If the two games are played in isolation, the same strategy (cooperate or do not cooperate) is adopted in each (since the two situations are symmetrical in all respects). If the parallelism of the two games is then acknowledged, the decision of one player to defect from cooperation in one game will lead his counterpart to retaliate by defecting from the cooperative solution in both games. Thus the same outcomes will obtain in both games, and the incentives to cooperate are exactly the same as when the two games are played in isolation.

This irrelevance result is useful, of course, only as a benchmark against which to compare the implications of various asymmetries. Consider a particular asymmetry—namely, response lags that differ across games. Retaliation, which still takes the form of the severest possible punishment in both arenas, will be swift if it is elicited by deviation in one game, slow if caused by deviation in the other. Imagine, for example, that American retaliation against the EC is swift if the latter shirks on its agreement to contribute to defending the interests of the North Atlantic alliance, but U.S. retaliation (in the form of trade sanctions) against subsidies extended to European semiconductor and aircraft industries takes place only with a lag. Such an assumption is plausible insofar as actions in the defense sphere are relatively transparent. (The United States knows whether

---

*The optimal collusive Nash equilibrium to a repeated game is that subgame perfect Nash equilibrium in which the expected welfare of the players is highest. Optimal collusive Nash equilibria satisfy the requirement of dynamic consistency: players act in their own best interest under all circumstances, thereby ruling out incredible threats.

[†]Intuitively, the most severe possible punishment is optimal since it minimizes the probability that other governments will deviate and hence maximizes the likelihood of cooperation.

or not European nations are contributing troops and materiel to Operation Desert Shield, but the scope and nature of subsidies to industry can be disguised.) If the parallelism of the two games is not recognized, cooperation between the United States and Europe will be easier to sustain in the economic game than in the defense game. The country that renegs on its agreement to behave cooperatively reaps benefits until retaliation occurs and suffers costs thereafter; the longer the response lag, the greater the present value of the benefits relative to the costs. Hence the incentive to reneg is greater in the market with the longer response lag. In our example, the United States and the EC may cooperate in economic affairs but not in defense.

Suppose that the United States and the EC previously played these games without acknowledging their parallelism, cooperating in economics but not in defense. Suddenly their parallelism is recognized. From the assumptions of optimal collusive equilibria, it follows that failure to cooperate in one game will lead to retaliation in both. Although each party previously had an incentive to play the game with the long response lag noncooperatively, parallelism raises the stakes by increasing the scope for retaliation. Parallelism serves to "pool the incentive constraints" in the two areas (Bernheim and Whinston 1990). Rather than comparing the costs and benefits of defection for each game and choosing strategies accordingly, governments pool costs and benefits across games before deciding whether to cooperate or defect across the board.

Removing the assumption that an identical set of players is involved in both games may similarly alter the scope for cooperation. Imagine, for example, that the United States and EC are engaged in both the economic and defense arenas as before, but in addition Japan participates in the economic game.* Holding constant other features of the games, it is generally the case that the

---

*One could argue that it is equally plausible to assume that Japan should be involved in the defense game. All that matters for the present argument, however, is that the extraneous player, in this case Japan, be more intimately involved in one game than in the other. I would argue that Japan is much more involved in Europe's economic affairs than in its security affairs. On the one hand, Japanese penetration of the European automotive and high-technology sectors is viewed as a pressing issue; on the other hand, Japan's constitution continues to severely limit its involvement with the United States and Europe in attaining security goals.

larger the number of players, the less the likelihood of cooperation. It is harder to hold together large coalitions than small ones, or to cartelize markets with many firms than markets with few since the larger the number of players, the smaller the share of the costs suffered by the player who deviates. If two players contribute equally to their common defense, each suffers half the consequences of either one's decision to deviate from their agreement to cooperate. But if three countries contribute equally to the maintenance of an open trading system, each suffers only a third of the consequences of the decision to deviate from their collective agreement.

If when considered in isolation the defense game was played cooperatively while the economic game was not, then recognition that these games were proceeding in parallel will alter the likelihood of a cooperative outcome in each. The countries involved in both games (in this case, the United States and Europe) realize that they are rivals in both arenas. If they fail to cooperate in either game, then optimal retaliation dictates noncooperation in both. Hence if the countries are better off when cooperating in both games than when playing both noncooperatively, parallelism increases the likelihood of cooperation in the game previously played noncooperatively. Recognizing that erecting Fortress Europe will provoke not just U.S. trade retaliation but also undermine the prospects for cooperation on defense with the United States, Europe may maintain low tariffs even if, when taken in isolation, the strategy is undesirable.

What of the extraneous player, in this case Japan? Whether other players' recognition of parallelism encourages the extraneous player to cooperate depends on the nature of the spillovers involved. In our example, from Japan's point of view the benefits of continuing to contribute to the maintenance of an open trading system (rather than dumping goods in Europe or following other practices that yield returns in the short run but court costs subsequently insofar as they may lead to U.S. and European retaliation and to a proliferation of trade restrictions) will be increased if economic cooperation by the United States and Europe means that they maintain open markets to exports from all sources. If U.S.-EC cooperation takes the form of open trade between them but barriers against exports from Japan, the incentive for Japan to follow a noncooperative strategy is enhanced rather than diminished.

IMPLICATIONS FOR ECONOMIC POLICY*

What are the implications of this analysis for the interaction between European economic integration and European security? First, the realization that the process of economic integration and the restructuring of European security have reached critical junctures simultaneously raises the stakes. The framework developed here suggests that it is unlikely that a satisfactory outcome will be reached in one of these arenas but not in the other. The pooling of incentive constraints points strongly to the probability that intra-European cooperation and EC-U.S. cooperation will obtain or not obtain in both arenas.

This heightens the importance for governments to resist pressure for favors from special interest groups with little reason to take into account the broader implications of the policies for which they lobby. In the present situation, subsidies to European industries which antagonize their American competitors threaten to undermine not just U.S.-EC economic cooperation but U.S.-EC defense cooperation as well. Daimler-Benz's recent request for $4 billion in government aid to subsidize the development costs of producing a small regional airliner is disturbing in this light, as is the French government's decision to provide $1.5 billion in subsidies to two struggling state-owned electronics companies and to give Air France $390 million above and beyond the emergency aid allowed by the EC during the Gulf War. The United States has already announced plans to file a second GATT complaint against Airbus and threatened to impose special duties and quotas on Airbus sales in the U.S. market. (See Betts 1991.) Imagine the impact on U.S.-European relations, and not just in the economic sphere, of subsidies to European airlines that permit the latter to buy up American carriers on the cheap. Imagine Washington, D.C.'s reaction if France and other European nations subsidize their electronics firms with capital and research funds, and if the latter expand their presence in the U.S. market or try to take over their U.S. competitors.

Policies that violate the Community's Subsidies Code threaten not only to throw a wrench in the works of economic integration, but also promise to increase the difficulty of agreeing on a new

*In this section I draw directly on Alt and Eichengreen (1989).

European defense architecture. The example cited above of prospective German government subsidies for developing a small commercial airliner is a case in point. These subsidies are antagonizing the British because of Britain's stake in Airbus, which would compete directly with the new product, and also because of the British government's strong preference for unsubsidized development. Not only do they represent an obstacle on the road to economic integration, but also they complicate discussions of the prospective role of a standing German army in the WEU.

A final set of policy implications follows from the fact that the structure of the economic and security games in which Europe and the United States are engaged is not simply a datum to which the players must adapt. The principals have some capacity to shape the structure of their economic and strategic interaction. Attempts to artificially segment the two games from one another are probably unrealistic. More promising are initiatives to shorten response lags in arenas where they are relatively long. Shorter response lags, as shown above, increase the costs of reneging on cooperative agreements and thereby raise the likelihood that cooperation will be sustained. International conventions, like the GATT, which enhance the transparency of economic policies and provide mechanisms for quickly imposing sanctions against nations that violate commercial norms, shorten response lags in the economic sphere. The argument of this paper suggests that this will enhance the prospects for EC-U.S. cooperation on matters of security as well as economics.

REFERENCES

This paper draws freely on my previous publications on European integration (Eichengreen 1990, 1991, 1992). I thank Beverly Crawford for helpful comments.

Abreu, Dilip. 1988. "Infinitely Repeated Games with Discounting: A General Theory." *Econometrica* 56: 383–96.

Alt, James, and Barry Eichengreen. 1989. "Parallel and Overlapping Games: Theory with an Application to European Gas Trade." *Economics and Politics* 1: 119–40.

Bernheim, R. Douglas and Michael D. Whinston. 1990. "Multimarket Contact and Collusive Behavior." *Rand Journal of Economics* 21: 1–26.

Betts, Paul. 1991. "U.S. Plans Fresh GATT Complaint Against Airbus." *Financial Times,* 7 May, pp. 1, 20.

Caballero, Ricardo, and Richard Lyons. 1990. "Internal Versus External Economies in European Industry." *European Economic Review* 34: 805–26.

Cooper, Richard. 1985. "Trade Policy as Foreign Policy." In *Trade Policy in the United States,* ed. Robert Stern. Cambridge, Mass.: MIT Press.

Edwards, Corwin. 1955. "Conglomerate Bigness as a Source of Power." In National Bureau of Economic Research, *Business Concentration and Price Policy.* Princeton: Princeton University Press.

Eichengreen, Barry. 1990. "One Money for Europe: Lessons from the U.S. Currency and Customs Union." *Economic Policy* 10: 118–87.

————. 1991. "Coûts et avantages de l'unification monetaire l'Europe." In *Vers l'union economique et monetaire européenne,* ed. Pierre Beregevoy. Paris: Ministry of Finance.

————. 1992. "Is Europe an Optimum Currency Area?" In *European Economic Integration: The View from Outside,* ed. Herbert Grubel. London: Macmillan.

Goldstein, Morris, and G. Woglom. 1991. "Market-Based Fiscal Discipline in Monetary Unions: Evidence from the U.S. Municipal Bond Market." Unpublished manuscript, International Monetary Fund.

Goulder, Lawrence, and Barry Eichengreen. 1991. "The Impact of Temporary and Permanent Import Surcharges on the U.S. Balance of Trade." In *Empirical Studies of Commercial Policy,* ed. Robert Baldwin. Chicago: University of Chicago Press.

Hooper, Peter, and Catherine Mann. 1989. "The Emergence and Persistence of the U.S. External Deficit." *Princeton Studies in International Finance* no. 65.

Olson, Mancur, and Richard Zeckhauser. 1966. "An Economic Theory of Alliances." *Review of Economics and Statistics* 48: 226–79.

Tiebout, C. 1956. "A Pure Theory of Local Government Expenditures." *Journal of Political Economy* 64: 416–24.

Wightman, David. 1956. *Economic Co-Operation in Europe.* New York: Frederick A. Praeger.

EUROPEAN ECONOMIC SECURITY IN THE NEW GLOBAL ENVIRONMENT

Stephen D. Krasner

INTRODUCTION

Economic security could involve the welfare of groups within a country, the electoral prospects of parties, the freedom of action available to government policy-makers, the stability of a particular regime, or the aggregate economic welfare and growth prospects for the country as a whole. Regardless of how economic security is understood, however, it could be threatened by changes in external economic conditions.

These threats could be generated in two ways. First, external economic conditions could deteriorate as a result of systemic changes. Global economic regimes could break down because of the unintended consequences of choices made by one or more actors. Major world depressions are the clearest examples of such phenomena. Dramatic price changes could be prompted by natural disasters such as a wide-scale drought or global warming. There need not be any effort by any actor in the system to target a particular country or set of countries. Second, external economic conditions might also change as a result of policies taken by other states explicitly designed to affect the behavior of one or more target countries. A donor country might, for instance, threaten to withhold aid unless the potential recipient alters its policy. The use of economic resources for coercive purposes can be effective only if the opportunity costs of change are asymmetrical. The opportunity cost of change is a function of the degree of external exposure and the ability to adjust.[1]

Holding other factors equal, external exposure is inversely related to size. Large countries are likely to be less involved in external transactions and therefore are less vulnerable to external changes. The ability to adjust is also a function of the mobility of factors, which, in turn, depends on the behavior of both governments and markets. More developed markets facilitate adjustment because they make it easier to reallocate factors across different kinds of activities. Governments that encourage the development of markets and provide social safety nets also facilitate adjustment. Governments that promote rigidities in their economies or are unable to provide social safety nets impede the ability to adjust.

In contemporary Europe the most vulnerable states are the smaller countries of Eastern Europe. Although Poland is larger than Romania, the Czech and Slovak Republic, Hungary, Yugoslavia or any of its parts, and Bulgaria, the economies of all these countries are all relatively small. Their markets are not well developed. Their political institutions are fragile. The developed states of Western Europe, both large and small, can more readily adjust to external shocks, and are therefore less vulnerable and more economically secure. While the economic situation of Russia is problematic, its economy is both large and relatively isolated from the world economy. The economic security of Russia might be at risk, but not because of external shocks or pressures.

Because of the decline of American power, the international economic system is now more susceptible to a general breakdown than it was in the two or three decades immediately following World War II. The most likely source of such a shock would be international energy markets. All states would be affected by an international energy crisis, although the small states of Eastern Europe would probably be most severely affected. Bulgaria, the Czech and Slovak Republic, Hungary, Poland, Yugoslavia, and Romania are also the most likely targets of any specific efforts at economic coercion. The most likely source of such coercion would be Germany. The strains of the 1930s, when Germany did use its economic resources to threaten the security of Eastern Europe, could reappear, however, only if the European Community (EC) disintegrated and the economy of Russia collapsed; only then would the asymmetries of opportunity costs be significant enough to give Germany real coercive leverage.

Hence while the end of the cold war and the decline of American power have made the economic security of Europe more problematic, the continent and the individual countries within it—even the countries of Eastern Europe—are relatively secure from external economic shocks and pressures. A collapse of world energy or financial markets, the only potential threat to the stability of the international economy as a whole, is not likely. Imbalances of power which have undermined the stability of the center of Europe in the past are now contained by the integration of Germany into Europe and by the balancing role of Russia and the United States. If the economic security of any part of Europe is threatened, it is because of endogenous political developments—notably ethnic conflicts— rather than external economic strains.

THE EUROPEAN SITUATION

It is possible to map the European countries with regard to their size and their ability to adjust. Gross national product (GNP) can be taken as a measure of size; per capita income can be taken as a measure of the ability to adjust.[2] The European countries fall into four groups: large and highly developed, small and highly developed, large and less highly developed, and small and less highly developed.

Group I: Large and Highly Developed
   Germany
   France
   Britain
   Italy

Group II: Small and Highly Developed
   Belgium
   Netherlands
   Austria
   Switzerland
   Sweden
   Norway
   Denmark
   Finland

Group III: Large and Less Highly Developed
   Russia

Group IV: Small and Less Highly Developed
   Spain
   Portugal
   Ireland
   Bulgaria
   Czech and Slovak Republic
   Hungary
   Poland
   Romania
   Yugoslavia or parts thereof
   Members of the former USSR, excepting Russia

These are simpleminded categories, but they offer a rough map. The large and highly developed countries are the least threatened with regard to economic security. Even these countries, however, are relatively small compared with the United States and even Japan, and they are much more involved in the world economy. For the large and highly developed European countries the share of trade (exports plus imports) in aggregate economic activity varied from about 35 percent for Italy to nearly 60 percent for Germany in the late 1980s.* For the United States and Japan the comparable figure is about 20 percent.

For smaller European countries, both highly and less highly developed, the ratio of trade to GNP can exceed 100 percent. In 1988, for instance, the ratio of Irish exports plus imports of goods and NF Services to GNP was 1.69.[3] If per capita income is a good proxy for factor mobility and adjustment, the small, less highly developed European states, which are very dependent on trade, are the most vulnerable to external shocks and pressures.

The extent to which the economic security of a country could be threatened is, obviously, not fully indicated by these crude categories. Domestic political structures can play a critically important role. As the work of Peter Katzenstein and others has demonstrated, the small highly developed European states have developed political institutions that enhance their ability to adjust to changes in an external

*The German figure will probably decrease as a result of unification because there was substantial trade between East and West Germany.

environment over which they have little control but from which they cannot extricate themselves. These states have developed what Katzenstein terms democratic corporatist structures. There is a commitment to consultation. Consensus decision-making prevails among a limited number of elite groups. Individuals may circulate among several critical sectors. One person, for instance, might be the leader of a union and the director of a company, and might even at the same time be a member of the government. Democratic corporatist political systems make an effort to incorporate all significant groups into the decision-making structure and even to overrepresent relatively weak groups. Perhaps most important, these political systems attempt to spread the burden of adjustment, providing for generous unemployment benefits and retraining programs. This political structure reflects a functional adaptation to an economic situation that demands rapid and flexible responses to the external environment.[4]

The situation for all of the highly developed European countries, whether large or small, can be contrasted with smaller developing countries in the Third World. Such countries are usually extremely vulnerable to external shocks. Their exports are often highly concentrated and dependent upon macroeconomic conditions in advanced countries over which they have no control. The economic well-being of copper-exporting states, for instance, may be more dependent on interest rate policies in the United States and Europe than on any policy that is under the direct control of their own governments because the demand for copper is sensitive to the level of activity in the automobile and housing industries, and these industries are, in turn, directly affected by interest rate levels. No policy was more damaging for the well-being of Third World countries than the decision in the first years of the Reagan administration to manage American macroeconomic policy almost entirely through monetary rather than fiscal measures. This pushed real interest rates to very high levels around the world, as well as in the United States, and greatly increased the debt obligations of Third World states, whose payments were determined by floating rate loans.[5]

Poverty and bureaucratic limitations have made it very difficult for small developing states to throw themselves with open arms into the uncertainties of the global marketplace. The World Bank, the IMF, and many industrialized countries have been extolling the benefits of free trade. Many less developed countries have recently adopted the same position, at least rhetorically. A fascinating empirical investigation by Robert Bates and colleagues shows, however, that countries will adopt freer trade policies only if they can provide their populations with an adequate social safety net—that is, if they can offer some insurance against unexpected shocks from the international environment.[6] Very few developing countries are in a position to provide such a safety net.

In sum, compared with most of the rest of the world, the economic security of the European countries is not much at risk. There is, however, considerable variance within Europe. The highly developed countries, especially the large highly developed countries, are the least vulnerable. The small less developed countries are the most vulnerable. Because of their fragile political institutions and weak markets, Bulgaria, the Czech and Slovak Republic, Hungary, Poland, Romania, most of the former USSR, and Yugoslavia and its successor states are almost certainly the most vulnerable.

THE EXTERNAL ENVIRONMENT

The external environment can pose threats to economic security through two different paths—systemic collapse and specific pressure. Even very large states might not be able to insulate themselves from a systemic collapse. All of the major industrialized countries suffered major economic deprivation during the Great Depression of the 1930s, an event which Charles Kindleberger and others argue was related to the failure of the United States to exercise effective leadership.[7]

In contrast, only vulnerable states can become the target of specific pressures. The more asymmetrical the relative opportunity costs of change, the more susceptible a country is to external targeted pressure. If, for instance, Country A can engage in a foreign economic policy that would have little impact on its own well-being but a great deal of impact on Country B, then Country A is in a position to exercise pressure against Country B. Country A can pressure Country B into changing its policies because the implementation of the threat would have little impact on Country A but a great deal of impact on Country B. Country B will accede to the threat if the costs of bowing to Country A's pressure are less than the costs that Country B would have to bear if Country A implemented its threat.[8] Given the level of interaction among the highly advanced European states, both large and small, it is not very likely that they would become the target of explicit economic pressure. The most likely targets for such pressures would be Bulgaria, the Czech and Slovak Republic, Hungary, Poland, Romania, most of what was the USSR, and Yugoslavia and its successors.

SYSTEMIC STABILITY AND AMERICAN POWER

Optimistic assessments of systemic stability point to growing levels of interdependence and knowledge as firm foundations for the growth and prosperity of the international economy as a whole and individual states. A replay of the 1930s could not happen. States, multinational corporations, international financial institutions, global banks, and many exporting industries have high stakes in the stability of the global economy. Public actors now have a much higher level of knowledge than they did in the 1930s, especially about macroeconomic management. The policy mistakes of the 1930s—the failure to support the international banking system, the imposition of very high tariffs by the United States, the orthodox monetary policies followed by some countries in the wake of the initial downturn—would not be repeated. If these kinds of arguments are correct, then there is little or no threat of a systemic crisis. We can say, with Alfred E. Newman, an old American cartoon character, "What, me worry?"

A more cautious assessment points to the importance of political leadership. In the past, that leadership has come from the United States. While the main rival of the United States, the Soviet Union, has imploded, the world is moving toward a more equal distribution of power. Effective global management is more difficult in a multipolar world. Public goods problems are more acute. More powerful states might be less and less willing to bear a disproportionate share of the costs of maintaining the system, whether acting as lenders of last resort in financial markets or intervenors of first resort to stifle local instabilities such as unrest in the Persian Gulf. It is more difficult to manage the global economy if the United States is less willing to absorb the costs of adjustment for others, if

American policy-makers place less emphasis on the stability of the international economic system as a whole and more on the specific economic interests of the United States.

The relative position of the United States has changed since the end of World War II and the general pattern of that change is clear. The United States emerged from World War II with extraordinary resources across a very wide range of issue areas. It had by far the largest GNP. It was the only state that possessed nuclear weapons. Although its army was partly demobilized after the war, it had a formidable blue water navy. It held far more international financial reserves than any other state and was the only significant source of international capital. Its industries possessed the lead in cutting edge technologies.

The relative position of the United States declined from the late 1940s until about 1970. There has not been much change in the last two decades, as indicated by overall economic output, the single best indicator of underlying capabilities, albeit a very crude measure. The U.S. share of aggregate production for all OECD countries fell from 58 percent in 1953 to 38 percent in 1975. Since that time it has remained relatively stable, accounting for 35 percent of output in 1988.[9]

Per capita output can be taken as a very rough proxy for technological capability and factor mobility, variables that are consequential for the ability of a state to redeploy its resources to either resist a foreign threat or increase its leverage on another actor. The pattern here is similar to that in aggregate production, with the position of the United States vis-à-vis other industrializing countries falling until the 1970s and remaining more or less stable since then. Only Japan has continued to close the gap with the United States.*

The American share of world trade has followed a similar pattern to that of aggregate output, declining in the immediate postwar period and stabilizing over the last two decades. The U.S. share fell sharply in the late 1940s and 1950s, and then more or less

---

*The situation in the advanced industrialized market economy countries can be contrasted with that in many LDCs, which have limited capital markets and where labor is relatively immobile. Such countries are vulnerable to shocks from the external environment which they cannot control or easily adjust to. (This argument is developed in Krasner, note 5 below.)

stabilized between 24 and 28 percent. The composition of its share has, however, changed dramatically. In the 1950s, the U.S. share of world exports was greater than its share of world imports; in the 1980s, the U.S. share of world imports was greater than its share of world exports.[10]

One area where American capabilities have dramatically declined is monetary reserves. The U.S. share of world monetary reserves fell from 50 percent of world reserves in 1948 to 15 percent in 1970, remained at 13–17 percent during the mid-1980s, and then fell to under 10 percent in 1988. Japan passed the United States as the country with the largest international reserves in 1987, the first time that the United States had not ranked first in the postwar period.[11]

Most dramatically for global economic performance, the United States no longer has, as it did before 1970, surplus crude oil production capacity that could be used to offset cutbacks by Third World oil-exporting states. Moreover, by the early 1970s the seven major oil companies (five of which were American) had made considerable concessions to host country governments. The companies could no longer dictate production levels.

In the Gulf War the United States acted to prevent further price increases that would have resulted from the ability of Iraq to dictate production levels in the Arabian peninsula (Kuwait, Saudi Arabia, Abu Dhabi). This military action, which involved moving 450,000 troops halfway around the world, was an impressive demonstration of continued—indeed enhanced—American military power.* It would, however, have been easier to deal with the prospects of higher oil prices if the United States still had had surplus production capacity of its own. In that case increasing production rates in Texas could have been a substitute for sending troops.

In sum, American power has declined since the peak immediately after the conclusion of World War II. This is hardly surprising. Western Europe and Japan were destined to recover from the devastation of the war, even if it was difficult to predict that they would recover so well.[12] This decline in relative American

---

*Had the Soviet Union opposed this action, as it almost certainly would have at any point before 1985, it is difficult to believe that American intervention would have taken place, although the Soviets might have kept their military client, Iraq, from invading Kuwait in the first place.

capability was most pronounced before 1970. Some major indicators of capabilities—especially share of world GNP—have remained fairly stable since then. The United States still remains by far the world's largest and most diverse economy.

Nevertheless, the recovery of Europe and Japan and other shifts in capabilities have eroded the relative position of the United States, even if it remains exceptionally formidable.[13] The United States has moved from being a net creditor to a major net debtor, making American financial markets sensitive to external developments and constraining the freedom of action of U.S. policy-makers. Japan has challenged the pre-eminence of the United States in many high-technology industries. Most pointedly, the United States lost control of the world oil market shortly after 1970.

The changes in the relative international capabilities of the United States have resulted in a shift in American policies from the pursuit of very open-handed milieu goals in the immediate postwar period to a much greater concern with specific American economic interests in more recent years. The United States has become increasingly focused on pursuing its own specific economic interests and less concerned with preserving the stability of the system as a whole, although, as the Gulf War demonstrates, it is still prepared to accept major leadership responsibilities.

During the first part of the cold war, American leaders presumed that all good things would go together, that they could accomplish all of their core objectives—the promotion of economic development in the non-Communist world, economic growth for the United States, and increasing utility for American consumers—by pursuing a policy of liberal internationalism.[14] The possibility that promoting prosperity for the Western bloc as a whole could impede American growth, weaken the relative position of the United States, damage particular American industries, and even threaten the ability of the United States to effectively assume global leadership was not seriously confronted by American policy-makers.

In recent years American policy has begun to change in the face of increased external pressures, but there is as yet no articulated alternative to the guiding philosophy of liberal internationalism, even as the principles and norms of this approach are violated by an increasing number of specific American policies. While the general principles and commitments of American policy-makers have not changed, however, both external and internal pressures have led to the adoption of new policies that are based more on specific than diffuse reciprocity.[15] American foreign economic policy has not been characterized by the replacement of one set of principles by another but rather by the accretion of new practices on top of earlier policies that were based on different principles and norms.[16]

Trade legislation since 1970 has, on balance, been less concerned with multilateralism and the stability of the global economic system as a whole and more concerned with specific American interests. American legislation eased provisions for invoking escape clause actions, introduced unfair trading as a basis for American retaliation in section 301 of the 1974 Trade Act, encouraged bilateral free trade agreements (a move away from multilateralism), and reduced the power of the State and Treasury Departments, the two agencies most committed to free trade. In the summer of 1991 the United States concluded a semiconductor agreement with Japan which for the first time explicitly set targets for the entry of American products into a foreign market.

The growing American concern with specific interests has not been limited to the area of trade. In international monetary policy the United States moved from concern for global stability in the 1960s to a focus on more narrow American interests. In the early 1960s the Kennedy administration was willing to impose deflationary pressures on the American economy to preserve the international value of the dollar. In August 1971, American policy-makers suspended the gold convertibility of the dollar and imposed an almost across the board 10 percent import surcharge, unilaterally ending the Bretton Woods system.[17] In the area of telecommunications, American officials have pressed other countries to open their markets to both American products and companies.

There has been a relationship between declining American power, changing American policy, and the performance and stability of the international economic system. The critical link in that relationship has been oil. International economic flows have continued to grow, in most areas and for most countries, at higher rates than national economic activity. This is especially true for finance. Changes in American power and policy have not led to a collapse of the global economy or anything even resembling such a development. While the commitment of the United States to the stability of the global order may have flagged, that order itself appears to be robust.

While various measures of international economic transactions—trade, finance, investment—are either growing or only marginally declining, the performance of national economies has been more problematic. Overall economic performance has declined since 1970: growth rates are slower, and unemployment and inflation are higher, as shown in Table 1. Growth rates for poor, middle-income, and developed market economy countries have all declined since the 1960s. With the exception of the industrialized countries, inflation rates have also grown steadily since the 1960s. Public debt service has increased dramatically from 7.1 percent of the export of goods and services for low-income countries in 1970 to 21.9 percent in 1987, and from 11.7 percent for middle-income countries to 23.9 percent.[18]

At least to some extent these negative aspects of international economic performance can be attributed to the declining power of the United States via changes in international energy markets. Higher and less stable oil prices are directly attributable to the declining power of the United States in this issue area. The United States lost control of the international energy market after 1970, primarily because it became a net oil importer, and secondarily because oil-exporting states were able to nationalize their oil fields. Nationalization ended the full vertical integration that had previously been enjoyed by the major international oil companies, most of which were American. As a result, oil prices rose precipitously in 1973–74, 1979–80, and 1990. Fuels accounted for 10 percent of world exports in 1963, 11 percent in 1973, 20 percent in 1979, and 21 percent in 1983. By 1987, however, fuels had fallen back to 11 percent of world exports.[19]

Higher and less stable oil prices worsened global economic performance. Many companies were forced to scrap some capacity and to alter their allocation of factors. This led to a fall in real wealth, a decline in aggregate demand because of government attempts to control rising inflation, and, for the United States, a worsening trade balance because of rising dollar exchange rates. These macroeconomic changes reduced the rate of productivity growth.[20]

The Third World debt crisis, which began partly as a result of the exceptional incentives that international banks had to recycle

Table 1

OVERALL ECONOMIC PERFORMANCE, 1960–87
(Percent)

Country/Economy	Average Annual Growth of GDP			Average Annual Rate o f Inflation		
	1960–70	1970–79	1980–87	1960–70	1970–79	1980–87
Low-income countries excluding China and India	4.3%	3.8%	1.7%	3.0%	10.9%	13.3%
Middle-income countries excluding oil exporters	6.1	5.5	2.8	3.0	13.3	62.3
Industrial market economies	5.1	3.2	2.6	4.3	9.4	5.2

Source: World Bank, *World Development Report, 1981 and 1989*, tables 1 and 2.

petro-dollars, also revealed an absence of American leadership—or any leadership for that matter. The funds flowing into these banks grew so precipitously as a result of the revenues generated by petroleum-exporting states that the banks almost pushed oil-importing Third World states into higher levels of borrowing, despite the fact that high rates of inflation in the mid-1970s made real interest rates negative for some loans. When real global interest rates rose in the late 1970s, many Third World countries found themselves in a debt squeeze which contributed to economic downturns more severe than anything they had experienced in the 1930s. Debt service ratios (debt payments as a percentage of the export of goods and services) for non-oil developing countries increased from 11.5 percent in 1974 to 22.3 percent in 1982 and remained at about the same level through the late 1980s.[21] Mexico experienced a growth rate of only 0.5 percent for the period 1980–87, compared with 6.5 percent for the period 1965–80; Argentina had a negative growth rate of -0.3 percent for the period 1980-87, compared with a positive rate of 3.3 percent for the period 1965–80.[22]

There was an absence of any leadership, including American leadership, in dealing with the problem of petro-currency recycling. Little guidance was given to banks. Little effort was made to steer the activities of oil-exporting states with surplus revenues. Most significantly, the decision by the Reagan administration to manage

American macroeconomic policy virtually exclusively through monetary measures led to a large increase in interest rates around the world which severely disadvantaged highly indebted Third World countries. Only when Mexico threatened to default in the early 1980s did American officials begin to take a more decisive role, and even then such leadership was initially limited to the chair of the Federal Reserve, Paul Volcker. The United States has subsequently floated several plans to manage Third World debt which have had some modest impact.

In sum, there has been a relationship between American power, American policy, and global economic stability. Declining American power led to unstable oil prices, and unstable oil prices have contributed to lower growth rates, higher inflation, and lower productivity growth. The failure of American leadership contributed to the international debt crisis of the Third World and (to a lesser extent) some countries of Eastern Europe.

Nevertheless, these systemic shocks have been fairly easily absorbed by the advanced industrialized countries. Their economic security has not yet been jeopardized by the loss of American power and leadership. Oil remains the most likely market that could pose future risks; managing price stability through military intervention does not indicate a stable market. Financial markets could also imperil the stability of the global system, but these markets have functioned well, at least for the wealthier countries of the world, despite the absence of American leadership. Unintended external shocks are not likely to threaten economic security in Europe.

NATIONAL VULNERABILITIES AND ECONOMIC COERCION

Economic security could be threatened not just by some systemic shock, but also by specific policies in which one country targets another. Such policies can be implemented only if the opportunity costs of change for the two parties are asymmetrical—that is, if it would be much more costly for one of the parties to accept change than for the other. Opportunity costs are a function of exposure to the external environment and the ability to adjust.[23] The large highly developed European states—Germany, Italy, France, and Britain—are not subject to such pressure from each other. Their economies are too locked together, the opportunity costs of change too symmetrical, for such pressures to be credibly applied. It is difficult to imagine that some external actor, even the United States, could apply such pressure. The major European economies are too large, too diverse, and too flexible to be vulnerable.

Russia may be in a somewhat more vulnerable position because its domestic situation is so fragile. Given the transition problems being experienced by Russia, adjustments to external shocks or direct pressures could be problematic. Russian involvement with the rest of the world is, however, still very limited, both because the Russian economy is large and because the legacy of central planning and socialism in one country restricted external contact.

Western agencies have been reluctant to offer estimates of Russian aggregate economic activity. The population of Russia, however, is about two times larger than that of the former Communist countries in Eastern Europe. In 1989, the gross external debt of the Soviet Union was $50.6 billion, compared with $39.9 billion for Poland, $20.6 billion for Hungary, and $9.0 billion for Bulgaria—all much smaller countries in terms of aggregate economic activity. The gross external debt of Bulgaria, the Czech and Slovak Republic, Hungary, Poland, and Romania combined was about $76 billion, while the debt of the Soviet Union was only $51 billion. In 1989 the total exports of Eastern Europe to the West were $30.9 billion, while the exports of the Soviet Union were $29.3 billion.[24] The Soviet Union was relatively uninvolved in the world economy and therefore not very vulnerable to external pressure. The former Soviet economy may collapse, but it will not be because of pressure from the West. Nor is it likely that rewards from the West in the form of higher levels of aid or trade concessions would be decisive.

The small highly developed states of Western Europe are also in a relatively strong position for opposite reasons. They are very heavily involved in the international economy, but so are their major trading partners, and, unlike the former Soviet Union, they have political and economic structures that facilitate adjustment to external pressures.

The interesting cases for Europe with regard to targeted external threats to national economic security are the countries of the former Eastern bloc. The smaller states of Central and Eastern Europe—including parts of the Commonwealth of Independent

States (CIS)—are relatively undeveloped. For some of them, involvement in the international economy is substantial; they are, or will be, more dependent on their trading partners than their trading partners will be on them. They are attempting major economic restructuring.

The East European countries are poor; per capita incomes for even the better-off countries, such as Poland and Hungary, are probably one-third less than the poorest countries of Western Europe and little more than 10 percent the per capita GNP of the wealthiest countries.[25] They are in a period of transition. They do not have the highly developed economic and political institutions of the small democratic corporatist states of Western Europe. Bulgaria, Hungary, and Poland have fairly high external debt burdens. Trade is becoming relatively more important as a percentage of GNP, although it is still lower than for most of the countries of Western Europe. Merchandise exports as a proportion of GNP ranged from a high of 34 percent for Bulgaria in 1988 to a low of 7 percent for Poland. These figures could rise to between 19 and 23 percent, which would be comparable to the smaller highly interdependent countries of Western Europe.[26] In sum, the countries of Eastern Europe are more susceptible to external pressure than the countries of Western Europe or than Russia.

The smaller states of Eastern Europe were very dependent on Germany before the creation of the Soviet bloc. Germany exported sophisticated consumer and capital goods in exchange for agricultural products, raw materials, and cheap manufactures. This pattern of trade prevailed from the middle of the nineteenth century until the 1940s.

At the same time, Germany was not very dependent on Eastern Europe. In 1929 Germany accounted for 30 percent of Polish trade, but Poland accounted for only 3 percent of German trade. Germany absorbed 28 percent of Czech exports and supplied 40 percent of Czech imports.[27] In 1928 Germany was the most important export market for Bulgaria, Romania, Poland, and the Czech and Slovak Republic, and the third most important export market for Yugoslavia and Hungary.[28] This situation, in which the relative opportunity costs of change were highly asymmetrical, invited, as Hirschman so elegantly demonstrated, the use of economic coercion. The Nazi regime established a set of trading relationships with the smaller countries of Eastern and Central Europe, including the use of non-transferable currencies, which made these countries very suscepti-ble to German economic pressure.

The creation of the Communist bloc radically altered the tra-ditional trading patterns of Eastern Europe. In 1987, 4 percent of exports from the Eastern trading bloc (which then included the GDR) went to West Germany, and 5.5 percent of the imports of the Eastern trading bloc came from West Germany.[29] In 1988, 81 percent of Bulgarian exports, 73 percent of Czechoslovak, 45 percent of Hungarian, 41 percent of Polish, and 41 percent of Romanian ex-ports went to other members of the CMEA. The Soviet Union was the most important export market for all of the countries of Eastern Europe, ranging from a low of 25 percent of Poland's export market to a high of 58 percent of Bulgaria's.[30]

The new political situation in the center of Europe will radi-cally change trading patterns and make Germany once again the economic linchpin of the middle of the continent. Germany has substantial economic resources in the form of capital, technology, and markets. One study estimates that had the East European countries never become socialist and had they developed along the same path as countries in Western Europe, Germany would account for 23 percent of Poland's exports, 19 percent of Romania's, 20 percent of Czechoslovakia's, 14 percent of Hungary's, and 21 per-cent of Bulgaria's. Germany would be the single largest export market for all of these countries. In contrast, exports to these coun-tries would account for between 1 and 8 percent of German exports and imports.[31] Although the socialist experience has undoubtedly altered the pattern of trade that will actually emerge, there will be a forceful redirection of East European trade toward the West and especially toward Germany.

Hence the potential for exercising political leverage against the countries of Eastern Europe may exist. The relative opportunity costs of change are highly asymmetrical. Western Europe as a whole, and perhaps Germany as an individual country, could make credible threats. Leverage could, however, be used for many differ-ent purposes. In the 1930s, the Nazi regime used economic threats to encourage conformity with Germany's foreign policy. In contrast, in the 1990s either Germany or the European Community (EC) could use its economic power to support developments in Eastern

Europe that would ultimately create more resilient domestic institutional arrangements, both economic and political, which would make these countries less vulnerable to external shocks or pressures.

A replay of the 1930s, in which economic asymmetries were used for coercive purposes, appears remote. Germany has a liberal democratic rather than an autocratic nationalistic polity. German policy has been closely bound to the European Community. The vision of a united Germany in a united Europe, so strongly articulated by Chancellor Helmut Kohl and Foreign Minister Hans-Dietrich Genscher, is a slogan designed to put to rest fears of German revanchism. Indeed the current leadership in Germany seems anxious to tie its own hands, to limit its freedom of action by binding itself to the Community. German support for the creation of the European Bank for Reconstruction and Development, headquartered in Britain with a French president, indicates a policy designed to weaken rather than enhance German leverage.

Even if the character of Germany's polity and its policies are ignored, there are severe constraints on any unilateral exercise of coercive leverage. Russia could act as a balancer because it is a much more important economic partner for the states of Eastern Europe than was the case before World War II. In 1928, the Soviet Union had virtually no trade whatsoever with Bulgaria, Romania, Hungary, and Yugoslavia and accounted for less than 2 percent of the trade of Poland and Hungary.[32] In the later 1980s, the Soviet Union was the most important trading partner for all of these countries. Even if there is dramatic readjustment of trade toward the West, Russia will still offer some counterbalance to Germany. In addition, the governing regime for international trade, which emphasizes multilateralism, nondiscrimination, and the reduction of trade barriers, also limits the opportunities for unilateral economic leverage. In an open system potential target states would have other options. More important, such an international regime makes it more difficult to engage in discriminatory trade practices, a necessary condition for the use of economic leverage.[33]

Germany has found it possible, however, to use economic leverage for benign objectives. In these cases, Germany has offered incentives rather than threatened sanctions. In the mid-1950s Germany linked grain trade with Poland to the repatriation of German nationals. In September 1989, the EC, at Germany's prodding, delivered $300 million in aid to Hungary to encourage an opening of the border for East German refugees. In the 1950s and again in the 1980s, Germany provided aid to Poland to encourage political reform.[34] In recent years, groups within Germany have provided political support to specific parties in East European countries.[35]

There are three developments that could change this relatively benign situation, that could make the German problem again a problem, that could raise anew the issue of Mitteleuropa and the inherent danger presented by a Germany that is powerful enough to threaten its neighbors but not powerful enough to impose a stable order. These are the collapse (or at least severe deterioration) of the European Community; the degeneration of the Russian economy, or the economies of the successor states of the Soviet Union, to a point where they could not act as an economic counterbalance to Germany; and the inability or unwillingness of the United States to offset German capabilities. To revive issues of economic security in Eastern Europe in anything like the form which they took before World War II, all three of these developments would have to take place.

If the European Community weakened, Germany would be compelled to pursue an independent foreign policy. At the present juncture, it is not evident whether the Community should be understood as a supranational institution of which its member states are component parts, or as an international organization created and controlled by its individual members.[36] Regardless of which of these characterizations is correct, the level of economic and political integration and cooperation within the Community has been increasing since the adoption of the Single European Act.

The most manifest threat to a continuation of this trend is the fact that the Community must now confront, for the first time since its creation, foreign policy issues in which it is compelled to take the leading role, issues that could be divisive because the member states of the Community have different interests. The cold war removed fundamental foreign policy issues from the European agenda. The end of the cold war has restored them. The disintegration of Yugoslavia is the first major crisis in which the Community has been the leading player. The response to Yugoslavia, and potentially other ethnic clashes in Eastern Europe, could make the Community stronger if a coherent and effective policy could be developed. Ethnic conflicts could, however, undermine the Community if it is unable to act forcefully, and the consequences of civil strife, such as large-scale migrations, differentially impact on its members.

If the Community weakens, Germany will be confronted with a new, or perhaps old, set of problems. It would be the dominant power in the center of Europe. Its economic, if not its military, situation would be affected by the fate of the smaller states of Eastern Europe. It would have the economic resources to influence political developments in these states. The nature of that pressure would depend upon the objectives of any given German regime. From the perspective of the Czech and Slovak Republic, Bulgaria, or Hungary, however, Germany might again become a threat to their economic security.

The ability of Germany—even a Germany in a Europe without a European Community—to threaten the economic security of East European states would, however, depend on what economic alternatives these states had. One reason Germany was able to exercise leverage during the 1930s was because the Soviet Union was not a significant trading partner. Since the 1940s the economies of the East European states have been oriented toward the East. Even with the end of the CMEA, the economic complementarities that have been developed over the last forty years will not disappear. Unless the Russian economy and the economies of the other members of the CIS collapse, the smaller states of Eastern Europe would have an alternative to trade dependence on Germany, and German economic leverage would be reduced.

Finally, even if the European Community weakens and the economy or economies of the CIS falter, the United States could play a balancing role for Central Europe. This is, however, improbable. The United States is not likely to account for more than 3 or 4 percent of the trade of Eastern Europe.[37] This contrasts sharply with the situation in Asia, where the United States is a more important export market than Japan for the countries of South and East Asia. In the absence of some overarching ideological struggle, it will be difficult for American leaders to legitimate substantial support for Eastern Europe.

In sum, despite the structural weakness of East European countries, they are not likely to become the targets of specific economic coercion that could significantly threaten their economic security. Germany is the only country that could make such a threat. Contemporary institutional arrangements in Europe, however, limit Germany's freedom of action and the current political atmosphere in Germany has encouraged self-abnegation rather than self-aggrandizement. Moreover, Russia is a natural economic balance against Germany, a more important balance than the United States. Only if the European Community fell apart and the economy of the CIS states collapsed would Germany be in a position to exercise significant leverage against Eastern Europe.

The most obvious threats to economic security in Eastern Europe come not from specific targeting but from political disorder, prompted in the first instance by ethnic conflict. The most attractive way to manage and contain instability in Eastern Europe would be for the United States and the European Community to play an active peace-keeping role in the region.[38] The Community, however, may have troubles enough of its own, and the willingness of the United States to intimately involve itself in European affairs in the absence of some overarching ideological as well as political and military threat is problematic. The very ambitious policies followed by the United States after World War II were legitimated domestically by ideological opposition to communism. Realpolitik has never sold very well in the United States. The invasion of Panama had to be rationalized as an effort to halt drug trade, not to defend the security of the Panama Canal. The Gulf War could not be sold as a defense of oil prices; Saddam Hussein had to be compared with Hitler. Hence if the economic security of Eastern Europe is threatened, the threats are most likely to come from political developments within Eastern Europe itself, not from external economic shocks or pressures.

CONCLUSION

While the economic security of Europe is more at risk than it has been in the recent past, the risks are not very great. Global economic collapse could be precipitated only by developments in energy or financial markets. The supply of oil at stable prices cannot, as recent developments in the Persian Gulf have demonstrated, be taken for granted. Had Iraq's invasion of Kuwait not been challenged, Saddam Hussein would have been in a position to dictate world oil prices either through intimidation of Saudi Arabia and the United Arab Emirates, or conquest of their oil fields. American military power mattered decisively. Oil is one area where the decline in American power, resulting from the increase in American energy imports and loss of production control by American international oil companies, has affected global economic stability. To date, the consequences of this loss of power have not been catastrophic, although aggregate global economic performance has deteriorated as a result of instability in international energy markets. Future developments could, however, have a destructive impact on global economic security.

Finance is the only other market that could have such widespread repercussions. Financial breakdown, of the sort that initiated the depression of the 1930s, is unlikely, not so much because international coordination is so significant, but because national monetary authorities are more committed and able to act as lenders of last resort.[39] Spectacular banking failures during the last decade, including the American savings and loan crisis, have not undermined the stability of international financial markets.

Threats to economic security in Europe arising from specific targeting policies are also unlikely. It is difficult to see how the larger and most highly developed European states could be subject to significant pressure. The smaller highly developed states have been able to reduce their opportunity costs of change by developing factors markets and political and social institutions that facilitate adjustment. Russia is very large and not much engaged in the international system. Only the smaller, less highly developed states of Central and Eastern Europe could be targeted. The most likely candidate to exercise such pressure would be Germany. Anything like a repeat of the coercive German policies of the 1930s could, however, occur only if the European Community weakened, the Russian economy collapsed, and the United States failed to actively play a balancing role. Ethnic strife and political disorder, rather than global economic deterioration or specific economic targeting, are the most likely threats to the economic security of Europe.

NOTES

1. This analysis draws on Albert Hirschman's seminal study, *National Power and the Structure of Foreign Trade* (Berkeley: University of California Press, 1945).

2. The breakpoint for size was a GNP of $500 billion in 1987. The breakpoint for development was per capita income of $10,000 in 1987. Figures from World Bank: *World Bank Atlas*, 1988, and *World Development Report*, 1989, table 1.

3. Calculated from figures in World Bank, *World Tables*, 1989–90, p. 313

4. Peter J. Katzenstein, *Small States in the World Economy* (Ithaca: Cornell University Press, 1985).

5. The ultimately unsuccessful effort of Third World states to deal with this situation through the creation of authoritative rather than market-based international economic regimes is explored in Stephen D. Krasner, *Structural Conflict: The Third World against Global Liberalism* (Berkeley: University of California Press, 1985).

6. Robert Bates et al., "Risk and Trade Regimes," *International Organization* 45 (Winter 1991).

7. Charles Kindleberger, *The World in Depression* (Berkeley: University of California Press, 1973).

8. This is the essence of Hirschman's brilliant analysis (note 1).

9. U.S.-USSR comparisons, 1960–84, from CIA, *Handbook of Economic Statistics*, 1985; U.S.-OECD comparisons, 1960–86 based on OECD, *National Accounts 1960–1988*, Vol. 1, *Main Aggregates* (1990), table 13, and *National Accounts 1960–1986*, p. 145. U.S.-OECD comparisons for 1953 calculated from UN, *Yearbook of National Account Statistics 1965*.

10. UN: *Yearbook of International Trade Statistics 1960* and *1970–71*, and *1984 International Trade Statistics Yearbook*; GATT, *International Trade*—various years.

11. Data on reserves can be found in IMF, *International Financial Statistics Yearbooks 1987 and 1989*. Susan Strange, "The Persistent Myth of Lost Hegemony," *International Organization* 41 (1987): 568–69, argues that the United States is less constrained than other countries.

12. Kenneth Organski and Jacek Kugler have argued that states which are defeated in war ultimately return to the trend line of GNP growth established by their prewar experience (see *The War Ledger* [Chicago: University of Chicago Press, 1980]).

13. Bruce Russett,"The Mysterious Case of Vanishing Hegemony; Or, Is Mark Twain Really Dead?" *International Organization* 39 (1985). For other studies which emphasize the continued leadership position of the United States, see Joseph Nye, *Bound to Lead* (New York: Basic Books, 1990), and Henry Nau, *The Myth of American Decline* (New York: Oxford University Press, 1990). Both of these studies place considerable strength on the potency of American ideology, its endorsement of democracy, the market, and (especially in contrast with Japan) its universalism.

14. The argument that American leaders were unable to make trade-offs, that they believed that all good things would go together, is developed in Robert Packenham, *Liberal America and the Third World* (Princeton: Princeton University Press, 1973).

15. The distinction between diffuse and specific reciprocity is developed in Robert Keohane, "Reciprocity in International Relations," *International Organization* 40 (1986).

16. Judith Goldstein, "Ideas, Interests, and American Trade Policy"; unpublished manuscript, Stanford University, October 1990.

17. Joanne Gowa, *Closing the Gold Window: Domestic Politics and the End of Bretton Woods* (Ithaca: Cornell University Press, 1983). John Odell, *International Monetary Policy* (Princeton: Princeton University Press, 1983), has pointed out that American policy was consistent with and could be rationalized by new economic ideas that extolled the virtues of flexible exchange rates. The specific decisions taken by American leaders, however, in the summer of 1971 reflected specific interests, not new intellectual ideas, as evidenced by the fact that efforts to reestablish a fixed exchange rate system continued until the mid-1970s.

18. World Bank, *World Development Report 1989*, table 24.

19. Figures from GATT, *International Trade 87–88*, vol. 2 (Geneva, 1988), tables AB 1–3.

20. Zvi Griliches, "Productivity Puzzles and R & D: Another Nonexplanation," *Journal of Economic Perspectives* 2 (1988).

21. IMF, *World Economic Outlook 1982*, p. 173.

22. Figures from World Bank, *World Development Report 1989*, table 2.

23. Again, the analysis here follows Hirschman (note 1).

24. Figures from UN, Economic Commission for Europe, *Economic Survey of Europe in 1989–90* (New York: 1990), appendix tables C.4 and C.11.

25. Peter Kenen, "Transitional Arrangements for Trade and Payments among the CMEA Countries," *IMF Staff Papers* 38, 2 (June 1991): table 1.

26. Susan M. Collins and Dani Rodrik, *Eastern Europe and the Soviet Union in the World Economy* (Washington: Institute for International Economics, May 1991), table 2.2

27. Robert Mark Spaulding, Jr., "German Trade Policy in Eastern Europe, 1890–1990: Preconditions for Applying International Trade Leverage," *International Organization* 45, 3 (Summer 1991).

28. Collins and Rodrik (note 26), tables A.3–A.9.

29. Derived from figures in GATT, *International Trade 87–88*, vol. 2, tables AA 10 and AB 11.

30. Collins and Rodrik, (note 26), tables 2.1 and 2.4.

31. Collins and Rodrik, *Ibid.*, tables A.3–A.9 and 2.6.

32. *Ibid.*, tables A.3–A.9.

33. The consequences of the international regime for encouraging or discouraging the use of trade as an instrument of political coercion are made by Spaulding (note 27).

34. *Ibid.*

35. Based on interviews in Budapest in July 1991 but not confirmed.

36. For two analyses arguing that the Community is best understood as a product of national power and policies, see Andrew Moravcsik, "Negotiating the Single European Act: National Interests and Conventional Statecraft in the European Community," *International Organization* 45, 1 (Winter 1991), and Geoffrey Garrett, "The European Internal Market: The Political Economy of Regional Integration," *International Organization* (forthcoming).

37. Collins and Rodrik (note 26), tables A.3–A.9.

38. Ronald Steel, "Europe after the Superpowers," in *Sea-Changes: American Foreign Policy in a World Transformed,* ed. Nicholas X. Rizopoulos (New York: Council on Foreign Relations, 1990), pp. 17–18.

39. There have been greater efforts at international coordination, including agreements on responsibility for the failure of multinational banks and on capital requirements. See Ethan Kapstein, "Resolving the Regulator's Dilemma," *International Organization* 43 (Spring 1989).

THE PROSPECT OF WORLD ECONOMIC CONFLICT: IMPLICATIONS FOR THE GLOBAL SYSTEM AND FOR EUROPE

Richard Rosecrance

INTRODUCTION

A number of observers have suggested that growing economic conflict will take place among major industrial nations in the future.[1] There is also a wider group of policy-makers and politicians who are concerned that a new recession-depression may make the world vulnerable to a round of economic conflicts like those of the 1930s. A third group sees the construction of somewhat exclusivist trading blocs in Europe, North America, and East Asia leading to a greater conflict among trading units.[2] From all three points of view, as international trade and production decline (or fail to rise), conflict burgeons if trading nations or blocs do not cooperate to stabilize the economic system. According to one main line of scholarly argument, they may have little reason to do so if there is no hegemonic stabilizer in place willing and able to pay the public goods costs of maintaining a cooperative international economic system. From this point of view, the decline of a hegemonic leader will likely lead to conflict. A declining leader cannot provide emergency credit (act as a lender of last resort) or offer a market for distress goods (act as a market of last resort) if it has a shrinking market, no current account surplus, or no store of foreign currency or gold. If these tasks cannot be performed, lesser nations facing payments imbalances will be forced to take drastic action (levying tariffs, establishing exchange control, or imposing quotas), thereby diminishing or cutting their ties with the world economy. Ultimately, according to this view, world economic stagnation or crisis will unfold. Since, it is held, the United States has already "declined," we may be in for a crisis like that of the 1930s in the mid-to-late 1990s.[3] It is possible that the future consequences of economic conflict could be as severe as they were in the past.[4]

Pessimists (realists?) contend that even if the leading economic nation does not appreciably weaken, other rising states will thrust themselves into the industrial market, winning new market shares and generating economic competition and conflict for the remainder. Since the established industrial powers will not readily yield market share to newcomers, games of ruin could ensue, jeopardizing the future growth of the world economy.[5]

For a variety of reasons which I will outline below, I reject these two conclusions. The analytical basis for the argument that American decline will cause conflict is flawed, to say the least. The contention that the intrusion of new economic competitors or new trading blocs into the world economy will lead to conflict or chaos cannot be sustained at least on the basis of recent economic and political experience. It is likely to be confuted even more definitively by future developments in the international trading system. Neither so-called "hegemonic decline" nor the rise of new economic units heralds a breakdown in the international economic and political system.

If this is true, the new Europe and the global international system will *not* have to absorb a rash of "beggar thy neighbor" policies like those of the 1930s. The lower levels of economic conflict which may actually occur are not likely therefore to be transformed into political or military disorder. This suggests that Europe can and will remain a part of the global trading network and not an isolated, self-sufficient, inward-looking entity. Dependent on markets, technology, and resources from the outside world, Europe cannot become a "fortress." Rather, East European states and possibly later the Soviet Union will be drawn into stronger economic ties to a broader European community, and a larger Europe will continue to have crucially important links to a still wider world economy.

THE HEGEMONIC STABILITY ARGUMENT

It is not clear, according to the theory of hegemonic stability, why the world has experienced at least two relatively benevolent hegemonic leaders, nineteenth century Britain and the twentieth century United States. The conclusion of most arguments on the subject is that a benevolent hegemonic power does not benefit from such labors, and a predatory hegemon does not last.[6] It is therefore questionable whether any reliance should be placed on the likely emergence of hegemonic leaders playing beneficent roles in the future. Future potential leaders may very well recognize the disabilities of hegemony and seek instead a more limited role in the system.[7] But even if there is no benevolent hegemonic stabilizer, the system need not founder. Duncan Snidal has shown that strategic bargaining can produce cooperation even in the absence of a hegemon or in the presence of a declined hegemon.[8] Fundamentally, Snidal's work demonstrates that while a declined hegemon may be able to work with a large second power to produce cooperation by creating a *k-group* offering public goods, three or more cooperators do not emerge unless the declined hegemon threatens to withdraw cooperation if the others do not contribute to the provision of the collective good. If this contention is true, then the presence or absence of an existent or failed hegemon is not central to the result; the outcome depends, rather, on successful strategic bargaining among the leading players in the system. Rosecrance and Taw have also shown that states that start out trying to be predatory hegemons typically metamorphose into more benevolent system stabilizers. Partly this is because they can no longer impose "optimum tariffs" when their now more powerful competitors are capable of retaliating. Also, "once they have an export surplus and have become leading creditor powers, they face the alternative of allowing others to pay back their loans or of forcing default."[9] To solve this problem, late nineteenth-century Great Britain and the post-World War II United States opened their markets to debtors. Today, Japan is in the process of gradually doing so as well.[10] If these arguments are valid ones, a new hegemonic power will either fail to materialize, or if it does, it will be progressively forced to assume a benevolent role. Most likely, two or three large units will act to run the system on the basis of strategic bargaining among them, one playing lender of last resort; another, market of last resort; and so on. Thus the key question for the future is whether such large states or units will have the incentive to reach agreement should there be conditions leading to growing economic conflict.[11] My answer to this question is Yes, but I reserve full discussion of the reasons for this conclusion to the section on the containment of conflict below.

THE RISING COMPETITORS ARGUMENT

The contention that new rising industrial nations will cause chronic and continuing economic conflict is based on the assumption that "inside-out" influences today dominate "outside-in" effects in international relations (see Figure 1). It has always been true that domestic causes have generated important international effects. What is less recognized is that today the "outside-in," or "second image reversed," relationships are also very strong.[12] Small trading states have to behave differently from large, more self-sufficient nations and may require a degree of social corporatism to cope with the effects of the external market.[13] A trading state needs electoral systems that do not cause great political and economic change in policy if it is to compete effectively in the international market. In response, trading nations do not simply act to protect uncompetitive domestic sectors; they seek to fashion more effective national responses to the economic world at large.[14] In the process, typical inside-out responses of the past have been modified and reshaped. The matrix in Figure 1 displays the possible causes and outcomes of the international relations field in terms of two levels of analysis, domestic and international. Traditional views can here be particularly associated with boxes I and IV, in each of which subdisciplines maintain their entity and autonomy. International influences determine international outcomes, and domestic pressures cause domestic political patterns. Of greater interest are boxes II and III, in which subdisciplines change their independent and dependent character. From an "inside-out" perspective domestic politics determine international outcomes; inversely, from an "outside-in" perspective it is the pressure of international politics which reshapes domestic politics. Strictly speaking, there is no causal pattern which is more or less associated with conflict than another. Domestic determinants can have a very pacific or very disruptive effect on international events. The occurrence of a highly ideological revolution, the development of extreme nationalism, the installation of a domestic totalitarian regime—all these can be dramatic forces for conflict at

Figure 1

PATTERNS OF CAUSATION

	International Effects	Domestic Effects
International *Causes*	Systemic Effects "Realism" I	Outside-In Domestic Response II
Domestic *Causes*	Inside-Out Domestic Stimulus III	Comparative Political Analysis IV

the international level. On the other hand, the emergence of democracy or liberal government domestically may produce peace among previously contending countries. In the realist-traditional box (I) international determinants can produce equilibrium or disequilibrium, depending on patterns of power and polarity. In the domestic-traditional box (IV) changes in the domestic economy and polity can lead to different governing regimes. In the "outside-in" box (II), international determination of domestic politics can, say, at the end of a major war dictate the installation of repressive regimes. Alternatively, the pressures of international trade can gradually modify domestic patterns and political arrangements, permitting mutual adjustment of international economic interests and diminishing economic nationalism.

In the aftermath of World War II, the Soviet Union as a conquering power was able to impose its will, dictating domestic arrangements in the defeated states of Eastern Europe. Even the much more benign U.S. hegemony in occupied Germany and Japan helped to form the basis of new domestic and democratic governments. Since 1950, however, no newly victorious hegemonic power has been able to call the tune in occupied territories, least of all the Republic of South Africa or the State of Israel. Thus since World War II, international influence upon domestic politics has come typically to refer to the peaceful influence of trade, foreign investment, or currency change upon the demand and supply of domestic welfare in a range of countries.*

"Inside-out" influences (Box III), in contrast, have referred either to internal democratization and its effects or to nationalism. Democratization has worked a generally beneficial influence, reducing the possibility of war with like-minded powers. Nationalism has represented a more malign effect. Typically, it involves a perverse domestic introversion which seeks to subjugate international forces to internal requirements. It may nonetheless be the case that certain forms of internal and external regimes may be mutually reinforcing. A democratic domestic regime tends to strengthen trading strategies in international relations. An international trading system equally may enhance transparency and open domestic economies tending in a liberal direction. Alternatively, domestic repressive regimes are likely both to cause and to encounter opposition at the international level. At the present time, the most signal nexus is the link between liberalization domestically and responsiveness to international trade at the global level.

This has not always been true and may not always be true in the future. In the nineteenth century the development of world trade initially fostered a nationalist reaction to strive to discipline its domestic effects. German historian and economist Friedrich List stressed the need for a national system of political economy to control foreign trade and to tailor it to internal political purposes. According to List, the historical development of countries suggested five stages of maturation: from the savage to the pastoral, then to the agricultural, the agricultural-manufacturing, and finally to the agricultural-manufacturing-commercial stage.[15] A nation fully achieves its unity and power only when it enters the last stage:

> It is only at this stage that a nation can nourish a vast population, ensure a complete development of the arts and sciences, and retain its independence and power.[16]

List believed that to fulfill Germany's destiny, it required "an extension of territory," particularly the annexation of Holland and Denmark. List frequently spoke of making a nation independent of

*This point holds quite generally for the developed world. Among the developing countries, however, international influence, via debt pressures, has even more strongly constrained domestic outcomes, sometimes channeling them in a repressive direction.

foreign markets by means of industry. He considered that nation highest which

> has cultivated manufacturing industry in all its branches within its territory to the highest perfection, and whose territory and agricultural production is large enough to supply its manufacturing population with the largest part of the necessaries of life and raw materials which they require.[17]

List did not go quite as far as Johan Gottlieb Fichte, who had favored a policy of *autarchy*. An early nineteenth century German philosopher, Fichte in his *Der gleschlossene Handelsstaat* contended that a country should be completely independent, economically speaking. This objective could be attained by two methods only: either by restricting national needs to the level of its own resources, or acquiring territory through conquest or exchange to meet enlarged economic requirements.

A more contemporary "inside-out" perspective is depicted by Robert Gilpin. Citing a tradition which links List with Gautam Sen, Gilpin summarizes the argument in the following terms:

> All states want to possess modern industries because of the linkages among industry and overall economic development, the goal of economic self-sufficiency and political autonomy, and the fact that industrialism is the basis of military power and hence of national independence. This nationalist desire for industrial power leads states to promote industrialization based on the importation of foreign technologies. The less developed economy attempts to acquire the most advanced technology from the hegemonic power and from other highly developed economies. . . . The follower has the great advantage . . . of being able to skip economic stages and to overtake the industrial leader.[18]

Gilpin then observes:

> The political consequences of this diffusion of comparative advantages and of the rise of the new industrial powers are powerfully affected by the speed at which the changes take place and how long is required for the rising challenger to take a significant share of world markets. The shorter the time period the greater will be the adjustment problem imposed on other states and the greater

the resistance of domestic interests. Rapid shifts in comparative advantage give rise to intense economic conflicts between rising and declining economies.[19]

Later Gilpin notes:

Initially, the less developed economy pursues nationalist policies in order to protect its infant industries and overcome the advantages possessed by the earlier industrializers. Eventually, it must attempt to break into world markets to achieve efficient economies of scale and to obtain foreign currency to finance imports of required resources and capital goods. To the extent that this industrialization is successful, the developing economy, with its lower wage structure, undercuts the industrial position of the more advanced economies. The resulting generation of surplus industrial capacity in the world economy is intimately related to the process of the relative industrial decline of the hegemon, intensified trade competition, and the possible onset of a global economic crisis.[20]

In this way Gilpin depicts one well-known strand of the "inside-out" argument. He admits that the spread of industrialism has both trade-creating and trade-destroying effects. Technically, it is open to advanced economies either to protect their threatened industries or to transform their economies to adjust to the new international economic realities. It appears, however, that there is a strong temptation to try to push the adjustment costs on to other nations (as President Richard Nixon did with his New Economic Policy of 15 August 1971) or to assume a protectionist stance.[21] When a leading country enjoys a monopoly of the three factors of production (land, labor, and capital), the total population may benefit from a liberal economic policy. Once that monopoly is broken, however, the scarce factor of production loses ground, and the national consensus supporting a liberal and open trading position declines. Labor or land may become highly protectionist.

According to Gilpin, adjustment becomes most difficult in a welfare state. Powerful organized interests can then resist paying the costs of openness.[22] The slow pace of global economic growth also makes adjustment more difficult. With a smaller economic pie, there are more losers: "These obstacles to economic adjustment threaten the world economy with the possibility of slow growth and failure to adjust that could deteriorate into economic warfare."[23] At various places Gilpin makes clear that he is unsure whether large-scale economic conflict will actually result from the intrusion of rising industrial powers, but the argument he proffers tends to reinforce a pessimistic conclusion.

THE CONTAINMENT OF CONFLICT

Whatever one says about the possible emergence of an "outside-in" orientation among modern trading nations, at least the effect and durability of an exclusive "inside-out" approach has been thoroughly challenged today. The reason for this is simple: autarchy and self-sufficiency simply cannot be attained, even by the largest geographic entities. Thus even if domestic politics supposedly requires military conquest of foreign nations to eliminate the noxious influence of the world economy upon internal politics, such attacks cannot possibly succeed. And when the aggressor nation has been defeated in its attempt at autarchy, the country will still remain dependent on others and possibly even more so. If this is true, policy-makers, however well disposed to their own peoples, will not generally pursue domestic political tendencies to the point where they imperil the long-term survival of the state.*

The pursuit of self-sufficiency and autarchy in the nineteenth century and then later in the 1930s was conditioned on the supposed fact that total national independence could somehow actually be achieved. In the 1930s and under conditions of a severely depressed world economy, perhaps an approximation to self-sufficiency at a low standard of living might even have been attained by aggressor states, realizing Fichte's aim. If Japan had been able to cling to Manchuria and to its market in eastern China and to conquer Southeast Asia as well, it might have been able to find viable substitutes for Western oil and minerals and for export markets located in Europe and the United States. If Nazi Germany had been powerful enough to subdue Eastern Europe and the Soviet Union, gaining new food supplies, oil, coal, and minerals in the bargain, it might

---

*This key realist insight remains the heart of deterrence theory, as well as of the explanation of state policy.

have been capable of creating a European empire that would have made it less dependent on the markets of the outside world. Neither eventuality, of course, took place, though calculations that they might have done so were not entirely unrealistic.[24]

In the future, however, the objective of practical self-sufficiency verges on fantasy. Even the new, larger "trading blocs" in process of creation in Europe, North America, and East Asia will not achieve effective economic independence from foreign suppliers, capital, technology, and markets.[25] They will almost certainly stimulate an even greater interpenetration of foreign direct investment within each others' tariff zones than existed previously.* As we shall see, this investment will create an even greater stake in foreign economies than presently obtains.

Further, the objectives of "late developers" have changed in the past hundred years. Alexander Gerschenkron was correct in his analysis of nineteenth century political and economic practice.[26] Late and late, late developers would have crucial advantages in the structure of comparative advantage and in the trading system as a whole. Late developers like Germany, Russia, and Japan might buy the latest industrial technology off the shelf from mature industrial nations and expect to fare extremely well against them. Britain and Belgium might not be able to keep up with new and rising challengers. Moreover, the advantages won might become enduring ones, in that the returns from new technology would continue to be higher than those from outdated plant and equipment, and the new industrial powers could expect to use those revenues to invest more and to stay ahead. Applied in political and international terms, late developers could expect to gain a degree of independence that their industrial predecessors had not achieved. Ultimately they could turn their industrial power to military expansion and, by conquering new territory, hope to win a further emancipation from world markets and sources of supply. There seems little doubt that German and Japanese expansionism on the threshold of the twentieth century was designed to acquire local territory or far-flung empire that would lend Berlin and Tokyo a greater approximation to economic self-sufficiency. In the late nineteenth century no doubt the depression of 1873–96 and the slowing of growth

---

*Johnson & Johnson-Merck's acquisition of pharmaceutical companies from Rhone-Poulenc is further evidence of this tendency.

in world trade fostered the illusion that this outcome was both possible and desirable.

A century later, however, the once-for-all advantages of late development are no longer so clear. This does not mean that newly industrialized countries (NICs) do not gain from the application of new technology to low-wage industries. Nor does it suggest that there are built-in limits to the benefits the NICs derive from entering the trading system after industrialization. Post-1945 Japan has not made the mistakes of its predecessors in seeking to translate economic power into military and imperial dominion—to win new territories.

The key point, however, is that *today* new, "late, late, late developers" cannot remain satisfied with indigenous industrial development once they have received the initial contribution of high technology from other nations. Not only must they develop and refine this technology further to stay ahead, but they must also receive and benefit from the continuing stimulus that only open world markets and research and development findings in other nations provide. They cannot be content to rely only upon their own indigenous efforts. In this particular sense, Gerschenkron's findings for the late twentieth and early twenty-first centuries appear to be modified today. Late developers have advantages, but they do not bar the door to still later developers in newer fields, or to resurgent predecessors.* Countries which seek to remain content with indigenous development will not, ultimately, be able to keep pace with the fast-changing world technological marketplace.†

Some may believe that the new "strategic trade theory" may alter this conclusion. According to this view, a nation seeking to find a new industrial metier does not consult its traditional strengths in "comparative advantage." Rather, it seeks to make critical investments in a new area of technology and then to sustain them through gains in market share. In this manner, Paul Krugman showed how a country can intervene in a developmental process

---

*In many respects the resurgence of older economies like those of Germany and Japan after World War II shows that more recent developers like the United States, Argentina, Australia, China, or India obviously do not have once-for-all advantages.

†India's strategy emphasizing "import replacement" instead of high-technology exports undoubtedly slowed New Delhi's economic adjustment and progress toward steady economic growth.

as Japan did, for example, with the 16K memory chip and then gain an advantage in the follow-on 64K, 256K, and 1 megabyte chips. If Japan had not made the initial investment, it would now have completely lost out to the United States in the semiconductor field.[27] But Japanese progress does not rule out others' opportunities to make similar investments in an unfolding technology of strategic trade. The United States can leap in with microprocessors and *risc* technology. It can seek to vault over analog HDTV with digital transmission via fibre optic cables and much higher fidelity. The technology of supercomputers is not learned simply by innovating more powerful memory chips. The "teraflop" computer (capable of performing one trillion calculations per second) does not sprout from the head of Zeus simply because a few critical investments were made at the beginning of the semiconductor road. Superconductivity is another area in which previous research on low temperature conductors does not guarantee future gains. We know that superconductivity provides new magnetic fields, abundances of electricity at cheaper prices, and new devices for transportation. But success in this difficult and complex field is not achieved by making sequentially phased investments beginning with the most elementary technology of conductors. It is possible for newcomers to overleap a development stage. Thus in a whole range of fields, early investments yielded returns, not because higher benefits automatically flowed from them, but because one technological problem helped with the solution to the next one, and perhaps to a declining cost and "experience curve" in that strand of technology. The initial technological investments do not produce gains later on if the new developer does not continue to plumb open markets and to do research on the basis of the highest technological achievements attained in foreign countries. Thus the "strategic trade approach" yields long-term national benefits only if the country's society and government are willing to continue to invest in new fields in which foreigners are already making advances.[28]*

Further, there is a point at which the progressive modification of innovations derived from others' off-the-shelf technology may

*This, of course, is a major policy question in the United States today, where DARPA efforts to develop an industrial policy have been checked by the White House staff. New "pre-competitive" technologies, however, are now being supported by the Department of Commerce.

lose efficacy. When the late developer has already fully exploited the technology available from someone else, it can progress only through new, risky technology in which its guesses are no better than those of its competitors.* New technological discoveries are far more difficult than technological adaptation and application of the proven innovations of others.

Thus at some point Gerschenkron's approach for the nineteenth century is modified and even reversed for the late twentieth and twenty-first centuries. Late developers do not automatically remain ahead of industrial pioneers or other new developing states. The advantages of the late, late developer do not permit disengagement from the international economic system through tariffs and policies of economic nationalism. Building upon their initial economic gains, new industrial states cannot expect permanently to translate their initial strengths into economic dominance. Nor can they assume that initial economic advantages will produce military independence. In fact powers that seek transformation and ultimate economic self-sufficiency through either economic isolation or military conquest of new territory will be likely to lose their advantages in economic terms.[29] This means, practically, that new developers today must remain open and cooperative participants in the international trading system to be sure of keeping up. As twenty-first century trading states, they can continue to benefit only so long as they continue to maximize their economic returns. At minimum, this means controlling their military costs.[30]

This lesson was borne home on the contemporary Soviet Union. As a late, late developer, Russia and then the USSR had hoped to advantage itself against the mature industrial countries of England and Germany. Under Count Sergei Witte's leadership, Russia developed very rapidly on the basis of English and Scottish industrial designs, creating a new railway system and a large steel industry. After the 1917 Revolution, Lenin and then Stalin sought to turn Russia's industry increasingly to the solution of military tasks. In the New Economic Policy (1921–27) period the USSR gained new industrial designs from the West which it hoped might lead to ultimate economic independence from the Western economy. De-

---

*Japan's failures with the "fifth-generation computer" are particularly in point here.

spite the galvanic effect of the first five-year plans and the further stimulus of World War II (in which much of Russian industry was moved East and modernized), the great economic gains which Nikita Khrushchev envisioned in the 1950s never materialized. In heavy industry, the Soviet Union recorded growth rates of 5–7 percent per year. But while heavy and machine industry prospered, chemicals were neglected. The agricultural system languished. Modern information processing, miniaturization, and high technology were slighted. Consumer and light industry were sidetracked. By 1976 Soviet growth rates had declined to 2–3 percent per year, and in the 1980s there was very little growth at all in the Soviet product. In the past three years, the Soviet economy has declined each year. Cutting itself off from the rest of the world, the USSR has not been able to develop the latest technology on its own. And even where it has developed new designs, as in the space program or the supersonic transport, the Soviet Union has not been able to "commercialize technology," so that it might produce it reliably and efficiently and sell it at reasonable prices in competitive Western markets. Russia must advance beyond the production of minerals and oil, sturdy tractors and snowblowers, beyond caviar, vodka, furs, and leather if it is to generate an enduring impact on the world marketplace

Even Japan cannot expect to advance rapidly in the years to come if it shuts itself off from Western economies and from Western technological progress. The failure of the fifth-generation computer project shows that Japan still needs to do more work to solve the problems involved in massively parallel processing in super-computers. In pharmaceuticals Japan remains behind; in chemicals, laggard. Its aircraft industry has not progressed to the level of Boeing or even Airbus. In computers and microprocessors Japan's NEC remains behind America's IBM and Intel. Japanese software does not compare to the innovations offered by Microsoft and Lotus. Its workstations are not equal to Sun's. To keep up with new Western technology Japan has established a strong foothold and a production base inside Western economies to remain abreast of the latest theoretical knowledge. An open and internationally oriented Japan will be able to remain abreast of the high-technology market. If Japan retreats to its island fastnesses, however, it cannot expect to prosper in world competition. Hence an insular, exclusionary nationalism is not a realistic policy for the Japanese.

Further, its direct investment in the United States, Europe, and East Asia inevitably transfers some technological and managerial know-how to its most significant competitors. Japan is in fact investing in the economies (lending great supplies of capital) which are now or will become its strongest challengers in the future. They will benefit from the infusion and the technological stimulus. As British investment in Australia, America, New Zealand, Canada, and South Africa rendered these nations into industrial competitors, so Japan is in the process ineluctably of creating and sustaining its own competition through its contribution to the dynamic development of other countries. The Japanese attempt in the Pacific to structure a "flying geese" V-shaped pattern of industrial sophistication (with Japan permanently leading the East Asian flock) is unlikely to succeed for political as well as economic reasons. Korea, Taiwan, Singapore, and Hong Kong will not forever remain inferior to Japan, and their rates of economic growth are of course much higher than Japan's. As China comes to participate fully in East Asian development, the idea of Japan leading a new co-prosperity sphere assumes an air of political as well as economic unreality.

Foreign investment spreads technology; domestic investment safeguards it. The internationalization of Japan's production is proceeding apace, and the process will continue and accelerate. Finally, Japan's need to allow its debtors to repay their loans and to finance its investments in foreign countries will require a growing Japanese import surplus.* Otherwise those who have borrowed from Japan may ultimately be forced to default. In short, Japan faces in the next twenty years the same dilemmas that confronted Britain in the fourth quarter of the nineteenth century. Then Britain reinvested its trade surplus into the countries which formed its overseas market, fostering and speeding their economic growth. In response, it had to open its economy and market to allow them to pay back their debts and finance British investment. The redoubled effect was ultimately to undermine British exports. Japan faces the same long-term dilemma

---

*Some contend that if this surplus is only in raw materials, food, or low-tech items, Japanese industry faces no disadvantage. But a U.S. export surplus in Japan (however composed in terms of products) would increase the American pool of savings, make it easier to finance the government deficit, and reduce interest rates. This would facilitate new investment in a wide range of new and high-technology products.

today. Its domestic stimulus strategy conjoined with the Structural Impediments Initiative foreshadows a gradually opening Japanese market along with the creation of new competitors overseas. Japanese rice and construction industries will gradually admit American and Asian competition. This is an eventuality which, like that faced by the United States in the 1950s, Japan cannot today avoid. It must act as an international stabilizer even when the role may be an uncongenial one, possibly inimical to its own long-term economic interest. Ultimately Japan will pass its climacteric and move into a phase of gradual decline in relative terms.[31]

But even if this does not occur in the next decade or two, the pressures of Japan's foreign investments and markets will remain very heavy. Japanese investments and overseas markets create a stake in the success of foreign economies and societies. If they fail to prosper, the profits to Japanese producers and investors themselves decline. The point can be generalized: for many economic and trading powers in world politics today there is an approximation to *economic deterrence* that provides a stabilizing influence in world politics that extends beyond *military deterrence*. Military deterrence holds the enemy population hostage. The resulting influence process, however, is a very crude one. The alternative is basically like that of an "on-off switch": to kill or not to kill the enemy population. Russian influence upon U.S. policy is thus entirely negative in character; it is also very gross.

Economic deterrence refers to the stake that one economy holds within another in terms of markets and productive investments. If that stake is a broadly symmetrical one, then each country has much to lose if the other's economy does not prosper. The influence process is much more subtle: the home economy can influence and reshape the foreign economy's stake through taxation and expenditure policy, inhibitive or enabling legislation. Unlike the situation in military deterrence, in which the "hostage" is outside the political and legal borders of the home country, in economic deterrence the stake or hostage exists within the domestic jurisdiction. Not only that, but also a government can decide to reward foreign investment and exports as well as to punish them. The influence is positive as well as negative. As the stake that individual trading units hold within the confines of another's economy rises in value and symmetry, deterrent mechanisms progressively come

to interdict the outbreak of radical economic conflict. The importance of these mechanisms should not be understated.

In a pair of studies a few years ago, Cornell University inves-
tigators examined the pattern of cooperation among the Group of
Six in international monetary negotiations during 1960–70.[32] In each
case a measure was prepared of the amount of cooperation each
nation gave and received in the negotiations. This was then correlated with a series of indicators of economic influence or power
such as growth rates, size of foreign exchange holdings, and trade
balance. The result was negative. What turned out to be much more
influential than these indicators of economic power was the degree
to which one country had a stake in the economic success of another
country. At that time, the United States had a very significant stake
in the fate of European economies, though the stake was not yet
fully reciprocal: European investment in the United States remained
quite low. Not surprisingly, European countries such as France and
Germany did particularly well, receiving a great deal of cooperation
in the negotiations. The United States was in the middle. Last of
all, of course, was Japan, the country in whose economy no other
country had been allowed to develop a significant stake, in either
export markets or direct investment in Japanese productive assets.*
Fortunately today Japan has become aware of the problem and is
seeking to draw in imports through a domestic stimulus strategy
and also to permit greater foreign and direct investment in the
Japanese economy. It appears, therefore, that with the possible
exception of China and Russia, each major industrial economy is
extending its stake in the economies of other nations.[33] Production
is being internationalized, and a greater proportion of erstwhile
national production is now taking place outside national borders.
According to Japanese estimates, American production overseas
may now be nearing 20 percent of U.S. domestic production. Japanese production abroad has increased from 2 percent of GNP to
something like 7 percent.[34] It will increase further as Europe integrates and the North American free trade area develops. Even aside
from these powerful economic stimuli, Japanese direct investment
in productive facilities has spread into East and Southeast Asia,
reducing the costs of production for Japanese manufacturers.

*As of March 1990 U.S. direct investment in Japan had attained a total of only
$14.7 billion. The amount, however, was expected to rise rapidly.

The net effect of growing and reciprocal economic stakes among major world trading units is to deter the outbreak of economic conflict between them. A fully symmetrical pattern would guarantee to impoverish any economic "aggressor," preventing a repetition of the economic conflict of the 1930s in the later 1990s. This is true despite the gradual construction of larger trading units in Europe, North America, and East Asia. Larger trading units with a higher external tariff will provide powerful incentives to jump over the tariff barrier and invest directly in production within the market unit.* Only if capital flows were controlled would new trading units begin to move toward greater economic autonomy. With capital flows unfettered, the integration of Europe after 1992–94 will lead to a great resurgence of American and Japanese investment in European productive facilities. If American and Japanese goods cannot be exported over the tariff wall, they will be produced and sold within the protected market. This new investment will not simply go to set up assembly plants because the European Commission has indicated that 80 percent of the product must be produced within Europe for the commodity to meet "local content requirements." Thus American and Japanese investment will include component plants as well as plants devoted to final manufacture. When the North American Common Market is created, huge new Japanese and American (as well as European) investment will go into Mexico. Thus the existence of larger (and possibly slightly more self-sufficient) trading blocs does not foreshadow growing economic conflicts among the new units. Each will be so tied up with the success of others—their bets will be so hedged—that no unit will be able to afford a trade war. Reciprocal economic stakes will forge a reliable economic deterrence among them.

These claims are buttressed by statistical comparisons. Table 1 shows the relatively low dependence of major countries on foreign trade in the 1930s as compared to today. Table 2 indicates the degree of dependence of particular countries or trading units upon specific markets today. While European dependence upon the U.S. market has been declining as it integrates, America remains highly dependent upon the European market. Japanese dependence upon the

---

*Partly as a result, foreign production is now rising more rapidly than foreign trade. In 1991 foreign trade was forecast to reach $3.7 trillion, while the total of (book value) foreign direct investments exceeded $1 trillion.

Table 1

FOREIGN TRADE AS A PERCENTAGE OF NATIONAL PRODUCT

Country	Year	
	1938	1989
United Kingdom	12.69%	42.25%
France	11.59	38.92
Germany	4.04	51.32
Japan	--	17.45
United States		16.48

Source: B. R. Mitchell, *European Historical Statistics: 1750–1975* (London: Mac-Millan, 1975); *International Financial Statistics* (Feburary 1991); *OECD Economic Surveys: Japan*; *International Financial Statistics Yearbook* (1990).

Table 2

PERCENT EXPORT DEPENDENCE ON PARTICULAR MARKETS

Country/Market	Year	
	1986	1989
European Community (EC) on U.S. market	9.29%	7.45%
United States on EC market	24.46	23.80
Japan on U.S. market	38.88	34.22
Japan on EC market		c. 17.00

Source: *Direction of Trade Statistics Yearbook*, 1990; *International Financial Statistics Yearbook*, 1990.

American market remains extremely high (34–38 percent). The next best market takes only 6 percent of Japanese exports.

While Europe has become more self-sufficient in trade (though not in investment), its dependence upon energy imports continues at a high level, as shown by Table 3. It is difficult if not impossible to think that Europe could ever become self-sufficient in energy. Economic stakes of one nation or trading unit in another are strengthened by the pattern of investment. Unfortunately, the statistics for this are typically incommensurable, but we know that the U.S. investment stake in Europe is very large, and that of Europe and Japan in the United States is growing rapidly. The most pronounced asymmetry occurs in American and European direct investment in Japan

Table 3
**ANNUAL ENERGY IMPORTS AS A PERCENTAGE OF TOTAL
CONSUMPTION**

Country/Unit	Year 1985	1988
EC total	43.85%	47.51%
Germany	50.64	53.19

Source: Energy, Statistical Yearbook, 1987, 1988.

which, because of Japanese restrictions, remains much lower than Japanese investment in America and Europe. At the moment, Japanese investments in the United States are many times those of American investments in Japan.[35] Table 4 gives general (though not always particular) figures.

IMPLICATIONS

The range and variety of these statistics is sufficient to establish a few central points. Japan is extremely dependent upon foreign trade and it is growing dependent upon its foreign investment abroad as well. It must sell 36 percent of its exports every year in the U.S. market and 17 percent in Europe. There are no other consumer markets which can absorb such large amounts of Japanese products. The Japanese economy may actually be twice as large as it needs to be if it were meant solely to serve the needs of the Japanese domestic consumer. To support the rest of the productive plant, Tokyo is dependent upon sales to the outside world. There is no way in which Japan can withdraw from this market or substitute for it at home.

The United States is also heavily dependent upon foreign markets (though not yet as dependent as Japan). It must sell 23 percent of its exports each year within the market of the European Community. Most self-sufficient is the European market area. It exports mainly to itself. But it is still not fully independent. Europe must import about 50 percent of its energy needs. It is not self-sufficient in technology—certainly not in computers, electronics, software, or biotechnology. It is dependent upon returns from the huge

Table 4

**WORLDWIDE FOREIGN DIRECT INVESTMENTS:
SOURCE AND TARGET, 1988**
(Percent of total)

Country	Source	Target
United States	31.7%	33.4%
Japan	10.7	--
United Kingdom	17.8	9.7
West Germany	9.4	--
Developing countries	--	25.9
Asia (including Japan)	--	7.3

Total world direct investment: $1.03 trillion

Source: JETRO (note 33 below), p. 2.

foreign direct investment which it maintains and increases within
the markets of other countries (principally North America), as well
as upon the funds that foreigners invest in its own market. As a
result, individual countries in Europe have been required to develop flexible domestic economies to meet the continuing challenge
of both European and extra-European exports.

One pioneering analysis contends that support for increased
trade depends upon the existence of abundant factors of production
within the local economy.[36] For most of the nineteenth century continental Europe did not even enjoy capital abundance. Today it
possesses both capital and labor abundance. Only agriculture (land)
exists as a scarce factor of production and obviously it favors a policy
of protection. Thus low tariffs now enjoy majority group support in
most European countries. In certain respects the economic adjustment to outside industrial pressures may even be easier in Europe
than in other regions in the years ahead. Individual European states
(unlike the United States or Russia) never had self-sufficiency in
resources or markets. They could not depend upon a domestic stimulus (consumption) strategy to meet their needs but had to rely on
exports. And an integrated Europe today will also not achieve self-
sufficiency. As it broadens and enlarges in scope, it probably will
not even be able to achieve full domestic economic integration.*

*National economic policy-makers have three policy levers that they can pull:
they can seek to control capital flows, to maintain monetary policy autonomy,

Some will claim that the creation of new, larger trading blocs will lead to multilateral economic conflict in the future. But one should remember, first, that these blocs will not be self-sufficient. Second, their very existence will hugely stimulate inward flows of foreign direct investment, leaping over the tariff barrier into the free trade zone. Thus the stake of countries in the welfare and prosperity of other economies may actually deepen in the future.

A final point which cannot be fully elaborated here is that the emergence of a *central coalition* in world politics will help diminish the divisive effect of economic conflicts. In two other periods (at the end of divisive wars) a central coalition briefly emerged to govern Europe and the world. The first, the Concert of Europe, failed when Britain withdrew from continental concerns after 1822. The second, the League of Nations Council, failed when the United States failed to participate. In the future, however, a central coalition will not likely be stunted by a refusal to participate by one or more of the leading powers of the world. Drawn by the stimuli of strong economic interests, the United States and the Soviet Union will remain intimately involved in the political and economic process of European politics. Japan will not be able to stand aside because of its new and heavy investment in both Western and Eastern Europe. The question will be whether China, confronting this strong central group, will seek to remain outside. If it does, following the argument of this paper, it will suffer economically and politically. Actually, and for the first time in the history of the modern state system, there is the prospect that concentrated power, far from repelling other magnetic poles, will begin to attract them. From a balance-of-power standpoint, it is very difficult to understand what is now happening in Europe. The integrating and enlarging Europe is becoming an ever stronger force. On typical historical precedents, one might expect the fringe countries to form an alliance against

---

and to control exchange rates. The Mundell-Fleming conditions suggest that they can   govern only two of the three. If there is capital mobility (as there will be in an integrated Europe after 1992) and fixed exchange rates (in the ERM and EMU), then governments will have lost control over monetary policy. This makes the final stage of a single currency and a single central bank very hard to swallow for most economic policy-makers, and not only for the British. It is therefore possible that the final stages of European monetary unification will not be achieved.

this strong central group. Instead, the fringe nations—including Eastern Europe, the Soviet Union, Turkey, Morocco, and others—are trying their best to win an association if not direct admission to the councils of the European Community.[37]

The result is that one of the main features of the post-1989 world is that typical balance-of-power effects are absent. Instead, a central coalition, centering on the European Community, but drawing in the United States and Japan as well, is in the process of formation. For economic reasons this group is highly interdependent. Violating all historical precedents, the USSR, rather than seeking to balance *against* this strong central coalition, is rather trying to join it. It seems impossible in these circumstances to imagine, say, that China and India would form an opposing bloc to balance against the central group. They too, in time, will be drawn into association with it.

Thus the possibility of greater economic conflict in the future will be conditioned and limited by a greater political association of leading states in a central coalition. In this respect, the very large economic stakes that separate trading units already have in the welfare of others, conjoined with a new system of international and power governance, will tend to reduce the excesses of economic conflict. Under these conditions, Europe will not be able to lapse into interwar economic squabbles, but will resume an open and cooperative posture toward the outside world.

WHAT FORM WILL COOPERATION TAKE?

If the argument of this paper is correct, the ultimate outcome of economic conflict will be growing cooperation among three major blocs in world politics: the European Community—progressively drawing in Eastern Europe and even an emerging Russian federation—a North American bloc, and an East Asian bloc centered on Japan. These blocs will not be homogeneous, however. In the North American and East Asian cases, they are organized around a single economic dynamo, the United States or Japan. In the European case, while the united Germany is very strong, it does not dominate the European twelve, and it would even less control the European eighteen (with EFTA), or twenty-three (with Hungary, Poland,

Czechoslovakia, Turkey, and Morocco), or twenty-four (with a re-formed Soviet Federal Republic). Neither does it appear that full economic and political union will be achieved by members of the European Community.[38] There will also be security tensions among Eastern and Western portions of the partly integrated unit. Tensions will exist outside this unit as well with the possible breakup of Yugoslavia, and territorial disputes between Romania and Hungary, Romania and the Soviet Union, and Poland and the Soviet Union.

It is of course possible to imagine that new European federal institutions will quickly solve these problems and move to create a self-sufficient, all-European defense force replacing NATO. For various reasons this result seems unlikely. While it is true that Europe as a collectivity is more economically self-sufficient than other regions (though still heavily dependent on the outside world), it is less militarily self-sufficient. It is the participation of the United States in European security that offers reassurance when the West European partners ponder their long-term relationship with the Soviet Union. The Soviet Union offers two challenges to an integrating, economically preoccupied Europe. The first, short-term challenge is the possibility of a reversion to militarism in Moscow to put down the seceding republics and enforce political calm. During any such crisis Europe will need the presence of American forces to moderate the challenge that might then be posed to Eastern Europe or even to Western nations themselves. The second, longer-term challenge will occur when a reunited Russian federation solves its economic problems and resumes producing at a significant rate. As Halford Mackinder knew, there was no necessary balance between land and naval powers in Europe. Industrialization, new modes of transportation, and new products could always change the equilibrium between land and sea, west and east. A new economic powerhouse in Moscow and Leningrad (or Petrograd?) would alter the relation between Russia and Germany, between Russia and Europe. It is at this point that a close Euroatlantic partnership would make the difference in producing a stable outcome.[39] As we have already seen, none of the three regions is self-sufficient in economic terms. Of these, Europe is the least self-sufficient in security terms. It is because of the cooperation of the United States that a Europe that stretches to the Urals can remain stable and peaceful.

It is also that tripartite combination of the United States, Europe, and Russia which gives Europe a weight in world politics which it would otherwise not have. It brings Europe into a central coalition which is so strong that it draws other nations in; it does not call forth a balancing response against itself. The strength of that central coalition is great enough to draw in Japan and ultimately China. With China added, India and the Third World will not be able to stand aside. The key to the entire structure lies in the links that integrating Europe holds out to outside nations: they can participate in the customs union and benefit from funds and institutional support. Without these initial efforts to draw erstwhile feuding nations together, the structure would not have a core. The European core of economic and political stability makes possible links to other nations, diminishing the scope of economic conflict.

The united Germany will play a large role in the new economic and perhaps also security structure. It will be the strongest European state with the Soviet Union on the sidelines. Germany's key interest is to draw East European countries under the European political umbrella without necessarily admitting them to the fully integrated structure of the twelve. In economic terms Germany will seek to help finance the economic stabilization and development of the satellite countries. The problem in the Soviet Union, however, is too great for Germany to tackle alone. Nor can the Soviet Union be admitted to the "inner" integrated Community. Neither political nor economic criteria would sanction such an admission. If Germany is to remain as a critical linchpin between East and West, however, Moscow should not be driven off as a result of failing to meet the most rigorous integrative criteria. This means that Germany ultimately will wish to maintain an open Europe, not a closed one. Enlargement will become more important than the continued deepening of the integrative process among existing members. This is probably for the best, for an open Europe can more easily associate itself with others. A wider Concert of Europe then becomes possible.

ADDENDUM ON DEVELOPMENTS IN THE FORMER SOVIET UNION AND EASTERN EUROPE

Nothing that has recently transpired in the breakup of the Soviet Union and Yugoslavia greatly changes the preceding analysis.

If anything, these trends suggest that a connection between the European Community and the United States is even more imperative than before. The present centrifugal tendencies in the East could in time produce a probably ineffective attempt to reassert centripetal control. If the Commonwealth of Independent States remains both a titular and relatively ineffective economic unit, attention will shift to integrating Russia and possibly also the Ukraine, Belarus, and Kazakhstan into the Western economy. Russia's degree of interdependence with the West in both technology and capital would then be (if anything) more marked. Would this mean that it might then become too weak to act as a pillar in the emerging concert of nations discussed above? Not necessarily. Since it would need capital from Europe and the United States and would ultimately depend upon selling a new line of consumer products in the West, the connection could strengthen. But it would be based on the very great long-term strengths of a highly educated Russian population, abundant natural resources, and not inconsiderable ability to master complicated information-processing and software problems. Russia will not remain on its economic knees, and its successes will be largely attributable to a close association with the United States and Europe.

NOTES

1. See, inter alia, Robert Gilpin, *The Political Economy of International Relations* (Princeton, N.J.: Princeton University Press, 1987), and Stephen Krasner, "State Power and the Structure of International Trade," *World Politics* 28, 3 (April 1976): 317–47. A more general argument for the likelihood of such conflict is given in R. Gilpin, *War and Change in World Politics* (Cambridge: Cambridge University Press, 1981), esp. chs. 4 and 5. For contrasting views, see Duncan Snidal, "The Limits of Hegemonic Stability Theory" *International Organization* 39, 4 (Autumn 1985), and John A. C. Conybeare, *Trade Wars: The Theory and Practice of International Commercial Rivalry* (New York: Columbia University Press, 1987).

2. See Gilpin, *Political Economy* (note 1), pp. 397–401.

3. The dubiety of this conclusion is underscored by the fact that writers have tended to argue that the 1980s would be like the 1930s. Paul Erdman wrote a book titled *The Crash of '79* (New York: Simon and Schuster, 1976); when that did not transpire, he crafted another one titled *What's Next? How to Prepare Yourself for the Crash of 1989 and Profit in the 1990s* (New York: Doubleday, 1988).

4. John Zysman and Michael Borrus offer a different version of the traditional argument. It is essentially that the United States was in the 1950s and 1960s in a position to compel cooperation from its allies, wholly dependent upon the United States for protection and for capital. See "Trade Wars, Economic Threats, and an Independent European Defense"; paper presented to the conference on "The Future of European Security," Berkeley, 24–25 April 1991.

5. William Fellner first talked of this situation in *Competition among the Few* (New York: Augustus M. Kelley, 1960). He concluded that oligopolistic disagreements would not long persist (pp. 29–30). A major factor in settling disputes would be the ability of parties to take and to inflict losses during stalemates. If this and the degree of short-term loss, the long-run consequences of excessive asymmetric outcomes, and the willingness or unwillingness to yield in the range in which the other party was expected to yield are taken into account "and the zero-profit limits are appraised correctly for all parties from the outset, a permanent stalemate would have to rest on a series of mutual errors. . . . It is unlikely that this would persist" (p. 29). Fellner also argues, however, that "the periods of established quasi-agreement will be interrupted by intervals of strength-testing (aggressive) competition; and also by periods of tentative price-setting aimed at testing their market views of rivals"(p. 34). He concludes that joint maximization will not be achieved and that "Economic behavior under fewness is imperfectly co-ordinated; it remains competitive in a limited sense" (p. 35). Robert E. Keunne writes: "Mature oligopolistic industries, in which major rivals have coexisted for extensive periods of time, are much more peaceful communities than [game theoretic] frameworks picture. They are blends of the rivalrous and the cooperative, with coexistence generally frankly accepted, and, indeed, with some positive and motivating concern for the image or welfare of the industry. Each rival is solicitous of the impacts of his decisions upon the welfares of each of his major rivals. A great source of this concern, of course, is the fear that if that impact is too painful, the rival or rivals will respond with punishing reaction" (*Rivalrous Consonance: A Theory of General Oligopolistic Equilibrium* [Amsterdam: North-Holland, 1986], p. 4).

6. See particularly Arthur Stein, "The Hegemon's Dilemma: Great Britain, the United States, and the International Economic Order," *International Organization* 38 (Spring 1984): 355–86, and Conybeare, *Trade Wars* (note 1), ch. 3. The benevolent hegemon does not benefit because it loses relatively. The predatory hegemon does not last because the preconditions of successful predation—the existence of small price-taking competitors—only endure for a short period of time. See also David Lake, *Power, Protection, and Free Trade: International Sources of U.S. Commercial Strategy 1887–1939* (Ithaca: Cornell University Press, 1988).

7. For the advantages of being "Number 2," see Thomas Schwartz, "The Paradox of Power in International Relations" (Los Angeles: University of California, Department of Political Science, August 1990), and Zeev Maoz, "Power, Capabilities, and Paradoxical Conflict Outcomes," *World Politics* 61 (January 1989): 239–66.

8. Snidal (note 1) pp. 579–614.

9. R. Rosecrance and J. Taw, "Japan and the Theory of International Leadership," *World Politics* 62 (January 1990): 203–04.

10. See argument and data in Rosecrance and Taw (note 9). See also Jeffry Frieden, "The United States and Inter-War Money and Finance: Lessons for Japan's Future from America's Past," in *History, the White House, the Kremlin: Statesmen as Historians*, ed. Michael Fry (New York: Columbia University Press, 1992).

11. See Kenneth Oye, "The Sterling-Dollar-Franc Triangle: Monetary Diplomacy 1929–1937" in *Cooperation under Anarchy*, ed. K. Oye (Princeton: Princeton University Press, 1986). Oye argues that there was no collective action problem between 1929–33; rather the central participants were playing *deadlock* against each other. When common interests returned in 1936, three powers could solve the collective action problem in the Tripartite Agreement. Though Oye disputes the "fable" of the 1930s, he contends that the "moral" is both sound and applicable to the future: "The specter of international economic disintegration brought about by the mindless and short-sighted pursuit of narrow national interests provides a powerful spur to cooperation" (p. 199).

12. See, e.g., Ronald Rogowski: *Commerce and Coalitions* (Princeton: Princeton University Press, 1990), and particularly "Trade and the Variety of Democratic Institutions," *International Organization*, Spring 1987, and Peter Gourevitch, "The Second Image Reversed: The International Sources of Domestic Politics," *International Organization* 32 (Autumn 1978).

13. See Peter Katzenstein, *Small States and the World Market* (Ithaca: Cornell University Press, 1985).

14. See R. Rosecrance, *The Rise of the Trading State: Commerce and Conquest in the Modern World* (New York: Basic Books, 1986).

15. See Charles Gide and Charles Rist, *A History of Economic Doctrines: From the Time of the Physiocrats to the Present Day* (Boston: D.C. Heath, 1948), p. 280.

16. Quoted in *ibid.*

17. *Ibid.*, p. 294.

18. Gilpin, *Political Economy* (note 1), p. 112.

19. *Ibid.*, p. 112.

20. *Ibid.*, p. 113.

21. *Ibid.*, p. 115.

22. *Ibid.* See also Mancur Olson, *The Rise and Decline of Nations* (New Haven: Yale University Press, 1982).

23. Gilpin, *Political Economy*, p. 116.

24. See Paul M. Kennedy, *Strategy and Diplomacy, 1870–1945: Eight Studies* (London: Allen and Unwin, 1983). In addition, in 1939 a Japanese-German alliance to attack Soviet Russia might have had more long-term effectiveness than a German-Italian alliance to attack France and England.

25. Here Zysman and Borrus seem to suggest that separate trading units in Europe and East Asia can be well nigh self-sufficient. They provide no data to reach this conclusion, however, and Japan's dependence on the U.S. market in which it must sell more than one-third of its exports (an amount which cannot possibly be sold anywhere else) raises serious questions about their analysis. As applied to Europe, the conclusion has more merit, but even here an integrated Europe appears likely to depend on energy imports for 50 percent of its needs for the foreseeable future. These imports must be balanced by exports, not to Europe, but to the rest of the world.

26. See particularly Alexander Gerschenkron, *Economic Backwardness in Historical Perspective: A Book of Essays* (Cambridge, Mass.: Belknap Press, 1962).

27. See Paul Krugman, *Rethinking International Trade* (Cambridge, Mass.: MIT Press, 1990), ch. 13. In certain ways Krugman may even too strongly disagree with Gerschenkron, by focusing too exclusively upon the strategic significance of early investments (not late or late, late investments) in a new technological field.

28. See R. Rosecrance, *America's Economic Resurgence: A Bold New Strategy* (New York: Harper/Collins, 1990).

29. This surely is the major thesis of Paul Kennedy's *The Rise and Fall of the Great Powers* (New York: Random House, 1987).

30. See particularly Rosecrance, *Rise of the Trading State* (note 14).

31. In the 1960s Japan was improving its relative world economic position at an increasing rate. In the 1980s Japan improved its world position at a decreasing rate. After 2020 it appears likely that China's great gains may well thrust Japan into a position of relative decline. For further analysis see Rosecrance and Taw (note 9).

32. Brian Healy, "Economic Power Transition in the International System: The Translation of Economic Power into Political Leverage in the International Monetary System"; Ph.D. dissertation, Cornell University, 1973, and William Gutowitz, *The Interrelationship of Economic Factors and Political Relations among Nations: A Quantitative Analysis* (Cornell University, 1978).

33. It is perhaps significant that of present world gross national product of about $20 trillion, more than $1 trillion is lodged in foreign direct investment (see JETRO, *White Paper on Foreign Direct Investment*, Tokyo, March 1990, pp. 1–2).

34. These are based on Japanese estimates. Others have calculated that total Japanese investments abroad (portfolio and direct) total about 14.64 percent of Japanese 1988 GDP (Elizabeth Bailey, Department of Political Science, UCLA, May 1991).

35. See JETRO (note 33), p. 16, which contends that U.S. investments in Japan are more than one-third of Japanese investments in the United States. These figures, however, do not appear to take into account the latest Japanese acquisitions in America.

36. See Rogowski, (note 12).

37. For a further analysis of this phenomenon see Rosecrance, "A New Concert of Europe?" (Berlin: Kennedy Institute, Free University of Berlin, June 1991).

38. See the contribution to this volume by Barry Eichengreen for the variety of economic powers which governments would have to give up to attain full economic integration. This list may be too long and too important to be fully conceded to supranational authority.

39. See speech by James Baker, 18 June 1991.

CHANGING THE ORDER THAT WORKED: PROSPECTS AND ALTERNATIVES FOR EUROPEAN SECURITY

Alexei B. Arbatov

As a popular maxim goes, if something works, don't fix it—i.e., don't change it. European security has worked during the last forty plus years. It was based on the divisions of Europe and Germany by two powerful political-military alliances. The standoff maintained stability because of the massive military presence on the continent of the two superpowers and mutual nuclear deterrence, and because no *casus belli* arose that was serious enough to justify a third devastating war on the continent in one century. The paradox is that the very success of NATO and U.S. security commitments means the old organizations will have to be rearranged quite radically.

Whatever stability the old security order provided, it will have to be fundamentally restructured to adapt to the new balance of power with its changing interests and security concerns. Otherwise, stability may suffer serious setbacks that simply cannot afford another period of confrontation, much less any kind of large-scale armed violence. As we have recently learned only too well in the former Soviet Union, keeping the situation under control requires keeping ahead of events, or at a minimum abreast of them.

There are four principal models of European security arrangements: 1) the preservation of NATO; 2) the spread of nuclear capabilities, in particular to Germany; 3) the collective security system based on CSCE; and 4) European integration based on the European Community (EC). In the next decade the actual institutional arrangements may not embody any one of these in their pure forms. The future will belong to some combination of all the models, their relative role changing over time and according to circumstances. Even now all of them (except the nuclear proliferation variant) are present in Europe.

What is really important—how and when these priorities will change—will be determined by a set of relatively predictable trends in combination with a number of largely unpredictable variables. The interaction of these constants and variables of the basic economic, political, and military circumstances will shape the superstructure of security arrangements on the continent, and it is to these scenarios that we shall turn. Acknowledging the secondary nature of arms control and political security agreements right now, it is necessary to point out their strong back-channel influence on pending concerns. Some specific arms control recommendations will be presented in other sections of the essay.

CONSTANTS, NEW PROBLEMS, AND NEW DILEMMAS

Some trends in and outside of Europe are sufficiently predictable and cannot easily be reversed by the political actions of leaders and parties. These trends are driven by powerful dynamics of economic, social, and technological momentum. Still, their intensity and particular forms are tangibly affected by outside events.

First, the dominant process at work is European economic, social, and political integration. This process has occurred in stages, with development in depth (a closer merger of the countries) superseded by development in width (new states entering the EC), but the momentum is inexorable.

The second predictable trend is the curtailment of foreign military and political activities of Russia and of any of the other states in the former Soviet Union in the Third World.

The third obvious constant for the 1990s is the decline in United States military and political dominance in Europe and the Western Pacific. American activity will at the same time increase in the Third World, although after the Gulf War the United States will hardly be eager to act unilaterally as the world policeman. Rather, Washington will seek cooperation with other Western powers and regional states. Prospects for U.S. cooperation with the Soviet states and the probability of the UN taking charge in Third World crisis-resolution will largely depend on developments in the former Soviet Union, and on U.S. readiness to exercise flexibility in accommodating the legitimate interests of Moscow and local states.

The fourth probability is continuing turmoil in the Third World: economic, demographic, social, and ecological troubles which will present the industrialized world with hard dilemmas: armed intervention or abstention, inflicting devastating losses on innocent populations or letting aggressors get away with their acquisitions.

The fifth trend among the developed and newly developed nations is the growth of economic, financial, and technological instruments of political influence abroad. To a certain degree these will decrease the significance of traditional military levers as attributes of world status.

The sixth phenomenon is the expanding agenda of arms control. The rapid development of technology and a changing geostrategic environment will place a growing burden on traditional arms control processes and regimes including START, defense and space talks, CFE, nuclear tests limitation, chemical weapons disarmament, and NPT. New issues are TNF talks in Europe, naval arms control, limitation of missile proliferation, arms trade limitation, and talks on cooperation and burden-sharing in peace-keeping missions and in the Third World. Things will not be easier for the international arms control community, even in a benign political climate, which is by no means assured.

The above-mentioned constants will interact with the variables of new interests and concerns on the parts of the states involved. Of particular significance to Europe are the four following problems:

- Future internal developments in the former Soviet Union;
- Evolution of the situation in Eastern Europe;
- Possible changes in relations between the United States and Western Europe within the NATO framework; and
- Evolution of relations among West European states, primarily among a reunited Germany, France, and Great Britain.

The first variable, the future of the former Soviet states, is of paramount importance and deserves some elaboration.

SOVIET UNCERTAINTY

The new political thinking in foreign policy, initiated in 1985, softened the internal rigidity of the regime. Attempts at political democratization dealt a blow to the Soviet empire. And the dismantling of the centralized economy undermined the military-industrial complex and the traditionally privileged position of the army within the state. Efforts to preserve the centralized economy and the empire would have led to a revival of political totalitarianism, and hence to a revival of confrontational policy abroad, with the cold war resumed at the new frontiers.

A more hopeful alternative is a continuation of consistent political, economic, and military reforms in the former Soviet Union; this would preserve and improve the foundation for a Shevardnadze-type foreign policy—i.e., improving political and economic relations with the West, cooperating in organizing regional security systems and conflict-resolution in the Third World, and stabilizing the military balance and reducing the role of military power in world politics by way of arms control agreements and unilateral force reductions.

In particular, promoting reforms would mean conceding real sovereignty and a freedom of choice to the republics and national minorities, leaving it up to them to choose the degree of their integration in the union and to delegate certain functions to the central authorities. Economic interdependence, unified energy and transportation systems, and an intermixing of nationalities across the country—all these make it absolutely certain that most of the republics cannot separate and survive without each other at least for the next two decades.

If Russia does not try to impose its will on the republics in order to perpetuate its hugeness and preponderant power, then the centrifugal forces in the republics—a counteraction to this policy— would immediately diminish. The republics would begin to establish the framework of economic, ecological, social, and political cooperation on the basis of treaties and contracts. At the same time, they would immediately delegate important functions, including broad areas of foreign policy and common defense, to the central structures of the Commonwealth of Independent States (CIS), with a proper representation of the interests of individual republics and national minorities.

It is certain that the nature and form of the union will change. Most likely the inner core of the new federal state will be represented by the "big four": Russia, the Ukraine, Belorussia, and Kazakhstan, which have already started establishing independent horizontal ties. Bilateral treaties among the big four, in addition to economic obligations, postulate the inviolability of national borders (not surprisingly like the fundamental principle of the CSCE Helsinki Final Act of 1976) and the protection of human rights. Other republics will probably choose a looser type of economic and political association. Still others (like the Baltic states) will maintain close economic and humanitarian relations while becoming politically independent. The contribution of the republics to a common defense and the status of armed forces deployments and a military infrastructure on their territories would be defined by special treaties.

There is only one alternative to this kind of arrangement: a reanimation of empire with an extremely militarized core, a centralized state economy, and an oppressive totalitarian political regime. It would not necessarily retain a Communist ideology. Extremist versions of Russian chauvinism and imperialism would do just as well. It would again inflict hardships on the peoples at home and present an expansionist threat to the outside world. Of course it would be virtually impossible to recapture the Soviet positions in Eastern Europe. Still, a lot can be done to build up conventional and nuclear forces and to greatly expand arms sales, including ballistic missiles, to the volatile areas of the Third World. Earning hard currency would serve as a powerful motive and justification of such a policy.

Clear-cut alternatives are hardly possible in practical terms. For the near future there will be some complex and changing mixture of these two paths. During the next decade the dominant trend will become evident, and it is just as obvious that this will be the primary factor affecting European security and exerting a tremendous influence on the other variables of European politics.

OTHER VARIABLES

While developments in the former Soviet Union will undoubtedly exert an influence on European politics, other variables might be important too. Eastern Europe will remain a quite unstable subregion in the 1990s. Economic difficulties and hardships of transfer to a market economy may cause violent political shocks. National problems within some states (e.g., the Slovaks in Czechoslovakia, the Hungarians in Romania, and the Turks in Bulgaria) will continue to be exacerbated, bringing about additional conflicts. Even worse, if combined with escalating national collisions in the former Soviet Union, these problems might lead to a confrontation with former allies: Romania against Moldavia, and Poland or Lithuania against the Ukraine.

Another variable is U.S.–West European relations. Depending on what happens in the former USSR and Eastern Europe, the extreme variants bracketing the range of possibilities in the 1990s are as follows:

- A retention of the present NATO structures with Western Europe assuming 60–70 percent of the slightly reduced cost of common defense, and U.S. forces in Europe reduced to 100,000–150,000 personnel, 2,000–3,000 tanks, and the present number of aircraft (about 700); development of long-range conventional and tactical nuclear systems capable of striking Russian territory "over the head" of Eastern Europe (bombers, strike aircraft, air-launched cruise missiles, TASM systems, etc.); the upgrading of tactical mobility to reinforce Eastern Europe in a crisis; and arms supplies, military training, and political security guarantees to former Soviet allies;

- A deep restructuring of the NATO establishment, with Western Europe assuming 80–90 percent of substantially cut defense expenditures (and appointing SACEUR); U.S. ground forces completely withdrawn; U.S. tactical nuclear weapons relocated to CONUS; a U.S. military presence consisting of 100–200 aircraft and newly deployed air defense units manning the logistics infrastructure, POMCUS storages, and keeping officers in command structures; and U.S. and allied navies securing SLOCS;

- European security integration may occur outside of NATO structures. This will become a high priority when Soviet forces withdraw from Central and Eastern Europe;
- Joint power projection forces oriented toward Third World contingencies;
- Coordination of arms trade and arms transfer policies;
- Joint development and production of conventional weapons systems, especially in the area of high technology;
- Joint development of new air defenses and probably anti-tactical ballistic missile defenses;
- Joint early-warning, reconnaissance, and command-communication systems, including space-based systems;
- Joint operational planning, development, production of components, and eventually (after the year 2000) joint deployment of European nuclear deterrent forces.

As suggested, the development of European military integration is an objective process which will go on under all circumstances. Its rate, scale, and priorities, however, will depend on the relations of Western Europe with the former USSR and the United States. Any worsening of Europe's relations with Moscow will leave the United States to play a predominant role in the Third World. Relative stability in Europe, on the contrary, would prompt coordination and bargaining with Washington over collective actions in the Third World. WEU military programs will provide West European states with greater autonomy.

Prospects for the latter alternative depend on the evolution of relations among major West European states; once again these have acquired a degree of uncertainty after the reunification of Germany. It seems obvious that the more Western Europe is independent of the United States, the less important NATO will be and the larger will be the German strategic, security, and political roles. For instance, Bonn is likely to demand to be "plugged in" to the European nuclear deterrent talks through the WEU or other, special, out-of-NATO structures.

INTERPLAY OF CONSTANTS AND VARIABLES IN
EUROPEAN POLITICS

Given the major uncertainties of European politics in the 1990s, the issue is not whether to preserve NATO and encourage European integration as a constructive supplement to the Atlantic alliance. The real problems to be resolved concern how to fit both into the new security framework enveloping Eastern Europe and the former Soviet Union; how to avoid a new cold war and deep shocks within the Western alliance, and how to use arms control and security arrangements to facilitate reforms and stability in the former USSR and Eastern Europe.

Will it be possible to adapt NATO to the new conditions in Europe after the transitional period (which may last until the end of the 1990s)? Can NATO with some modifications assume the role of a European security system? What may be the relationship between NATO and the CSCE? Will some new security structures emerge to supplement these institutions?

In addressing these issues, we must keep in mind that the term "NATO" has a quite concrete meaning, rather than simply suggesting a political community and partnership of Western Europe and North America. NATO was born of global bipolarity and the division of Europe and Germany, with the overt aim to defend against the perceived threat of Soviet aggression. NATO structure, functions, and plans are directed to this goal. American leadership is embodied in all alliance institutions and procedures, beginning with a U.S. general as SACEUR and ending with the U.S. custody of nuclear weapons and the double-key locks on nuclear munitions. U.S. nuclear guarantees are supported by large-scale TNF deployments with targets assigned in the East. Overall operations planning, allocation of sectors of the front to national contingents, U.S. reinforcement plans and capabilities, POMCUS sites, maritime strategy designed to secure Atlantic sea lines of communications, air-land battle and Follow-On-Forces Attack (FOFA) systems and planning—all these and more are geared to a clear and definite purpose. That is what "NATO" means.

Certainly missions and forces may be modified, reduced, or rearranged. That has been done many times during the last forty years. But the nature, purpose, and instruments of the institution cannot be changed without changing the institution per se. NATO's major properties simply cannot be adapted to the tasks of ensuring the internal stability of East European states, preventing conflicts among them, or involving the former USSR in the collective security system by guaranteeing the absence of hostile surroundings on its western borders. Nor can NATO be adapted to the task of keeping Germany under control after the removal of the threat from the East. Still less can FOFA and TNFs be used to address the continent's economic, social, and environmental problems.

Under the worst possible scenario, if the cold war is revived along the western borders of the former Soviet Union or Russia, NATO will be inadequate in that circumstance as well. For instance, massive deployments of ballistic missile defenses (BMD) by either side—almost certain in this case—would make U.S. nuclear commitments (i.e., limited strategic strike options) dubious. While protecting U.S. territory, BMD systems would be incapable of defending Western Europe against theater nuclear weapons. France and Britain would have to expand their nuclear forces. But then what about Germany? Would it continue to rely on huge U.S. commitments or demand participation in French-British nuclear cooperation? Or would it go on its own? Would a U.S. general remain SACEUR if the core of European defense—nuclear retaliatory capabilities—stays out of his control? Would the United States retain its tactical nuclear weapons in Europe—the basis of commitments and leadership in NATO—if SACEUR were no longer American?

Since the watershed of the new cold war most certainly would be East European–Soviet border areas, how would NATO provide for the defense of the threatened region with its forces deployed 600 to 1,000 kilometers from the front? Would the United States take upon itself the still greater burden of protecting Poles, Czechs, and Hungarians or leave the task to integrated Europe and the WEU under German leadership? How would NATO handle intervention in the Third World? The resolution of all these and many other issues would require such a profound revision of NATO that, apart from the title, not much would be left of it.

If, however, reforms in Eastern Europe and the former Soviet Union and economic and political cooperation on the continent developed successfully, NATO would be even less relevant. The

Atlantic alliance is a tool for confrontation; if it is sustained at all costs, that in itself will generate confrontation. It cannot be transformed into a new type of collective security system.

At the same time, under an optimistic scenario, the CSCE framework probably would not work either. Even Russia alone would still be too big and much stronger than any single European state. Most probably Europe in the future will be able to counterbalance this power without U.S. leadership and massive participation through the joint efforts of major nations. But this would constitute bipolarity all over again (which actually might ensue under the worst scenario), and bipolarity can no longer serve as a basis for a collective security system.

Moreover, the CSCE has geographic boundaries—from the Atlantic to the Urals. Future arms control and confidence-building arrangements will be complicated by the fact that one major player's territory is mostly beyond the area and the other's is entirely removed from it. The problems with the CFE-I treaty—in particular the massive redeployment of former Soviet weapons to the east—are a harbinger of future troubles. Fortunately the earth is round, so extending the CSCE zone to the east is possible. The new zone would include Siberia, Japan, the United States and Canada, and would return to Europe from the West. Hence the appropriate extended framework of the security system would be a North Atlantic and Pacific Security Organization. Actually this fits quite well with prevailing economic, political, and military realities and concerns.

It seems that all kinds of envisioned follow-ups to arms control negotiations require an extended geostrategic format and would be ineffective if artificially limited to Europe (from the Atlantic to the Urals). Equally important, this would provide for the kind of multipolarity which is essential for a system of collective security (as opposed to an alliance). With four major players (including Japan), this system would make it certain that any potential troublemaker would face an overwhelming coalition of the three other major centers of power.

One important reservation is in order. Under even the most optimistic of scenarios, transition to such a system would require at least a decade. The rapid dismantling of NATO is not only unnecessary, but would also be highly destabilizing. The proper approach is to undertake a planned, gradual, and coordinated "Europeanization" of NATO, parallel to the multi-lateral arms control and CBM arrangements of the 1990s. The same goes for expanding the CSCE, which cannot be done in one step.

With more radical measures in Europe, less stringent agreements may be applied to Siberia, the Far East, Canada, and U.S. territories. Tokyo, perhaps initially by way of politically binding declarations and indirect limitations, would join Russian-American agreements on the Western and Northern Pacific CBMs and arms control measures.

However lengthy the transition, it is necessary to keep in mind the main direction—in particular the gradual transformation and dissolution of NATO and the CSCE. In this way intermediate steps may be worked out accordingly. As an illustration, several transitional agreements on arms control are presented below.

CHANGING THE PARAMETERS OF CFE

There is no question that the obstacles to CFE-I ratification have to be removed by Russia. At the same time, these steps will become easier with the West showing some flexibility—in particular declaring its readiness in the course of CFE-I implementation to discuss naval CBMs and eventually naval arms control, reduce U.S. TNFs in Europe, and address Russian security concerns in view of the changed situation in Eastern Europe during the CFE-II stage.

With respect to CFE-II (unlike CFE-IA), an incremental approach would hardly be sufficient since the basic assumptions of CFE-I were suited to very different geopolitical realities—i.e., two opposing alliances led by the two superpowers; a meridional border of direct military juxtaposition running through Central Europe and Germany, with the highest force concentrations lying near the border; and mutual fears of direct surprise attack and large-scale offensive penetrations. Correspondingly the grand design of CFE-I was

- To alleviate any external insecurity of Western Europe and West Germany as a source of East-West tensions and to encourage economic and political cooperation between the two alliances;

- To enhance the security of both alliances by reducing the offensive land superiority of the East and the offensive air superiority of the West;
- To provide legitimacy to Soviet forces stationed in Eastern Europe and East Germany and to fix force allocation among former Warsaw Pact (WTO) members; and
- To remove the quantitative across-the-board superiority of the East in order to avoid an expensive program of qualitative modernization on the part of the West.

It goes without saying that all of the former realities no longer exist. Hence the grand design of CFE-I is inadequate and the incremental approach will not work, although some of its elements may serve as means for other goals.

The political tasks of the follow-up talks and new CBMs (and more generally the whole CSCE process) have to be fundamentally revised in light of the new geopolitical realities. Some of new priorities might be

- To ensure the security of Eastern Europe, which will be "sandwiched" between the united Germany and the former USSR and which threatens to become a source of European instability;
- To take into account security concerns of the former Soviet republics over being left alone against a NATO that might possibly include Eastern Europe;
- To resist East European states' joining NATO; their joining would deal a mortal blow to European security and dramatically strengthen the positions of the enemies of democratic change in the former USSR;
- To provide for the deep integration of the united Germany's arms and forces into the WEU and into the framework of multilateral arms control limitations; and
- To ensure the irreversibility of lowering the military postures in Europe by dealing with the Russian fears beyond the Urals; this in turn would require some measures on U.S. force reductions.

Translating this general design into the treaty structure will demand a great amount of elaboration. As an illustration let us take only one CFE parameter. The basic principle of the first Vienna treaty was the quantitative parity of NATO and WTO arms in Europe. It is obvious that a simple further lowering of the levels—say by 25 or even 50 percent—will not do since most of the East European countries no longer consider themselves to be part of a counterbalance to the West. But this does not mean that in CFE-II the new parity has to be established between the CIS and the whole of NATO in Europe, or between the CIS and NATO plus some East European states. The basis of the new arrangement might consist of three equations, corresponding to the new realities and concerns of the states involved:

- An equality of armed forces (by TLEs and perhaps also by personnel) at levels lower than CFE-I levels between the NATO forces in Europe and former Soviet forces in the European part of its territory (for instance, these levels could be 10,000 tanks, 4,000 aircraft);
- An equality of armed forces among the four major European states (Germany, Great Britain, France, and Italy) and forces in the Baltic, Belorussian, Carpatian, and Kiev/Odessa military districts (for example, 6,000 tanks and 3,000 airplanes);
- An equality of the German, Danish, and Benelux forces and the military forces in the Baltic, Belorussian, and Carpatian districts, with Poland, Czechoslovakia, and Hungary entitled to the same collective levels of armed forces (tentatively 3,000 tanks and 1,000 airplanes).

In addition, the United States and other countries should unilaterally commit themselves not to exceed some fixed ceiling of forces stationed in Central Europe (for instance 1,000 tanks and 300 airplanes), provided that the former USSR does not create a "strategic reserve" in western Siberia (for example, not to exceed the level of 2,000 tanks and 500 aircraft, including storage).

Since the above proposals would cut quite deeply into U.S. and West European forces while reducing and limiting former Soviet forces, an agreement might be reached not necessarily to destroy or convert reduced equipment, but to place it, partially dismantled, in secured storage facilities and under international control. Since for all sides storage at the production plants will be covered as well and stored equipment will be limited by some percentage of deployed forces, this measure would indirectly limit arms production. The same quota on stored (nondeployed) equipment might be extended to U.S. and non-European Soviet territories, thus limiting their reinforcement and mobilization potential.

To further stabilize these conditions some measures may be applied beyond Europe—for instance, transparency; exchange of data; and confidence-building notifications related to U.S. forces in CONUS and in Japan, Canadian and Turkish forces outside Europe, and military forces beyond the Urals. In addition, former Soviet troops deployed in the zone under negotiation with China will probably be limited separately.

In the next CBM stage the new steps might be

- Limiting the scale of military exercises on the continent;
- Lowering still further the thresholds on notifications;
- Developing transparency;
- Extending CBMs on naval forces;
- Extending CBMs at least to certain parts of the United States, Canada, and Soviet Asian territories.

Certainly variants may be quite different, but the main principle is clear: instead of East-West parity, the goals are meticulous regional balances and trade-offs, stringent limitations on redeployment, and a lowering of military readiness.

TACTICAL NUCLEAR ARMS

With the withdrawal of Soviet armed forces (including tactical nuclear weapons) from Central and Eastern Europe the justification for the heavy deployment of U.S. nuclear arms will be seriously weakened. Agreements on TNF may provide a good arms control framework for stabilizing reductions of tactical nuclear forces. This would ensure the following:

- Strengthening the non-nuclear status of a united Germany, which France and Britain may find difficult to guarantee without arms control agreements on tactical nuclear weapons on German territory;

– Soviet satisfaction that its security is not jeopardized by its withdrawal of forces from Central Europe;

– Alleviation of European concerns about the threats created by tactical nuclear weapons on their soil;

– U.S. commitment to maintaining a strategic link with Western Europe, despite the deep reductions of American conventional forces on the continent.

As one possible option in an extended Central Europe (including a unified Germany, the Benelux states, Denmark, Poland, Czechoslovakia, and Hungary) a totally denuclearized zone could be established. All nuclear munitions (warheads, bombs, shells, ADMs, tactical nuclear SSMs, and SAMs) would be withdrawn completely to CONUS and former Soviet territory. U.S. nuclear-capable aircraft and artillery would not be totally withdrawn but would be limited by CFE treaties.

Verification will principally focus on nuclear storage facilities, which have to include provisions for on-site inspections. Since for safety reasons these facilities are quite conspicuous, cheating would be extremely risky and unlikely. Thus any large-scale reintroduction of nuclear munitions would be time-consuming and easily detectable.

In order to have the minimum levels of military deterrent, both sides might agree to limit their TNF in the rest of Europe to no more than 300 weapons. The systems which might be subject to this limitation are surface-to-surface missiles with a range between 50 and 500 kilometers, nuclear bombs, and air-to-surface (or air-to-air) missiles with ranges up to 600 kilometers (in order to differentiate from strategic ALCMs). Each side should have the freedom to mix these systems within the 300 limit. In order not to overcomplicate verification, other nuclear munitions withdrawn from Central Europe may not be limited at the first stage of agreement. They would be out of range from each other.

It is clear that the above option and almost all other variants of TNF agreements are achievable only in the context of the implementation (but not necessarily the fulfillment) of the CFE-I treaty—in conjunction with the negotiations on CFE-II. Hopefully these arrangements would alleviate German nuclear concerns for a long time. At the next stage U.S. and Soviet TNF could be further reduced to the 100 level, with French and British tactical nuclear weapons of the same types limited by the same combined ceiling. If in the future Germany still feels entitled to some form of participation in nuclear deterrent negotiations, special arms control arrangements could be established.

NAVAL ARMS CONTROL

If an arms control regime is to be enhanced, the problem of naval stability will also have to be addressed. Regardless of the merits of various proposals on this subject, it had been a major political issue in the Soviet Union. Western intransigence is still portrayed in the former USSR as a tremendous threat to security and a symptom of the West's desire to retain a unilateral advantage in any global strategic balance.

On the regional level, extending incident avoidance agreements to all European states would be quite expedient. Next, in the European seas it would be useful to extend confidence-building measures to the Russian, Ukrainian, U.S., and European navies, providing early notification of naval exercises above a certain level of forces. Taking into account Western interests and existing asymmetries, the trade-off might consist of notification of attack submarine deployments and land-based naval aircraft take-offs involving simultaneously more than a certain number of subs and planes, compared to day-to-day practice.

Real reductions and limitations in selected areas would be more effective at first on a global level and on a bilateral U.S.-Russian basis (like START, INF, and TNF). For example, the limitation of anti-submarine capabilities is important for strategic stability between the United States and Russia as the two powers proceed to cut their strategic offensive forces. However, strategic ASW is closely linked with tactical ASW—that is, the protection of sea routes against attack submarines. In both strategic ASW and SLOC interdiction the key and most threatening weapons system is nuclear attack submarines. A possible U.S.-Russian treaty might limit nuclear subs on the global level by a ceiling of 50–60 for each side.

Since Russian nuclear subs are the main defense against U.S. aircraft carriers, a limitation of the latter would be appropriate as well. One of the possibilities would be to limit not the ships per se, but rather the fixed wing carrier aircraft (which is actually what is of concern with carriers). Land-based naval airplanes should be included as well in these agreements because they are designed to strike at carriers and because they present a threat to SLOCs and to European states. There are currently about 1,000 naval bombers and fighter-bombers in the former USSR; the United States has approximately 1,500 strike aircraft in the navy and marine corps. A ceiling of 800-900 naval strike aircraft, with the freedom to mix land-based and carrier-based aircraft (and different classes of ships), is an attractive option. While limiting mutual threats, this treaty would leave more than enough forces to deal with any Third World contingencies.

The above global naval arms control options might directly and positively affect stability on the regional level, in particular in the Atlantic and Arctic Oceans. In addition, within the framework of global treaties it may become feasible to fix special regional limitations.

CONCLUSION

Arms control, for all its importance, is only one facet of the much broader and more intricate subject of European security. Economic, financial, political, social, and psychological aspects of the problem are no less—and probably more—important.

The above arms control proposals are based on an optimistic scenario of economic, social, and political developments in the East and elsewhere. Nevertheless, if exercised vigorously and innovatively, arms control may serve as an effective tool for rearranging the European security order. Some of the problems we now face are the result of past security negotiations that were conducted too cautiously, slowly, incrementally, and generally lagged behind political events. Instead of being used as an instrument, they were often treated as the goal and final product of security. The failures associated with these strategies are among the most important lessons to be learned in the 1990s.

THE DOMESTIC SOURCES OF PEACE AND WAR IN THE NEW EUROPE

Stephen Van Evera

RUMORS OF WAR

This chapter explores two questions. First, how will the end of the cold war affect the likelihood of war in Europe? In particular, what risks will arise from the retraction of Soviet power from Eastern Europe and the disintegration of the Soviet Union itself? Second, what U.S. and Western policies would best preserve peace?

Some observers warn that Europe may return to its historic warlike ways once Soviet forces are gone from Eastern Europe, especially if American forces also leave Western Europe. One such view holds that bipolar state systems are more peaceful than multipolar systems; that Europe's post-1945 peace grew largely from the bipolar nature of the cold war international system; that the retraction of Soviet power from Eastern Europe and the internal collapse of Soviet power will probably trigger a complete American withdrawal from Western Europe; and that these withdrawals will return all of Europe to a war-prone multipolar system like the one that spawned Europe's many wars before 1945.[1]

A second pessimistic perspective suggests that Germany may return to the aggressive course that caused both world wars, once it is free from the police presence of the superpowers. Proponents of this view believe that past German aggression was driven largely by flaws in German national character, that Germany has behaved well since 1945 only because it was not free to behave badly, and that a united and more autonomous Germany may return to its old ways.* This fear is often thought, sometimes whispered, but rarely

*A variant of this view suggests that Germany was aggressive in the past because it found itself surrounded by strong neighbors with borders that offered few physical barriers to invasion; hence it expanded to bolster its security. In

stated baldly.[2] Still, it underlies the common fear that Germany will be the focus of instability in post–cold war Europe.

Third, some worry that the post-Communist regimes of Eastern Europe and the former USSR may fail to become healthy democracies, instead evolving into "praetorian states"—flawed democracies that lack the institutions required to channel growing popular participation. In such states, governments are often captured by narrow interest groups. If this occurs, these groups may pursue aggressive policies that benefit themselves, even if these policies harm the larger society. As a result, praetorian states are more warlike than healthy democracies, and the rise of praetorianism in Europe would raise the risk of war.[3]

A fourth school of thought suggests that Europe's virulent ethnic hatreds and latent border conflicts will reemerge, like plagues from Pandora's box, as the calming presence of the superpowers dissipates. These conflicts are most likely in Eastern Europe and the former USSR because these regions are more ethnically heterogeneous than Western Europe, the ethnic groups of the East are more intermingled, and many national borders in the East lack legitimacy.[4]

I argue that the first three of these pessimistic views rest on false fears, but the fourth danger is real. As a net result the risk of war in Western Europe is very low, but the risk of war in the East is significant.

The first three fears are false partly for military reasons—the nuclear revolution has raised the price of aggression and dampened security motives for expansion—but mainly for domestic reasons: the domestic structures of most European states have changed in ways that make war far less likely than before 1945. The most significant domestic changes include the waning of militarism and hypernationalism. Others include the spread of democracy, the leveling of formerly stratified European societies, the resulting evaporation of "social imperial" motives for war, and the disappearance of states governed by revolutionary elites. These changes have removed important causes of Europe's past wars, especially the two world wars.

---

this view, these unchanging geographic facts may stir renewed German aggression once Germany is reunified and unoccupied.

Europe's past multipolar systems would have been far more peaceful without these conditions and factors, and a return to multipolarity poses no special risks in their absence. The social transformation of Germany since 1945 has removed the roots of its past aggressiveness, and reunited Germany will remain a responsible member of the European community. The risks of imperfect or stunted democratization are real, but these problems are confined to a few Eastern states. Even in that region, communism has removed much of the social and economic stratification that gives rise to hypernationalism, militarism, and aggressive praetorianism.

However, the Soviet withdrawal from Eastern Europe raises the risk of renewed border and ethnic conflict in that region, and the disintegration of the Soviet Union raises the risk of war among its successor states and of civil war within them. Such conflicts could spread westward; this gives the Western states a major stake in preserving peace in the East.

Overall, the risk of major war in the new Europe may be greater than under the cold war order, but only slightly so. The risk of war in Western Europe seems very small, and any dangers that might arise in that region could be dampened by appropriate American policies. The main dangers lie in the East, where potential causes of war are more potent (and have already manifested themselves in the 1991–92 Serbo-Croatian war), and where the West has less capacity to promote peace.

To bolster peace in the East, the Western powers should use economic leverage to encourage all Eastern governments to adopt democracy, protect the rights of national minorities, accept current borders or reach a settlement on new borders, foreswear the propagation of hypernationalism, and adopt market economic reforms. The United States should also maintain a substantial military force in Western Europe, under the auspices of a NATO alliance revamped into a collective security system.

The next section reviews the many causes of past European conflicts that have disappeared over the past few decades, or are now disappearing, and offers reasons why these causes are unlikely to recur. In the section that follows, I assess the specific dangers of German aggression and praetorianism and indicate why they pose little danger. Factors that raise the risk of war in the East are noted in the subsequent section. The last section offers prescriptions for American and Western policy.

REASONS FOR HOPE: VANISHED AND VANISHING CAUSES OF WAR

The case for optimism about Europe's future rests chiefly on the diminution or disappearance of many of the prime causes of the wars of the past century. Specifically, eight significant causes of past wars have markedly diminished or are now diminishing. All but the first are domestic in nature, and even the first has a domestic component.

OFFENSE-DOMINANCE

War is far more likely when offense appears easy and conquest seems feasible, for five main reasons.[5] First and most important, arguments for territorial expansion are more persuasive: states want more territory because their current borders appear less defensible, and the seizure of others' territory seems more feasible.

Second, the incentive to launch preemptive attack increases because a successful surprise attack provides larger rewards and averts greater dangers. When the offense is strong, smaller shifts in the ratio of forces between states create greater shifts in their relative capacity to conquer and defend territory. As a result, a state has greater incentive to strike first—in order to gain the advantage of striking the first blow or to deny that advantage to its opponent—if a first strike will shift the force ratio in its favor since such a shift can be converted into larger territorial gains. This increases the danger of preemptive war and makes crises more explosive.

Third, arguments for preventive war are more powerful. Since smaller shifts in force ratios have larger effects on relative capacity to conquer or defend territory, smaller prospective shifts in force ratios cause greater hope and alarm, bolstering arguments for shutting "windows of vulnerability" by force.

Fourth, states are quicker to use diplomatic tactics that risk war in order to gain diplomatic victories. Since security is scarcer, more competitive behavior seems justified when assets that provide security are disputed between states. As a result, states use more competitive tactics, like brinkmanship and presenting opponents with *faits accomplis*, that increase the risk of war.

Fifth, states enforce tighter political and military secrecy since national security is threatened more directly if enemies win the contest for information. Hence states try harder to gain the advantage and avoid the disadvantage of disclosure, leading them to carefully conceal military plans and forces. This can lead opponents to underestimate one another's capabilities and blunder into a war of optimistic miscalculation.[6] It also may ease surprise attack, by concealing preparations from the opponent, and may prevent arms control agreements by making compliance more difficult to verify.

These dangers have been ubiquitous causes of past European wars, and faith in the relative ease of conquest played a major role in the outbreak of both world wars, especially the first.[7] However, three changes since 1945—the nuclear revolution, the evolution of industrial economies toward knowledge-based forms of production, and the transformation of American foreign policy interests and thinking—have greatly strengthened the defense and largely erased the rationale for security competition among the European powers.

The Nuclear Revolution. Many observers note that nuclear weapons have bolstered peace by vastly raising the cost of war; as a result states behave more cautiously.[8] If this were the sole effect of the nuclear revolution, however, it would represent little net gain for peace and would provide little basis for optimism about Europe's future. Wars would be far fewer, but far more destructive. Over the long run the number of war deaths might be as large as always; the difference is merely that the dead would die in a smaller number of more violent conflicts.

A second effect of nuclear weapons is far more important: they strengthen defending states against aggressors. States with developed nuclear arsenals can annihilate each other even after absorbing an all-out attack, giving rise to a world of mutual assured destruction (MAD). In a MAD world conquest is far harder than before because international conflicts shift from tests of will and capability to purer tests of will—to be won by the side willing to run greater risks and pay greater costs. This strengthens defenders because they nearly always value their freedom more than aggressors value new conquests; hence they have more resolve than aggressors, hence their threats are more credible, hence they are bound to prevail in a confrontation.

For these reasons the nuclear revolution makes conquest among great powers virtually impossible. A victor now must destroy almost all of an opponent's nuclear arsenal—an enormous task requiring massive technical and material superiority. As a result, even lesser powers can now stand alone against states with far greater resources, as they never could before.

Britain, France, and the former Soviet Union are Europe's only nuclear powers today, but a number of others could develop powerful deterrents if they ever faced serious threats to their security. This potential diminishes the risk of war. Before 1945, states sought to redress insecurity by territorial expansion and preventive war. The nuclear revolution has given states the option of achieving security without resort to war by peacefully acquiring superior defensive weapons. As a result of this increased security, competition for security will be muted in the new Europe; arguments for preemptive and preventive war will be less common; diplomacy will be conducted with less reckless search for unilateral advantage; and foreign and security policies will be relatively open.

The possibility of nuclear proliferation should thus be seen as a net benefit to peace in Europe. Proliferation would entail obvious dangers. For example, new nuclear states might develop frail deterrents that are not secure from accident, terrorist seizure, illegal sale, or surprise attack, raising the risk of terrorist use, sale to unsavory governments or groups, and accidental or preemptive war. (For example, these risks could arise if the new states emerging from the former Soviet Union opt to acquire nuclear forces and attempt to do so by retaining control over Soviet nuclear weapons now on their territory, since such states might lack the capacity to manage their new arsenals.) However, these dangers can probably be managed. Widespread proliferation within the former Soviet Union now seems unlikely since most of the emerging Soviet republics have renounced nuclear weapons. Proliferation there and elsewhere can also be dampened by taking active steps to prevent aggression and preserve peace (see below, last section), thus reducing the non-nuclear powers' need for nuclear weapons. If any states do opt to acquire nuclear weapons, the existing nuclear powers can minimize the risks this poses by giving new nuclear states the technical help required to build secure arsenals. If proliferation is constrained and managed in this fashion, it can bolster Europe's peace by making conquest infeasible. Things would be safest if all European states that might someday desire nuclear deterrents already possessed them; the dangers of the proliferation process would then be avoided. Overall, however, the possibility of proliferation makes Europe safer than it would be if that possibility did not exist.

Economic Change: The End of the Age of Extraction. The shift toward knowledge-based forms of production in advanced industrial economies since 1945 has reduced the ability of conquerors to extract resources from conquered territories. This change, too, lowers the risk of war in Europe by making conquest more difficult and less rewarding.

Today's high-technology post-industrial economies depend increasingly on free access to technical and social information. This requires a free domestic press and access to foreign publications, foreign travel, personal computers, and photocopiers. But the police measures needed to subdue a conquered society require that these technologies and practices be forbidden because they also carry subversive ideas. Thus critical elements of the economic fabric now must be ripped out to maintain control over conquered polities.

These changes mean that states can now afford to compete less aggressively for control of industrial areas since control adds less to national power, and control by others would give them less power gain. Hence it poses less threat. This change undercuts the geopolitical motives that produced past European balance-of-power wars. It is now far harder to conquer Europe piecemeal, using each conquest to gain strength for the next, since incremental conquests would provide less gain in power and might even produce a net loss. Hence would-be aggressors have less motive to expand and defenders less reason to compete fiercely to prevent others' gain.[9]

This is a marked change from the smokestack economy era, when societies could be conquered and policed with little collateral economic harm. The Nazis sustained fairly high levels of production in France and Czechoslovakia, even while they subjugated the conquered populations. Likewise, the Soviet regime was able until recently to squeeze high production from a society that was also subject to tight police controls, including severe limits on information technology, foreign publications, and travel. The slowdown of Soviet economic growth after 1970 and the stall in Soviet economic growth during the 1980s reflect the new economic reality. The Soviet economy stalled partly because Soviet means of political control now collide with the imperatives of post-industrial economic productivity. The Soviet Union had to institute *glasnost* and other democratic reforms if it hoped to restart its economy because the police measures required to sustain the Bolshevik dictatorship would also stifle Soviet efforts to escape the smokestack age.

Any expansionist European state would confront the same dilemma. It would have to adopt harsh police measures to control its newly acquired empire, but these measures would wreck productivity. Industrial economies could once be domesticated and milked; now they would wither in captivity. Hence any future European state that pursued successful military expansion would then face only two options: liberalize and lose control politically, or maintain tight political control and impoverish the empire. This change dampens the balance-of-power concerns, and the attendant competition for control of industrial regions, that helped cause both world wars.*

America as Balancer: The Transformation of American Foreign Policy Interests and Ideas. When diplomatic coalitions fail to form against aggressors, aggression becomes easier, making war more likely. Such failure represents a diplomatic variety of offense-dominance and has the same effects as the military variety. Thus the two world wars were caused partly by American and British failure to balance firmly against German aggression in both 1914 and 1939, and Soviet failure to balance in 1939. This left Germany's neighbors less secure and allowed Germany to believe that hegemony was possible. Peace has been preserved since 1945 partly because the United States and

---

*This change does have a downside: by slackening the impulse to balance against aggression, it could weaken the resistance that aggressors face, weakening deterrence. However, the new economics would cause net damage to peace through this effect only if aggressors' motives to commit aggression are not reduced by the new economics, while defenders' will to defend is weakened. This asymmetry might develop, but there is no clear reason why it should be expected.

Britain reversed course after 1945, actively counterbalancing Soviet power on the European continent.

American foreign policy interests and thinking have changed dramatically since the 1930s. The United States is therefore likely to continue playing an active balancing role, at least in Western Europe, even after the Soviet withdrawal from Eastern Europe.* As a result, the danger of inadequate diplomatic balancing is unlikely to recur in the new Europe.

The nuclear revolution reduces the threat posed by a hegemonic European state to American sovereignty since a nuclear-armed America could defend itself against such a hegemon far more easily than it could in the pre-nuclear era. This lowers America's geopolitical interest in balancing actively against a potential European hegemon. However, the nuclear revolution also heightens America's interest in avoiding war in Europe since such a war would now inflict far more harm on America if it spread to engulf the United States. America could well be drawn into such a war because it has strong cultural and ethnic ties to Europe, and would find it difficult to stand aside while the homelands of American ethnic groups were conquered or destroyed. A future European war could also harm American commercial or other interests, drawing in the United States by a process parallel to that which pulled it into the French revolutionary wars and World War I. Thus while one argument for balancing has diminished, another has become more persuasive. As a result, the United States is unlikely to return to its pre-World War II policy of isolation.[10]

The experience of the two world wars has also changed American foreign policy thinking in ways that will probably not be reversed. Before both wars, the United States remained aloof from Europe in the belief that it could stand aside from Europe's wars, but this proved impossible both times. National historical learning

---

*A continued American military commitment to Europe will not diminish the risk of war in Eastern Europe unless the United States guarantees the security of the East European states against attack by one another—a policy I do not expect or recommend—but it will inhibit aggression in Western Europe and dampen the spread of war from Eastern to Western Europe. Moreover, the United States can use measures short of military commitment, such as economic incentives, to punish aggressors and reward good conduct in Eastern Europe, as I note below. This would constitute a balancing policy implemented by nonmilitary means.

is often ephemeral, but this experience forms a large part of American historical consciousness, and its main lesson—that the United States could be drawn into a future European conflagration and should therefore act to prevent it—is relatively unambiguous. As a result, it is difficult to imagine a return to the simple isolationism of the 1930s. The disastrous results of that policy are too difficult to explain away. Moreover, during the cold war the United States developed a large military establishment whose main justification lies in the American commitment to Europe. This establishment has an institutional interest in reminding Americans of the grim history of 1914-45, should they begin to forget it.

The post–cold war world has yet to emerge, but early signs indicate that those who forecast a complete American withdrawal from Europe will be proven wrong.[11] During the 1980s some Americans called for such a withdrawal, but these voices have now largely faded away.[12] The current American administration is committed to staying in Europe even after the Soviet withdrawal from Eastern Europe, and there is little serious dissent from this policy in the United States.[13]

MILITARISM

World War I and the Pacific war of 1941–45 were caused in part by the domination of civilian thought by military propaganda that primed the world for war. This domination has now disappeared in Europe.

As a general matter, professional military officers are nearly as cautious as civilians in recommending decisions for war.[14] However, militaries sometimes cause war as a side effect of their efforts to protect their organizational interests. They infuse the surrounding society with organizationally self-serving myths; these myths then have the unintended effect of persuading the rest of society that war is necessary or desirable. Militaries purvey these myths to convince society to grant them the size, wealth, autonomy, and prestige that all bureaucracies seek—not to provoke war. Yet these myths also support arguments for war; hence societies infused with military propaganda will be warlike, even if their militaries want peace.[15] Wilhelmine Germany and imperial Japan are prime examples of societies that were infused with such myths and waged war because of them.[16] Other European powers also fell under the sway of militarist mythology before 1914, although to a lesser extent than Germany.[17]

Five principal myths have been prominent in past military arguments and propaganda. First, militaries exaggerate the power of the offense relative to the defense, and the ease of conquest among states. Before World War I the German army's chief propagandist, General Friedrich von Bernhardi, expressed the common military prejudice when he wrongly asserted that "the offensive mode of action is by far superior to the defensive mode" and that new technology favored the attacker.[18] Such illusions bolster arguments that larger forces are needed to defend against aggression and support arguments for the offensive military doctrines that militaries strongly prefer.[19] However, they also cause war by conjuring up the many dangers (noted above) that arise when national leaders believe that security is scarce and conquest is easy.

Second, military propaganda exaggerates the hostility of other states, painting neighbors as malevolent and aggressive. This bolsters the military's case for large budgets by exaggerating the likelihood of war, but also causes war by bolstering arguments that enemies should be forestalled by launching preemptive or preventive war.[20]

Third, militaries exaggerate the tendency of other states to give in to threats—to "bandwagon" with the threat instead of "balancing" against it.[21] Such myths bolster the military's arguments for larger forces by reinforcing claims that a bigger force can be used to make diplomatic gains, but also cause war by feeding confidence that belligerent behavior will bring political rewards.[22]

Fourth, militaries commonly overstate the strategic and economic value of empire.[23] These exaggerations strengthen arguments for forces required to gain or defend imperial conquests, but also feed arguments for waging imperial wars.

Finally, militaries often understate the costs of warfare, sometimes even portraying it as healthy or beneficial.[24] This raises the prestige of the military by increasing the apparent utility of the instrument it wields, but it causes war by encouraging states to behave recklessly. The bizarre pre-1914 popular belief that a European war would "cleanse" and "rejuvenate" society largely sprang from such military propaganda and helped set the stage for war.

The scourge of militarism kept the world in turmoil until 1945 but has now almost vanished in Europe. European militarism diminished sharply after World War I, when Europe's militaries were widely blamed both for causing the war and for waging it foolishly. This reduced the military's ability to shape public opinion by lowering its prestige.

Since World War II the potential for militarism has diminished further, with the end of the deep social barriers between the military establishment and civilian society. Before 1914 European militaries stood apart from society in two ways. First, military officers were socially segregated and isolated. This allowed them to develop a separate culture, including an arrogant sense of a right to command civilian ideas on foreign and military policy. Second, the military officer corps were preserves of the upper class, especially in Germany and France, and were seen by that class as pillars of its social dominance.[25] Hence militaries had a double motive to sow propaganda that enhanced their prestige: to advance the interests of military institutions, at the expense of wider societies with which they felt little identification, and to advance the interests of the upper class as a whole.[26] Three changes, which began after World War I and gathered momentum after World War II, have now diminished these motives: European officers are more integrated into civilian society; the officer corps are no longer an upper-class preserve, instead representing a wider cross-section of society; and European societies have undergone a process of social leveling which has sharply reduced class conflict.

In addition, new barriers have been built against a militarist revival. These barriers are embodied in the spread of democracy in Europe, the development in the West of governmental institutions for the civilian evaluation and control of defense policy, the growth in Western Europe of university-based civilian expertise in military affairs—which is weaker than in the United States but is nevertheless significant—and the awareness of European military officers that their institutions did great harm in the past. The growth of official and unofficial civilian defense analysis, combined with democracy and norms of free speech, guarantees that military propaganda would face greater public criticism than before 1914. The greater historical awareness of European military officers—a product of their greater social integration, which connects them with general historical discourse—causes militaries to use more self-restraint than before in defending their institutional interests.

The permanent disappearance of European militarism is not guaranteed, however, and logic suggests that militarism could make a modest comeback in the future. This danger lies in the same dynamic that makes great powers more vulnerable to militarism than medium powers. Great powers must provide for their own security. This causes them to maintain larger militaries, which then have larger effects on the discourse of surrounding society. More important, great power militaries stand to gain more from the propagation of militarist myths than do medium-power militaries because great powers address the foreign threats that these myths depict by counter-buildup, while medium powers more often respond by seeking support from allies. Hence great power militaries gain a greater budgetary payoff from propagating such myths, giving them greater incentive to do so.

This dynamic helps explain the marked confinement of past militarism to great powers or to isolated medium powers that lacked allies to provide security. It also suggests that Central and West European states will become more prone to militarism as the superpower presence diminishes. These states will then be forced to provide more of their own security; hence their security policies will come to more closely resemble those of great powers, restoring one condition for militarism. The risk of militarism may also appear in the former Soviet Union. The end of the Bolshevik dictatorship has lifted the long-standing Communist Party monopoly on political ideas; this will free the new militaries of the emerging post-Soviet states to purvey their views. Moreover, unlike the West, these societies lack established academic or governmental civilian institutions with military expertise that can offer a competing perspective, raising the risk that military views will dominate.[27] However, a resurgence of European militarism to the levels seen during 1900–14 seems unlikely because pre-1914 militarism arose partly from social conditions unique to those times and because European societies are at least partly immunized against a repetition by the memory of its results.

HYPERNATIONALISM AND ITS MYTHS AND MISPERCEPTIONS

During the period 1871–1939, a great wave of hypernational-ism swept over Europe. Each state taught itself a mythical history of its own and others' national past, and glorified its own national character while denigrating that of others.[28] The schools, the uni-versities, the press, and the politicians all joined in this orgy of mythmaking and self-glorification. Boyd Shafer summarized the common tenor of European education:

> Text and teacher alike, with a few notable exceptions, taught the student that his own country was high-minded, great, and glori-ous. If his nation went to war, it was for defense, while the foe was the aggressor. If his nation won its wars, that was because his countrymen were braver and God was on their side. If his nation was defeated, that was due only to the enemy's over-whelmingly superior forces and treachery. If his country lost territory, as the French lost Alsace-Lorraine in 1870, that was a crime; whatever it gained was for the good of humanity and but its rightful due. The enemy was "harsh," "cruel," "backward." His own people "kind," "civilized," "progressive."[29]

This chauvinist mythmaking poisoned international relations by convincing each state of the legitimacy of its own claims, the rightness of its own cause, and the wrongfulness and maliciousness of the grievances of others. Oblivious that its own past conduct had often provoked others' hostility, each country ascribed hostility to others' innate and boundless aggressiveness. This led each to as-sume that others could not be appeased and should be dealt with harshly.[30] Countries also approached war with a reckless confidence engendered by a sense of innate superiority. Such ideas fed the climate that fostered both world wars.[31]

The stability of postwar Europe has been partly due to the remarkable decline of nationalist propaganda, especially in Euro-pean schools.[32] As I note below, this decline resulted in part from the social and economic leveling of European societies after the 1930s and the less competitive relations that developed among West European states after 1945. It also grew from the Allied occupation of Germany, which destroyed the Nazi textbooks and imposed a more honest history curriculum in German schools;[33] and from the concerted efforts of international agencies and educational institutions, most notably the U.N. Educational, Scientific, and Cultural Organization (UNESCO) and the Brunswick International Schoolbook Institute in Germany.[34] These institutions oversaw textbook exchanges whose purpose was to force the educators of each country to answer foreign complaints about their curricula, with the aim of causing Europe to converge on a single shared version of European history. Their efforts were a dramatic success, largely ridding Western Europe of hypernationalism. Nothing suggests that this achievement will soon be undone. Moreover, the social leveling of Eastern Europe should limit hypernationalism in that region as well, as I note below.

SOCIAL IMPERIALISM

During the late nineteenth and early twentieth centuries European elites sometimes sought to bolster their domestic position by distracting publics with foreign confrontations or by seeking successful foreign wars.[35] Russian bellicosity toward Japan before the Russo-Japanese War of 1904–5 has been ascribed partly to such motives.[36] Hans-Ulrich Wehler likewise argues that the Prussian government launched the wars of 1864, 1866, and 1870 partly "to legitimize the prevailing political system against the striving for social and political emancipation of the middle classes."[37] Before 1914 some Germans feared the domestic effects of war,[38] but others favored bellicose policies because they thought a victorious war would strengthen the monarchy.[39]

This cause of war has been dampened by the democratization of European politics and the leveling of European societies. The coming of democracy has legitimized Europe's regimes, and social leveling has reduced popular discontent with the existing social order. Both changes have reduced the elites' need to use foreign policy to bolster their legitimacy.

There is some risk of "social imperial" wars in Eastern Europe and the former Soviet Union during the economic crisis that will grow from the marketization of the East's command economies. If this crisis is deep and prolonged (as I fear it will be), it will generate great popular anger at the newly elected Eastern governments, producing a crisis of political legitimacy throughout the East. The governing elites may then be tempted to distract the public from its economic woes and restore the government's legitimacy by pursuing foreign confrontations. Indeed this dynamic may have already occurred in Yugoslavia, where some observers suggest that Serbian leader Slobodan Milosevic launched the Serbo-Croatian war in June 1991 in part to bolster his waning popularity. However, these problems are confined to Eastern Europe. In Central and Western Europe elites face far less pressure from below than in the past, and hence have less motive to divert that pressure by foreign adventurism. Even in the East the problem is temporary and should diminish once market economies are established.

UNDEMOCRATIC POLITIES

European societies are more democratic than before 1914 or 1939, and democracy is spreading rapidly in Eastern Europe. This trend is bound to continue because key preconditions for democracy—high levels of literacy and industrial development and a relatively equal distribution of land, wealth, and income—are now far more widespread in Europe than they were eighty years ago.[40] This change bolsters peace.

Empirical evidence suggests that democracies are not generally more peaceful than other states, but that relations among democracies are more peaceful than relations among nondemocratic states or between democracies and nondemocracies.[41] Logic suggests two related reasons why relations among democracies should be peaceful.[42]

First, the ideologies of democracies do not incorporate a claim to rule other democracies, so they have no ideological motives for expansion against one another. The democratic presumption of the right of peoples to choose their own political path precludes the idea that world democracy should be run from a single center or that any democracy has a claim to rule another. The Communist world has long been rent with conflict over who would be the leader, most clearly manifest in the Sino-Soviet and Yugoslav-Soviet conflicts.[43] The Arab states have likewise clashed over leadership of the Arab world.[44] The democratic world has suffered no parallel conflict because democratic ideology preempts the question "Who should lead?" with the answer that "No one should lead."[45] This dampens expansionism among democratic states and eases their fears of one another. Second, democratic elites would have more difficulty legitimating a war against another democracy. They could not claim that they fought to free the people of the opposing state since these people would already be free. The elite would also face arguments that warring to overthrow another democratic regime is antidemocratic since such a war would seek to undo the popular will of the other society. Thus democracies have less motive to attack each other and would face greater domestic opposition if they chose to do so.

Logic also suggests two additional reasons why democracies should be more peaceful. First, war-causing national misperception—militarist myths, hypernationalist myths, or elite arguments for "social-imperial" wars, for example—should be dampened by norms of free speech, which permit the development of evaluative institutions that can challenge errant ideas. Even in democracies the evaluation of public policy is seldom very good, and fatuous ideas can often influence state action; but this danger is smallest in societies that permit free debate, as all democracies must to some degree. Second, democracy tends to limit social stratification. This limits the elite's motive to purvey nationalist myths or to pursue war for social-imperial reasons and removes a past cause of militarism.*

These last two deductions suggest that democracies should have more peaceful relations with both democracies and non-democracies; hence they are contradicted by empirical studies showing that democracies have in fact not been more pacific in their relations with nondemocratic states.[46] However, these studies have not controlled for perturbing variables that may explain the discrepancy; hence they do not definitively disprove these deductions.[47] Moreover, this question need not be resolved to establish the effect of the spread of democracy in Europe. It has created a homogeneously democratic Western Europe, and most Eastern states are likely to become democracies also. If so, nearly all international relations in Europe will be intrademocratic, and most scholars agree that intrademocratic relations are more peaceful.

*Thus democracy and social leveling are reciprocally related; each bolsters the other.

SOCIAL AND ECONOMIC STRATIFICATION

European societies are now far less socially and economically stratified than they were before 1914 or 1939.[48] In Western Europe, stratification was ended by democracy and the political mobilization of the working class. In Eastern Europe it was ended by communism. This transformation has operated as a remote cause of peace by contributing to the four changes just discussed—the growth of democracy, and the decline of militarism, hypernationalism, and social imperialism.

These four effects of social leveling vary in importance. The demilitarization and democratization of Europe have removed important causes of war, but social leveling was not the sole cause, nor perhaps even the main cause, of these changes. It played a large role in eliminating social-imperial motives for war, but this cause of war, while significant, probably mattered less than others. The most significant effect of leveling has been the reduction of hypernationalism; leveling removed the taproot of the great wave of hypernationalism that swept Europe during 1870–1939.

This hypernationalism was a largely artificial phenomenon, engineered by elites who fomented nationalism to persuade publics to tolerate the steep stratification of late nineteenth-century and early twentieth-century European societies. As the nineteenth century progressed, Europe's elites faced increasing challenges because industrialization weakened previous methods of social control. The spread of mass literacy and the rural migration to the cities broke the elites' monopoly of information and caused the spread of egalitarian ideas. The development of mass armies, caused partly by the invention of mass production methods to make small arms, forced each state to arm its citizenry to avoid defeat by mass foreign armies; this broke the elites' monopoly of force. These changes impelled elites to seek new instruments of social control—so they switched from coercion to persuasion. Hypernationalism, purveyed chiefly through public education, was their prime weapon. This hypernationalism was crafted to persuade publics to continue to serve and obey the state loyally.[49]

The leveling of European societies, however, now allows European elites to command public loyalty without resort to hypernationalism. Hence this motive for the propagation of nationalism has largely disappeared, which suggests that hypernationalism will not return in force.

Social stratification was not the sole cause of European hypernationalism: a secondary cause lay in the felt need to mobilize publics to support the costly defense efforts required by the competitive international politics of the era.[50] This cause may reappear as the European states begin providing more of their own security, and their elites may be motivated to propagate somewhat more nationalism in order to persuade publics to back enlarged defense programs. The elites of the newly freed states of Eastern Europe and the former Soviet Union will also fan nationalism to mobilize popular support if they become embroiled in conflicts with one another, as some surely will (see, e.g., the Serbo-Croatian and Azeri-Armenian conflicts already underway). However, the United States can dampen security motives for the propagation of nationalism in Western Europe by continuing its military presence in Europe. And any nationalism-fanned conflict among the emerging Eastern states will be weakened by the absence of the social inequities that nourished hypernationalism in the past.

AGGRESSIVE REVOLUTIONARY STATES

War spawned by revolution is another danger absent from the new Europe. States led by movements that seized power through mass revolution are more war-prone for a number of reasons. Once in power, revolutionary elites fear counterrevolution, leading them to defensive wars of expansion to remove threatening counter-revolutionaries from their borders. They infuse themselves with self-glorifying myths to motivate supporters during the revolution; these myths live on after the revolution, fueling chauvinism toward other countries. They frequently adopt universalist aims and rhetoric to inspire supporters to sacrifice for the revolution, but these universalist aims often become dogma that outlives the revolutionary struggle, fueling messianic expansion later on. They demand a monopoly of ideas and suppress dissent during the revolution itself; this habit later leads to the suppression of free speech and public debate, which allows misperceptions and illusions to govern state conduct and raises the risk of war-causing folly or miscalculation in foreign policy. Neighboring regimes with different social systems may fear the contagious impact of a revolutionary example on their own publics—especially if these regimes lack domestic legitimacy— and may foment the counterrevolution that the revolution fears, or even attack it directly. Neighbors may also be influenced to attack by emigres who flee the revolution and then work to persuade neighboring states to restore them to power. Thus revolutionary states are more prone to attack others and more likely to be attacked.[51] Revolutionary France, the Soviet Union, Khomeini's Iran, and Castro's Cuba all suffered these syndromes and sparked these reactions, leading them into international confrontation.[52]

This cause of war will not arise in the new Europe because Europe is devoid of revolutionary states and of illegitimate regimes that might be threatened by them. Soviet Bolshevism has finally disappeared. The new regimes of Eastern Europe gained power in popular upheavals, but these were not mass revolutions; they involved no long insurgencies of the sort that nurture battle-hardened, myth-ridden revolutionary organizations. Moreover, the older regimes of Europe would feel less threatened by revolution and would respond more temperately if a revolutionary regime did appear because they are now democratic, socially leveled, and legitimate.

AGGRESSIVE CAPITALIST STATES

Some scholars, mostly Marxist, have blamed distempers of capitalism for past troubles in Europe. Such arguments have been overblown, but they also contain a grain of truth. During the 1890s many Europeans and Americans came to believe that the conquest of colonies could avert or cure economic depression by providing a market for unsold goods. Such ideas played a major role in American imperial expansion during 1898–1902.[53] They soon lost fashion, with the worldwide recovery from the great depression of the 1890s and with the failure of markets to appear in conquered colonies. However, after-echoes of these ideas continued in Germany, where arguments that Germany should seize territory to create markets for unsold goods played a minor part in the expansionist propaganda that fueled German chauvinism and set the stage for war in 1914.[54] After-echoes also continued in the United

States; after World War II American policy-makers feared a new depression, and America's early cold war belligerence was given an extra push by arguments that the United States should acquire or protect overseas markets to avert it.[55]

This problem, never large, has now disappeared completely. Fears of economic depression have abated throughout the West with the development of fiscal and monetary tools for managing the business cycle. The often tragic European and American colonial experience has delegitimated the concept of colonialism in general, and with it the concept of regulating the business cycle by imperial expansion. Reflection has brought the realization that any attempt to relieve depression by one-way colonial trade could last only until the colony's currency reserves were exhausted, which would happen quickly. These changes remove the main causes of any past capitalist belligerence.

SUMMARY: ABSENT AGGRESSOR STATES

If all states accept the status quo and none wish to change it, wars are far fewer. Indeed if no aggressor state is on the scene, war can occur only by accident or misunderstanding.* The causes of war discussed above all operate primarily by fueling expansionism, thereby creating aggressor states that reject the status quo. Aggressor states will be rare in the new Europe because both domestic and systemic factors will provide little stimulus to aggression and powerful dissuasion. This is a vast change from 1914, 1939, and 1945.

This auspicious condition is likely to persist. Today's West European states are far less bellicose in their general approach to foreign relations than the European states of 1914 and 1939. In part this reflects their status as smaller powers, which are generally less bellicose than great powers because their militaries are smaller and tamer. This could fade as the West European states assume their own security burdens, if both superpowers withdraw from Europe

---

*I use the term "aggressor state" to refer to states that seek to expand for any reason. Others often use the term to refer only to states that seek to expand for reasons other than security, while classifying expansionist states that are driven mainly by security concerns as status quo powers. (See, for example, Charles Glaser, "International Political Consequences of Military Doctrine"; unpublished manuscript, July 1990, p. 4.)

completely. But it also reflects the nuclear revolution, the knowledge revolution in economics, and the transformation of European
domestic societies, which are far more healthy than those of the
European states of 1914 or 1939. The emerging societies of Eastern
Europe are likely to develop eventually along similar lines—although they may take some unfortunate detours along the way.*

FALSE FEARS: ILLUSORY NEW CAUSES OF EUROPEAN WAR

Pessimists about the future peace of Europe have said little
about these propitious changes, focusing instead on four dangers:
the multipolar character of the emerging Europe, the possibility of
renewed German aggression, the risk of praetorian states emerging

---

*Some observers have suggested that two additional changes since 1945 may
prevent renewed conflict in Europe. John Mueller has argued that the great
horrors of past conventional wars have delegitimated even conventional war,
and that warfare is therefore now largely obsolete (see *Retreat From Doomsday:
The Obsolescence of Major War* [New York: Basic Books, 1989]). Others point to
the spread of free economic exchange in Europe since 1945, the greater prosperity and economic interdependence that this change produces, and the development of international institutions, including the European Community
(EC) and the General Agreement on Tariffs and Trade (GATT), to foster and
protect these changes. They argue that prosperity and interdependence promote
peace by dampening economic motives for war and by raising the economic
cost of war. Some also argue that international economic institutions could grow
stronger, developing into a kind of superstate that could bolster peace by
playing a police role. I find both views largely unpersuasive. Even the horrors
of World War I failed to delegitimate war, and if World War I cannot do the
job, nothing can. (Germany developed a large war-celebrating literature only a
decade after World War I ended; see Wolfram Wette, "From Kellogg to Hitler
(1928–1933): German Public Opinion Concerning the Rejection or Glorification
of War," in *The German Military in the Age of Total War*, ed. Wilhelm Deist [Dover,
N.H.: Berg, 1985], pp. 71–99.) For a general criticism of Mueller's argument, see
Kaysen, note 9 below). The prosperity promoted by economic liberalism probably promotes peace indirectly by bolstering democracy and by pushing economies further toward knowledge-based forms of production. However, there is
little reason to believe that prosperity directly reduces economic motives for
war. Economic interdependence is more likely to cause war than peace by
inducing states toward aggressive policies to relieve dependence on other states
they feel they cannot trust. Such motives drove Germany and Japan to seek
economic autarky through expansion in World War II, and arguments that
America depends on Third World raw materials have often been advanced by

in the East, and the problem of national and border conflicts in Eastern Europe and the former Soviet Union. However, the first three dangers (discussed immediately below) are largely illusory; only the fourth poses large risks, as I note in the subsequent section.

A MULTIPOLAR EUROPE?

Some scholars have argued that bipolar systems are more peaceful than multipolar systems. John Mearsheimer recently used this theory to predict that the emergence of multipolarity in Europe will raise the risk of war.[56]

The European system is indeed losing its bipolar cold war character with the decline of Soviet power and the Soviet withdrawal from Eastern Europe. It will become fully multipolar if the United States also withdraws from the West. However, those who fear this development rest their case on weak theory. Some aspects of bipolarity favor peace, but others favor war. Still other aspects of bipolarity have indeterminate effects. Overall, I believe, the two types of systems seem about equally prone to war. Moreover, even if bipolarity is somewhat safer, the difference between the two systems is not dramatic and forms a frail basis upon which to argue that the risk of war will rise sharply in the new Europe.[57]

GERMAN AGGRESSION?

The argument that a free and united Germany will return to its past aggressiveness is refuted by the dramatic transformation of German society since 1945. Five specific changes have erased the roots of past German aggressiveness.

American advocates of U.S. Third World intervention. Finally, the European liberal economic order is likely to dissolve if other causes of war appear to produce conflict in the new Europe; instead of dampening these causes, the European economic order will succumb to them. John Mearsheimer persuasively criticizes both theories on these and other grounds: see "Back to the Future" (note 1 below), pp. 29–31, 40–48; and "Correspondence: Back to the Future, Part II: International Relations Theory and Post–Cold War Europe," *International Security* 15, 2 (Fall 1990): 194–99. On interdependence see also Gaddis, "Long Peace" (note 8 below), pp. 110–14; for examples of arguments for American intervention premised on American raw materials dependence, see Van Evera, "Why Europe Matters" (note 10 below), pp. 19, 43n.

First, German society, like the rest of Europe, has undergone a dramatic social leveling process.[58] The Junkers and big industrial barons have disappeared into history. Their departure removed the arrogant elite whose stubborn defense of its class privilege helped provoke World War I and, less directly, World War II.

Second, Germany is an established democracy. German society contains all the preconditions for democracy in abundance, so we can be confident that this democracy is robust and durable.

Third, flowing in part from the first and second changes, German hypernationalism has dissipated, and a powerful barrier against its return has been erected by a strong movement in Germany for the honest discussion of German history. German secondary schools and the German media generally provide accurate coverage of Germany's past crimes.[59] German academic historians have largely abandoned the nationalist cheer-leading of their Wilhelmine predecessors, often taking a more critical view of German conduct than foreign historians do. For example, Fritz Fischer and his students have assigned more of the blame for World War I to Germany than many British and American historians.[60] A few German historians have tried to justify Germany's conduct in World War II, but many others have beaten them down.[61]

If historical mythmaking did make a comeback in Germany, it would raise an acute danger. Germany was badly mutilated by the two world wars, losing 34 percent of its pre-1914 territory,[62] and suffering the expulsion of 13.8 million Germans from the lost territories.[63] Germans who forget that German conduct was the main cause of this mutilation would begin blaming others and could develop an extreme sense of grievance. The potential danger is even larger than in 1914 and 1939 since Germany was whole in 1914 and had less lost territory in 1939 than it has now. Hence German behavior is highly dependent upon German historical memory, and benign German behavior depends on sound memory. However, the Germans' commitment to honest history now seems very strong, and the main causes of past historical mythmaking have disappeared with the leveling of German society and the growth of German democracy.

Fourth, German civil-military relations have been transformed since the 1930s. The German military is no longer an upper-class preserve and is integrated into German society. As a result, German officers understand the civilian viewpoint and accept the civilian right to determine foreign and defense policy. German military officers are taught the history of the German military's past misdeeds; this inoculates the officer corps against repeating these misdeeds.[64] German mass media contain no echoes of past military propaganda.

Fifth, the nuclear revolution has made available weapons of absolute security, should Germany ever need them. If Germany again faces a serious external threat, it will not need to reach for more defensible borders or for wider territories to provide economic autarky, as it once did; now it can secure itself by building a nuclear deterrent. Germany's transition to nuclear power would not be without danger, in the form of possible preventive attack by outsiders. However, outside powers, most notably the United States, have the power to deter such an attack. Moreover, they would have good reason to do so, since a secure Germany is a more benign Germany, and is thus in the common interest.

In short, the new Germany is very unlikely to launch a new campaign of aggression. Its benign behavior since 1945 has been due less to its divided and occupied condition than to the postwar transformation of German society, which removed the causes of its past belligerence. The time has come for the wider world to stop viewing the German people with suspicion and to begin according them the respect that their responsible conduct deserves. The world should require that Germans remember their past, if they ever need reminding. It should also ask that Germans accept an enduring obligation to reassure Germany's victims that Germany's past crimes will not be repeated. But the world should not demand penance from a German generation that was not yet born in 1945 and should not make them pariahs for crimes committed by Germans who are long gone.

PRAETORIAN STATES IN THE EAST?

Jack Snyder has suggested that the tide of democracy in Eastern Europe and the former Soviet Union may produce flawed praetorian polities, reminiscent of Wilhelmine Germany rather than the civic-democratic or corporate-democratic states now found in the West.[65] Fledgling democratic institutions may be inadequate to channel growing popular political participation. This could leave control in the hands of narrow elites. These elites might then pursue aggressive foreign policies that would profit these elites, even if they produced net harm for the whole society. However, this danger has been sharply reduced by the social leveling imposed by Soviet Communist rule. Praetorianism is largely a disease of stratified societies; in praetorian states political institutions are inadequate to channel rising participation chiefly because elites want to exclude the public from politics, not because democratic channels for participation would be hard to establish if elites wished to create them. Communism has done great harm throughout the East, but its egalitarian policies have ended steep class stratification and thereby reduced the elites' motive to constrict democracy and create praetorianism.

The possibility of praetorianism is not gone altogether because some social stratification persists in the East. The upper-class elites are gone, but the Communist Party bureaucracies and military establishments still cling to power in parts of Eastern Europe and the former USSR, where they form elites of a different sort. Nevertheless, praetorianism will probably be muted across Eastern Europe because the old guard is fast losing power and because the net stratification of post-Communist Eastern states seems smaller than in past states where praetorianism flourished, even in places where the old guard retains strength.

The newly free Eastern states might suffer from other maladies of new democracies. Most notably, they lack developed nongovernmental institutions for the evaluation and criticism of public policy—free universities, a skilled free press, and free research institutions. This raises the risk of debased public discourse, political demagoguery, and the domination of dishonest propaganda purveyed by the government or private special interests. As a result, these states are likely to elect more than a few crackpot politicians of the Joe McCarthy–Jesse Helms–Gus Savage variety and find their public debates polluted by European Al Sharptons. (Such leaders have already won elections in Serbia and Croatia and have plunged the region into war.) However, this is a short-term problem; these societies have the resources to develop evaluative institutions and should be able to build them fairly quickly.

WHY PEACE IS NOT ASSURED: EMERGING DANGERS IN THE EAST

The main risk of war in the new Europe arises in Eastern Europe and the former Soviet Union and stems from the collapse of the Soviet empire. History warns that the international system deals poorly with the collapse of great empires; their demise often sparks war. War occurs because actors inside and outside the former empire are suddenly brought face-to-face in the former imperial zone without guidelines to regulate their interaction—no agreed spheres of influence, no accepted rights and responsibilities, and no "rules of the game." As a result, outside powers collide as they compete for influence in the old empire, and the newly freed peoples collide with the outsiders and one another. Moreover, internecine conflicts that were previously suppressed by the imperial metropole boil to the surface, fueling these collisions. Thus the slow collapse of the Turkish empire during 1832–1914 was the catalyst for four great crises, two great wars, and several smaller wars.[66] The disintegration of the Austrian empire likewise helped spark World War I, by spurring Austria to lash out against Serbia for its subversion in Bosnia-Herzegovina. The dismantling of the European empires in Asia and Africa was often followed by great violence among the newly independent peoples.[67]

The demise of the Soviet empire has brought the end of the cold war and freedom for millions who have suffered Moscow's subjugation, and should be celebrated for these reasons. However, it also conjures up dangers like those that accompanied the demise of other empires, and that might trigger war. The newly freed states now find themselves thrown together with no preexisting agreements on their rights and responsibilities toward each other, or on the rules of the game that should govern their interactions. Moreover, three specific triggers for conflict are present: national borders in Eastern Europe and the former USSR are unsettled, giving rise to many border disputes; the nationalities of the region are geographically intermingled; and these nationalities harbor intense animosities toward each other. Finally, these dangers are magnified by the ongoing collapse of the former USSR's economy: this collapse is bound to sharpen intercommunal conflicts, and it may bring to power fascist demagogues who pursue aggressive foreign policies.

Many borders in the region lack legitimacy, especially those in the former USSR, which were arbitrarily established by Stalin. This sets the stage for border wars in the region as the former Soviet republics assert their independence.[68]

Wars could also spring from the bitter national conflicts that are reappearing with the retraction of Moscow's power. These conflicts are made more dangerous by the intermingled distribution of the peoples of the region. A survey of Eastern Europe reveals more than a dozen minority group pockets that may seek independence or be claimed by other countries.[69] In the former Soviet Union, nationalities are even more intermingled. The former USSR's population totals some 262 million, comprising 104 nationalities living in 15 republics. Of these, a total of 64 million (24 percent) either live outside their home republic or are among the 89 small nationalities with no titular republic who will thus be minorities in the Soviet Union's 15 successor states (assuming that these republics are not further subdivided).[70] Of these 64 million, some 39 million (15 percent of total Soviet population) are members of nationalities that have a titular republic but live outside it; these include 24 million Russians (17 percent of all Russians) and 15 million members of other nationalities (15 percent of all such nationalities). Another 25 million people (9 percent of the total Soviet population) are members of the 89 smaller nationalities without titular home republics who will be minorities wherever they live.[71]

The dismantled Soviet Union will thus be riddled with national conflicts. These will arise from nationalities' demands to annex territory other republics inhabited by their own members; from complaints against the oppression of national kin who live across accepted borders;[72] and from demands by the small, stateless nationalities for autonomy or secession from the republics where they reside. If large numbers of people are expelled from their homes, these expellees may call for revenge or recovery of lost land and property.* Border disputes may also arise among the republics because some nationalities may claim larger borders dating from their days of independent precolonial greatness.[73]

---

*For example, it seems quite possible that millions of Russians will be expelled from non-Russian republics; if so, these expellees could form the core of a Russian nationalist movement that poisons Russian politics, just as the *pieds noirs* poisoned French politics after the Algerian war.

Meanwhile, the economy of the former Soviet Union is in free fall and will continue imploding at a rapid rate for some time to come. The old Soviet command economy was driven by coercion; that coercion has now been lifted, but it has not been replaced by the positive incentives, which only a free market can provide. In short, the "stick" is gone, but no "carrot" has replaced it; hence the entire economy is freezing up. This freezing will continue until free-market institutions are established—but marketization has barely begun and will take years to accomplish. In the meantime, tens of millions will face unemployment and poverty. Under such conditions, people will search for other groups to blame for their suffering and will be drawn to demagogues. As a result, nationalist or fascist antidemocrats may win power, and intercommunal conflict will intensify.

If these conditions spawn an Eastern war, could it spread into Central or Western Europe? The risk of westward spread is less than in the past because the nuclear revolution has made conquest harder, and the high-technology revolution has reduced the strategic value of empire. These changes reduce the security implications of events in the East for West European states, which lowers their impulse to intervene in Eastern wars. However, some nationalities in Eastern Europe (most notably the Poles) have ethnic kin in the West, and many Soviet nationalities (including the Lithuanians, Latvians, Estonians, Ukrainians, Poles, Germans, Moldovans, Armenians, Azeris, Turkmen, Tadjiks, Uzbeks, and Kazakhs) have ethnic kin just outside the former USSR or farther afield in Western Europe and North America. If these peoples were threatened by violence, their conationals in other countries would understandably pressure their governments to intervene. As a result, a war among the peoples of the former USSR could involve East European, Middle Eastern, or South Asian states, and a war in Eastern Europe or the Middle East could affect others farther west.

An Eastern war could also affect the West in other ways. Large-scale fighting could generate millions of refugees needing humanitarian assistance or asylum. It could also produce vast environmental damage that could affect the West, especially if nuclear weapons were widely used, or if the former Soviet Union's many nuclear reactors were damaged or mismanaged in the chaos of war. Together these dangers create a general Western interest in ensuring that the Soviet transition occurs peacefully.

POLICY PRESCRIPTIONS

The United States has a major interest in preventing war in Europe; it should therefore take concerted action to keep the risk of war as low as possible. Two specific policies are recommended.

CONTINUE AMERICA'S MILITARY PRESENCE IN EUROPE

The Soviet collapse will allow large American troop withdrawals from Western Europe, but the United States should leave a sizable residual force in Europe. Such a presence will allow the United States to deter aggression and play the balancing role that it failed to play in 1914 and 1939. It will also strengthen America's ability to influence events in the East and to bound and manage proliferation. The European deployment should be small enough to forestall taxpayer complaints, but large enough to symbolize America's commitment to both Europeans and Americans and to carry some weight in the European military balance. A force of roughly 75,000–125,000 U.S. troops, backed by large additional forces in the United States, would seem to fit this requirement.

Such a deployment requires an institutional framework to define its purpose and to bolster its legitimacy in the eyes of the American and European publics. The current NATO framework is inadequate for this purpose. A continued American deployment would have the purpose of deterring aggression from any quarter, while NATO exists only to address the now vanished Soviet military threat; hence NATO's aim and the aim of the American deployment no longer match.

One solution might be to broaden NATO's purpose by adding a collective security function (under which its members would guarantee each other against attack by other member states) to its current collective defense function (under which members guarantee each other against attack by non-NATO members).[74] This would clarify that NATO now has a new mission—peace-keeping in the West—that is not made obsolete by the demise of the Soviet threat and that deserves and requires an American contribution.[75]

Collective security systems have a dismal history; the hapless League of Nations is the main exemplar. However, a NATO collective security system need not work like a Swiss watch. Its main purpose would simply be to provide a public rationale for a continued American (and Canadian) presence in Europe and to legitimate American action if action is ever needed. This task is far less demanding than the tasks faced by the League. Moreover, the League of Nations failed because it lacked strong leaders, but if the United States decides to continue playing a peace-keeping role in Europe, this gives NATO the strong leader it needs.

USE ECONOMIC LEVERAGE TO PROMOTE PEACEFUL CONDUCT IN THE EAST

To address the risk of war in the East, the U.S. government should organize a common Western policy that would condition Western economic relations with the states of Eastern Europe and the former USSR on their willingness to behave peacefully.* The logic supporting such a policy is straightforward: if the West wants *peace in the East*, it should encourage the states of the East to *behave peacefully* by offering appropriate economic incentives.

This would require that the Western powers first define a common standard of peaceful conduct. That standard could be framed several ways, but I think it should include seven main elements: (1) renunciation of the threat or use of force; (2) robust guarantees for both individual human rights and the rights of national minorities;† (3) acceptance of current national borders or

---

*The agency for this common Western policy should probably be the Group of Seven (G7) states (the United States, Japan, Germany, France, Britain, Italy, and Canada) since they have the world's largest economies, and they share a common interest in a peaceful and orderly transition in the East.

†Minority rights should be defined broadly, to include fair minority representation in the legislative, executive, and judicial branches of the central government. The definition of minority rights used in most international human rights agreements is more restrictive: it omits the right to share power in the national government and includes only the right to political autonomy and the preservation of minority language, culture, and religion (see Edward Lawson, *Encyclopedia of Human Rights* [New York: Taylor and Francis, 1991], p. 1070). Should minority rights be defined to include the right to secession and national independence? On this question the Western powers face a difficult decision. Some writers recommend that minority rights should sometimes be construed to include a right to secession (Vernon Van Dyke, "Collective Entities and Moral Rights: Problems in Liberal-Democratic Thought," *Journal of Politics* 44, 1 [February 1982]: 21–40, esp. 36–37). However, universal recognition of this right

agreement to promptly settle contested borders through peaceful means; (4) willingness to adopt a democratic form of government; (5) willingness to portray history honestly in the schools and to renounce the propagation of nationalist, chauvinist, or hate propaganda; (6) adoption of free-market economic policies and disavowal of protectionist or other beggar-thy-neighbor economic policies toward other Eastern states; and (7) cooperation with Western efforts to safely consolidate the Soviet nuclear force.* Then the Western powers should pursue a common economic policy toward the states of the East, offering the carrot of full membership in the Western economic system to states that behave "peacefully," while threatening the unpeaceful with the stick of exclusion and economic sanctions.[76]

---

would require massive redrawing of boundaries in the East and would raise the question of Western recognition of scores of now unrecognized independence movements worldwide. One solution is to recognize the right to secede in instances where the central government is unwilling to fully grant other minority rights, but to decline to recognize the right to secede if all other minority rights are fully recognized and robustly protected. In essence, the West would hold its possible recognition of a right to secede in reserve, to encourage governments to recognize other minority rights.

*The argument for the first five conditions is straightforward: wars are fewer if states use less force; states that oppress their minorities may provoke nearby states to intervene to protect these minorities; states without settled borders will have more border conflicts with their neighbors; democratic states generally have relatively peaceful relations with other democratic states and may have more peaceful relations with all states; and states whose schools teach false, self-glorifying history and whose public discourse is infected with nationalist propaganda are more prone to agressive foreign policies. The logic of the sixth condition is that the Eastern states must transit from command to market economies sooner or later; they will magnify the economic dislocations produced by marketization if they procrastinate this decision; these dislocations will be even more severe if the Eastern states fail to adopt cooperative economic policies toward one another; the resulting economic cataclysm will raise the risk of fascism, dictatorship, and war; and, therefore, early decisions to adopt radical market reforms and cooperative economic policies toward their neighbors will reduce the overall risk of war. The danger posed by the possibility of nuclear proliferation flowing from the breakup of the Soviet Union, and thus the logic of the seventh condition, is detailed in Kurt M. Campbell, Ashton B. Carter, Steven E. Miller, and Charles A. Zraket, *Soviet Nuclear Fission: Control of the Nuclear Arsenal in a Disintegrating Soviet Union* (Cambridge, Mass.: Harvard University, Center for Science and International Affairs, November 1991); CSIA Studies in International Security No. 1.

The rationale for these seven conditions is that an effective code of "peaceful conduct" must require that states renounce the use of force against others (condition 1), but cannot stop there: it must also require that states refrain from policies that would provoke others to use force against them (conditions 2 and 3), avoid creating domestic conditions that would foster their own decisions to use force (conditions 4, 5, and 6), and refrain from policies that endanger the worldwide nonproliferation regime (condition 7).*

Such a policy has a fair chance of working because the West enters this situation with more leverage than usual, for two reasons. First, the impending Eastern economic implosion will leave the Eastern states desperate for Western economic aid and for membership in the Western economy—far more so than they would be in normal times. Hence the promise of Western economic help, and the threat of economic sanctions, will carry great extra weight. (It may be that Eastern leaders now exaggerate the value of economic relations with the West and that the West cannot help as much as Eastern leaders think. If so, however, the West should exploit these misconceptions while they last, if this assists Western efforts to build a peaceful order.)

*In speeches on 4 September and 13 December Secretary of State James Baker outlined a similar set of standards and indicated that American policy toward the Eastern states would be conditioned on their acceptance of these standards ("Baker's Remarks: Policy on Soviets," *New York Times*, 5 September 1991, p. A12, and "Baker Sees Opportunities and Risks as Soviet Republics Grope for Stability," *New York Times*, 13 December 1991, p. A24). Baker later conditioned American recognition of the new Eastern governments on their acceptance of these standards (Michael Wines, "Ex-Soviet Leader is Lauded by Bush," *New York Times*, 26 December 1991, p. 1). Thus the overall approach of the Bush administration has closely resembled the option 5 approach. However, it is weaker than the one I recommend in five respects: (1) it omits condition 5 (the renunciation of nationalist propaganda); (2) it does not define minority rights, leaving Eastern governments free to adopt a restrictive definition that omits the right to fair representation in the national government; (3) the assistance it offers to cooperating governments is quite meager—far below the $4–5 billion I recommend below; (4) the administration has not yet moved to forge a common Western policy toward the East that incorporates these standards; and (5) the administration has sometimes failed to apply these principles with adequate firmness to Eastern governments. For example, during early 1992 Secretary Baker agreed to recognize the government of Azerbaijan despite Azeri atrocities against Azerbaijan's Armenian minority and Azeri unwillingness to offer more than lip service to Baker's principles (see "Winking at Aggression in Baku," *New York Times*, 14 February 1992, p. A28).

Second, the West has cultural leverage that should not be underestimated. The peoples of the East admire the people and culture of the West. Perhaps they exaggerate the West's virtues, and someday they may recognize that Western societies also have warts. Right now, however, they see Western societies as role models, they respect Western opinion, and they want Western approval. Hence the threat of chastisement and exclusion by the West is a sanction that carries real weight. The West also derives leverage from the unformed nature of Eastern political thought. The collapse of communism has left an intellectual void, leaving the East more than normally receptive to Western notions of appropriate political conduct.[77]

Two basic variants of this option should be considered: an expensive ("large aid") variant and a less expensive ("little or no aid") variant. In the expensive variant the West would offer a substantial economic aid package (perhaps $15–20 billion per year for several years), focused on providing the resources needed to transit from command to market economies and conditioned on Eastern compliance with the above-noted seven-point peaceful-conduct standard.* The less expensive variant would keep aid to a minimum, offering only free access to Western capital, markets, and technology in exchange for peaceful Eastern conduct.

The first variant is far superior, if Western publics will accept the cost. It would give the West greater leverage over Eastern policies and would ease the economic pain of marketization, thus lowering the risk of antidemocratic reaction and fascism. These rewards are surely worth the price, which is a pittance relative to the cosmic stakes at issue. However, even the second variant could

*This variant follows the "Grand Bargain" proposed by Graham Allison and Robert Blackwill, except my variant would attach more conditions to Western aid than would the Grand Bargain proposal (see Graham Allison and Robert Blackwill, "America's Stake in the Soviet Future," *Foreign Affairs* 70, 3 [Summer 1991]: 77–97). Allison and Blackwill suggest an aid package offer of $15–20 billion per year for three years, with costs to be spread among the United States, Western Europe, and Japan. They would condition aid on full market reforms and democratic reforms. Also recommending sizable economic aid to the former Soviet Union is Anders Aslund and Richard Layard, "Help Russia Now," *New York Times*, 5 December 1991, p. A33, suggesting an aid package of $17 billion for 1992, including a once-only $5 billion currency stabilization fund, $6 billion in food aid, and $6 billion to finance imports required to restart the economy.

give the West substantial leverage because the emerging Eastern states will place a high value on membership in the Western economic system. In short, the West should use large carrots in its carrot-and-stick policy, but even small carrots can produce significant results.*

This program is vulnerable to several telling criticisms,[78] and some observers would rely instead on other means to bolster peace in the East; some favor extending NATO eastward, for example, while others favor establishing a Europe-wide collective security system. Thus the case for a program relying on economic carrots and sticks is not open and shut, and other approaches should be considered as well.

However, it is very important that the Western powers develop a program of some sort—perhaps a hybrid of these approaches—to manage the Eastern transition. In essence, these powers face the task of designing a new political order following a decisive great war, for only the fourth time since Waterloo. The decisions they make will match the importance of those that shaped the peace settlements of 1815, 1919, and 1945. If wise, these decisions can lay the foundation for a durable peace; if not they may sow the seeds of a new war, as the errors of 1919 sowed the seeds of World War II—despite the favorable conditions that now exist in the West, since Eastern troubles could spill Westward. Therefore, this is not a time for letting small considerations guide policy. The West's leaders should stand ready to invest the intellectual and financial resources needed to produce a stable settlement—even if these prove substantial—and to run political risks to bring that settlement about.

---

*The Western powers should also consider offering to help the Eastern powers devise specific policies to implement these seven principles, and offering active assistance with peace-making if conflicts nevertheless emerge. Specifically, Western governments and institutions should offer to share Western ideas and experience on the building of democratic institutions, the development of political and legal institutions that protect and empower minorities, the development of market economic institutions, and the best means to organize the control of nationalism in education. Finally, if serious conflicts emerge despite the West's preventive efforts, the West should offer active mediation, just as the Nixon-Ford, Carter, and Bush administrations have actively mediated the Arab-Israeli conflict.

NOTES

I wish to thank Beverly Crawford, Charles Glaser, Robert Jervis, Teresa Johnson, Chaim Kaufmann, John Mearsheimer, Jack Snyder, Marc Trachtenberg, Stephen Walt, and David Yanowski for their advice and comments on earlier drafts. Research for this article was supported by the Ford Foundation through the Consensus Project of the Olin Institute at Harvard University.

1. See John J. Mearsheimer, "Back to the Future: Instability in Europe after the Cold War," *International Security* 15, 1 (Summer 1990): 5–56. Mearsheimer does not forecast a complete return to the levels of danger of 1914 or 1939, and he sees some possibility of dampening the dangers he outlines. He also recognizes the importance of factors other than the polarity of the international system in causing war, although he believes these factors are less important than the structure of the international system. However, he warns that the new European order will be substantially more dangerous than the cold war order, largely because the system will be multipolar.

2. A crude example is Leopold Bellak, "Why I Fear the Germans," *New York Times*, 25 April 1990, p. A29. Bellak argues that German children are abused more often than children in other societies and grow up to become aggressive adults "whom I don't trust to be peaceful, democratic people." For replies, see letters to the editor by Werner M. Graf, Mark Tobak, and Joseph Dolgin, *New York Times*, 10 May 1990, p. A30. See also Dominic Lawson, "Saying the Unsayable about the Germans" (an interview with British then secretary of state for industry Nicholas Ridley), *The Spectator* (London), 14 July 1990, pp. 8–10, in which Ridley expressed fears of Germany. Prime Minister Margaret Thatcher reportedly shares Ridley's views; see Anthony Bevins, "Bitter Memories Shape Views on Germany," *The Independent* (London), 13 July 1990, p. 3. Likewise, former NATO Secretary General Joseph Luns warned that a united Germany someday might seek to expand beyond its current borders, adding: "Ridley said out loud what many Europeans think. We all know about the German character, don't we? Germans naturally become a little arrogant when they are powerful" (Robert Melcher and Roman Rollnick, "Axis Urged to Counter Bonn," *The European*, 27–29 July 1990). *The Economist* reported that "Mr. Ridley's words . . . reflect the visceral feelings of millions of fellow-Britons, thousands of Tory party workers and scores, if not hundreds, of Tory MPs" ("Nick and His Mouth," 14 July 1990, p. 33).

3. See Jack Snyder, "Averting Anarchy in the New Europe," *International Security* 14, 4 (Spring 1990): 5–41; for historical background on the problem of praetorianism, see Jack Snyder, *Myths of Empire* (Ithaca: Cornell University Press—forthcoming). Snyder is the main exponent of the praetorian scenario, but others also fear the emergence of flawed democracies in the East. See, for example, Timothy Garton Ash, "Eastern Europe: Après Le Deluge, Nous," *New York Review of Books*, 16 August 1990, pp. 51–57, and Valerie Bunce, "Rising above the Past: The Struggle for Liberal Democracy in Eastern Europe," *World Policy Journal* 7, 3 (Summer 1990): 395–430.

4. See Zbigniew Brzezinski, "Post-Communist Nationalism," *Foreign Affairs* 68, 5 (Winter 1989/90): 1–25; F. Stephen Larrabee, "Long Memories and Short

Fuses: Change and Instability in the Balkans," *International Security* 15, 3 (Winter 1990/91): 58–91; Paul Kennedy, "The 'Powder Keg' Revisited," *Los Angeles Times*, 1 November 1989, p. B7; and Samuel R. Williamson, "1914's Shadow on the Europe of Today," *Newsday*, 27 July 1989, p. 61.

5. These and other dangers are detailed in Robert Jervis, "Cooperation under the Security Dilemma," *World Politics* 30, 2 (January 1978): 167–214, and Stephen Van Evera, "Causes of War"; Ph.D. dissertation, University of California at Berkeley, 1984, pp. 77–123.

6. On wars of optimistic miscalculation, see Geoffrey Blainey, *The Causes of War* (New York: Free Press), pp. 35–56.

7. On World War I, see Stephen Van Evera, "The Cult of the Offensive and the Origins of the First World War," in *Military Strategy and the Origins of the First World War*, ed. Steven E. Miller (Princeton: Princeton University Press, 1984), pp. 58–107, and Jack Snyder, *The Ideology of the Offensive: Military Decision Making and the Disasters of 1914* (Ithaca: Cornell University Press, 1984). The effect of offense-defense calculations on the outbreak of World War II is more complicated; a "cult of the defensive" among the states opposing Hitler also played a role in setting the stage for that war. See Barry R. Posen, *The Sources of Military Doctrine: France, Britain, and Germany between the World Wars* (Ithaca: Cornell University Press, 1984), p. 232, and Thomas Christensen and Jack Snyder, "Chain Gangs and Passed Bucks: Predicting Alliance Patterns in Multipolarity," *International Organization* 44, 2 (Spring 1990): 137–68, esp. 166. However, this defensive cult was not universally shared. Specifically, Hitler believed that offensive military action was feasible, if not easy, and exaggerated the ease of conquest overall by underestimating the political forces that would gather against an aggressor. Thus a key player embraced his own "cult of the offensive" and launched war partly because of it.

8. See, for example, John Lewis Gaddis, "The Long Peace: Elements of Stability in the Postwar International System," *International Security* 10, 4 (Spring 1986): 99–142, esp. 120–23.

9. Carl Kaysen notes further reasons why conquest now pays smaller strategic and economic rewards than in the past. See "Is War Obsolete? A Review Essay," *International Security* 14, 4 (Spring 1990): 42–64, esp. 48–58. However, most of the factors he identifies have evolved over several centuries and thus provide little reason to hope that the world is significantly safer now than it was in 1914 or 1939.

10. For further discussion of America's post–cold war interest in Europe, see Stephen Van Evera, "Why Europe Matters, Why the Third World Doesn't: American Grand Strategy After the Cold War," *Journal of Strategic Studies* 13, 2 (June 1990): 1–51, esp. 2–12.

11. Mearsheimer suggests that the dissolution of NATO and the complete withdrawal of American and British forces from the European continent are likely if the Soviet Union withdraws fully from Eastern Europe ("Back to the Future," note 1 above, pp. 5–6).

12. For examples, see Van Evera, "Why Europe Matters" (note 10), pp. 1, 34–35n.

13. President George Bush has declared that American forces will be needed to provide a "stabilizing presence" in Europe even after Soviet power is gone from Eastern Europe (see Michael Gordon, "American Troops Needed in Europe, President Asserts," *New York Times*, 13 February 1990, p. 1).

14. The only empirical study on this question is Richard K. Betts, *Soldiers, Statesmen and Cold War Crises* (Cambridge: Harvard University Press, 1977). Betts found that America's cold war military leaders were as cautious as American civilian leaders in recommending war, although military leaders were notably more hawkish than civilians when the escalation of warfare was considered.

15. I develop this argument in Van Evera, "Causes of War" (note 5), pp. 206–398.

16. Thus Hans-Ulrich Wehler notes "the spread of military values throughout German society" before 1914 and argues that "this 'social militarism' not only placed the military highest on the scale of social prestige, but permeated the whole of society with its ways of thinking, patterns of behavior, and its values and notions of honor" (*The German Empire 1871–1918*, trans. Kim Traynor [Leamington Spa/Dover, N.H.: Berg, 1985], p. 156). German Admiral George von Muller later explained German pre-war bellicosity by noting that "a great part of the German people . . . had been whipped into a high-grade chauvinism by Navalists and Pan-Germans" (quoted in Fritz Stern, *The Failure of Liberalism* [London: George Allen and Unwin, 1972], p. 94). For more on the role of the military in Wilhelmine Germany, see Gordon Craig, *The Politics of the Prussian Army, 1640–1945* (New York: Oxford University Press, 1955); and Martin Kitchen, *The German Officer Corps, 1890–1914* (Oxford: Clarendon Press, 1968). On Japan, see Saburo Ienaga, *The Pacific War, 1931–1945* (New York: Pantheon, 1978), pp. 13–54. A survey on the problem of militarism is Volker R. Berghahn, *Militarism: The History of an International Debate 1861–1979* (New York: St. Martin's, 1982).

17. I summarize the beliefs purveyed by European militaries before 1914 in Stephen Van.Evera, "Why Cooperation Failed in 1914," *World Politics* 37, 1 (October 1985): 80–117, esp. 83–99.

18. Friedrich von Bernhardi, *How Germany Makes War* (New York: Doran, 1914), p. 155. Before 1914, British generals likewise declared that "the defensive is never an acceptable role to the Briton, and he makes little or no study of it," and that the offensive "will win as sure as there is a sun in the heavens" (Generals W. G. Knox and R. C. B. Haking, quoted in T. H. E. Travers, "Technology, Tactics, and Morale: Jean de Bloch, the Boer War, and British Military Theory, 1900–1914," *Journal of Modern History* 51 [June 1979]: 275). For more details on British thought and practice, see Tim Travers, *The Killing Ground: The British Army, the Western Front and the Emergence of Modern Warfare, 1900–1918* (Boston: Allen and Unwin, 1987). On offensive thinking in Germany, France, and Russia before 1914, see J. Snyder, *Ideology of the Offensive* (note 7), pp. 41–198; on France, see also Basil Liddell Hart, "French Military Ideas before the First World War," in *A Century of Conflict, 1850–1950*, ed. Martin Gilbert (London: Hamish Hamilton, 1966), pp. 135–48; for further examples see Van Evera, "Causes of War" (note 5), pp. 280–324, 571–607.

19. The reasons for this preference are detailed in Posen (note 7), pp. 47–51, 58, 67–74; and J. Snyder, *Ideology of the Offensive* (note 7), pp. 24–25.

20. Thus German officers in the Wilhelmine era depicted a Germany encircled by envious neighbors about to attack, and naval officers in imperial Japan warned of an aggressive encirclement of Japan by America, Britain, China, and the Netherlands in the 1930s. Such warnings created a general belief that war was inevitable, which strengthened the arguments of German and Japanese advocates of preventive war. For an example from Germany, see Imanuel Geiss, *German Foreign Policy, 1871–1914* (Boston: Routledge and Kegan Paul, 1976), pp. 121–22, quoting General Alfred von Schlieffen; for other pre-1914 examples from Germany, Britain, and Russia, see Van Evera, "Why Cooperation Failed" (note 17), p. 85. On Japan, see Asada Sadao, "The Japanese Navy and the United States," in *Pearl Harbor as History: Japanese-American Relations 1931–1941*, ed. Dorothy Borg and Shumpei Okamoto with Dale K.A. Finlayson (New York: Columbia University Press, 1973), pp. 225–60, esp. 243–44, 251.

21. On bandwagoning and balancing, and the prevalence of the latter over the former, see Stephen M. Walt, *The Origins of Alliances* (Ithaca: Cornell University Press, 1987), pp. 17–33, 147–80, 263–66, 274–80.

22. Thus the Wilhelmine German navy justified its big fleet with its famous "risk theory," which proposed that a large German fleet could be used to cow Britain into neutrality while Germany moved aggressively (see Theodore Ropp, *War in the Modern World*, rev. ed. [New York: Collier, 1962], p. 212–13; Paul Kennedy, *Strategy and Diplomacy, 1870–1945* [Fontana, 1984], pp. 127–62, and specifically on the intimidation of Britain, pp. 133, 135, 139). Germany's General Schlieffen similarly contended that even if Britain fought to contain Germany, it would abandon the war in discouragement once the German army had defeated France (Gerhard Ritter, *The Schlieffen Plan: Critique of a Myth*, trans. Andrew and Eva Wilson [London: Oswald Wolff, 1958; reprint ed., Westport, Conn.: Greenwood, 1972], p. 163). These notions strengthened the arguments of German war hawks in 1914.

23. For example, before 1914 German admiral George von Muller saw Germany locked in a "great battle for economic survival"; without new territories "the artificial [German] economic edifice would start to crumble and existence therein would become very unpleasant indeed" (Muller memorandum to the Kaiser's brother, quoted in J. C. G. Rohl, ed., *From Bismarck to Hitler: The Problem of Continuity in German History* [London: Longman, 1970], pp. 56–57, 59). General Bernhardi likewise declared that "flourishing nations. . . . require a continual expansion of their frontiers, they require new territory for the accommodation of their surplus population" (Friedrich von Bernhardi, *Germany and the Next War*, trans. Allen H. Powles [New York: Longmans, Green, 1914], p. 21; see also 82–83). In France, Marshal Ferdinand Foch spoke in similar terms; see Foch, *The Principles of War*, trans. de Morinni (New York: Fly, 1918), pp. 36–37. For more examples, see Van Evera, "Causes of War" (note 5), pp. 339–47.

24. For examples, see *ibid.*, pp. 348–60; and Van Evera, "Why Cooperation Failed" (note 17), pp. 90–92.

25. On Germany see Wehler, *The German Empire* (note 16), pp. 125–27, 145–46, 155–70; on France, see Snyder, *Ideology of the Offensive* (note 7), ch. 3.

26. In France the military also believed that its social purity could best be preserved by an offensive doctrine that would require a fully professional army, untainted by masses of middle-class reserves, and for this reason as well it purveyed offensive ideas (see *ibid.*).

27. Civilian experts have always been in short supply in the Soviet Union; see Stephen M. Meyer, "Civilian and Military Influence in Managing the Arms Race in the U.S.S.R.," in *Reorganizing America's Defense: Leadership in War and Peace,* ed. Robert J. Art, Vincent Davis, and Samuel P. Huntington (Washington, D.C.: Pergamon-Brassey's, 1985), pp. 37–61.

28. For examples from before 1914, see Van Evera, "Why Cooperation Failed" (note 17), pp. 93–95. On the doctoring of history in Germany during the interwar years and its consequences, see Holger H. Herwig, "Clio Deceived: Patriotic Self-Censorship in Germany after the Great War," *International Security* 12, 2 (Fall 1987): 5–44. A general survey on nationalism is Boyd C. Shafer, *Faces of Nationalism: New Realities and Old Myths* (New York: Harcourt Brace Jovanovich, 1972). See also Louis L. Snyder, *Encyclopedia of Nationalism* (New York: Paragon, 1990).

29. Boyd Shafer, *Nationalism: Myth and Reality* (New York: Harcourt, Brace, 1955), p. 185.

30. I suspect that such nationalist mythmaking is the main cause of the "spiral model" pattern of conflict described by Robert Jervis, *Perception and Misperception in International Politics* (Princeton: Princeton University Press, 1976), pp. 58–113. Jervis emphasizes psychological causes; empirical research comparing these explanations would be useful.

31. During World War I an American historian reflected on the responsibility of chauvinist historical writing for causing the European war: "Woe unto us! professional historians, professional historical students, professional teachers of history, if we cannot see written in blood, in the dying civilization of Europe, the dreadful result of exaggerated nationalism as set forth in the patriotic histories of some of the most eloquent historians of the nineteenth century" (H. Morse Stephens, "Nationality and History," *American Historical Review* 21 [January 1916]: 225–36, esp. 236).

32. See Paul M. Kennedy, "The Decline of Nationalistic History in the West, 1900–1970," *Journal of Contemporary History* 8, 1 (January 1973): 77–100.

33. A survey of this often mismanaged but ultimately successful endeavor is Nicholas Pronay and Keith Wilson, eds., *The Political Re-Education of Germany and Her Allies after World War II* (Totowa, N.J.: Barnes and Noble, 1985).

34. An account is E. H. Dance, *History the Betrayer* (London: Hutchinson, 1960), pp. 126–50. The Brunswick Institute has since been renamed the Georg Eckert Institute for International Schoolbook Research, after its founder, Dr. Georg Eckert.

35. On social imperialism in Germany, see Wehler, *The German Empire* (note 16), pp. 24–28, 103–4, 171–79, 200; Volker Berghahn, *Germany and the Approach of*

War in 1914 (London: Macmillan, 1973), pp. 81–82, 93–94, 97, 185; Fritz Fischer, *War of Illusions: German Policies from 1911 to 1914*, trans. Marian Jackson (New York: W.W. Norton, 1975), pp. 253–54; and Arno Mayer, "Domestic Causes of the First World War," in *The Responsibility of Power*, ed. Leonard Krieger and Fritz Stern (New York: Macmillan, 1968), pp. 286–300. Some have ascribed Soviet cold war expansionism to similar causes; a discussion is Gaddis, "Long Peace" (note 8), pp. 118–19. A criticism of the social imperial explanation for German conduct is Marc Trachtenberg, "The Social Interpretation of Foreign Policy," *Review of Politics* 40, 3 (July 1978): 328–50, esp. 341–44. A more general discussion of social imperialism and other scapegoat theories of war is Jack S. Levy, "The Diversionary Theory of War: A Critique," in *Handbook of War Studies*, ed. Manus I. Midlarsky (Boston: Unwin Hyman, 1989), pp. 259–88; a criticism of these theories is Blainey (note 6), pp. 72–86.

36. The Russian minister of the interior, Viascheslav Plehve, stated at the time: "What this country needs is a short victorious war to stem the tide of revolution" (quoted in Levy, note 35 above, p. 264).

37. Wehler, *The German Empire* (note 16), p. 26.

38. For examples, see Berghahn, *Germany* (note 35), pp. 82, 97, 185, and Wehler, *The German Empire* (note 16), p. 200.

39. Thus shortly before the war, former chancellor Bernhard von Bulow wrote that an expansionist policy was the "true antidote against social democracy," and Chancellor Bethmann Hollweg noted in June 1914 that belligerent German agrarian interests "expected a war to turn domestic politics in a conservative direction" (quoted in Wehler, *The German Empire* [note 16 above], pp. 177–78; and Berghahn, *Germany* [note 35 above], p. 185).

40. The prerequisites for democracy are discussed in Robert A. Dahl, *Polyarchy: Participation and Opposition* (New Haven: Yale University Press, 1971), pp. 48–188, and Seymour Martin Lipset, *Political Man: The Social Bases of Politics*, expanded ed. (Baltimore: Johns Hopkins University Press, 1981), pp. 27–63.

41. For empirical studies, see Steve Chan, "Mirror, Mirror on the Wall . . . Are the Freer Countries More Pacific?" *Journal of Conflict Resolution* 28, 4 (December 1984): 617–48; and Erich Weede, "Democracy and War Involvement," *ibid.*, pp. 649–64.

42. Developing these arguments is Michael Doyle: "Kant, Liberal Legacies, and Foreign Affairs," Parts 1 and 2, *Philosophy and Public Affairs* 12, 3–4 (Summer, Fall 1983): 205–35, and 325–53, and "Liberalism and World Politics," *American Political Science Review* 80, 4 (December 1986): 1151–69.

43. A general account through the early 1960s is Richard Lowenthal, *World Communism: The Disintegration of a Secular Faith* (New York: Oxford University Press, 1964).

44. See Walt, *Origins of Alliances* (note 21), pp. 206–12.

45. Making this point is Walt, *ibid.*, pp. 35–37, 211–14.

46. See Chan (note 41), and Weede (note 41).

47. For example, these studies did not control for the strength of states. This omission may make democracies appear more warlike because democracy tends to develop in industrialized states, industrial states tend to be strong states, and strong states tend to be involved in more wars. See Quincy Wright, *A Study of War*, 2d ed. (Chicago: University of Chicago Press, 1965) pp. 220–22, who notes that European great powers have averaged twice as many wars as lesser states since 1700. Moreover, case studies of the origins of wars indicate that hypernationalism, unchallenged official propaganda, and social imperialism have sometimes played a role in their outbreak; this supports the argument that democracies are more peaceful overall since democracy should dampen these diseases. Thus the total body of empirical evidence points both ways.

48. For data on the evolution of income inequality in Europe, see Peter Flora, Franz Kraus, and Winfried Pfenning, *State, Economy, and Society in Western Europe 1815–1975: A Data Handbook in Two Volumes*, vol. 1: *The Growth of Industrial Societies and Capitalist Economies* (Chicago: St. James, 1987), pp. 611–74. They report inequality diminishing over the past several decades in eight of nine countries covered. For example, the share of national income received by the top 10 percent of the British population fell from 38.8 percent to 25.8 percent between 1938 and 1976 (p. 672); in Germany the share received by the top 10 percent fell from 40.5 percent to 31.7 percent between 1913 and 1974 (p. 652). Inequality in the distribution of wealth in Europe has diminished even more markedly. For example, in England and Wales the share of total wealth controlled by the richest 1 percent of population fell from 61 percent to 32 percent between 1923 and 1972; in Sweden the share of total taxed net worth controlled by the richest 1 percent fell from 50 percent to 17 percent from 1920 to 1975. (See A. B. Atkinson and A. J. Harrison, "Trends in the Distribution of Wealth in Britain," in *Wealth, Income and Inequality*, 2d ed., ed. A. B. Atkinson [Oxford: Oxford University Press, 1980], pp. 214–29, esp. 218, and Roland Spant, "Wealth Distribution in Sweden, 1920–1983," in *International Comparisons of the Distribution of Household Wealth*, ed. Edward N. Wolf [Oxford: Clarendon Press, 1987], pp. 51–71. On the United States, see H. P. Miller, "Income Distribution in the United States," in *Wealth, Income and Inequality*, ed. A. B. Atkinson [Harmondsworth: Penguin, 1973], pp. 111–35, esp. 113, 125–26.)

49. Overall, as Wehler notes, the German "teaching of history was used as an anti-revolutionary mind-drug for the inculcation of a patriotic mentality" (*The German Empire* [note 16 above], p. 121). However, see also Geoff Eley, *Reshaping the German Right: Radical Nationalism and Political Change after Bismarck* (New Haven: Yale University Press, 1980). Eley argues that nationalist propaganda had its main effect on the German middle class, while leaving the working class relatively unaffected. For a different view on the causes of nationalism, see Ernest Gellner, *Nations and Nationalism* (Ithaca: Cornell University Press, 1983). Gellner explains nationalism without reference to social stratification.

50. Thus the Kaiser's government instructed German teachers to produce "self-denying subjects . . . who will be glad to pay the supreme sacrifice for king and country" by teaching "the power and greatness of our people in the past and in the present" (quoted in Walter Consuelo Langsam, "Nationalism and

History in the Prussian Elementary Schools Under William II," in *Nationalism and Internationalism,* ed. Edward Mead Earle [New York: Columbia University Press, 1950], pp. 243–45).

51. Advancing these hypotheses is Stephen Walt: "The Foreign Policy of Revolutionary States: Hypotheses and Illustrations"; paper prepared for the annual meeting of the American Political Science Association, Chicago, 1987, and "Revolution and War"; paper prepared for the annual meeting of the American Political Science Association, San Francisco, 1990.

52. See T. C. W. Blanning, *The Origins of the French Revolutionary Wars* (New York: Longman, 1986); Marvin Zonis and Daniel Brumberg, *Khomeini, the Islamic Republic of Iran, and the Arab World* (Cambridge: Harvard Center for Middle East Studies, 1987); Jorge I. Dominguez, *To Make a World Safe for Revolution: Cuba's Foreign Policy* (Cambridge: Harvard University Press, 1989).

53. See David Healy, *U.S. Expansionism: The Imperialist Urge in the 1890s* (Madison: University of Wisconsin Press, 1970), pp. 42–46, 159–77.

54. Thus German journalist Arthur Dix explained in 1901 that a world power requires "extensive territory . . . as a market for [its] manufactures," and General Bernhardi in 1911 saw a Germany "compelled to obtain space for our increasing population and markets for our growing industries" (Wallace Notestein and Elmer E. Stoll, *Conquest and Kultur: Aims of the Germans in Their Own Words* [Washington, D.C.: U.S. Government Printing Office, 1917], p. 51). German chancellor Bethmann Hollweg's famous "September Program" of 1914 posited a commercial treaty that "secures the French market for our exports" as a German war aim (Fritz Fischer, *Germany's Aims in the First World War* [New York: Norton, 1967], p. 104). France's Marshal Foch explained that modern states needed "commercial outlets to an industrial system which produces more than it can sell, and therefore is constantly smothered by competition" and argued that "new markets are opened by force of arms" (Foch [note 23 above], p. 37).

55. For examples see Walter LaFeber, *America, Russia, and the Cold War 1945–1980,* 4th ed. (New York: Wiley, 1980), pp. 10–11, 18, 27, 45, 52, 55, 59–61, 110–11, 179–80, 235. It may not follow that these ideas helped cause the cold war, however; perhaps they fueled American belligerence, but this belligerence may have deterred the Soviets from further aggression, thus dampening the cold war, as much or more than it provoked it. Making this argument is Vojtech Mastny, *Russia's Road to the Cold War: Diplomacy, Warfare, and the Politics of Communism, 1941–1945* (New York: Columbia University Press, 1979). A good survey of the debate on cold war origins is John Lewis Gaddis, "The Emerging Post-Revisionist Synthesis on the Origins of the Cold War," *Diplomatic History* 7, 3 (Summer 1983): 171–204.

56. Mearsheimer, "Back to the Future" (note 1), pp. 13–19, 21–29; Kenneth N. Waltz: "The Stability of a Bipolar World," *Daedalus* 93, 3 (Summer 1964): 881–909, and *Theory of International Politics* (Reading, Mass.: Addison-Wesley, 1979), pp. 161–76; Gaddis, "Long Peace" (note 8), pp. 105–10.

57. I develop this argument in "Primed for Peace: Europe After the Cold War," *International Security* 15, 3 (Winter 1990/91): 7–57, esp. 33–40.

58. See World Bank, *World Development Report 1990* (New York: Oxford University Press, 1990), p. 237. The distribution of income in Germany is more equal than in most other major industrialized states, including the United States, Canada, Britain, France, Italy, Switzerland, Finland, Denmark, Australia, and New Zealand; it is less equal than in Sweden, Japan, the Netherlands, and Belgium; and it is roughly comparable to the distribution in Norway and Spain.

59. See Anne P. Young, "Germans, History, and the Nazi Past," *Social Education* 4, 2 (February 1981): 86–98, and Hildegund M. Calvert, "Germany's Nazi Past: A Critical Analysis of the Period in West German High School History Textbooks"; Ph.D. dissertation, Ball State University, 1987. Calvert notes some objectionable omissions but concludes that German "textbooks satisfactorily covered the majority of the topics examined" (p. ii.)

60. The Fischer school's views are summarized in Geiss (note 20), and Fischer, *War of Illusions* (note 35). A good survey of the controversy stirred by the Fischer school is John A. Moses, *The Politics of Illusion: The Fischer Controversy in German Historiography* (London: George Prior, 1975). As Moses notes, most German historians now accept Fischer's argument that Germany deliberately unleashed World War I in June–July 1914, disputing only Fisher's contention that the war was planned long in advance (p. 73). An example of a non-German interpretation far more sympathetic to Germany than the Fischer school is L.C.F. Turner, *Origins of the First World War* (London: Edward Arnold, 1970).

61. On this dramatic debate, see Richard J. Evans, *In Hitler's Shadow: West German Historians and the Attempt to Escape from the Nazi Past* (New York: Pantheon, 1989), and Peter Baldwin, "The Historikerstreit in Context," in *Reworking the Past: Hitler, the Holocaust and the Historian's Debate*, ed. Peter Baldwin (Boston: Beacon, 1990), pp. 3–37. Noting the defeat of the German apologists in this debate are Baldwin (*ibid.*, p. 29) and Hans-Ulrich Wehler, "Unburdening the German Past? A Preliminary Assessment," in Baldwin, ed., *Reworking the Past*, pp. 214–23, esp. 214–15. Noting the absence of chauvinism in Germany today is Hans Mommsen, who concludes that "Germany today is ahead of its neighbors in its wariness of patriotic appeals and violent solutions to domestic conflicts" ("Reappraisal and Repression: The Third Reich in West German Historical Consciousness," in Baldwin, ed., *Reworking the Past*, pp. 173–84, esp. 183).

62. *World Almanac and Book of Facts 1990* (New York: World Almanac, 1989), pp. 712–13.

63. At the end of World War II a total of 13,841,000 Germans were expelled from formerly German territories annexed by Poland and the Soviet Union, and from other East European countries; of these, 2,111,000 died during the expulsion, leaving 11,730,000 expellees alive during 1945–50. Most settled in West Germany, some in East Germany, and a small fraction in Austria and other Western countries (Alfred M. de Zayas, *Nemesis at Potsdam: The Expulsion of the Germans From the East*, 3d rev. ed. [Lincoln: University of Nebraska Press, 1988], p. xxv).

64. I am indebted to Dr. Roland E. Foerster, Director of the Department of Education, Information, and Special Studies at the Military Historical Research

Institute at Freiburg, and to Professor David Large of Montana State University for sharing information on this question.

65. J. Snyder, "Averting Anarchy" (note 3), pp. 18–38.

66. Disputes arising from the collapse of the Ottoman empire spawned the great European crises of 1832–33, 1839–40, 1875–78, and 1908; the Crimean War and World War I; the Balkan wars of 1885 and 1912–13; and the Greek-Turkish war of 1919–22. A general account is M.S. Anderson, *The Eastern Question 1774–1923* (New York: Macmillan, 1966). A summary is Rene Albrecht-Carrie, *A Diplomatic History of Europe Since the Congress of Vienna* (New York: Harper and Row, 1958), pp. 40–55, 84–92, 167–77, 196–97, 259–72, 280–86, 321–34, 401–4.

67. During the post-1945 era five newly independent regions saw more than a million killed in local warfare (Cambodia, India-Pakistan-Bangladesh, Nigeria, Sudan, and Vietnam), and eight others saw at least 100,000 killed (Angola, Burundi, Indonesia, Lebanon, Mozambique, Rwanda, Uganda, and Zaire). Casualty data on these wars is from William Eckhardt, "Wars and War-Related Deaths, 1945–1989," in Ruth Leger Sivard, *World Military and Social Expenditure 1989*, 13th ed. (Washington, D.C.: World Priorities, 1989), p. 22.

68. For a map of border conflicts in the former USSR, see Graham Smith, ed., *The Nationalities Question in the Soviet Union* (New York: Longman, 1990), appendix 1.

69. Frontiers that may be disputed include the Romanian-Moldovan-Ukrainian, Romanian-Hungarian, Polish-Lithuanian, Polish-Ukrainian, Polish-Belorussian, Polish-Czechoslovakian, Hungarian-Czechoslovakian, Hungarian-Yugoslav (Serbian), Yugoslav (Serbian)-Albanian, Greek-Albanian, Greek-Turkish, and Greek-Yugoslav (Macedonian)-Bulgarian. Ethnic pockets include Hungarians in Romania and Czechoslovakia; Poles in Lithuania, Belorussia, Ukraine, and Czechoslovakia; Germans in Poland, Czechoslovakia, and Romania; Turks in Bulgaria; Greeks in Albania; and Albanians in Yugoslavia (Serbia). Summaries include Larrabee (note 4); Istvan Deak, "Uncovering Eastern Europe's Dark History," *Orbis* 34, 1 (Winter 1989): 51–65; and Barry James, "Central Europe Tinderboxes: Old Border Disputes," *International Herald Tribune*, 1 January 1990, p. 5.

70. All demographic figures are for 1979 and are calculated from John L. Scherer, ed., *USSR Facts and Figures Annual*, vol. 5 (Gulf Breeze, Fla.: Academic International Press, 1981), pp. 49–51.

71. This excludes the Kazakh residents of Kazakhstan, although a strict accounting based on the 1979 census should include them because that census showed the Russians outnumbering them in Kazakhstan, 41 percent to 36 percent. However, data from 1989 indicate that Kazakhs again outnumber Russians in Kazakhstan, 40 percent to 38 percent (see Alan P. Pollard, ed., *USSR Facts and Figures Annual*, vol. 15, 1991 [Gulf Breeze, Fla.: Academic International Press, 1991], p. 501). In all other former Soviet republics the nationality after whom the republic is named was the majority or (in Kirgizia) a plurality in 1979, and all were a majority in 1989.

72. By mid-1990 the Soviet Union already had over 600,000 internal refugees who had fled from such oppression, and hundreds had died in communal

violence (Francis X. Clines, "40 Reported Dead in Soviet Clashes," *New York Times*, 9 June 1990, p. 1). By late 1991 that toll had risen to 3,000–4,000 deaths and nearly 2 million refugees, according to U.S. State Department officials.

73. Western Europe itself is largely free of such problems; its borders are well settled, and its populations are not significantly intermingled. The Polish-German boundary is the only Western frontier that conceivably might be disputed. However, before unification the East and West German governments agreed to guarantee the current German-Polish border; if the united German government adheres to this agreement, this border dispute is settled (see Serge Schmemann, "Two Germanys Adopt Unity Treaty and Guarantee Poland's Borders," *New York Times*, 22 June 1990, p. 1, and Thomas L. Friedman, "Two Germanys Vow to Accept Border with the Poles," *New York Times*, 18 July 1990, p. 1).

74. The term "collective security system" has been debased over the years, often being used to refer to an alliance directed against an external threat. However, it properly refers to a system in which members guarantee one another against attack by other members. On the debasement of the term, see Inis L. Claude, Jr., *Power and International Relations* (New York: Random House, 1962), pp. 115–23.

75. In November 1991 NATO took a large step toward such a policy. Specifically, the alliance replaced its secret basic strategy document, MC 14/3, with a new unclassified basic strategy document, "The Alliance's New Strategic Concept," which contains language suggesting that the alliance now guarantees its members against any aggression, including aggression by other members (see "The Alliance's New Strategic Concept," NATO Press Communique S-1(91)85 [Brussels, 7 November 1991], para. 21, subpara. I and III). In contrast, in the past the alliance refused pleas from member states for guarantees against other NATO members (see, for example, Athanassios Platias, "High Politics in Small Countries: An Inquiry into the Security Policies of Greece, Israel, and Sweden"; Ph.D. dissertation, Cornell University, 1986, pp. 165–66, recounting NATO rejection of Greek requests for NATO guarantees against Turkey on grounds that NATO's purpose did not include the defense of NATO members against each other). I am grateful to Col. Robert Ulin for enlightenment on this topic.

76. Some Eastern states will embrace many of these standards without Western pressure. See, for example, Francis X. Clines, "Yeltsin Plan Wins a Quick Approval," *New York Times*, 2 November 1991, p. 7, reporting the Yeltsin government's decision to implement the market reforms that it launched on 2 January 1992.

77. To put the matter in Kuhnian terms, the East's dominant political paradigm has been shattered, leaving it for the moment highly receptive to Western paradigms (see Thomas S. Kuhn, *The Structure of Scientific Revolutions*, 2d ed., enl. [Chicago: University of Chicago Press, 1970]).

78. I discuss these in "Managing the Eastern Crisis: Preventing War in the Former Soviet Empire," *Security Studies* 1, 3 (Spring 1992).

DOMESTIC POLITICS AND INTERNATIONAL CHANGE: GERMANY'S ROLE IN EUROPE'S SECURITY FUTURE

Beverly Crawford and Jost Halfmann

INTRODUCTION

The end of bipolarity in Europe, German unification, and the restoration of German sovereignty have catapulted Germany into a new position in world affairs. In the aftermath of World War II "security" in Europe meant not only deterring a Soviet attack; it also meant dividing Germany and "anchoring" the emerging West German economic giant in the Atlantic alliance and the European Community (EC). Now fully sovereign, united Germany is capable of playing an independent and influential role in global politics and markets. Since the events of 1990 Germany has been transformed from a divided, "front-line" state vulnerable to an attack from the Warsaw Pact to the most powerful state in Europe in both economic and conventional military power.[1] Located in the heart of Europe, Germany is now capable of eastward expansion. Although its GDP is smaller than that of Japan, as the world's leading exporter, it plays a larger global economic role.[2]

Realist theories of international politics tell us that as a nation develops its power resources, the range of its interests widens and the country assumes a more prominent role in international politics. Countries with great-power economies have increasingly acquired far-flung interests. If those interests conflict with the interests of other powerful states, the temptation to augment economic power with appropriate military capabilities arises. And other states in the system expect this of them. Capabilities drive behavior and incentives in an anarchic self-help world.

Many argue that Germany is no exception. At least in the rhetoric of its leaders, the first signs of Germany's global influence

216

may have already appeared. A top adviser to Chancellor Helmut Kohl has said, "We *want* to lead. Perhaps in time the United States will take care of places like Central America, and we will handle Eastern Europe."[3] According to Kohl, "Germany has closed a chapter of its history, and in the future it can assume its role as world power. . . . It is expected of us now that we offer more participation in the solution of world political problems."[4]

Germany's growing weight is not reflected only in the public statements of the political leadership. Indeed Germany has begun to pursue independent policies in line with its new power. The terms of German unification and Germany's relationship with the Soviet Union were negotiated *not* in concert with the allies but between Kohl and Mikhail Gorbachev alone. There are also signs that Germany is playing an increasingly important role in shaping multilateral military strategies. German opposition to short-range nuclear weapons on German territory led to the canceling of "Wintex," NATO's planned nuclear war game that would have tested command procedures.[5]

There are a number of indicators, however, that Germany's international status and willingness to play the role of a great power will not rise in step with its material resources, even when some of its allies might demand this. This is most evident in the German government's acceptance of constraints on military power. In the "Two-plus-Four" negotiations on German unity, Germany agreed to reduce its army from 490,000 to 370,000 soldiers and to not acquire nuclear or chemical weapons, thereby refraining from arming itself with the military capabilities appropriate to its great-power status.[6]

It is clear that the NATO allies expect Germany to be prepared to undertake collective military action in response to threats in the Middle East and instability in Eastern Europe and the Soviet Union. Nonetheless, during the Gulf War, Kohl told the allies that the German constitution prevented troop deployment in "out-of-area" conflicts. Germany hesitated before sending its eigthteen alpha jets to defend Turkey—a NATO ally—against a possible attack by Iraq. Turkey's President Turget Ozal charged that "Germany has become so rich that it has completely lost its fighting spirit."[7]

What will be Germany's role in determining Europe's future? Will it again attempt to dominate Europe? Will it begin to act as a global military power? Or will it be an isolationist nation, playing a role similar to that of the United States in the first half of the twentieth century? How will Germany's preferences shape Europe's multilateral security institutions? Can Germany provide leadership? Will the security partnership with the United States continue? How will that partnership be transformed with the end of the cold war and the end of Europe's division? Answers to these questions are essential because of Germany's growing weight in the world and because most of NATO's weapons and troops are located on German soil. As one British observer put it, "The German approach to disposing of the cold war will probably become the kernel of the yet-to-emerge European defense order."[8] Thus in order to more fully understand the future of European security, we need to understand German preferences and investigate their origins.

In this essay we shall examine the interplay between international and domestic forces in order to explain those preferences. We shall make three arguments. First, we shall argue that both the restoration of German sovereignty and the cold war's end have made domestic politics increasingly important in that explanation, but that domestic politics are overwhelmingly influenced by commitments to working through multilateral institutions. This commitment was imposed by Germany's security dependence on the United States but took root among the political elite across the political spectrum and continued after that dependence waned. This commitment is both ideological and pragmatic: ideas such as *Westbindung* and "common security" dominate the current security debate, and German politicians have sought international support for their positions in domestic political debates.

Second, we shall argue that the restoration of sovereignty and the cold war's end have only partially resolved the historic tension between Germany's commitment to the West and "normal" relations with the East. The confluence of a commitment to multilateralism with Germany's historic interest in drawing closer to the East has created the beginnings of a new domestic consensus which will shape Germany's diplomatic position in European security issues. Based on that consensus, Germany will use its growing international influence in *regional* security debates in order to build and support multilateral security institutions which include all of Europe, including Eastern Europe and the former Soviet Union. Since, however, Western commitments and Eastern ties will still be difficult to reconcile, and a domestic consensus may not be possible on the more difficult issues (such as the level and direction of financial aid to Eastern Europe), those institutions may not be robust.

Finally, we shall argue that Germany will refrain from acquiring the capabilities that would enable it to become a *global* military power for three reasons: the fragmentation of the German party system, the lack of a sense of "mission" in the world, and the entrenched commitment to multilateralism.

Our evidence for these predictions comes from the historical development of German political party positions on security issues in the postwar period and the relative success of parties in and out of power to reconcile the tension between commitment to the West and ties to the East. Parties are the foci of political power in German politics. They form governments and design the programs top politicians are supposed to execute once they are elected. The party machines select candidates for parliamentary seats or governmental positions, and the election laws are designed so that the electorate votes on parties, not individual candidates.

We shall also trace changes in public opinion within the Federal Republic throughout the postwar period. Although we recognize that public opinion is shaped by political elites and that those elites in government have often made policy decisions which were directly opposed to prevailing public preferences, it is also true that public opinion sets the parameters within which political elites can operate and correlates with support for party positions.

The argument will proceed as follows: We shall begin by briefly discussing the causes for the postwar disappearance of aggressive hypernationalism and militarism in Germany and present evidence to show that even with the emergence of right-wing extremist parties, these impulses are not likely to dominate the political agenda. We shall then show that Germany's past security dependence on the United States shaped its preference for military multilateralism. Third, we shall show how a decreasing security dependence on the United States led to the prominence of domestic forces in shaping Germany's security priorities, as well as the growing domestic dissatisfaction with the exclusiveness and vulnerability imposed by Germany's commitments to NATO's security policies. Finally, we shall show that in the 1990s a new domestic consensus on European security is emerging which will permit Germany to play an important role in shaping pan-European security institutions. The inclusion of the East in those institutions will change the terms upon which Germany's commitment to the West is renegotiated. Nonetheless, the security debate in the wake of the Gulf War demonstrates that domestic forces will constrain Germany from playing an independent and prominent global military role.

FROM CAPITULATION TO UNIFICATION: THE GRADUAL WIDENING OF GERMAN SECURITY OPTIONS

THE END OF HYPERNATIONALISM AND THE PREFERENCE FOR MULTILATERALISM

The period from the Kaiserreich to the Third Reich is a well-documented history of intense and aggressive German nationalism. During the Kaiserreich the elite ideologies of Social Darwinism and pan-Germanism were brought forward for legitimating expansionist ambitions.[9] These ideologies permeated all classes of German society. Domestic elites portrayed Germany as a state which had not achieved the international status and influence which a powerful industrial society in the heart of Europe supposedly deserved. And extreme social and political inequalities fed the belief within the commercial and working classes that aggressive nationalism could improve their social conditions.

During the postwar period, the Nazi power elite was dislodged, national political institutions became more democratic, and income was more evenly distributed. Between 1950 and 1980 the size of middle-income groups (in which the majority of German households can be found) grew slightly; beginning in the mid-1970s, however, the number of Germans below the poverty line also grew due to rising unemployment.[10] It is this growing minority of unemployed poor which began to look for radical right-wing and potentially aggressive nationalist solutions to their domestic economic plight.

The growth of the Republikaner Party in the late 1980s was one consequence of these changing economic conditions. In addition to its call for reunification, the Republikaner platform rejected

Germany's membership in NATO and the EC in favor of an ethno-centric approach to the protection of German "national interests." The platform also called for the expulsion of all foreigners from Germany. By 1989 it was estimated that the Republikaner Party could claim 5 percent of the votes in West Germany and received "sympathy" (but not actual votes) from 15 percent of the electorate.[11] Republikaners began to appear in the European Parliament as well as the Berlin City Parliament, and in March 1989 the Republikaner as well as the National Democratic Party (NDP) had a good showing in the communal elections in Hessen.* To some this signaled the reappearance of aggressive nationalism in Germany.

This, however, is not the case. Survey research data suggest that Germany maintains a relatively high standard of living and that a large majority of people with secure incomes want to continue established economic and political practices. This majority shows few signs of any nationalist impulses, much less a tendency toward aggressive nationalism.[12] The unification of Germany under Kohl in 1990 took most of the ideological wind out of the Republikaners' sails, and the party failed to gain the 5 percent vote in the December 1990 elections needed to establish itself at the national level. Indeed none of the right-wing parties has ever collected more than 5 percent of the votes in federal elections and overcome the *Sperr-klausel*, which bars small parties from entering the Bonn parliament.[13] And although not many data are available for the former German Democratic Republic (GDR), an analysis of voting behavior during the *Volkskammer* elections in March 1990 shows that the distribution of left and right voters is similar to the former Federal Republic, although compared to the Western states the Eastern

*The 1989 Hessen elections returned gains for the Republikaner and NDP and losses for the Christian Democratic Union (CDU) and the Free Democratic Party (FDP). Forty percent of those who voted for the Republikaner were former CDU/CSU (Christian Socialist Union) supporters, and most of these voters came from small-town rural areas in the south of Germany. They were primarily farmers who feared international freer trade agreements which would reduce their incomes. Those coming from the north were predominantly Social Democratic Party (SPD) voters located in the major industrial cities in areas where housing is both inferior and hard to get. The majority of these voters were blue-collar workers and unemployed men. One out of five Republikaner voters had never voted before, and almost twice as many men as women voted for the Republikaner. Overall, Republikaner voters have the lowest level of education of all voters in Germany (see Veen [note 11 below], pp. 13–19).

states seem to have a slightly stronger right-wing potential.[14] As Wolfram Hanrieder writes,

> Affluence brought with it a certain hedonistic utilitarianism; the general attrition of political ideologies in the Europe of the 1960s encouraged political parties to become more pragmatic in their platforms and policies; and in the German case the electoral system promoted appeals to the middle-of-the-road majority by penalizing political parties that had narrow programs and small constituencies.[15]

This latter point held true in Germany at least until the end of the 1970s.

An opinion poll conducted in 1981–82 confirmed these claims. It found that only 59 percent of West Germans claimed to be proud of their country, as compared to 96 percent of North Americans; while North Americans scored highest in patriotism among fifteen nations, Germans were last in national pride.[16] Whether there will be more nationalism after unification is unclear at this point. An opinion poll of May 1990, however, revealed that only 28 percent of (West) Germans considered unification the most pressing task for the near future; unification came in tenth place on a list of "most important tasks," way behind support for environmental protection, the fight against unemployment, and the stabilization of the Deutsche mark.[17] This is not to say that there are no aggressive nationalist feelings or groups that espouse (or will espouse in the future) nationalist ideologies in Germany. However, voting behavior has become increasingly consumer-oriented and tied to economic interests and personal views rather than ideology or religion, so the majority of the German population will not easily be persuaded to see any benefit from the state's efforts to couch a German identity in nationalist terms. As long as economic inequalities are not exacerbated, even in times of economic downturns, it is safe to predict that hypernationalism will not take hold again in Germany.

Nor does it appear that domestic forces will push Germany toward neutrality, despite the fact that many Germans would like to see their country become a larger version of Switzerland.[18] Although opinion polls have consistently shown throughout the postwar period that almost one-third of the German population would like Germany to be neutral, this view has not affected the general course of German defense and foreign policy since it does not correspond to a change of outlook within the German political elite itself.[19] The impulse toward neutrality has resonated only in the fundamentalist wing of the Green Party. Fundamentalist Greens prefer the full denuclearization of Europe and the dissolution of all military alliances. The "realist" or more pragmatic wing of the party, however, opposed the dissolution of NATO before 1989, arguing that Germany's membership in multilateral security arrangements would prevent the resurgence of a new German *Grossmachtpolitik*. Since then, they have seen the CSCE as the most promising institution for safeguarding European security.[20]

WESTERN MULTILATERALISM: IMPOSED SECURITY CHOICES IN THE POSTWAR PERIOD

With the disappearance of the forces that fed aggressive nationalism in West Germany, German security policy in the postwar period was almost entirely shaped by German dependence on the American defense shield. That dependence rested on three pillars which were in turn founded on cold war security assumptions: U.S. *commitment* to defend the FRG against a Soviet attack; the *credibility* of extended deterrence as an expression of that commitment (U.S. troops in Germany as a "tripwire" which would bring the United States into a European war); and the *necessity* (and thus reliability) of an American commitment, given the unambiguous nature of the Soviet threat. Although West Germany became a sovereign state in 1955 and the rights of the occupying powers were rescinded, both its domestic and foreign policies were clearly subject to U.S. scrutiny. Even after its establishment as a sovereign state, it was an instrument of U.S. policy rather than an independent actor. American ideas about the impending Soviet threat precluded any German impulse to work with the Soviet Union or rebuild economic relations with the East. And it was within the confines of this ideology that the majority's views on West Germany's defense policy (if not views on foreign policy as a whole) were forged.

According to that ideology, the Soviet Union was seen as an aggressive power bent on the domination of Europe. Security for the free world required deterring it from invading Western Europe.

Security for NATO meant superiority in the balance of military forces. In addition, "economic containment"—a national security approach to foreign economic policy—became a central component of this ideology.[21] Economic containment was based on the assumption that economic strength was a key foundation of Western security and that foreign economic policy was its essential building block.[22] International economic relations, then, were first and foremost a weapon in the Western multilateral security arsenal.

The weapon was two-pronged. First, relations with other industrial democracies were guided by liberal economic ideology and policies of economic "openness." Open markets in democratic societies would nurture economic growth, vitiate internal communist movements, and build a bulwark against Soviet expansion. The second prong of the economic weapon was an explicit refusal to trade with the Eastern bloc. Because these economies were geared to drive the Soviet military machine, the argument ran, and because Western exports to the Soviet bloc would simply satisfy its thirst for power, East-West trade would lead to the West's vulnerability. Anti-communism, then, was harnessed to build broad-based support for an alliance whose mission was to deter a Soviet attack in Europe and defend Europe if deterrence failed, and for international economic institutions which would create and maintain an international market economy from which the socialist countries would be excluded.[23] Thus U.S. officials took steps to ensure that America's major trading partners would also be military allies, and at the same time, they constructed a multilateral policy of economic warfare against the Soviet Union, making sure that the allies would go along.

Given the dominance of these ideas and the U.S. military, Germany had no choice but to cut old ties with new rivals. Alignment with the West meant the severing of ties with the East. The pervasive role of the United States in the rebuilding of Germany and Germany's division into two states with opposing political and economic systems provided a powerful basis for domestic political consensus on security issues. According to Konrad Adenauer,

In this world situation, there was only one possibility that made sense for Germany: to make common cause with the West and to take its place in a free Europe, economically, militarily and politically. It was a policy of pure self-preservation. It was a policy of the smaller risk—and there was no policy without risk.[24]

Genuine fears of a Soviet takeover merged with commitment to a strong NATO alliance—whose mission rested on the unwavering assumption of the inevitability of a confrontation with the Soviet Union.

But to many Germans, Eastern Europe especially, and even the Soviet Union, were part of Europe in historical heritage and culture. The division between East and West, Europeans knew, was largely artificial, and at some indefinite point in the future broken ties would again be resumed.[25] European elites questioned the "essentialist" view of the Soviet Union that prevailed in Washington, one which held that the Soviet Union was an aggressive power bent on destroying the West. In contrast, they saw the USSR as a formidable adversary, but nonetheless one they could bargain with, even live with.[26] Positive incentives, like trade, the argument ran, could draw the Soviet Union into a web of interdependent relationships with the West, and the ties created could reduce the military threat in Europe.[27] Indeed, as if to foreshadow Gorbachev's notion of a "Common European Home," the belief prevailed among many West European elites—even in the darkest days of the cold war—that trade was an avenue of communication and conciliation which should not be closed.[28] As long as the division of Europe could not be overcome, it should at least be softened and made more palatable.

Major political forces in Germany adhered to this latter view. The SPD had actually wanted to avoid integration with the West and test the possibilities for accommodation with the Soviet Union on the basis of a neutral united Germany. The SPD fought multilateral commitments to the West which had been pressed upon Germany by the United States and supported by the CDU. The party opposed membership in the European Defense Community, the Coal and Steel Community, and NATO. As early as 1957 the SPD came out against American nuclear weapons deployed on German territory.[29]

The SPD was adamantly opposed to German armament on four major grounds: it would damage the prospects for reunification by aligning West Germany with one of the cold war camps; it would antagonize the Soviet Union and increase world tensions; it would support militarist elements in domestic German society; and it would bring Germany into a conservative West European union that could split non-Communist Europe.

During this early period, the FDP had pursued a pro-West line but always made it clear that the party wanted to explore openings to the East which would advance unification. Even in 1961 the FDP called for a more "independent" foreign policy and argued that Germans themselves, not the Four Powers, were ultimately responsible for unification.[30] SPD and FDP views were opposed by the United States.

West Germany's dependence on the United States and the U.S. zero-sum notions of how the cold war should be conducted precluded these options. Under Adenauer, therefore, the West German government defined its values and priorities both in terms of U.S. preferences and in opposition to the totalitarianism on the other side of the iron curtain. By invoking the specter of communism and totalitarianism, it was possible to silence the opposition within by pointing to the acute threat posed by the enemy without.[31] The alliance was really the only choice.

INTERNATIONAL FORCES AND THE BREAKDOWN OF THE DOMESTIC CONSENSUS

These cold war choices imposed by the United States and fully accepted by Adenauer were never universally shared among political elites in Germany (except perhaps during a brief period after 1961, when the Berlin Wall was built). In 1969 a coalition government of the SPD and FDP was elected, united in a determination to develop fresh approaches to the East. These approaches, though originating in domestic politics, were facilitated by changes at the international level. East-West tensions were diminishing and Germany was unambiguously anchored in NATO and firmly under the U.S. nuclear umbrella. It made overtures to the East in issue areas of "low politics." The policy of *Ostpolitik* was officially proclaimed and implemented in the Moscow and Warsaw treaties and the inter-German accord on Berlin in 1972.[32] It was immediately opposed by the CDU/CSU for the same reasons they had opposed it all along: in the zero-sum atmosphere of the cold war, overtures to the East were seen by the CDU as weakening the bonds to the West.[33] The CDU argued that Ostpolitik would undermine long-range German and West European security interests, weaken the Western defense effort, and bring about a reduced American commitment to Europe.[34] But when the SPD won the 1972 elections with a solid majority, indicating, among other things, clear approval of Ostpolitik, the CDU was forced to accept the policies, and Kohl had little choice but to carry them forward in the 1980s. In this period, detente with the East was accompanied by a lessening of Germany's dependence on the U.S. defense shield.

Three episodes loosened the bonds of dependence; the first was the U.S. attempt to modernize INF by placing Pershing II and Cruise missiles on German territory. This plan sharpened doubts among political elites and within the public at large as to NATO's flexible response strategy. Despite the fact that both Helmut Schmidt and Kohl argued for the placement of intermediate range missiles on German territory, the debate surrounding that placement weakened the credibility of the nuclear deterrence upon which Germany had depended for three decades. Second, the INF treaty and U.S. calls for burden-sharing within the alliance gave both German elites and mass publics the impression that U.S. commitment to maintaining the defense shield was weakening. Third, perceptions of the decline in the Soviet threat made the defense shield seem increasingly unnecessary. Each of these issues contributed to a widening of Germany's defense options and enhanced the role of domestic politics in setting a new course for German security policy.

THE "DOUBLE-TRACK" DECISION OF 1979: WAS DETERRENCE CREDIBLE?

In 1979 NATO announced its "double-track" decision: to begin deploying 108 Pershing II missiles and 464 ground-based Cruise missiles in Europe in 1983. These were intermediate range missiles capable of reaching the Soviet Union. At the same time, NATO would initiate arms control negotiations with the Soviet Union that would make the deployment of these weapons unnecessary.

All of the Pershing missiles were to be deployed in Germany. Many German political elites, however, had begun to feel that Germany was being singled out as the target in a potential nuclear war in Europe, and the German government did not want the Federal Republic to be the only NATO member to deploy weapons which were a strategic threat to the Soviet Union. Citing the "singularization" of Germany, the West German government persuaded NATO to deploy only 96 of the cruise missiles in Germany. This deployment seemed necessary to some experts because the Soviet Union had deployed intermediate range SS-20s in the mid-1970s, causing a "gap" on an important rung of the "escalation ladder" which in turn created a "gap" in NATOs flexible response strategy.[35]*

The problem was simple: if NATO failed to stop a Soviet attack with conventional forces and was forced to resort to the battlefield with tactical nuclear weapons, the accuracy and reduced yield of the Soviet SS-20s would allow Moscow to escalate the conflict by striking NATO's nuclear-equipped aircraft capable of reaching the Soviet Union. In this scenario, the United States would have to choose either *not* to respond or resort to intercontinental ballistic missiles. Nuclear parity had, in the eyes of many Germans, increased the American temptation not to respond (since response to a threat in Europe would mean suicide for the United States), and the imbalance in theater nuclear weapons would have a "decoupling" effect. As Hanrieder writes,

> For Chancellor Helmut Schmidt, restoring the Eurostrategic military balance, whether by deploying modernized NATO weapons or by reducing Soviet weapons, was the essential prerequisite for sustaining the European political balance and retaining an important German voice in the management of the Western alliance. The chancellor feared that the SU could convert its Eurostrategic nuclear advantage into political pressures within Germany and Eu-

---

*This strategy of flexible response was designed in the 1960s to graduate the scale of Western response in order to counter the perceived Soviet threat. It emphasized "regional nuclear options" as a response to Soviet aggression under which NATO would have access to a continuum of military threats in order to bolster nuclear deterrence. These threats included conventional forces, tactical nuclear forces, theater nuclear weapons, and ultimately strategic nuclear weapons. The various "rungs" on the escalation ladder were considered important to the credibility of NATO's deterrent since U.S.-Soviet strategic parity (codified in SALT I) strengthened mutual deterrence between the United States and the Soviet Union but simultaneously weakened the U.S. strategy of extended deterrence in Europe.

rope, and worried that the United States might not resist such pressures firmly enough.[36]

Thus Schmidt supported the double-track decision. The Christian Democrats, of course, came out strongly in favor of the modernization of intermediate nuclear forces.

But for some political elites, a restoration of the balance on that particular rung would have a different kind of decoupling effect and thus increase the odds of nuclear war in Europe. Defense planners in Washington had argued that the United States could fight a conventional war in Europe and avoid nuclear escalation. But because nations involved in war can be expected to reach for their most potent weapons if they are losing, the risk was high that any conventional war in Europe would escalate to nuclear war. By substantially improving NATO's capability to strike the Soviet Union from Western Europe, modernizing NATO's nuclear forces might give the United States the option of limiting such a war on the European continent.[37]

The deployment of INF, then, raised the question of the real credibility of NATO's deterrent strategy. Doubts about the extended deterrence and deterrence itself began to be openly voiced in Germany. If deterrence failed, the world would be lost in a nuclear war, and if nuclear war-fighting strategies were a key part of NATO's defense doctrine, the odds of a nuclear war in Europe increased. Therefore, whether the United States chose to modernize weapons or not, the effect for Europeans on both sides of the issue seemed to be the same: an increased danger of nuclear war in Europe. From 1979 to 1980, the proportion of people who considered a new world war probable increased from 20 percent (a figure which had been consistent since 1950) to 59 percent.[38]

This increased fear of nuclear war gave birth to the idea of "common security"—an idea which quickly began to compete with the idea of nuclear deterrence in Europe. In 1982, the Independent Commission on Disarmament and Security Issues (the Palme Commission) published a report entitled *Common Security* which argued that in a nuclear age, the notion of security based on deterrence and military superiority was no longer feasible. It suggested that with the survival of all countries at stake, real security involved a reduction of tensions and mutual efforts to achieve security.[39] Implementing the concept of common security would break down the postwar division of Europe and create conditions for a pan-European order of nonmilitary and demilitarizing forms of competition and cooperation.

Some political elites within the SPD began to argue that once the notion of common security began to define the military situation in Europe, NATO could start to develop new force postures which were less aggressive. These included "nonprovocative defense," "reasonable sufficiency," "no first use," further arms control talks, and the withdrawal of offensive forces from forward areas.[40] As the credibility of America's deterrence strategy in Europe weakened, room had been created for the birth of alternative definitions of security.

These alternative definitions and the peace movement which propagated them received growing support beginning in the early 1980s. Public support for the peace movement peaked in 1983–84, after the deployment of INF missiles.[41] The movement's immediate goal was the prevention of the INF deployment; in addition, it fought for the dissolution of the military alliances. Nonetheless, new strategies for common security and defensive force postures in Europe were not accepted by the majority of the German population. The double-track decision initially received more support than opposition, mostly because people hoped that successful negotiations between the United States and the Soviet Union would make deployment unnecessary.[42] As deployment neared, however, two-thirds of the population opted against deploying the new missiles.[43] Despite doubts about the credibility of the U.S. nuclear commitment, the "habit of multilateralism" had clearly been entrenched. Most Germans wanted to remain in NATO and supported nuclear deterrence. In the end, a two-thirds majority of the population opted against the deployment of the INF despite an obvious commitment to the West.[44]

In sum, the double-track decision and INF deployment undermined the cold war consensus on German security policy. As the 1980s began, domestic politics were characterized by the sharp antagonism between exclusive supporters of the alliance (CDU/CSU) and those who tried to reconcile support for the alliance with detente with the East (SPD in coalition with the FDP). Because a reconciliation was not possible and political forces in favor of tight Westbindung were stronger, the decision for deployment was assured.

THE INF TREATY AND BURDEN-SHARING: DOUBTS ABOUT THE U.S. DEFENSE COMMITMENT

While the INF deployment controversy raised the possibility of alternative notions of security and cast doubt on the credibility of NATO's basic deterrent strategy, the Reykjavik summit of 1986 and the INF treaty cast more doubt on U.S. willingness to defend Europe in case of Soviet attack. Most military elites and political elites within the CDU had believed that the Soviets would leave some INF missiles in Europe , so that some U.S. INF range missiles would remain as well. This would have relieved fears of decoupling. Decoupling was perceived as a growing problem because the INF Treaty prohibited the United States from placing nuclear weapons in Europe with a range sufficient to reach Soviet territory. NATO's flexible response doctrine after the INF Treaty relied on a mixture of nuclear artillery, mines, aircraft-delivered ordinance, and eighty-eight Lance missile launchers with a range under one hundred miles. With the mid-range rung in the escalation ladder removed, decoupling seemed inevitable.

President Ronald Reagan's goal at the Reykjavik summit to "eliminate all ballistic missiles from the face of the earth" by 1996 confirmed long-held European (and especially French) military elite fears of Washington's unwillingness to defend their continent. In Reykjavik's wake, France moved toward closer military contacts with West Germany, so as to revive the West European Union (WEU) and to build a more integrated and independent West European defense effort. Atlantic unity seemed threatened in the face of increasing French-German coziness.

Furthermore, throughout the 1980s, the burgeoning budget deficit in the United States pressured the country to cut back on its forces in Europe and push for increased European defense contributions. European political and military elites, however, had a different response to America's changing role. For them, leadership of the alliance, not burden-sharing was the key issue. But it was the end of the cold war which contributed most clearly to the expansion of Germany's defense options.

THE WANING OF THE SOVIET THREAT: DOUBTS ABOUT THE NECESSITY OF DETERRENCE

The rapid introduction of Soviet foreign policy initiatives and concessions under Gorbachev in the late 1980s reduced the fear of the Soviet threat and thereby reduced public perceptions of the need for dependence on the U.S. defense shield. Gorbachev's proposal to unilaterally reduce Warsaw Pact troop strength in Europe, as well as the Soviet agreement to withdraw troops from Afghanistan, negotiate peace settlements in southern Africa and Cambodia, and relax control over Eastern Europe, triggered important changes in the West European public perception of the Soviet threat. The nightmare of a Soviet military invasion which had haunted many Europeans began to fade. In 1962, 63 percent of the population believed in a "Communist threat." In 1988, only 11 percent of those polled felt that the Soviet Union threatened world peace, as opposed to 71 percent in 1980.[45] In 1989, 59 percent of the population had "trust" in Gorbachev, and 9 percent had "great trust" in Gorbachev. In 1990, fear of the Soviet military threat placed seventeenth in a list of possible public concerns.[46]

These sentiments put yet another strain on German-American relations.* The debate over Lance missile modernization was a quintessential symbol of this strain. As noted, eighty-eight Lance missile launchers were deployed mostly in Germany because their short range and small yield made them especially suitable for use on a relatively narrow battlefield such as the two Germanies. Pressure for modernization came from the United States, which made it an issue of loyalty to the alliance. In the wake of the INF Treaty, U.S. officials argued that these aging short-range missiles must be modernized to preserve deterrence. Gorbachev's initiatives and the increasing popularity of the common security idea, however, dimmed support for early modernization. Many viewed arms control talks as a more stable road to peace than nuclear modernization. Many

---

*Indeed relations between the two countries had reached a nadir with the embarrassing exposure of the participation of German firms in the construction of the Rabta chemical weapons plant in Libya and the Kohl government's inept response. The coalition parties were extremely weak in winter/spring 1989. In the Berlin state elections on 29 January 1989, the CDU/FDP ruling coalition lost its majority, while the FDP failed even to get 5 percent. In addition, the CDU/CSU was facing a challenge on its right flank from the Republikaner.

West Germans, fearing that in a war such weapons would fall on German soil, argued that improvements should be deferred until conventional stability talks between NATO and the Warsaw Pact countries were well underway. Progress in the talks, it was believed, would most likely result in public pressure not to modernize the Lance missile, despite U.S. protests that modernization was required for more negotiating leverage with the Soviets. Furthermore, short-range missiles had not yet been covered in any negotiating forum, and West Germany, Italy, Denmark, Norway, and Spain lobbied within NATO for the creation of such a forum.

In the face of growing opposition to the missiles in Europe, U.S. Defense Secretary Frank Carlucci threatened darkly that the United States might withdraw troops from Germany if Bonn banned nuclear weapons from German territory. Obsolete Lance missiles would mean a "structural disarmament" of NATO because the Warsaw Pact had deployed 1,400 comparable short-range weapons, most of which were stationed in the GDR.[47] U.S. officials were therefore determined to build a "firebreak" around these weapons to prevent the alliance from sliding any farther along the slippery slope of denuclearization.

Since the majority of these forces were on German territory and faced a Soviet force of some 1,400 short-range missiles, some German politicians began to raise the issues of singularization again. This view was quickly accepted across the political spectrum. It was felt that the majority of weapons would fall on Germany; therefore Germany was bearing an unequal burden. "The shorter the reach, the deader the Germans," the slogan became. Hanrieder writes,

> Considering the pro-American credentials of such prominent German conservatives, they could hardly be accused of harboring neutralist tendencies. Opposition in Germany to the new missiles ranged across the entire political spectrum, prompting the SPD to speak of the emergence of a "new consensus" on foreign and defense policy.[48]

Public opinion was rapidly corresponding to a shift in perceptions among the political elite. In early 1988, despite continued support of NATO and ties with the United States, 68 percent of Germans rejected modernization, 79 percent wanted the removal of all nuclear weapons from German territory, and 57 percent said they would not feel vulnerable to Soviet pressure without nuclear weapons.[49]

In 1989 Foreign Minister Hans-Dietrich Genscher began to publicly oppose the Lance modernization. In mid-April of that year, his office leaked a report on NATO's February/March Wintex-Climex exercises. In these exercises the American president orders a nuclear strike on advancing Warsaw Pact forces. All but one of the weapons is launched from Germany; three hit the GDR, one the Soviet Union, one lands in Turkey, and the rest in Eastern Europe. The exercise confirmed all the suspicions that war would be limited to German soil. Although Genscher had broken a NATO pledge not to take any action that might undermine public confidence in deterrence, the leak strengthened his position in the coalition.

Genscher's position on the Lance prevailed. Within days, the coalition produced a position paper which followed Genscher's line. The paper called for 1) modernization "where necessary," 2) a decision on a follow-on to the Lance in 1992 if this was necessary, and 3) immediate negotiations on the SNF. Only a few days before this position was made public U.S. Secretary of Defense Richard Cheney thought he had reached an agreement in which the United States would put off the decision to modernize if the Germans would back off from SNF negotiations. Now Kohl was in the uncomfortable position of alienating his allies and CDU Atlanticists.

President George Bush's solution at NATO's fortieth jubilee offered Kohl a way to accommodate the United States without making an unpopular political commitment. The compromise called for SNF negotiations to begin after a CFE agreement had been reached and reductions begun. The goal of negotiations would be a "partial" reduction in SNF. No decision on modernization would be made until 1992.

The Lance debate revealed positions within the ruling coalition which were reinforced by the cold war's end and which signaled the end of NATO's flexible response policy, as well as the end of extended deterrence in its current form. In the aftermath of the Lance debate, various proposals emerged for drastically reducing U.S. troop strength in Germany.[50] This was significant because in the past that idea had always met with deep concern among the German conservative political elite. Even before the cold war's end, these proposals had become acceptable, signaling Germany's declining dependence on the United States for defense. Although these positions were originally voiced in the SPD, they began to gather momentum across the political spectrum.[51]

In the May 1990 meeting of NATO defense ministers, German defense minister Stoltenberg urged the withdrawal of all nuclear artillery and ground-based missiles from German soil.[52] Germany's voice had weight within the alliance. At the July 1990 NATO summit, it was decided that all NATO nuclear-tipped artillery would be withdrawn from Europe and the Lance would not be modernized. The upshot of this decision was that there would be no ground-based nuclear weapons in Europe. Since these weapons will be withdrawn, most of the European "rungs" in the nuclear escalation ladder will have been removed. This means that NATO's nuclear capability will probably be air-based. Air-based systems are, of course, vulnerable to attack in a conventional war. This vulnerability may lead Europeans to call on the United States to continue its strategy of extended deterrence in a new form: long-range, sea-based ballistic missiles, cruise missiles, or missiles and bombers based in the United States.[53]

GERMANY'S EMERGING ROLE IN SHAPING EUROPEAN SECURITY ARRANGEMENTS

As the 1990s opened, the first stage in defining Germany's role in Europe's security future was shaped by the need to assure its neighbors that it would not revert to unilateral aggressive policies and to assure its allies that it would not resort to "neutralism." Germany was again trapped between East and West. Kohl affirmed a steadfast commitment to NATO, but he accepted limitations on German military power in order to allay Soviet fears of German military strength within NATO. Furthermore, Kohl, Genscher, and leading SPD politicians joined to endorse a much greater role in the CSCE, including the creation of permanent CSCE institutions.

Within the government coalition, commitment to multilateralism is strong: there is no support for German neutrality and steady commitment to NATO membership (including membership in the integrated command structure). Nonetheless, Kohl, Genscher, and Stoltenberg have suggested that NATO take on a greater political role in developing cooperative relations with Eastern Europe and that it change its strategy and structure to make it more acceptable to the Soviet Union.[54] The continuation of NATO is essential in order to maintain the West European security connection to the United States. At the same time, they have called for the greater "Europeanization" of security responsibilities, particularly bringing France into a new defense framework. German government officials frequently refer to a non-NATO security organization that could be built on the basis of the EC and the WEU and extended to include Eastern Europe. It is envisaged as eventually becoming a "European Security Union," a CSCE alternative with defense capabilities. For example, Willy Wimmer, the parliamentary state secretary in the defense ministry, endorses the creation of a new security structure within the EC. Such a structure, officials argue, would be an important component of European political integration. It should not be overlooked, however, that Germany, as the most economically powerful member of the EC, would be dominant in a European security structure. Thus this view appeals to the German "Gaulists" and members of the SPD who, for different reasons, want to circumscribe the influence of the United States in West European security matters.[55]

Finally, the chancellor and foreign minister have also endorsed the CSCE as the appropriate framework for "new peacemaking structures in Europe," but not as a replacement for NATO.[56] In these endorsements there is clearly a move to distribute some responsibility for security to an alternative institution that includes Eastern participation. It appears that the need to include the former Soviet Union in Europe "will remain a driving factor in a continuing German interest in the gradual institutionalization of the CSCE process."[57]

In contrast, the strategy of common security is accepted doctrine among Social Democrats.[58] The SPD advocates the gradual integration of the Soviet Union and Eastern Europe into a pan-European security order. The SPD differs from the CDU on the issues of German membership in NATO and the future role of the CSCE as a preferred substitute to the existing alliances. The SPD has reaffirmed its position that Germany's membership in NATO should continue during the transition to a new security order, but insists, as it did throughout the 1980s, that NATO fully transform its defense posture into one which is incapable of offensive operations. This would require abandoning traditional NATO policies such as forward defense, flexible response, and threatened nuclear first-use. SPD elites are not united in their view of German participation in NATO. Some believe that NATO membership requires the elimination of the integrated military command structure, while others stress continued German membership in that structure.[59] The SPD further advocates that all nuclear and chemical weapons be removed from Germany and that German armed forces be drastically reduced. Finally, the SPD endorses the CSCE as the preferred "architecture" for a new European security order. It calls for the creation of agencies within the CSCE to verify arms control agreements and establish confidence-building measures, manage crises, resolve conflicts, coordinate military aerial reconnaissance and air surveillance, and create a European security council that includes the foreign affairs and defense ministers of member states.

The FDP position is midway between the CDU and the SPD. In a speech before the German Society for Foreign Policy, Genscher outlined his view of future security arrangements for Germany and Europe. NATO has a place as a stabilizing factor during the transition period, after which the alliance's military emphasis must be reduced in favor of its political character. Ultimately NATO will become little more than a wing within an enlarged and institutionalized CSCE. The United States and Canada must remain linked to Europe through this institution, but a "new architecture" must govern the relationship of the North Americans with the European Political Union.[60]

In sum, although there appears to be an emerging consensus on Germany's future defense policy which both reaffirms the commitment to multilateralism and reconciles Germany's historic tension between bonds with the West and ties to the East, there will be domestic battles ahead over the institutional framework of the future European security order. The CSCE is a "security community" and NATO is a military alliance; the two may be incompatible, and the East-West tension in German foreign policy may rear its head yet again.

CONSTRAINTS ON GERMANY'S FUTURE GLOBAL ROLE

Although Germany has expanded its maneuvering space in foreign policy over the last forty years, its global freedom of action is constrained by three sets of factors: a slowly growing fragmentation of party politics; the lack of a German "mission" in international affairs; and the weight of the multilateral commitments of the past decades. While the defeat of German hypernationalism poses problems for forging a consensus on its role as a global player, the shifting terrain of domestic party politics may prove to be an even greater obstacle in determining Germany's new security positions (and other foreign policy stands). Further, the engagement of Germany in a number of international organizations and treaties will restrain Germany from formulating a fully independent foreign policy position.

PARTY FRAGMENTATION

The stability of German governments and their policy formation process has depended heavily on the fact that a small number of parties with noticeably different programs attract the majority of the votes. This has been assured throughout most of the history of (West) Germany by two measures: the system of proportional representation, and the 5 percent clause (Sperrklausel). The system of proportional representation has meant that German governments are coalition governments. The so-called 5 percent clause, which bars parties with less than 5 percent of the vote from representative political bodies, has prevented the fragmentation of the party system for a long time. Between the mid-1950s and the early 1980s one of the two large parties (the SPD or the CDU/CSU) has formed a coalition government with the small FDP.

This stable but flexible system whereby a big governing party could become a big opposition party and vice versa—with a small party switching sides—was slowly but steadily undermined during the 1980s. While until the mid-1970s the SPD and CDU/CSU could collect 91.2 percent of the vote, in 1987 their share had declined to 81.3 percent.[61] This trend continued during the first elections of the newly unified Germany; in the elections of December 1990, the SPD and CDU/CSU won 77.3 percent of the vote.[62]

New parties emerged and overcame—at least on the local and state levels—the 5 percent clause. The Greens, a new party, managed to stay in the federal parliament for almost a decade. Because of the uniqueness of the recent federal elections (where it sufficed for a party to overcome the Sperrklausel in either of the two former German states to gain entry to the parliament), there are now three small parties in the Bundestag. The emergence of a fourth party in the early 1980s and the threat of further small parties entrenching themselves for a longer time in state and federal parliaments upset the established routines of power.

There are three reasons for the erosion of the "two-and-a-half party system." First, party loyalty has disintegrated over the past decades. The long-held wisdom in political science that cleavages along religious, sociographic, and class lines determine party adherence has been falsified in some respects. New cleavages—materialism vs. post-materialism, ecological vs. industrial modernization—have evolved and superimposed themselves over the old cleavages. Second, the core constituencies of the big parties (industrial workers for the SPD, small business and farmers for the CDU/CSU) are shrinking as the German economy shifts from an industrial to a service economy. Finally, new forms of extraparliamentary political participation have emerged. Some social groups support "anti-party" parties such as the Greens or the Republikaner. These threads—if they continue to unravel further—will have one major consequence: it will be more difficult to form a stable and viable government. The securing of *Mehrheitsfahifkeit* for the big parties will become increasingly hard. These big parties will need to depend more on the small parties if they want to stay in power; hence they will become more open to the often extreme interests of their junior partners. Elections will become more embattled over time. There is now the prospect of the "Italianization" of German government politics—discord among the patchwork of coalition partners in government and the permanent reshaping of government coalitions.

GERMAN IDENTITY

Germany may have become independent again since the unification of the two former states, but for cultural and ideological reasons Germany is definitely not yet ready to act like a great power. The flip side of the thorough defeat of hypernationalism after two attempts at global (or at least trans-European) power status is the utter lack of any positive definition of Germany's role in the world. The acceptance of the defeat of its world-power ambitions in 1945 and the Westbindungs decision of the 1950s meant that for forty years Germany would not play an independent role in world (security) politics. In addition, Germany is still entangled in the moral consequences of its war crimes and the genocide of the Jews.

As we saw above, nationalism or patriotism, which feeds on a population's pride in the "achievements" of a nation and which has provided the ideological guidelines for Germany's past foreign policies, no longer functions as a basis for pursuing national security interests in today's Germany. In the early 1960s, philosopher Karl Jaspers summed up this widespread impression, one which still seems to be shared by a majority of Germans:

> The history of the German nation-state, not the history of the Germans, has come to an end. What we as a great nation can do for ourselves and the world is to understand the present world situation: that the idea of the nation-state is an evil for Europe and for all continents.[63]

In past decades liberals and conservatives have attempted to fill this ideological gap in German identity. The German "dilemma" was insufficiently patched over by the conservative distinction between Germany as a *Kulturnation* (nation as a culture) and *Staatsnation* (nation as a state); this distinction was meant to instill pride in the German cultural heritage even though the political history was not conducive to patriotic feelings. The liberal idea of *Verfassungspatriotismus* (pride in the constitution) was a similarly hapless effort to provide some ideological counterweight to the conservative patriotic program. The only source of satisfaction in national achievements for the Germans came from their economic prosperity. *Wirtschaftsnationalismus* (pride in economic achievement) is, however, only a *Schrumpfform* of nationalism.[64]

Until the unification of the two Germanies Wirtschaftsnationalismus was a sufficiently plausible form of nationalism. Now almost all pillars of the postwar domestic consensus in Germany are more or less eroding. As we saw above, the military aspect of Westbindung is becoming questionable the more concepts of common security or a Common European Home gain support in Germany.

GERMAN MULTILATERALISM

The third constraint on Germany's role in international politics is the web of affiliations and treaties by which Germany has bound itself to the system of international organizations. While this is also true for world powers like the United States, Germany's multilateralism has been the result of a combination of deliberate action and prodding by its European and transatlantic allies. This was expressed in Adenauer's initial decision to opt for Westbindung because—from a CDU/CSU perspective—it was seen as the only viable path toward regaining respectability in the "family of nations," and even toward reconstructing German unity.

German multilateralism has become a habit of self-restraint and even shying away from leadership, so much that one critic of Germany's role in international politics has blamed Germany for switching from *Machtversessenheit* (obsession with power) to *Machtvergessenheit* (being oblivious to power).[65] A recent example of the latter can be found in a statement of Bjorn Engholm, the new leader of Germany's opposition party, the Social Democrats. During an interview with the *New York Times* he stated:

> If in the place of General Schwarzkopf there had been a German general [in the Gulf War of 1991], and if that German general was on television every evening giving reports about the progress of German troops in the field, I don't think people in America or England or France would be so happy.[66]

REACTION TO THE GULF WAR IN GERMANY: A PARTIAL TEST OF THE ARGUMENT

As the 1990s began, it was the Persian Gulf which opened the debate over Germany's future military role in the world. The debate provided a testing ground for examining the willingness of the German public as well as political elites to take advantage of Germany's new weight in global politics.

The focus of the debate was on the *Bündnisfall*. The possibility that Germany might be dragged into the conflict by an Iraqi attack on Turkey, a member of NATO, was the source of much intraparty disagreement. While Article 5 of the NATO treaty binds all members of the organization to the collective defense of all other members, Article 11 says the partner states will act according to the corresponding procedures of their constitutions in doing so. Article 115A of the German constitution states that a two-thirds majority of the Bundestag must declare a *Verteidigungsfall* before German troops can be engaged. Whether Germany had automatically transferred authority to declare a defensive action to NATO was the source of heated political dispute in the Gulf War context.[67]*

The Gulf crisis revealed a split within the political elite over the appropriate role of the German military in international conflicts. Kohl suggested that the constitution be amended to allow the military to participate in out-of-area activities, arguing that the military had a responsibility to participate in actions defined by Chapter 7 of the UN Charter.[68] Some elements of the CDU and CSU (Teltschik, Boetsch) argued for fully sovereign German armed forces. But as we saw above, this would be unlikely to win FDP and SPD approval. In the Gulf War, Kohl would have liked to pursue Adenauer's traditional policy of winning autonomy by proving his trustworthiness to NATO, but instead found himself restricted by domestic and constitutional factors.

More than other German parties, the SPD was divided on issues rising from the war. Barely overcoming a challenge from its left wing, the SPD endorsed UN Resolution 678.[69] In contradiction to Stoltenberg and NATO General Secretary Woerner, the SPD rejected an automatic Bündnisfall if Iraq had attacked Turkey. Instead, according to the SPD, the Bundestag would have had to approve deployment by a two-thirds majority. This position found some resonance in the FDP and CDU. SPD foreign policy expert Karsten Voigt argued that no Bündnisfall would arise if an Iraqi attack was provoked by U.S. attacks from Turkish airbases. Internally the party remained split for several weeks between those who wanted an immediate unconditional cease-fire (Lafontaine, Schroeder) and those who wanted a cease-fire which was conditional on an Iraqi

*As the Bundesverfassungsgericht had decided in 1985 was the case with the Pershing II deployments.

pullout from Kuwait (Rau). In line with its preference for multi-lateralism—but not the same multilateral institutions preferred by the CDU—and in line with its criticism of Westbindung, the SPD used the occasion of the Gulf crisis to argue that German partici-pation in world conflicts should be linked to the United Nations rather than to the United States.

Genscher's overwhelming presence in all party discussions of security and foreign policy largely spared the FDP the kind of internal debate found in the SPD. On the other hand, the FDP was very vague about its position. Some internal dissent remains as to what constitutes a Bündnisfall. Feldman, a party expert on interna-tional relations, argued that an Iraqi attack on Turkey should not precipitate a NATO response since it would have been provoked by the United States, while Lambsdorff argued that even a rocket attack would represent a Bündnisfall.[70] The party also supported parliamentary consultation before troops are deployed, but hedged on the issue of whether such consultation would be binding on the government, and (if so) whether a two-thirds or simple majority could approve deployment. Genscher was determined to minimize Bonn's participation in the hostilities.

As long as Kohl wishes to base the new role of the military on a change of the constitution, the opposition has some influence on the decision (because of the necessity to win two-thirds of the parliamentary vote for a change of the constitution). If, however, the government decides to go ahead with out-of-area missions for the Bundeswehr without changing the constitution, public debate will intensify. It is easy to forecast the outcome of this debate: a decision for more German participation in UN actions will be made. But it is not at all easy to foresee answers to the more important question of what kind of preferences the government and the op-position will develop concerning the institutional frame of the future European security order: CSCE or NATO, including or ex-cluding the East European states?

CONCLUSION

Assuming that the factors that point in the direction of more maneuvering space for Germany weigh less than factors that restrain Germany's freedom of action, we come to the conclusion that Germany will continue to adhere to a policy of multilateralism in international security politics. The newly won sovereignty of Germany will, however, mean that its obligations and responsibilities will increase. Security politics will become more complicated for Germany because it has to play in different games at the same time: in the Western alliance (NATO), in a yet to be designed security order with Eastern Europe, and in the global system (the United Nations and out-of-area activities of NATO).

Three questions need to be answered in the immediate future. First, should Germany (and Europe) fully denuclearize, or should they rely on some (last resort) type of nuclear deterrence? Second, should Germany commit itself to NATO and other Western alliances, or should it participate in the construction of a European security system which would include the East European states and the former Soviet Union? Third, should Germany participate in global security politics through the United Nations, or should it restrict its security interests to Europe?

In many respects these are not polar alternatives, but points on a scale that might suggest a shift of emphasis to German political elites. It is, for instance, imperative for the German state to bind the former Soviet Union into a system of mutual trust and nonaggression. For this reason, Germany will not want NATO to pursue or resume an explicit deterrence strategy. On the other hand, Germany will not want to give up American nuclear protection as long as the former Soviet Union has nuclear weapons that can reach German territory.

The risks of German security policy lie in the form and consequences of the transformation process: how to give up a threatening posture toward the former Soviet Union and balance this with the American interest in securing an influential position in Europe. Germany has to make difficult decisions which no doubt will be made within the context of multilateralism. But the *Gestalt* of these multilateral institutions, depending on whether Germany is more interested in accommodating the former Soviet Union or the United

States, might vary substantially. It seems probable that the long-term trend will be the Europeanization of German security policy and that the main hardship for German security policy will lie in relinquishing its comfortable position of free-riding behind the American shield.

It seems possible that in the end Germany will be deprived of old security guarantees and confronted with insufficient new security arrangements. This might then set the stage for Germany's pursuit of full-fledged military sovereignty. This would not itself pose a risk to Europe if the international climate remains stable and the domestic resilience against nationalist definitions of a German mission stays intact.

NOTES

1. See the contribution by Jane M. O. Sharp in this volume.

2. "Unified Germany Is Top Exporter," *San Francisco Chronicle*, 26 March 1991, p. C1.

3. Quoted in Kenneth N. Waltz, "The Emerging Structure of International Politics"; paper presented at the American Political Science Association meeting, August 1990, p. 21.

4. "Kohl will raus aus Nische der Weltpolitik," *Die Tageszeitung*, 31 January 1991, pp. 1 and 8.

5. Michael Gordon, "NATO to Cut Back Training Program," *New York Times*, 24 May 1990.

6. Treaty on the Final Settlement with Respect to Germany, 12 September 1990; reprinted in *Survive*, November/December 1990, pp. 560–61.

7. Craig Whitney, "Gulf Fighting Shatters Europeans' Fragile Unity," *New York Times*, 25 January 1991, p. A7.

8. "The New Germany," *The Economist*, 3 June 1990.

9. Hans-Ulrich Wehler, *Das Deutsche Kaiserreich, 1871–1918* (Gottingen: Vandenhoeck and Ruprecht, 1988), pp. 179–82.

10. Stefan Hradil, *Sozialstrukturanalyse in einer fortgenschrittenen Gesellschaft* (Opladen: Leske and Budrich, 1987), pp. 19–20.

11. See Hans Joachim Veen, *A Protest Movement rather than a Political Party: The Republikaners between Right Wing Extremism and Pent-Up Discontent* (Washington, D.C.: Konrad Adenauer Stiftung, 1989), p. 12; Occasional Paper Series, no. 11–89.

12. Erwin K. Scheuch, "Die Suche nach der Besonderheit der heutigen Deutschen," *Koelner Zeitschrift fuer Soziologie und Sozialphychologie*, no. 4 (1990): 734–52.

13. Dieter Roth, "Sind die Republikaner die fuenfte Partei? Sozialund Meinungsstrunktur der Waehler der Republikaner," *Aus Politik und Zeitgeschichte*, 1989, pp. 41–42/89.

14. Scheuch (note 12), pp. 737–38. Eurobarometer analyses and other data show that most Germans do not support racist movements and parties (Scheuch, pp. 742–43). The overall impression that Germans make in the light of survey research is a comparatively high "acceptance of their societal conditions in conjunction with mild apathy toward public affairs" (*ibid.*, p. 748).

15. Wolfram Hanrieder, *Germany, America, Europe: Forty Years of German Foreign Policy* (New Haven and London: Yale University Press, 1989), p. 353.

16. Scheuch (note 12), p. 739.

17. Emnid-Institut, "Besonders wichtig ist die Einheit nur wenigen," *Der Spiegel*, 22/1990 (28 May 1990): 44.

18. See David Marsh, "Today's Germans: Peacable, Fearful and Green," *Financial Times*, 4 January 1991, p.2.

19. "Jeder Dritte fuer die Neutralitaet," *Der Spiegel*, 44/1984, p. 43, and 9/1989, p. 51.

20. See Europaeische Gruene, "Erklaerung der Europaeischen Gruenen zur KSZE-Sonderkonferenz in Paris, 27–28 October 1990" (1990), and Die Gruenen AG Gesamteuropa (Bundestagsfraktion), "Gesamteuropaeische Integration" (Bonn), 30 September 1990.

21. See Michael Mastanduno, "Strategies of Economic Containment: United States Trade Relations with the Soviet Union," *World Politics* 37 (July 1985): 503–31.

22. NSC 68, the blueprint for waging the cold war, stated that "foreign economic policy is a major instrument in the conduct of the United States foreign relations . . . particularly appropriate to the Cold War" (see "United States Objectives and Proposals for National Security"; a Report to the National Security Council, 14 April 1950 (NSC 68; mimeo), p. 28.

23. For an excellent history of the origins of this policy, see Robert A. Pollard, *Economic Security and the Origins of the Cold War, 1945–1950* (New York: Columbia University Press, 1985).

24. Konrad Adenauer, *Memoirs 1945–1953*, trans. Beate Ruhm von Oppen (Chicago: Henry Regney Company, 1966), p. 431.

25. An early statement of this view is spelled out in a study conducted by the Economic Commission for Europe (ECE), which stated that the flow of goods in Europe should be allowed to take its "natural" course (ECE Ad Hoc Committee on Industrial Development and Trade, United Nations, ECOSOC, E/ECE/10/2, 14 August 1948).

26. For a more extensive discussion of conflicting U.S. and European views of the Soviet Union, see Miles Kahler, "The United States and Western Europe: The Diplomatic Consequences of Mr. Reagan," in *Eagle Resurgent? The Reagan Era in American Foreign Policy*, ed. Kenneth A. Oye, Robert J. Lieber, and Donald Rotchild (Boston: Little, Brown, 1987), pp. 304–6.

27. During 1945–46 this was also the prevailing view in American official circles, but by mid-1947, tho goal of trade denial took the dominant position (see Pollard (note 23), p. 162.

28. For the British bxpression of this view see Elisabeth Barker, *The British Between the Superpowers, 1945–1950* (Toronto: University of Toronto Press, 1983), pp. 209–13.

29. See Hans-Karl Rupp, *Ausserparlamentarische Opposition in der Aera Adenauer* (Cologne: Pahl-Rugenstein, 1970). Policy platform also tended toward a more neutral role for Germany in international affairs. In 1959, however, the SPD "approved declarations ranging from approval of the 'defense of the country' to promises of the present and future allegiance to the Atlantic Alliance." This change was motivated by domestic electoral considerations rather than ideological beliefs (see Catherine Kelleher, *Germany and the Politics of Nuclear Weapons* [New York: Columbia University Press, 1975], p. 115).

30. See Hanrieder (note 15), p. 343.

31. Jost Halfmann, "After the Unification: A New German Assertiveness?," and Christine Schoefer, "The Discussion of National Identity in West Germany: A Discourse for Self-Assertion?," both in *The New Europe Asserts Itself*, ed. Beverly Crawford and Peter W. Schulze (Berkeley: International and Area Studies, University of California, 1990).

32. For an elaboration of the content of this accord, see Dietrich Traenhardt, *Geschichte der Bundesrepublik* (Frankfurt: Suhrkamp, 1986), p. 183.

33. See, for example, Wolf D. Gruner, *Die deutsche Frage: Ein Problem der europaeischen Geschichte seit 1800* (Munich: C. H. Beck, 1985), pp. 176–203.

34. See Hanrieder (note 15), p. 356.

35. *Ibid.*, pp. 110–11.

36. *Ibid.*, p. 112.

37. On the problem of escalation, see Barry Posen, "Inadvertent Nuclear War? Escalation and NATO's Northern Flank," *International Security*, 7, 2 (Fall 1982). On the relationship between escalation and decoupling, see Jeffrey D. Boutwell, Paul Doty, and Gregory F. Treverton, eds., *The Nuclear Confrontation in Europe* (Dover, Mass.: Auburn House, 1985).

38. "Mehrheit fuerchtet Weltkrieg," *Der Spiegel* 5/1980, p. 23, and "Jeder Dritte hofft auf die Null-Loesung," *Der Spiegel* 48/1981, p.57.

39. *Common Security 1982: A Programme for Disarmament*; Report of the Independent Commission on Disarmament and Security Issues under the Chairmanship of Olaf Palme, London, 1982.

40. For a detailed discussion of common security, the political coalitions which both support and oppose it, and the implications for NATO's force posture, see Michael Lucas, "The United States and Post-INF Europe," *World Policy Journal* 5, 2 (Spring 1988): 183–233.

41. Karl-Heinz Reuband, "Die Friedensbewegung nach Stationierungsbeginn," *Sicherheit und Frieden*, no. 3 (1985): 153.

42. Dieter Just and Peter Caspar Muehlhens, "Zur Wechselbeziehung von Politik und Demoskopie," *Aus Politik und Zeitgeschichte* , B 32/81 (1981): 63–68, and "NATO-Doppelbeschluss: Meinungswechsel unter den Waehlern," *Der Spiegel*, 6/1983, p. 90.

43. Reuband (note 41), p. 151.

44. *Ibid.*

45. Wolfgang T. Schlauch, "Defense and Security: The SPD and East-West Relations in the 1980's," *Politics and Society in Germany, Austria and Switzerland* 3, 1 (1990): 3.

46. "What West Germans Think," *The Economist*, 30 June 1990, p. 46.

47. See Hanrieder (note 15), p. 365.

48. *Ibid.*

49. Ronald Asmus, "West Germany Faces Modernization," *Survival*, November/December 1988, pp. 499–512.

50. Keith B. Payne and Michael Ruehle, "The Future of the Alliance: Emerging German Views," *Strategic Review*, Winter 1990, p. 38.

51. See Karsten D. Voigt, "Eine Europaeische Friedensordnung ohne den Ungeist des Nationalismus," *Europaeische Wehrkunde*, March 1990, p. 150.

52. See Craig R. Whitney, "NATO Allies, after 40 Years, Proclaim End of Cold War; Invite Gorbachev to Speak," *New York Times*, 7 July 1990, p. 1, and Michael R. Gordon, "A New Face for NATO," *New York Times*, 8 July 1990, p. 1.

53. Payne and Ruehle (note 50), p. 41.

54. See Whitney, "NATO Allies" (note 52), p. 4.

55. The most comprehensive discussion of these issues can be found in Payne and Ruehle (note 50), pp. 40–42.

56. See Christoph Bertram, "Old Europe Is Dead—Long Live the New," *Die Zeit*; reprinted in *World Press Review*, September 1990, p. 14.

57. Payne and Ruehle (note 50), p. 39.

58. Schlauch (note 45), p. 12.

59. See, for example, Karsten D. Voigt, "Sicherheitspolitische Konflikte in Mittel- und Osteuropa- potentielle Risiken und Wege zu ihrer Einhegung" (Bonn, 4 February 1991); mimeo.

60. See Hans Dietrich Genscher, "Die neue Europaeische Friedensordnung," *Europa-Archiv*, 8 October 1990, pp. 473–78.

61. Jost Halfmann, "Social Change and Political Mobilization in West Germany," in *Industry and Politics in West Germany*, ed. Peter Katzenstein (Ithaca and London: Cornell University Press, 1989) p. 71.

62. Wolfgang G. Gibowski and Max Kaase, "Auf dem Weg zum politischen Alltag," *Aus Politik und Zeitgeschichte*, B 11–12/91 (1991): 3.

63. Karl Jaspers, *Lebensfragen der deutschen Politik* (Munich: Deutscher Taschenbuch Verlag, 1963), p. 219 (translation by authors).

64. Jürgen Habermas, *Die nachholende Revolution* (Frankfurt: Suhrkamp, 1990), pp. 205–24.

65. Hans Peter Schwarz, Die gezaehmten Deutschen: Von der Machtbesessenheit zur Machvergessenheit (Stuttgart: Deutsche Verlagsanstalt, 1985).

66. Stephen Kinzer in *New York Times*, 16 April 1991, p. A4.

67. "Deutsche Soldaten kaum zu stoppen," *Die Tageszeitung*, 12 January 1991, p. 4.

68. "Kohl: Teilnahme an sogenannten Blauhelm-Missionen genuegt nicht," *Frankfurter Allgemeine Zeitung*, 15 March 1991, p. 4.

69. "SPD gegen den Kriegsautomatismus," *Die Tageszeitung*, 16 January 1991, p. 4.

70. "Bonner Angst vorm Buendnisfall," *Die Tageszeitung*, 19 January 1991, p. 5; "Parlamentarier widersprechen Woerner," *Die Tageszeitung*, 22 January 1991, p. 1.

CIVIL FOREIGN POLICY:
GERMAN DOMESTIC CONSTRAINTS AND NEW SECURITY ARRANGEMENTS IN EUROPE

Dieter Dettke

INTRODUCTION

The East-West conflict determined Western security policies for almost a half century after World War II. It had become such a dominant characteristic and structural element of foreign and security policies for scholars and governments in the East and in the West that many security specialists now face what Jürgen Habermas in a different context called "the new murkiness" (*die neue Unübersichtlichkeit*). Indeed security structures did not lack clarity and purpose during the cold war, but they do now, and it becomes more and more evident that the end of the East-West conflict and the demise of bipolarity is not *only* good news as far as security is concerned.

CHANGE AND SECURITY IN EUROPE

Certainly the danger of major war in Europe is radically reduced. Yet at the same time new forms of small-scale violence seem to be less constrained by the new environment. Ethnic violence in Yugoslavia is an example of the new dangers. Although we do not have to fear a situation like 1914 and an escalation of ethnic violence into a larger European conflict, security concerns for Europe remain a real problem. They are not only a pessimistic assumption. To be sure, there is no need for cold war nostalgia. After all, the cold war was not all that pleasant, with its enormous military burdens and ideological distortions. Under cold war conditions security costs were too high—politically, militarily, and economically. Now, for the first time since the end of World War II, there is an opportunity to demilitarize international relations. Today civilian policies have a much better chance for several reasons.

First of all, the revolution of 1989 was an enormous achievement for democracy and pluralism worldwide. Not only was there the implosion of communism, but also right-wing dictatorships experienced just as much pressure for change, and they too collapsed. With democracies gaining ground, peaceful international relations have a better chance too.

German unification has been part of this powerful change toward democracy. It was serendipity for the Federal Republic of Germany and was not the result of hard-driven national policies and aspirations. What paved the way for German unification was not so much a Western or German grand design, but rather the bitter consequences of political and economic failure of an authoritarian system, lack of freedom, and the absence of political legitimacy in the German Democratic Republic (GDR).[1] These enabled the democratic movements in the former GDR to take to the streets and force out the Communist leadership. At that point, large-scale repression of peaceful demonstrations was impossible.

Another important result of 1989 was a movement away from a command culture and collective interaction models toward an open exchange culture.[2] This is certainly a move in the right direction, but there is still a long way to go in order to achieve stability and functioning pluralistic institutions. The institutions of a civil society are still weak in the emerging democracies. Parties, unions, and civic groups have yet to build strength in order to be fully prepared for democratic interaction.[3]

Finally, as a third consequence of 1989, arms control in Europe has made enormous progress, unthinkable only a short time ago. Force levels in Europe are at an all time low as a result of drastic changes in the military and foreign policy of what once was the Soviet Union.

THE NEW SECURITY ENVIRONMENT

In the new security environment in Europe large standing armies like those of the former Warsaw Pact and NATO are no longer necessary. Major war in Europe can be ruled out in the foreseeable future. Russia today is still a strong military power, but it has given up a military posture that would have enabled it to launch a surprise attack on Western Europe. Today the West would have a long warning time if Russia ever contemplated such an attack. Major war would require months—not weeks or days—of mobilization for Russian forces under the present circumstances.[4]

The remaining problems of East-West military security are of a different nature, and there is some uneasiness in the new European security environment regarding the new type of conflicts and threats. These new threats are predominately non-Soviet. There are three different categories of new threats.

ETHNIC/NATIONALITY/MINORITY CONFLICTS[5]

Yugoslavia and the former Soviet Union are the two areas with the greatest potential for this type of conflict. Examples are the aspirations for independence in the Baltics, Georgia, and other republics. Yugoslavia is breaking up. Historical and religious factors add to the conflict potential in both federations. Other potential conflict areas are Czechoslovakia, where Slovaks seek more independence; Hungary and Romania, where the Hungarian minority in Romania could cause unrest; Bulgaria and its Turkish minority; and to a certain extent Poland with its German minority.

EAST/WEST AND NORTH/SOUTH MIGRATION

Although many people believe that migration is hardly a security concern, large-scale migration could well lay the ground for conflict, particularly with greater economic difficulties in Eastern Europe and the former Soviet Union. Precise figures for the possible impact of immigration in Western Europe are difficult to obtain because immigration depends on both economic conditions in the countries of origin and the capabilities of Western societies to absorb refugees. These conditions can change considerably, of course. However, there is a consensus among specialists that migration pressures will increase in the near future as a result of a combination of trends: ethnic and minority tensions, greater freedom of movement, and unemployment—according to recent figures, for example, some 20–25 million might be unemployed by 1995 in the former Soviet Union alone. These conditions will create an enormous migration potential. It will be difficult for the West to close the border for migration after so many years of pressuring the Eastern bloc countries for greater freedom of movement within the CSCE process, including the right to emigrate.[6]

REEMERGENCE OF RELIGIOUS CONFLICTS

Since the early 1980s, as a result of the Iranian revolution, Islamic fundamentalism and militancy have become an increasingly serious security problem. Islamic fundamentalism is a complex phenomenon. Although spiritual and religious in nature, it is also a social, economic, and political philosophy and vested with a propensity for violence in its political manifestation.[7] It would be wrong to perceive this as a military threat in the classical sense, but it is an additional concern for Israel and also a political and cultural challenge for the United States and the West.

As an ideology of protest against injustice, fundamentalism often articulates popular dissatisfaction and provides alienated Arab masses with a sense of commonality and assertiveness, in spite of economic misery and military humiliation.[8] There is little hope for mutual accommodation between "Western values" and Islamic objectives, particularly in view of the West's strong ties with Israel. This configuration does suggest a more protracted conflict pattern, at least as long as there is no settlement of the Arab-Israeli conflict.

These new types of conflict cannot be controlled by military means. The military in some cases might even be a problem and not a solution. For instance, in the case of ethnic and minority antagonisms, military intervention might fuel rather than stop a conflict. Also, it is impossible to stop migration with the military and refugees with rifles. There is no military solution to differences of development in North-South relations, the economic weakness of Eastern Europe and the former Soviet Union, and a lack of positive patterns of coexistence for ethnic, national, and religious minorities.

What is needed under these circumstances is economic assistance to bridge the economic gaps and provide support for democratic and federal institution-building. The crucial security problems of the future stem from the absence of functioning federal institutions and the lack of institutions of a civil society. The economic push and forward movement for human rights and democracy as a result of the crisis of authoritarianism and the collapse of dictatorship must be used for further demilitarization of security policies. What is needed in the new security environment are not large standing armies, but rather police and peace-keeping forces. These are the trends which foster and require civilian approaches to foreign policy.

The most appropriate security model for the future is neither *common security,* a concept developed by the Palme Commission which made sense in a bipolar international system,[9] nor *collective security,* a concept which threatens punishment of an aggressor by the international community after an act of aggression. The latter had been the security approach of the League of Nations, and its history is not the greatest success story. Instead a future security regime would need what John Steinbruner calls "cooperative security," a concept that is far more preventive in character and not only reactive.[10] Cooperative security is not only a superior idea in view of the remaining development tasks in North-South relations, but it is also a more realistic approach for European security issues.

In the next decade, West Germany alone will have to transfer over $1 trillion to East Germany in order to create roughly equal social and economic conditions in the two parts of Germany. To bring Eastern Europe up to West European standards of living would require ten times as much investment or more.[11]

Europe does have an interest in successful economic reform in Eastern Europe because if living conditions decline further, the potential for social and ethnic conflict will increase and possibly even endanger the emerging and still fragile democratic institutions. Economic reforms are impossible without democracy, but it is equally true that democracy can fail if economic reforms prove to be unsuccessful.[12] In Eastern Europe the task of democratic stabilization is aggravated by the poly-ethnic composition of societies. There are examples of successful poly-ethnic democracies—e.g, Switzerland. Here restraint on the part of the central government is an essential element of success. Yugoslavia and the Commonwealth of Independent States (CIS) might have to borrow some experience from the Swiss or Canadian models.

THE FOREIGN AND SECURITY POLICY OF THE NEW GERMANY IN EUROPE

With its commitment to keep the size of the German armed forces at 370,000 and to reconfirm the renunciation of nuclear, biological, and chemical weapons, Germany has made an important contribution to a European security regime based on much lower levels of military force. In addition, the German guarantee of the western Polish borders is an important element of stability. However, in order to avoid the possible danger of the psychological isolation of Germany in the new Europe, it is critical to achieve success in the area of European Community (EC) integration.

It would be a tragedy if German unity were achieved at the expense of European integration. It would be much harder to find a genuinely constructive role for Germany in Europe without a strong multilateralism based on the EC and open to Eastern and Central Europe. Even for Russia this scenario would be preferable to much more delicate bilateral ties with individual West European countries. Such a delicate bilateral relationship, for instance, would be a Rapallo-type of special relationship with Germany.

A policy of isolation vis-à-vis Russia does not make sense in the new European architecture, politically, economically, and otherwise, unless there is a relapse into authoritarianism and aggressive behavior. EC assistance programs for the former Soviet Union, like the aid program of December 1990, were designed to support the reform process.[13] The crackdown of independence movements in the Baltic in early 1990 prompted a temporary suspension of the $1 billion program, but it was resumed after the referendum on union issues.

After integration with the West in the 1950s and *Ostpolitik* in the 1970s, Germany is now in the midst of its third major foreign policy debate. The debate is still going on and far from over. The war in the Persian Gulf clearly complicated the search for a new foreign policy consensus. Expectations in other countries, particularly the United States, and German perceptions of the Gulf conflict were quite far apart, leading American observers to talk about the "expectation gap."[14] Moreover, what in American eyes under the microscope of the Gulf War appeared as German reluctance to participate in the coalition does not necessarily make the new

Germany narrow-minded, self-centered, or even isolationist.[15] Although absorbed by the process of unification, enormous economic difficulties in the East, and federal elections at the end of 1990, Germany did not renege on any of its international commitments. The German contribution to Gulf War costs—compared to that of Japan, which has a GNP three times as large as that of Germany—is substantial in financial terms alone. In addition to an $11 billion financial contribution, Germany provided essential services and facilities that contributed substantially to U.S. reinforcements and overall logistical efforts during the war.[16]

The German public, although in principle and generally in favor of the U.S. approach and its handling of the conflict, clearly wanted to stay out of direct military involvement. For good reasons, the German Basic Law (constitution) in Articles 26 and 87a limits activities of the armed forces in several ways and orders strictly defensive behavior. This has been interpreted in the past as a constitutional obstacle to an out-of-NATO-area deployment of German forces. In theory it might be possible to interpret Article 26 of the Basic Law in a way that would allow UN actions beyond the NATO area since the article opens up the possibility of joining a system of mutual collective security. Since Germany is a full member of the United Nations without any qualifications, the UN possibly could constitute such a system of mutual collective security. However, after so many years of restrictive interpretation of the constitution, it is difficult to conceive of an acceptable reinterpretation in order to participate in out-of-NATO-area contingencies. A clear and specific constitutional amendment that would allow for such activities would certainly be in order and would appear to be the only correct and consistent procedure to change the current situation, particularly since the current government and the ruling majority have used the restrictive interpretation in the past. The proper framework for out-of-NATO-area contingencies, however, should be the United Nations. NATO could not and should not try to replace the UN.

Germany has reacted in a civilian tradition toward the Gulf War, a tradition that began to take root only after World War II. Considering the former German tradition of militarism and the powerful historical influence of the military in German society—including the perversion of the military during the Third Reich—this civilian German reaction in the Gulf crisis does not deserve the strong criticism it received, especially in the United States. A recent poll published in *Süddeutsche Zeitung-Magazin* showed the interesting result that 75 percent of the Germans polled oppose involvement in military conflicts. The majority reject a German global role and view military power as unattractive. According to the poll results, Switzerland, with its concomitant values of well-being and independence, would be the model for the future Germany.[17]

A civilian orientation of German foreign policy does not necessarily prevent an international outlook and commitment. In fact, Germany is on record for having managed unification not only on the basis of the Two-plus-Four formula (the two German states plus the United States, France, Great Britain, and the Soviet Union). The process of unification has been a series of close consultations with the EC, NATO, and the CSCE as well. In addition, Germany has continued its pre-unification levels of expenditure for Third World development, despite its myriad economic difficulties. This policy signals Germany's ongoing commitment to multilateralism and global international cooperation.[18] To be sure, this is a civilian effort rather than a military one. This civilian impetus is at the heart of Germany's reaction to the Gulf War and its international political priorities. The fact that the new Germany did not use the first opportunity to expand its military role after unification should be seen as reassuring and not disturbing.[19]

THE NEW ROLE OF NATO

NATO has already started a process of transformation from a military alliance into a more political institution. U.S. Secretary of State James Baker emphasized this at an early stage of the revolution in Europe. In a major speech in Berlin on 12 December 1989, he pointed out that the new security architecture in Europe will require a reduction of the military component of NATO and an increased attention to the importance of the political element.[20]

Arms control is the key area for the new political role of NATO. In spite of the rather unceremonious death of the Warsaw Pact as a result of the changes in Europe, NATO's end is not an automatic consequence of the events of 1989. To the contrary, NATO can provide a key management role in the process of transition. It can also provide reassurance for countries with anxieties about Germany's future role in Europe. This is true not only for Central and Eastern Europe; the Soviet Union also must have seen some advantages in Germany's ties to NATO. For Russia, France, and Great Britain the expectation is that a united Germany in NATO will be less likely to develop nuclear ambitions. Fortunately, several American whisperings of a possible "managed proliferation" of nuclear weapons to Germany have not fallen on fertile ground in Germany.[21]

If Germany were to seek a nuclear role of its own in Europe, both the process of European integration and the Non-Proliferation Treaty regime would be endangered; as a result, Europe might fall back into great power competition, including a new risk of major war. The residual nuclear potential necessary to reassure Europe and to bolster extended deterrence is still an issue, but compared to the bitter debates of the early 1980s, it is much less of a problem. A zero solution for land-based short-range nuclear systems seems to be the natural course of events, and an agreement should be possible once the START Treaty is completed.

Nuclear weapons will be withdrawn from Hungary and Czechoslovakia. Germany is leaning toward the position that a withdrawal of both Russian and U.S. land-based nuclear armaments from its territory would enhance its security, not diminish it.[22] It would be difficult, if not counterproductive, for the United States to try to maintain land-based nuclear weapons in Europe, particularly since the military reasons for maintaining such weapons for extended deterrence purposes are much less compelling now. Clearly the new security environment in Europe could allow even further military reductions. If a Conventional Forces in Europe (CFE) II agreement could be reached, the remaining subregional force imbalances could be resolved too. One such imbalance is the force ratio of Russia (or the German forces, for that matter) vis-à-vis Poland, Hungary, and Czechoslovakia.[23]

It is a long way from the cold war and bipolarity to a pluralistic security community in Europe. Even with a smaller U.S. military presence, active American participation in European security policies will be necessary for maintaining stability. In the United States, this diminished military role in Europe could run into problems, especially under more difficult economic conditions. The United States and Europe are not only security partners, but they are also to some degree economic rivals. The management of transatlantic relations will become more difficult, and the quality of political consultations between Europe and the United States needs to be improved in order to prevent erosion.

For both Europe and the United States, Russia will remain a major concern. Without a U.S. role in Europe the quality of the U.S.-Russian relationship would change as well. All this indicates an even greater need for political consultation, and NATO could be helpful in this process, primarily because it is difficult to see a real alternative to NATO at the present time. Certainly the European Community needs to keep open the option of an independent security structure built around EC institutions. Full implementation of this option might take quite a while.

At the present time, the strengthening of the West European Union (WEU) seems to be the only practical avenue open to a common security policy within the EC. This would mean that the EC would concentrate on economic and political issues in the near future and achieve monetary and political union first, before shouldering the task of an independent military union. One important advantage of this new approach is that the WEU, although restricted to nine out of twelve EC countries, would constitute a bridge to the EC as well as to NATO.* This is also the most realistic approach to keep open the option of widening the EC to include the EFTA countries and the emerging democracies in Eastern and Central Europe (Poland, Hungary, Czechoslovakia).

Although the political priority for the EC has to be the deepening of EC institutions and complete political and monetary union, there is no alternative to simultaneously deepening and widening the EC structures. Deepening and widening must go together, even if Eastern Europe's "return to Europe"—as Vaclav Havel has formulated it—might take more time and preparation than anticipated.

For NATO these developments will require a certain degree of Europeanization, which should be mirrored in the future institutional framework.

---

*Denmark, Ireland, and Greece are not members of the WEU.

CONCLUSION

The demilitarization of the European security environment is not a threat for NATO. It is an opportunity for change and should be considered a chance to implement reforms. Both NATO's internal composition and structure as well as its policies and strategies are now very different from the original concept. NATO—in contrast to the Warsaw Pact—did not lose its legitimacy after the revolution of 1989. NATO never intervened in the way the Warsaw Pact did in 1968 in Prague. On the contrary, East and Central European states look at NATO as an instrument of reassurance in addition to the CSCE, in view of the security vacuum that emerged in this region following the collapse of the Warsaw Pact.

The CSCE will have to expand its role in terms of both substantive policies and institutionalization in order to deal with the issues at hand more effectively. NATO, however, will be needed in the foreseeable future to facilitate the necessary strategic cooperation with Russia and the CIS. Thus complementarity between NATO and the CSCE should be assured under the present circumstances. The ideal situation would have NATO become an executive component and serve as the foundation for CSCE institution-building. The only possible long-term alternative is full EC integration and the creation of a European security structure based on a deepened and widened European Community.

NATO and the EC are engaged in very similar political processes. They both are making an effort to allow for East European participation in response to demands from these countries. It would be foolish, however, to duplicate efforts. The North Atlantic Cooperation Council is an important enlargement of NATO's traditional tasks. For the EC or WEU to do the same does not make sense. There are also financial limitations. NATO, the CSCE, and the EC or the European Union are the three pillars of European security. It is not likely that these three institutions are going to merge into one single institution. They are interlocking institutions, and the issue is how to pool efforts rather than engage in senseless competition.

Furthermore, given the nature of the present international system, the Economic Summit, the Group of Seven, and the EC will play an extremely important role in the new Europe. It will be necessary to streamline policies and concentrate energies to avoid duplication of efforts. The United States has traditionally fulfilled this role, but it will be difficult for it to concentrate on building a new Europe when it has pressing domestic problems at home. The slogan "America First" is a powerful concept and will have an impact on American security and economic policy.

In response to the American preoccupation with domestic issues Germany should not try, nor should it be pushed, to replace the United States in Europe. An active U.S. role in Europe is essential for the internal power balance of Europe in the future. The European Community is a promising vehicle to bring about democratic multilateralism in Europe, but it will take a long time for the European Union to create stability.

NOTES

1. U.S. Congress, *Public Hearing on German Unification and the CSCE Process, April 3, 1990*; hearing before the Commission on Security and Cooperation in Europe, One Hundred-First Congress, Sec. Sess., Washington, D.C., 1990.

2. James M. Buchanan, "Tacit Presuppositions of Political Economy: Implications for Societies in Transition"; unpublished paper, pp. 5ff.

3. *Politics of Democracy in Eastern Europe*; contributions to an international conference of the Friedrich-Ebert Foundation's Washington office, "After the Wall: The New Politics of Democracy and Party Pluralism in Eastern Europe," 26–28 June 1990.

4. Paul Wolfowitz, speech at a seminar on "German Armed Forces in a Changing European Security Environment," sponsored by Eagle Research Group and the Institute for Foreign Policy Analysis, Arlington, Virginia, 30 March 1990.

5. For example, Zbigniew Brzezinski, "Post-Communist Nationalism," *Foreign Affairs* 68, 5 (Winter 1989/90): 1–25.

6. For general information on migration, see the issue paper of the Refugee Policy Group, *Emigration, Immigration and Changing Relations* (Washington, D.C., November 1989). More specific data are provided by Dieter Vogeley, "Nur weg, sobald die Reisepaesse ausgegeben sind," *Frankfurter Allgemeine Zeitung*, 19 June 1991, p. 10.

7. R. Hrair Dekmejian, *Islam in Revolution: Fundamentalism in the Arab World* (New York, 1985), p. 7.

8. *Ibid.*, pp. 175–76.

9. *Common Security: A Programme for Disarmament*; report of the Independent Commission on Disarmament and Security Issues, London, 1982.

10. John Steinbruner, "Revolution in Foreign Policy," in *Setting National Priorities*, ed. Henry J. Aaron (Washington, D.C.: Brookings Institution, 1990), p. 68.

11. Klaus Friedrich, "Financial Needs versus Financial Resources in Central and Eastern Europe: Prospects for Western Capital Investment," in *The European Monetary System and International Financial Markets*, ed. Dieter Dettke; contributions to an international conference, "The European Monetary System and International Financial Markets," organized by the Friedrich-Ebert Foundation, the European Institute, and the Center for European Studies at George Mason University; Washington, D.C., 19–20 November 1990, pp. 126–28.

12. *Politics of Democracy* (note 3), p. 2.

13. Text of the EC declaration on relations with the Soviet Union in *Europa-Archiv*, no. 1, 1991, pp. D36–38.

14. For example, Dan Hamilton, "United Germany: Closing the Expectation Gap"; paper for a manuscript review of the American Institute for Contemporary German Studies; Washington, D.C., 11 June 1991.

15. For example, Günther Gillessen, "Der Isolationismus der Deutschen," *Frankfurter Allgemeine Zeitung*, 4 July 1991, p. 12.

16. German Information Center, *News From Germany* (New York), 21 February 1991.

17. "Deutschland 2000: Der Staat, den wir uns wuenschen," *Süddeutsche Zeitung—Magazine*, no. 1, 4 January 1991.

18. As demonstrated by Beverly Crawford and Jost Halfmann in their contribution to this volume.

19. Theo Sommer, "Die Deutschen an die Front?," *Die Zeit*, no. 13, 13 March 1991, p. 3.

20. Text reprinted in *NSC/PR*, no. 245, 12 December 1989; German text in *Europa-Archiv*, no. 4, 1990, pp. D77–84.

21. For example, John Mearsheimer, "Back to the Future: Instability in Europe after the Cold War," *International Security* 15, 1 (Summer 1990), and Stephen Van Evera, "Primed For Peace: Europe after the Cold War," *International Security* 15, 3 (Winter 1990/91).

22. Jonathan Dean, "Building a Post Cold-War European Security System," *Arms Control Today* 20, 5 (June 1990): 1.

23. Ivo Daalder, "The Role of Arms Control in the New Europe"; paper for the 1991 NATO symposium on "European Security Arrangements for the 1990's and Beyond"; National War College, Washington, D.C., 18–19 April 1991.

EASTERN EUROPE AS A DESTABILIZING FORCE IN THE NEW EUROPE: A CRITICAL EVALUATION

Valerie Bunce

INTRODUCTION

The end of the postwar international order has generated a lively debate about whether the "new" Europe will be peaceful or prone to war. For John Mearsheimer, the shift to a multipolar international system, in combination with such factors as growing economic interdependence in Europe and the considerable potential for domestic and interstate conflict in Eastern Europe, means that the end of the cold war might lead to the end, as well, of what John Lewis Gaddis has termed the "long peace" in Europe.[1]* Others, such as Jack Snyder, Stephen Van Evera, and John Steinbruner, are less pessimistic.[2] While they share some of the concerns voiced by Mearsheimer, they also identify various domestic, regional, and global factors which could counteract a return in Europe to "war as usual."[3]

While there is considerable disagreement about where Europe is heading, there is one point of consensus which underlines these debates. That is that *the* major constraint on peace in post-Wall Europe is Eastern Europe. In particular, virtually everyone assumes, first, that the new regimes in Eastern Europe are unstable. Second, most assume—and this is even the case for realists—that domestic instability in Eastern Europe will necessarily present problems for the newly emerging order in Europe.

The purpose of this contribution is to evaluate whether these assumptions about Eastern Europe are in fact warranted.† In the first

---

*Of course the East Europeans are quite uncomfortable with the notion of the long peace after World War II. In their view, the postwar period, to paraphrase Clausewitz, was the continuation of war by political means.

†Here Eastern Europe will be understood to refer to Poland, Czechoslovakia, Hungary, Romania, Bulgaria, Yugoslavia, and Albania. I will not take on the

half, I will lay out in a systematic way the arguments in support of the proposition that Eastern Europe will be a destabilizing force in the international system. As we will discover, there are many reasons to be concerned about Eastern Europe. In the second half, I will complicate this pessimistic picture by both critiquing the ways scholars have tended to analyze Eastern Europe and providing some evidence of factors which in fact promote stability in this region.

What all this suggests is that we cannot *assume* that Eastern Europe will be in effect the "spoiler" of the newly emerging international order in Europe. Rather, the situation in Eastern Europe is too complex and too mixed to make such a call—and this will be the case for a very long time. Thus the future of Eastern Europe, like the future of the newly emerging international order in Europe, cannot be assumed. Both, in short, are empirical questions.

THE HISTORICAL ROOTS OF INSTABILITY IN EASTERN EUROPE

Let us turn first to the reasons why one should expect instability in Eastern Europe. The reasons to be pessimistic on this issue can be divided into two areas. The first has to do with the history of this region. As has been amply documented, Eastern Europe has a long history of political instability.[4]* Why this is so has to do primarily with geography—that is, the dual burdens of occupying both accessible and valuable real estate. Here I refer first to the topography of

---

question of the Soviet Union (which, as some forget, is in Eastern Europe), except insofar as the Soviet Union affects the countries noted above. I will also leave what was once the German Democratic Republic out of this discussion. I have decided to focus on these countries because 1) the Soviet Union and the unified Germany present quite different situations and would require separate papers; 2) the East European countries selected for concentration here can be treated as a group, given their similarities in being small, once state-socialist, quite vulnerable in the international system, and committed (albeit in varying degrees) to both substantial liberalization of politics and economics and participation in an economic and political-military alliance with the West.

*While the geographical burdens of Eastern Europe led to a number of difficulties in that region's historical evolution, these burdens also meant that Western Europe was freed from many difficulties. Eastern Europe, in short, functioned as a "sponge," giving Western Europe much latitude in its historical evolution.

this region and second to its location between East and West. What this meant in practice was that this was a region subject to countless and (by West European standards) quite late ethnic migrations. This, of course, delayed the process of nation formation and at the same time produced a late and unusual version of feudalism. The constant migrations and the particular pattern of mountains and plains, moreover, rendered the region an ethnic mosaic.

Second, when these factors were joined with the location of the region as the crossroads between Asia and Europe, the end result was to delay the process of state formation and to separate that process from the creation of nations. Thus the composition of these societies, the character of these states, and the relationship between states and societies and states and the international system were all a function of international and not domestic factors—that is, who was powerful, who was on the move, and who needed alliances with whom.

All this created in turn the optimal conditions for instability. Pummeled by East and West through tribal migrations, wars, and alliances which were at the convenience of the powers that be, the societies of Eastern Europe came to feature enormous ethnic, religious, linguistic, and therefore cultural diversity. That this diversity was exploited by international powers, that there were high correlations between ethnicity and access to power and privilege, and that once conquering groups invariably lived next door to those they had conquered, of course, merely made these societies even more explosive.

The states which emerged in this region were also affected for the worse by the legacy of being overrun by East and West. It was not just that the boundaries of these states were haphazard and ever changing and bore little relationship to national boundaries, and that this reflected their extraordinary dependence on the international system. It was also that these states combined despotism with little penetration, rendering them coercive enough to alienate the public, but not strong enough to extract resources or the compliance of their publics. This in turn meant that regime-society relations were quite testy and that economic development was slow and distorted.

Thus the first "Third World," so to speak, was Eastern Europe. A victim of imperialism, Eastern Europe was doomed to be unstable.

It was a region featuring weak but coercive states, fractured and divided societies, economic underdevelopment, and, at the regional level, considerable tensions among states. And to this powerful brew was added, of course, the ideas of the French Revolution. As a result, from 1848 onward, Eastern Europe became a region noted for its political instability. When the empires dominating the region collapsed in the wake of World War I, Eastern Europe was finally accorded some control over its destiny. But the legacies of the past, coupled with continued dependence on the international system and the collapse of the world grain market in the late 1920s, ended the myth of control. Also ended, except in Czechoslovakia, were the experiments with liberal democracy and any semblance of political stability. Finally, the interwar period featured numerous conflicts among these newly created states—which is hardly surprising, given the poor correspondence between state and national boundaries, competition with each other in the world market, and the rise to power of insecure politicians seizing international issues in order to build their claims to domestic power.

With the arrival of Stalinism in the region after World War II, the situation in Eastern Europe was both the same and yet different. It was the same in the sense that again an external power was dominant, again these states were despotic, and again divisions within and among these states were played up by the external power. What was different was that these states had become penetrative and were endowed with the necessary resources to carry through on their commitments to rapid socioeconomic development. But instability was still the norm—albeit prevented from having many international reverberations, given the cold war divide. East European publics rebeled against Communist Party rule—that is, against despotism, dependence, and the stress of Stalinist transformation— as they had rebeled against other rule in the region. Indeed instability was so central to these systems that domestic Communist Parties and the Soviet Union went to enormous lengths to placate the angry publics in Eastern Europe. Thus even the stability of this region in the 1970s and in the 1980s (except in Poland) was really testimony to the opposite—as the dramatic events of 1989 amply demonstrated.[5]

The history of Eastern Europe, then, is a history of domestic instability. That instability at home led to instability abroad is also without question. Lest one doubt this linkage, consider the following. The three major wars of the twentieth century—that is, World War I, World War II, and the cold war—were fought in and over Eastern Europe.

Such an unstable past bodes ill for stability in contemporary Eastern Europe. This is not just because what was left unsettled in the past is still unsettled, because instability can in effect become a habit since more peaceful forms of conflict-mediation have never been developed and/or utilized, or because so many of the earlier sources of tension in the region are still there since, among other things, geography is geography. It is also because the conditions in this region today harken back to this troubled past. While I will deal with the contemporary situation below, let me note here that there are some important parallels between Eastern Europe today and this region during the interwar period. As Peter Hayes, an historian of Germany, has so succinctly put it, there are three themes which are the same: Germany, nationalism, and debt. But there is a fourth—that is, instituting the forms of liberal democracy, but in the absence of its social base.

CONTEMPORARY SOURCES OF INSTABILITY

Historical legacies can be overridden—as the evolution of postwar Japan and Germany, for instance, remind us. The question then becomes whether factors operating in today's Eastern Europe promote stability or instability. Unfortunately, there are many reasons to assume that the present and future of this region will be similar to the past. Let us turn first to analyzing the events of 1989, wherein Communist Party hegemony collapsed in Eastern Europe. This is an important variable in the calculus of stability. The process by which systems (domestic and international) collapse, we must remember, plays a crucial role in shaping the structure and stability of the systems which emerge in their place.[6]

The new regimes in Eastern Europe were born in a process which is costly insofar as the future stability of these regimes is concerned. First, many people were mobilized in 1989; what is more, they quickly got the results they wanted and at precious little immediate cost (except in Romania). It is very easy, then, for citizens in

Eastern Europe to go to the streets again, if things are not developing the way they want. This is particularly the case since mass protests—in other places and other times at least—have tended to have a long life before they have spent themselves and since other mechanisms for expressing grievances are just developing and have, as a result, never been used and certainly never so successfully.[7] Moreover, the ease of getting rid of the Communist Party's political monopoly has led many to assume (particularly those who were not long-time dissidents) that achieving other desired results—for instance, the transition to capitalism and the economic benefits thereof—will be just as easy and just as fast. Thus high expectations, strong positive reinforcement for protesting, and (as will be noted below) an absence of institutionalized mechanisms for expressing dissatisfaction, when combined with the enormous costs of and difficulties in transforming the system, may very well mean that publics in Eastern Europe will vent their frustrations on the streets.

Second, the fact that the events of 1989 were but partial revolutions also creates problems. Here I refer to the fact that these were nonviolent processes of change. By being nonviolent, these revolutions allowed those in power the luxury of living, rather than dying or emigrating—the latter two being the usual outcomes of revolution. What this means is that citizens in these states still feel that scores have not been settled, get angry about whether the Communists are doing too well in the new order, and fear that the Communists will somehow manage to regroup. This causes enormous tensions within the society, makes citizens suspicious of regimes seen as too easy on the Communists, and opens up the possibility—which is being played out in Poland today, for instance—of politicians rising to power by appealing to these fears and resentments of the public.[8]

The events of 1989 were also partial revolutions in the sense that they left substantial portions of the old system intact. Here I refer first to the many cultural residues of Stalinism which are anti-democratic and therefore destabilizing when existing in systems committed to political liberalization. I also refer to institutional residues. As many have misunderstood, what happened in 1989 in Eastern Europe was the collapse of Commmunist Party hegemony, not the collapse of the Communist system. In particular, what has been left is the other half of the state-socialist equation—that is, the state apparatus.[9] This has made many East Europeans angry, not just because those who should have been punished were not, but also because this old elite shows signs of becoming a new elite— given, for instance, its considerable powers in these more liberal regimes and the possibility that these powers will undermine the transition to geniune liberal democracy. Thus the contradictions generated by a resilient state apparatus within a liberalized economic and political order and the anger created by a state apparatus intact and central to the transition may together lead to an explosive political situation.

The final cost of the events of 1989 is that they created a peculiar sequencing of systemic transformation, wherein political liberalization preceded economic liberalization. In the experience of the West, of course, the reverse was the case. In particular, the transition to capitalism preceded the transition to liberal democracy. By reversing this ordering, Eastern Europe is locked into a situation which is both no-win and destabilizing. Let me provide some examples. How can politicians, subject to the pressures of a fully enfranchised and fickle electorate and making decisions within a political framework which disperses power, possibly come to agreement on the necessarily divisive questions involved in creating a capitalist economy? Moreover, if politicians, courting voters with high expectations and short-term horizons, respond by avoiding making the hard economic decisions which the transition to capitalism requires, then they might be secure in the short run, but in the longer run they would face the wrath of citizens angry about long-term economic decline. If politicians decided to bite the bullet and carry out unpopular economic reforms, they might very well face mass unrest and, through ballots or battles in the streets, be thrown out of office. They would be replaced, of course, by a repressive state bent on forcing economic changes, by politicians eager to find scapegoats for economic miseries, or by politicians committed to making popular economic decisions. The end result for all cases would be to destabilize the system.

Thus there is a certain irony that just as politics sabotaged economics in the time of state socialism and a sabotaged economy produced in turn political instability and the eventual collapse of Communist Party rule, so the same scenario might develop for the liberalized political orders in Eastern Europe which succeeded state socialism. Politics in command, in short, is a real problem. This might even be the case when "good" politics is in command.[10]

This leads us to the final issue affecting domestic stability in Eastern Europe—that is, the difficulties generated by the nature of the transition itself. Here we must remember that what is going on in Eastern Europe today is truly revolutionary. It is not just that capitalism and liberal democracy are being constructed simultaneously—which has never before been done or done so quickly. It is also that the point of departure is state socialism, a system which (as I have argued elsewhere) is diametrically opposed in its operating principles, institutions, and procedures to capitalism and liberal democracy.[11] In this sense, while the events of 1989 were hybrids of reform and revolution and hence "refolutionary," as Timothy Garton Ash has argued,[12] developments in Eastern Europe since 1989 have been, if anything, hyper-revolutionary—that is, more revolutionary than what one often sees after "real" revolutions.* Rather than belabor this point, it will suffice to note that such incredible upheavals are by definition destabilizing since institutions, procedures, personnel, operating principles, and cultures are *all* in flux.

These transitions are particularly destabilizing since they are taking place within an already delicate and difficult context. Here I refer to several aspects of the current situation in Eastern Europe. One is that all of these countries are in dismal socioeconomic straits. This is particularly the case for Poland, Hungary, Romania, and Yugoslavia, all of which have undergone a full decade of decline in their standards of living. What that means is that the new regimes in Eastern Europe must orchestrate policies which do not just lay the base for a transition to capitalism—which is unsettling enough—but must also create, at the same time, a modern economy and a modern social and communications infrastructure and, in the bargain, provide for economic stabilization while providing some protection to those many who are already in severe economic straits. This is as contradictory and as destabilizing an economic situation as one can imagine.

---

*There is a certain irony, of course, that the most revolutionary of the changes in 1989—that is, the violent collapse of Communist Party hegemony in Romania—was precisely the one which seems to have had the least impact on the structure of politics and economics.

Another contextual difficulty has to do with ethnic tensions. Always a problem in this region, relations among ethnic groups have become more tense as a result of political and economic liberalization. Political liberalization has gone far enough to open up politics to competition and conflict, but not far enough to either structure public attitudes and behavior along nonethnic lines or to give every ethnic group equal access to the resources necessary to influence political outcomes. At the same time, economic liberalization has gone far enough to create uncertainty in outcomes, but not far enough to create the certain procedures necessary for capitalism or to mix up in effect ethnic experiences in the economy. As a result, people are angry, the benefits of liberalization are ethnically stratified, and ethnicity is rendered both the only source of certainty for individuals and a major source of uncertainty for the system.[13]

Perhaps the most serious constraint on political stability has to do with the turmoil caused by the transitions under way in Eastern Europe. It is commonplace in the West to assume that there are systems in place in Eastern Europe—that is, that these transitional regimes feature patterned regularities in their institutions, roles, and operating principles. But this is not the case. Everyday life in Eastern Europe is far from orderly; instead it is turbulent and full of uncertainties. For example, institutions are new, and new ones are cropping up every day, but no one knows what their functions are and whether they will survive; politicians are new and are overwhelmed in their jobs; and every day new policies are enacted which can suddenly transform rich into poor and vice versa. This massive uncertainty—in institutions, procedures, and even the calculation of self-interest—means that citizens in Eastern Europe are simultaneously mobilized, confused, and fearful. This is a sure recipe for political instability. This is particularly the case since this describes the situation of not just everyday citizens, but also of politicians.

Do these many pressures in the direction of domestic instability mean that this will translate into international instability? There are many reasons to think that it will—aside from the parallels between what I have just described and the turbulent interwar period. First, Eastern Europe faces several vacuums at the international level—that is, a political-military vacuum, given the collapse of the Warsaw Treaty Organization (which was made official in July

1991) and the impossibility, given Soviet concerns, of joining NATO; and a market vacuum, given the collapse in 1990–91 of the Soviet market and the collapse as well of the state-socialist market.[14] Second, there is the heritage of having been part of the Soviet bloc for so many decades. As a regional hierarchical system, the Soviet bloc functioned to isolate the East European states from each other and to force them to see each other in adversarial and zero-sum terms.[15] That the bloc shaped them for so long and built upon an extraordinarily long history of isolation from and hostility to each other means that the habits of the postwar period will die hard in Eastern Europe.* This is despite the fact that, as Vaclav Havel has so persuasively argued, these countries share so much—their pasts, the events of 1989, their current predicaments, and their agendas for the future. It is almost as though 1989 was the creation of a new hierarchical bloc, with the West the center instead of the Soviet Union and with horizontal ties among these states still absent.

Moreover, conditions in the new Eastern Europe have encouraged competition, if not conflict, among the states in the region. For example, the variance across these states in the approach to and the timing of economic liberalization has led to tensions between Czechoslovakia and Poland and between Hungary and Romania over interstate movement of peoples, goods, and currencies.† Another source of tension is the ongoing competition over the question of who is the furthest down the road to capitalism and liberal democracy. Each wants to be seen as ahead of the pack because this would support claims to having parted final company with state socialism—claims which are crucial for mobilizing domestic as well as international support. Furthermore, there are other gains to be had from being ahead in the race toward liberalization. If these states are perceived as making strong progress in liberalizing their politics and economics, the West Europeans will give these regimes in general and these governments in particular the scarce items they want and need—that is, legitimation, membership in European

---

*For example, when in Warsaw in November 1990, I found that Leszek Balcerowicz, the Polish finance minister, had no clue as to how either Hungary or Czechoslovakia were approaching economic liberalization

†This is not to mention the almost panic in Western Europe about the prospects of open borders there and the likely enthusiastic response of the Soviets and the East Europeans.

economic and political institutions, membership in Western financial institutions, access to Western capital, and the sense that they have at last become full-fledged members of the prosperous and liberal West.*

Finally, there is the issue of ethnicity and its impact on regional instability, if not regional conflict. The stresses and the inequalities generated by liberalization of politics and economics can, when interacting with ethnic pluralism, lead to a situation wherein insecure and angry politicians and citizens, seeking scapegoats, concentrate their fury on various ethnic groups. This becomes an international problem when 1) the target of blame is nationals in a neighboring state; 2) the target of blame is an ethnic minority within the state and a majority in a neighboring state; and 3) the ethnic tensions generated by the transition lead to the development of fascist governments which violate human rights at home and thereby antagonize the West and/or pursue a foreign policy which threatens the security of neighboring countries. That we have already seen some indications of such tensions arising in Eastern Europe—for instance, conflicts between the Romanian and Hungarian governments over the position of the Hungarian minority in Transylvania and the periodic surfacing of anti-semitism in Hungary and Poland—suggests that the extreme scenarios presented above could materialize.

Unfortunately, there are some other ways in which ethnic conflict in the domestic arena can become a source of international tension. For example, the combination of liberalized politics, ethnic pluralism, and ethnically based stratification of the burdens and benefits derived from liberalization can lead ethnic minorities to push hard for more rights, if not independence, and in the process to reach out to other countries and international organizations for help and legitimation. This process can wreak international havoc because it introduces the possibility of civil war, introduces the more general and frightening question of whether state boundaries are

---

*This shows up most clearly in the case of Hungary, where the Antall government has repeatedly emphasized the centrality of relations with the West and the virtual nonimportance of relations with East European neighbors, including the Soviet Union. This also shows up in the literature Hungary distributes to the West about privatization, where much is made of how Hungary is the leader of privatization in Eastern Europe.

ever fixed, demonstrates more often than not the weakness of international organizations as institutions mediating domestic conflicts,
and forces neighbors and powerful states to take a position on such
thorny issues as the rights of ethnic groups to claim sovereignty.

One good example of these complex dynamics is the ongoing
crisis in Yugoslavia. The republics of Croatia and Slovenia are
seeking at least renegotiation of Yugoslav federalism in the direction
of a loose-knit confederal state and, at most, full independence from
Yugoslavia. Toward this end, they have enlisted the support of their
publics through referenda on the question of independence, sought
international support, and approached international institutions
about mediating their conflicts with the Serbs (who are the dominant nationality in Yugoslavia, albeit not a majority, and who, not
incidentally, dominate the officer corps of the Yugoslav army). The
Croatian government (which was popularly elected in spring 1990)
managed to buy 15,000 machine guns from the Hungarian government.*

All this has set the stage for the crisis which began in summer
1991. The Serbs resisted responding to the various proposals by the
Croats and the Slovenes to decentralize the Yugoslav state throughout the spring of 1991, and in June 1991, prevented a Croat from
taking his rightful turn (according to the constitution) as the president of Yugoslavia (which the Serbs finally allowed in early July,
given severe international pressure). As of this writing (early July
1991), the Yugoslav army (which did not seem to be under the control
of Prime Minister Ante Markovic) has moved into Slovenia to
prevent a breakaway; the Austrians were pushing for international
settlement of this issue (in part because the Yugoslav army had
violated Austrian air space); and the German government was
severely cross-pressured, given its support of the status quo and
therefore the Serbs, versus the position of the German public that

*This was a very dangerous precedent for several reasons. First, the Hungar-
ian foreign minister denied in parliament that Hungary had made such a deal;
he was later forced to withdraw his denial. Second, there is some evidence from
sources in both Germany and in the Hungarian foreign ministry that Hungary
was in fact selling guns to Croatia on behalf of Germany. Finally, it must be
remembered that some of the East European states—most notably Czechoslovakia—have a huge armaments industry. The Czechoslovak government, after
initially declaring it would shut down such industries, has since changed its
mind, in part because of the concentration of such industries in Slovakia.

Croats and Slovenes should have the rights outlined by the Helsinki Accords.* The end result has been several unsuccessful international attempts to mediate this dispute, and growing fears that Yugoslavia is heading toward a civil war.

All this would seem to suggest that the common assumptions about instability in Eastern Europe are well placed. The history of this region, the nature of the events in 1989, the stresses of the transition to capitalism and liberal democracy, and the pressures working in the direction of fanning interstate tensions would all seem to render Eastern Europe a destabilizing force in the emerging international order in Europe.

Despite the power of these arguments, however, I am not convinced—especially if the question becomes one of *assuming* instability.† In the remainder of this contribution, I will both critique these perspectives on Eastern Europe and discuss various elements of the situation in this region which could be said to stabilize these countries and their relationship to the international system.

METHODOLOGICAL BIASES

Most of the concerns about the future of Eastern Europe rest on the arguments that these countries 1) are inherently unstable, 2) lack what is needed to build liberal democracy, and 3) will as a consequence become quite unstable as the struggle to liberalize politics, but without strong political organizations and institutions, leads to all kinds of social and interstate tensions. Central to the evaluation of the future of Eastern Europe, then, is how one understands political instability—its meaning, its origins, and its impact—and how one understands, as well, the preconditions for a transition to liberal democracy.

The problem with using the term "political instability" is that it lacks precise empirical referents. As Yegor Yakovlev, the editor of

---

*There is also trouble brewing in Czechoslovakia, given not just Slovak demands for more autonomy, if not statehood, but also Slovak approaches to the former Soviet Union. More generally, ethnic groups in search of a state in this region are likely to reach out to any state hoping to exert influence in this region.

†This is particularly the case since one cannot also assume that the West Europeans are so stable and so capable of working with one another.

Moscow News, once put it, "One person's instability is another's transformation." The same processes and events, therefore, can be coded in quite different ways—for instance, as stress versus innovation, as crises versus learning, or as dangerous change versus change which is necessary albeit discomforting. Instability, in short, is very much in the eye of the beholder.

What this means, of course, is that the analysis of instability is not very rigorous and can be, under certain circumstances, quite biased. Studies of revolution—an extreme form of political instability—are a case in point. What strikes one about the literature on revolution is its propensity to overpredict revolutions—that is, to predict more revolutions than actually occur. Why does this happen? The main reason is that these theories are underspecified. In particular, they lack the kinds of refined variables which might distinguish between states under stress versus states which are on the verge of collapse; between publics which are angry and expressing this versus publics which are not just mobilized and angry, but also resourceful and at the same time facing quite divided and weak states. These theories are also underspecified in the sense that they tend to ignore factors which might stabilize an unstable situation. After all, a strong theory of instability must be able to survive the test of inversion—that is, be sufficiently robust that it can specify the conditions under which regimes are stable.

There are similar difficulties with theories of liberal democracy. While the definition of liberal democracy is far more rigorous than the definition of instability, theories of what liberal democracy requires also feature a relatively poor batting average with respect to predicting whether regimes will become liberal democratic. Whereas theories of instability have the problem of predicting many false positives, however, theories of liberal democracy have the opposite problem—that is, they are guilty of predicting many false negatives. In other words, just as there is too little instability in the world, given our theories of instability, so there are far too many liberal democracies in the world, given our understanding of what liberal democracy requires!

While it is not so much a problem to have weak theories since the social sciences are limited in what they can do and may never be very good at prediction, it is a problem to have theories which bias our interpretations of social reality. In the cases of political instability and liberal democracy, the weakness of theory has meant that scholars tend to overstate instability (or at least its systemic consequences) and understate the capacity of systems to evolve into liberal democracies. Thus our theories have perhaps led us to read the data from Eastern Europe in a way which predisposes us to see instability, to be quite pessimistic about the prospects for liberal democracy, and to exaggerate the costs, domestic and international, when unstable systems with few preconditions for liberal democracy attempt to liberalize their politics. That so much is in flux in Eastern Europe and that this is an area which is a mystery to most only exaggerates the power of theory to structure reality.

One good example of how this bias has worked is the case of Poland. Many in the West have viewed the recent break-up of Solidarity as an indication of instability in Poland. The argument seems to be that without the unity forged by Solidarity, Poland will bust apart at the seams. But it could be argued just as persuasively that the break-up of Solidarity is an investment in both liberal democracy and political stability. Put more specifically, Poland is finally becoming a multi-party system (having switched in 1989, ironically, from a one-party system to another one-party system), Polish politics is finally recognizing and legitimating diverse values and interests, and Poland is making progress in differentiating between unions and political parties. Is it better, then, to squash diversity and prohibit competition, or is it better, in terms of stability and democracy, to institutionalize both?

Just as analysts have used theories to get a handle on a most confusing Eastern Europe and this has biased their interpretations because of the limitations of these theories, so analysts have used another device to get a handle on Eastern Europe—that is, analogies.[16] In particular, rather than relying heavily on contextual data, they have interpreted Eastern Europe through the lenses, variously, of the Western experience, the Stalinist past, the interwar period, or the Third World. Because they have not taken the time to establish whether these analogies are good ones, these analogies have often tended not to clarify social reality, but rather to distort it. The result, once again, has been to highlight the instability of this region, while ignoring its stabilizing aspects, and to weight heavily those factors which undermine liberal democracy while making light of those factors which favor a liberal democratic outcome.

Let me give some concrete examples of typical analogical thinking about Eastern Europe. Since Eastern Europe lacks institutionalized pluralism as in the West, has much less experience with liberal democracy, and certainly has weaker historical claims to a liberal state, then the liberalization of Eastern Europe must necessarily be not just a destabilizing process, but also one which will prevent liberal democracy from taking root. Since politics in Eastern Europe today is more combative than it was under Stalinism, then these systems are likely to be torn apart by political and social conflict. Since much of what we see today—for instance, ethnic squabbles, economic hardships, and rapid multiplication of political parties—is so reminescent of the turbulent interwar experience, then this most recent go-around with liberal democracy will have the same outcome—that is, praetorian politics. Finally, since Eastern Europe today shares with much of the Third World dependence on the global capitalist economy and what could be termed pushy societies and weak states, then Eastern Europe will experience the same political stresses that many Third World countries have experienced since they were liberated from colonial rule.

What is disturbing about these "since, then" statements is that the conclusions drawn seem to be primarily a function of forcing Eastern Europe to fit certain analogies and expectations. Let me respond to the arguments above. Is Eastern Europe unstable, or is politics there simply different from politics in the West—as it should be, given very different historical trajectories and the fact that liberal democracy is old in the West and new in Eastern Europe?* Is political conflict in Eastern Europe dangerous because it is so great, or is it simply the fact that we are not used to seeing conflict in these once Stalinist systems and have forgotten, as well, that the road to liberal democracy in the West was not without its conflictual aspects—and, for that matter, not without its detours? Is contemporary Eastern Europe like the interwar period, or does it matter that the liberalized regimes of today were created from the bottom up, that Europe and the West in general are much more "together" and politically and economically stable today, and that today's global economy, while

---

*The problem here is in part one of rushing to judgment. The fact is that these transitions are in their very early stages, and predicting outcomes at this point would be tantamount to predicting the outcome of a playoff game between the Chicago Bulls and the Los Angeles Lakers in the first thirty seconds of the game.

not terribly healthy, is certainly more healthy than it was in the 1930s? Finally, why assume that Eastern Europe is like the Third World when Eastern Europe is in Europe, has long had a participatory political system, had peaceful revolutions in 1989 which were in effect schools for democracy, and has a level of social development much closer to the First than the Third World?

What I am suggesting is that our assessment of stability in Eastern Europe should not be a function of primitive theories or less than well-thought-out frames of reference. Rather, it should reflect our reading of the liabilities and assets of these regimes and our reading, as well, of the factors which encourage and discourage conflicts among states in this region.

SOURCES OF STABILITY IN EASTERN EUROPE

While the new regimes in Eastern Europe, as noted, have many liabilities which might very well destabilize these systems and, more generally, the region, these new regimes also have important assets.[17]

One is what happened in 1989. Here I refer to several aspects of the collapse of Communist Party rule in Eastern Europe. One is the degree to which the events of 1989 were not a fluke of history or a product, plain and simple, of Gorbachev's actions. Rather, they were the result of a long-term historical process, wherein from the 1950s onward there was an informal and cumulative redistribution of power from the party to the society in Eastern Europe and, at the regional level, a redistribution of power as well from the Soviet Union to Eastern Europe. Thus if the events of 1989 were the result of a long-term process of liberalization at the domestic and regional levels, then one must conclude that 1) the historical claims to liberal democracy are stronger than what is commonly assumed, and 2) the regimes in this region today have historical and social roots and are therefore not so delicate nor so easily toppled as is commonly presumed. Of course,the process of redistributing power in Eastern Europe was different from what happened in the West, when, say, kings became more constrained in their powers, governments and then parliaments developed, civil liberties expanded and political parties became important actors. Indeed just as Eastern Europe has no bourgeoisie in its story, so the West had no Communist Party or

Soviet bloc. But the essence of the process is rather similar in both cases since constraints on the state grew along with the autonomy of society.[18] In this sense, Eastern Europe today is like the West—and very different from what this region was in the interwar period. In fact, this difference is also the case for the West—as many forget in the rush to look only at interwar *Eastern* Europe.*

Another aspect of the events of 1989 is that the transfer of political power from the Communists to the opposition (except in Romania) was a virtual school for democracy. After all, what we saw—in the streets and at the round tables between the Communists and the opposition—were such staples of democratic behavior as tolerance for political adversaries, peaceful demonstrations, peaceful mediation of conflict (and enormous conflict at that), and acceptance by those long in power of decidedly threatening political outcomes. If democracy has to do with bargaining, peaceful settlement of disputes, and acceptance of losing, then the very processes which ushered in liberal politics in Eastern Europe were themselves liberal in essence. That such practices were so successful, moreover, merely reinforced these values and behaviors.

Finally, we must realize how far these regimes have come in constructing the procedures and the institutions of liberal democracy. This is particularly true for Hungary, Poland, Czechoslovakia, Croatia, and Slovenia. What we must remember, in particular, is how long it took for representative institutions, political parties, and civil liberties to develop in the West. And the oldest popularly elected government in Eastern Europe—the Antall government in Hungary—is but fifteen months old! Thus the question may be less one of how far these regimes have to go than how far they have gone. All this would seem to imply that liberal democracy is easier to build than we once thought, that Stalinism contributed something to this outcome and left fewer negative residues than we might have thought, that the revolutions of 1989 created more of a consensus around liberal democracy than might have been immediately apparent, or that the talents and energy of the East Europeans are exceptional. My guess is that all of the above are probably true.

*This is also the case with respect to forgetting the lessons of postwar Germany and Japan. The evolution of liberal democracy in these regions was, in fact, quite slow, and the economic takeoff of these two countries was slow in the making as well. (See, for instance, Katzenstein, note 2 below.)

If the case for liberal democracy is stronger than what many seem to assume, then the prospects for political stability in Eastern Europe are better as well. This is, first, because liberal democracy seems to be a system of government which has some built-in mechanisms enhancing political stability.[19] Second, there is considerable evidence that democracies are peace-loving—albeit primarily when dealing with one another.[20] Third, there are more constraints on public protests than we might realize, given, for instance, the capacity of political and economic liberalization to not just anger people, but also to divide if not demobilize them. Fourth, the centrality of the ethnic question might be temporary—a feeling of one's oats before settling down to jockey for position in a liberalized economic and political order.

Finally, there may be a better fit than many have assumed between the political cultures in Eastern Europe and the political cultures, elite and mass, which liberal democracy seems to require. Indeed if we look at how these new regimes—particularly in Central Europe—have managed conflict thus far, we find reasons for optimism. Czechoslovakia, for example, has managed in a very short period of time to move to a very complicated confederal political arrangement; the Antall government in Hungary did not collapse in the face of the November 1990 taxi strike (though many in Hungary hoped or feared it would); and the Polish, Czech, and Hungarian governments seem to be preparing quite well for the coming deluge of Soviet emigres.

What I am suggesting, then, is that we would do well to disentangle the issues of levels of social conflict versus the capacity of these systems to manage such conflicts. What we have seen in Eastern Europe is considerable social conflict—as one would expect, given the history of this region, the public protests which led to the formation of the liberalized regimes, the newness of democracy, and the strains generated by a virtual and certainly simultaneous revolution in politics and economics. However, what we have also seen is the capacity of these embryonic democracies to manage conflict. It is the balance between levels of conflict and systemic capacity to adjudicate conflicts, then, and not simply the degree of conflict which should receive our foremost attention in assessing the stability of the new Eastern Europe.

If we need to disentangle levels of conflict from capacity to manage conflict, we also need to separate the issue of domestic unrest from the issue of the capacity of the international system to prevent such unrest from being played out at the level of interstate interactions. While there are many reasons, as noted, why domestic instability could become international instability in Eastern Europe, there are also some very good reasons why we should not assume that this will happen. One reason is that those countries best placed in a geopolitical sense to wreak havoc on Europe—that is, Hungary, Poland, and Czechoslovakia—are the countries which also happen to have the strongest claims to a future of political stability and liberal democracy. By contrast, the countries most likely to have severe domestic tensions—Yugoslavia being the most obvious case—are in areas which are more amenable, all else being equal, to international quarantining.

Moreover, there is some indication that these states can in fact adjudicate those tensions arising from shared ethnic groups. Here I refer, for example, to the success the Hungarian government had in encouraging the Slovaks to alter laws which discriminated against the Hungarian minority. I also refer to the ways in which the Romanian and Hungarian governments have managed to keep a lid on disputes about the position of the Hungarian minority in Transylvania.

There are, as well, the ties that bind these countries. Those now in leadership positions in the different countries in Eastern Europe are old friends in many cases and can, as a result, work together. This is one advantage of the dominance of the intelligentsia in these governments and the cross-national linkages which were developed in Eastern Europe in response to protests in the past and in response, as well, to the Helsinki Accords.

Indeed there has been some evidence of late that these governments can cooperate with one another. The February 1991 meeting of presidents, prime ministers and foreign secretaries from Hungary, Poland, and Czechoslovakia in Visegrad, Hungary, along with the communique issued after this meeting, is indicative of growing possibilities for regional cooperation. That such a meeting had not occurred since 1300 points not just to the age-old divisions among these states, but also to the considerable changes in Eastern Europe introduced by the events of 1989.[21] This meeting, moreover, has been followed up by other meetings involving, among other things, a considerable expansion of information exchanged about liberalization, responses to the collapse of the Soviet market and the Warsaw Pact, and what to do in response to the future opening of Soviet borders. Similar meetings, moreover, have been going on in the Pentagonale, which joins Southeast European countries, Austria, and Italy.

Finally, Western Europe can play and has played a crucial role in stabilizing politics in Eastern Europe. The West Europeans have helped not just with money and advisors, but also in other ways which are equally important. They have, in particular, encouraged the East Europeans to use European institutions to mediate domestic and interstate conflict—most recently with the crisis in Yugoslavia and the Conference on Security and Cooperation in Europe.

At the same time, the West Europeans have a great deal of leverage in Eastern Europe because of the desire of the latter to join the West, economically and politically. If Eastern Europe, for instance, is to follow in the footsteps of Spain, Portugal, and Greece and join the Council of Europe and then the Common Market, it must meet the same standards for liberalizing its politics and economics and somehow cushioning the stresses involved in the transition from dictatorship to liberalism. In this sense, the West has a way to discipline Eastern Europe, and East Europeans have enormous incentives to comply with Western demands.[22]

CONCLUSIONS

What are we to conclude from this complex mixture of factors suggesting both an unstable and a stable Eastern Europe? It would seem to me that two conclusions are warranted. First, the future of Eastern Europe—as stable countries, as liberal democracies, and as forces for stability in Europe—is quite open to question. This is not just because these regimes have such a mixture of assets and liabilities. It is also because they are new, what they are doing is so revolutionary and so historically unprecedented, and because there is no easy way—given how little we know about democracy and stability—to weight these many assets and liabilities.

Second, assuming that Eastern Europe will be the "spoiler" of the new Europe is not warranted. We simply do not know. While it would be nice to have one element of certainty upon which to base our predictions of the newly emerging international order in Europe, the situation in Eastern Europe cannot, unfortunately, give us that certainty. Just as only time and data will tell about the post-postwar international order, so only time and data will tell us about Eastern Europe's role in that new order.

NOTES

1. See John Mearsheimer, "Back to the Future; Instability in Europe after the Cold War," *International Security* 15 (Summer 1990): 5–56. For arguments about the long peace after World War II, see John Lewis Gaddis, "The Long Peace: Elements of Stability in the Postwar International Order," *International Security* 10 (Spring 1986): 99–142.

2. See Jack Snyder, "Avoiding Anarchy in the New Europe," *International Security* 14 (Spring 1990): 5–41; Stephen Van Evera, "Primed for Peace: Europe After the Cold War," *International Security* 15 (Winter 1990/91): 7–57; John Steinbruner, "The Goals and Instruments of American Foreign Policy under the Impetus of Revolutionary Change"; paper prepared for the Aspen Strategy Group, October 1990. On the question of whether a unified Germany will present a problem for stability in Europe, see Peter Katzenstein, "The Taming of German Power: Unification 1989–1990"; paper prepared for the conference on "Political Economy of the 1990s: The Past as Prelude," Northwestern University, 20–21 April 1991.

3. On the frequency of war in Europe prior to the post–World War II period, see Evan Luard, *War in International Society: A Study of International Sociology* (New Haven: Yale University Press, 1986), and Jack Levy, *War in the Modern Great Power System* (Lexington: University of Kentucky, 1983).

4. See, for example, Hugh Seton-Watson, *Eastern Europe between the Wars, 1918–1941* (New York: Harper and Row, 1967); Joseph Rothschild, *East Central Europe Between the Two World Wars* (Seattle: University of Washington Press, 1974); Barbara Jelavich, *History of the Balkans*, vols. 1 and 2 (Cambridge: Cambridge University Press, 1983); Perry Anderson, *Lineages of the Absolutist State* (London: New Left Books, 1974), Part 2.

5. On the domestic and regional dynamics of Stalinism in Eastern Europe, see, for instance, Valerie Bunce, "The Empire Strikes Back: The Transformation of Eastern Europe from a Soviet Asset to a Soviet Liability," *International Organization* 35 (Winter 1985): 1–46.

6. This argument is made most persuasively by David Stark and Laszlo Bruszt, "Negotiating the Institutions of Democracy: Contingent Choices and Strategic Interactions in the Hungarian and Polish Transitions," *Working Papers on Tran-*

sitions from State Socialism (Ithaca: Cornell University Press, 1990). More generally, this is an argument which analysts of international relations would do well to incorporate when speculating about the newly emerging international order. Rather than pretend that this order had in effect a virgin birth (which is what emerges in these studies, given the propensity to begin the analysis after 1989), they would do well to treat the transition from the old to the new order as an evolutionary process. This is, after all, how systems change; this would give clues to the future, and this would, as well, give due weight to the inevitable residues of the past. Moreover, this is particularly important since this international transition was without violence and therefore without the kinds of sharp boundaries that have been the norm for international transitions in the past. Indeed, even for earlier cases where change was violent, the emphasis is on the evolutionary character of systemic change. See, for instance, Richard Rosecrance, *Action and Reaction in World Politics* (Boston: Little, Brown, 1963), and Gaddis (note 1).

7. See, for instance, Sidney Tarrow, *Struggle, Politics and Reform: Collective Action, Social Movements and Cycles of Protest* (Ithaca: Cornell University). Western Societies Paper No. 21.

8. See, for instance, David Stark, "Privatization in Hungary: From Plan to Market or Plan to Clan?" *East European Politics and Societies* 4 (Fall 1990): 351–92; Voytek Zubek, "Walesa's Leadership and Poland's Transition," *Problems of Communism* 40 (January–April 1991): 69–83.

9. See especially Valerie Bunce and Maria Csanadi, "A Systematic Analysis of a Non-System: Post-Communism in Eastern Europe"; paper presented at the Hungarian-American Roundtable in Political Science, Budapest, 16 December 1991.

10. This has left the state in these new regimes in a quite contradictory position since, among other things, a strong state is needed to reduce the role of the state! For a good discussion of the many contradictions imposed by revolutionary change from above in support of liberalizing politics and economics, see Lena Kolarska-Bobinska, "The Role of the State in the Transition"; unpublished manuscript, Warsaw, Institute of Philosophy and Sociology, April 1991.

11. See Valerie Bunce, "Stalinism and the Management of Uncertainty," in *The Transition to Democracy in Hungary*, ed. Gyorgy Szobaszlai (Budapest: Hungarian Institute of Sociology, 1991).

12. See "Reform or Revolution," in Timothy Garton Ash, *The Uses of Adversity: Essays on the Fate of Central Europe* (New York: Random House, 1990), pp. 242–304.

13. See, for example, the discussion of the situation of the gypsies in *Report on the U.S. Helsinki Commission Delegation Visit to Hungary, Yugoslavia, and Albania, March 22–28, 1991* (Washington, D.C.: Commission on Security and Cooperation in Europe, 1991).

14. Of course, we are not used to thinking of state socialism as having a market, given the many distortions of economic transactions in this system. But there was a market, albeit with unusual structures and operating principles. See, for

instance, Vaclav Klaus and Tomas Jezek, "Social Criticism, False Liberalism, and Recent Changes in Czechoslovakia," *East European Politics and Societies* 5 (Winter 1991): 26–40.

15. See Bunce, "The Empire Strikes Back" (note 5).

16. This is also a problem, in my view, in analyses of the emerging international order in Europe. While the use of historical analogies is both necessary and legitimate in the study of international relations, given (among other things) the problem of having to go to Mars to construct a comparative standard (see E.H. Carr, *The Twenty Years' Crisis, 1919–1939* [Boston: Macmillan, 1949]), this does not mean that some analogies might not be far better than others. For example, rather than use World War I or the interwar period to get a handle on recent changes in the international system, it might be more useful to draw parallels between the Gorbachev era and its international characteristics, on the one hand, and the era of the "Great Reforms" of Alexander II (1855–81), on the other. See Valerie Bunce, "Sound Familiar? Domestic Reform and International Change in the Time of Gorbachev and Tsar' Alexander II"; paper presented at the conference on "Political Economy of the 1990s: The Past as Prelude," Northwestern University, 20–21 April 1991.

17. See, for instance, Valerie Bunce, "The Struggle for Liberal Democracy in Eastern Europe," *World Policy Journal* 7 (Summer 1990): 395–430; Stark and Bruszt, (note 6); Wlodzimierz Wesolowski, "Transitions from Authoritarianism to Democracy," *Social Research* 57 (Summer 1990): 435–62; Kolarska-Bobinska (note 10).

18. For an elaboration of this argument, see Bunce, "The Struggle" (note 17).

19. See Robert Dahl, "Transitions to Democracy"; paper presented at a symposium on "Voices of Democracy," University of Dayton, Center for International Studies, Dayton, Ohio, 16–17 March 1990.

20. See Michael Doyle, "Kant, Liberal Legacies and Foreign Affairs," parts 1 and 2, *Philosophy of Public Affairs* 12 (Summer and Fall 1983): 205–35.

21. On the Visegrad summit, see "Test of the Visegrad Summit Declaration," *Report on Eastern Europe* 2 (1 March 1991): 31–32.

22. See Richard Weitz, "The Expanding Role of the Council of Europe," *Report on Eastern Europe* 34 (24 August 1990): 12–19.

EUROPE'S NEW SECURITY ORDER:
A PLURALISTIC SECURITY COMMUNITY

Emanuel Adler

INTRODUCTION

In the beginning, Europe created the modern sovereign state and, later, the nation-state. And it saw that it was good—but only for three hundred years. Today Europe is experimenting again, this time with an approach to international relations that, while not transcending the sovereign nation-state, is nevertheless something new under the sun. The time has come to take cognizance of this experiment and, at the same time, to consider a major shift in our conceptual understanding of international relations and peaceful change among sovereign states.

The constitution of a community of values in Western Europe since the end of World War II and the conditions created by the end of the cold war and the mostly peaceful revolutions in Eastern Europe for the enlargement of this community demonstrate the growing inadequacy of both "realistic" balance-of-power thinking and "idealistic" world-government ideas in this part of the world. Somewhere "beyond the nation-state," but short of international governance, lies the domain of security communities composed of sovereign states that share stable expectations of peaceful change. Two hundred years ago Immanuel Kant predicted this phenomenon. More recently, students of international relations, aware of the social aspects of international life, have begun to relate the development of stable expectations of peaceful change to security communities, or what Karl Deutsch has called "pluralistic security communities."[1]

After a short excursion into Kantian thought, I shall proceed to describe and, I hope, to improve on the concept of pluralistic security communities, while trying to explain the transformation of common knowledge about sovereignty that must take place if such pluralistic security communities are to emerge. I shall then describe the pluralistic security communities that developed in Western Europe (and, almost certainly, in the entire Atlantic region) after World War II, and suggest that the enlargement of this community eastward to Vladivostok offers the best chance of maintaining and strengthening stability and peace in this important region. After reviewing the necessary conditions for the creation of such a community, I shall discuss the institutional kernel of this community, the Conference for Security and Cooperation in Europe (CSCE) and analyze how the CSCE has already been helping to create common values and expectations. Next I shall consider in greater detail several areas characterized by common values and institutions and by mutual responsiveness to liberal democracy, economic freedom, human rights, environmental protection, and new conceptions of security. I shall conclude with some thoughts about the dialectical relationship between integration and disintegration forces and about how the latter may hinder the evolution of a CSCE community.

THE CAUSES OF PEACE

Almost two hundred years ago, Kant predicted that nations who adopted the republican form of government and whose societies became interpenetrated by transnational relations would constitute themselves into a "league of peace" (*foedus pacificum*).[2] Distinguishing between a league of peace and a peace treaty—the latter merely seeks to stop one war, while the former seeks to end war as a means of settling international disputes[3]—Kant came to believe that ending wars depended not "on grandiose plans for the reform of the state system but on the internal improvement of states and, in particular, the achievement of republican government."[4]

Hence Kant rejected ideas of mergers between states and world government (*volkstaat*): "Unless all is lost, the positive idea of a *world republic* must be replaced by the negative substitute of a union of nations which maintains itself, prevents wars and steadily expands."[5] This "union of nations," in turn, should not seek any power of the sort possessed by nations, but only the maintenance and security of each nation's own freedom, as well as that of the other nations leagued with it, without their having thereby to subject themselves to civil laws and their constraints.[6]

Appearing "to be the limit of what is possible, given the constraints of state sovereignty and the importance of state autonomy on the one hand, and the need for a lawful framework for international relations on the other,"[7] a league of peace meant in essence a voluntary association of law-abiding nations that, due to the quality of their political system and the values of their societies, would informally constitute themselves into an association or union to prevent war. Kant believed that, one day, all nations would become republics and would therefore automatically join the union; thus "perpetual peace" would be guaranteed.

We must distinguish between Kant's idealistic vision of "perpetual peace," which I do not share, and his theoretical insight about the causes of peace, which is of value for the present and future of European security. I cannot improve on Hinsley's description of Kant's main theoretical insight—namely,

> Whatever league or international organization states might come to develop among themselves, it would not be that which would preserve the peace, but their voluntary acceptance as continuing independent nations of a rule of law that was not backed by international organization [meaning international authority] or physical force.[8]

Kant's theoretical insight—in contrast to his idealistic vision—has largely been lost on modern students of international relations, for several reasons. The fact that he believed that peace could become global and perpetual and that progress was inevitable, and that in writings other than *Perpetual Peace* he toyed with the ideal of a cosmopolitan/universal society,[9] obviously alienated sensible realist scholars like Martin Wight and Hedley Bull, who referred to the Kantian paradigm as most representative of idealist thought in international relations.[10] Perhaps more important, the modern realist line of thinking about international relations developed out of the ashes of two world wars and the Holocaust, against the backdrop of the cold war and the prospect of nuclear annihilation. Moreover, the way in which theoreticians thought about the nature of the state, sovereignty, and interstate practices led to a superficial dichotomy, according to which states either survive by means of a balance of power or achieve eternal peace through world government.[11] Not even those theoreticians who have recently shown that institutions help create some order in the Hobbesian state of affairs paid attention to the reciprocal influence between institutions and communities of values.[12]

Today, however, we can no longer overlook Kant's theoretical insights. While we were busy studying the cold war, Western Europe, together with North America, almost imperceptibly developed into a league of liberal republics, thus creating "an expanding separate peace."[13] The contemporary relevance of Kant's thought is also strengthened by "the validity of his prediction that the imperatives of economic modernization and the increasing destructiveness of war could make both the limits of the security of states and the obligations of a cosmopolitan morality even more important."[14] Furthermore, Kant's insights have received empirical corroboration from studies dealing with almost two centuries of warfare which have more or less conclusively shown that democracies do not fight each other.[15]

I cannot overemphasize the importance of these developments. First, we may have to transcend the narrow neo-realist thinking that considers international order to be dependent only on hegemonic power[16] and/or balances of power.[17] Second, such factors as the destructiveness of nuclear weapons[18] and economic interdependence[19] may explain states' reluctance to go to war, but only community bonds and the common identity that becomes established among democratic states can explain dependable expectations of peaceful change.

"Pregnant with implications of a general theory of international relations,"[20] the pluralistic security community idea may help clarify why liberal democracies do not fight one another. Outside the community, where non-democracies abound, power politics and security dilemmas may condition democracies to choose war. Within and through the workings of a community of the like-minded, however, democracies can express their identity—i.e., they can demonstrate their respect for the rule of law and human rights and may thus be able to turn their identity into a common identity that generates mutual trust. Moreover, within a community of sovereign democratic states peaceful change becomes possible because democracies transfer their domestic mechanisms of peaceful conflict-resolution to the international arena, turning them into both legitimate and habitual practices.[21]

PLURALISTIC SECURITY COMMUNITIES

In a pioneering 1957 study Karl Deutsch and his associates introduced the concept of the security community, a group of people that has become integrated to the point that there is a "real assurance that the members of that community will not fight each other physically, but will settle their disputes in some other way."[22] According to Deutsch, security communities may be either "amalgamated" or "pluralistic." Amalgamated security communities imply the formal merger of two or more previously independent units into a single larger unit, with some type of common government after amalgamation. On the other hand, a pluralistic security community, like Kant's league of peace,

> retains the legal independence of separate governments. The combined territory of the United States and Canada is an example of the pluralistic type. Its two separate governmental units form a security community without being merged.[23]

In such a community, settling a dispute by means of war is all but inconceivable. Thus a pluralistic security community is integrated to the point that its units entertain "dependable expectations of peaceful change"; the individual governments within the community together compose an "informal government to ensure peaceful change without subordinating all the differences in values, culture, and the like that make the separate units distinctively free and independent."[24]

Again according to Deutsch, there are two necessary conditions for the creation of a pluralistic security community: (1) compatibility of core values derived from common institutions; (2) mutual responsiveness—a matter of mutual identity, sympathy, and loyalty. The latter refers to "we-feeling," trust and consideration, partial identification in terms of self-images and interests, and successful predictions of behavior and cooperative action in accordance with it.[25] These conditions make war an increasingly less realistic possibility, lacking any practical purpose in the calculations of statesmen and the opinions of political elites.[26] Indeed

> Countries need not disarm suddenly, or even merge their armed forces. . . . As the prospect of war becomes gradually more remote, they can withdraw their troops from their common borders, unit by unit, while still retaining troops for more general disposition.[27]

Pluralistic security communities seem to develop most frequently around "cores of strength."[28] This finding leads to the important theoretical observation that once security starts to depend on community bonds, rather than on power balances, it is disequilibrium rather than equilibrium that promotes dependable expectations of peaceful change. Larger and stronger political units—such as the European Community (EC)—endowed with greater political, administrative, economic, and educational assets, are the cores of strength around which the integrative process almost always develops.

Sense of community also requires particular habits of political behavior which are acquired through processes of social learning and socialization. People learn the new habits slowly, as background conditions change; through various processes of communication they diffuse their "lessons" and expectations to one another. The most important lesson that societies need to learn for the emergence of a pluralistic security community, however, is the "increasing unattractiveness and improbability of war." War becomes unattractive because it promises to be both devastating and indecisive.[29]

Pluralistic security communities also benefit from intellectual movements and traditions that prepare the ground for them and from political decisions that have an aspect of the improbable and original.[30] The influence of functional organization lies mainly in the creation of habits of communication and responsiveness.[31] Deutsch also found that "a military alliance turned out to be a relatively poor pathway toward amalgamation and presumably also toward pluralism," and that excessive military commitments—bringing more burdens than rewards—had a "disintegrative effect."[32]

Deutsch's original concept of a pluralistic security community is not without its conceptual and operational problems. We do not really know how and why changes at the social-psychological level are converted into changes at the governmental level. In effect, said one student of Deutsch's, we cannot find any political structures or processes in pluralistic security communities; there are no groups or classes, no decision-makers, no decisions, very little voluntaristic behavior, and no politics.[33] Ernst Haas has characterized the concept of the pluralistic security community as lacking the political institutions that clearly differentiate communities from ordinary international relations.[34] Robert Lieber has pointed out that the concept is of little value since Western Europe constituted such an arrangement only soon after World War II.[35] Joseph Nye noted that the concept has proven resistant to precise operationalization.[36] Unfortunately, most of the research emphasis has been placed on counting communication interactions, while the broader, more philosophical argument was missed.[37] Below I shall offer a slightly different conception of the pluralistic security community.

Deutsch's conceptual variables constitute the starting point, of course. To sum them up: Pluralistic security communities consist of sovereign states and usually develop around cores of strength through communication and learning processes. The units need not be geographically contingent. The community becomes integrated to the point that the units entertain dependable expectations of peaceful change because of shared values and mutual responsiveness and trust which, in part, are triggered by the utter destructiveness of war.

Deutsch's analysis was incomplete, however, because he treated two key variables as descriptive rather than explanatory, while overlooking an important intervening variable. Members of pluralistic security communities hold dependable expectations of peaceful change not merely because they share just any kind of values, but because they share *liberal democratic* values and allow their societies to become interdependent and linked by transnational economic and cultural relations. Democratic values, in turn, facilitate the creation of strong civil societies—our key intervening variable— which also promote community bonds and common identity and trust through the process of the free interpenetration of societies, particularly as this affects the movement and exchange of people, goods, and ideas. Strong civil societies, for example, greatly facilitate the spread and strengthening of practices that promote human rights and environmental protection; these, in turn, help produce and reinforce community bonds and common identity. A common heritage, religion, and tradition may also condition the development of security communities, although the historical record shows that not all of these variables may be necessary, let alone sufficient.

We should therefore define a pluralistic security community as a group of democratic sovereign states that, agreeing on the unbearable destructiveness of modern war and on political, economic, social, and moral values consistent with democracy, the rule of law, and economic freedom, have transferred their domestic practices to the international arena and allowed their civil societies as well as their institutions to become integrated to the point that the idea of using force loses any practical meaning and even becomes unthinkable.

Deutsch's general treatment of values and expectations also suffered from empirical shortcomings. For example, how do we know whether a pluralistic security community has already been established? Quantitative accounts of communication exchanges may be important, but they are insufficient. Moreover, how can we be sure that values and expectations are part of the explanation of peaceful change? The first question may be approached by showing conclusively that nation-states sharing democratic values and expectations not only do not fight each other, but have also developed an entirely new set of international institutions and practices that transcend the balance of power and are consistent only with a community of values. The second question may be approached with the help of the counterfactual technique.[38] We may ask, for example, what would have happened if Germany had become reunited while not sharing a set of liberal values with the other Western powers? If the answer is that Germany would then have posed a security dilemma for these powers, we have a reason to suspect that, in this case, common democratic values are correlated with peaceful change.

Deutsch did not say much about institutionalization either. But pluralistic security communities must be, and are, institutionalized. It is by means of institutionalization that common identity and trust are translated into specific expectations of appropriate action and practices of peaceful change. Pluralistic security communities, however, need not be endowed with supranational, legislative, judicial, and administrative organs, which are more consistent with amalgamated communities.[39] When confronted by specific security threats, the pluralistic security community may formally organize to defend itself. Similarly, the community may delegate functional tasks to several organizations in order to deal with economic problems. The ideal institution of a pluralistic security community is, however, one that, by becoming the symbol and legitimator of democratic and liberal values, helps member states frame problems and solutions according to shared values and redefine security as a community, rather than a state or interstate problem.

It is very important to differentiate between a pluralistic security community, on the one hand, and alliances and international regimes, on the other. Steve Weber, in this volume, rightly argues that alliances and security communities have different kinds of institutions.[40] But he also argues that the North Atlantic Treaty Organization (NATO) has been both an alliance (against the Communist threat) and a security community (created to prevent intra-alliance conflicts). I do not share this view. First, nation-states do not create security communities; they become a security community by sharing democratic and liberal values and expectations. Second, some—but not all—of the countries of an emerging security community created NATO, and not the other way around. Third, as Deutsch found, alliances rarely produce pluralistic integration. Fourth, it was not NATO, but the voluntary acceptance of common democratic values and expectations by NATO members, that kept the peace. Finally, while NATO's conventional and nuclear weapons supposedly deterred the Soviets, what ultimately made them yield was the quality of the community's values. These values also helped preserve the cohesion of the alliance in times of stress.

We should also be careful not to confuse a security community with an international regime,[41] despite the propensity to do so, because both constrain the behavior of states without a world government or international authority.[42] International regimes usually set institutional-normative limits in one or several linked issue-areas. In this case, expectations converge either because of the existence of a hegemon, because of short-term rational decisions based on functional expectations, or because of a change in interests due to new knowledge or perceptions.[43] In the case of pluralistic security communities, however, expectations converge in a wide range of issue-areas, while common values are a necessary condition for policy coordination and cooperation. We may, however, find that international regimes are part of the institutional makeup of pluralistic security communities.

To finish off this reconceptualization of pluralistic security communities, we need to add an explanation of political change. The reasons why political units change their collective practices and institutions and evolve into something else are usually related to deep and long-lasting historical processes. For instance, the emergence of the modern state in the seventeenth century was preceded by changes in cosmological, philosophical, and religious ideas, in technology and weapons, and in economic systems and institutions, all of which pointed in the same direction—namely, that only the sovereign state could guarantee nations' security and well-being and the dominion of justice. War, experimentation, and practice later helped the sovereignty principle become habitual and be perceived as almost a law of nature. But as John Ruggie has demonstrated, sovereignty is not a given, but rather a legitimating practice based on common understanding or knowledge.[44]

Equally deep and wide-ranging historical forces may have prepared the stage for pluralistic security communities. The utter destructiveness of war, due to technological innovations, "battle fatigue,"[45] economic and ecological interdependence, the change in the meaning of power from territory to wealth, and the development of a global society of states maintained by modern telecommunications may have taught some nation-states to practice a slightly different kind of sovereignty—what we might call "internationalized sovereignty"[46]—when it comes to security issues:

> States within such an internationalized security structure might still try to exercise power or influence over each other. . . . But these effects could take place within a shared institutional context in which certain practices would be ruled out. . . . This is compatible with the institution of sovereignty because sovereignty does not imply *de facto* autonomy; if a state chooses to give up some of its autonomy by identifying its security with that of a collective that is its sovereign prerogative.[47]

In other words, it is a mistake to believe that state sovereignty necessarily leads to war and international anarchy; within a community of states, sovereignty may be collectively interpreted in ways that promote peaceful change.

We have not yet fully explained, however, how the units of a pluralistic security community give up, among themselves, the mutual use or threat of force. The most likely answer is that this surrender involves mutually reinforced reciprocal trust:

> Trust is the expectation that another's behavior will be predictably friendly. . . . Thus trust or distrust predisposes one to interpret another's actions as friendly or threatening when ambiguity exists.[48]

The security dilemmas that result from a state of international anarchy are a typical example of how distrust can turn unfriendliness into a self-fulfilling prophecy. By the same token, however, a commitment to the rule of law, common democratic values, and "we-feeling" may predispose nation-states that have a higher expected utility from peace than from war to trust one another, thereby allowing each sovereign nation to pursue its interests without having to plan for the contingency of war.

This is why nuclear powers sharing democratic values do not feel threatened by one another. By the same token, however, this is why the same powers would be threatened by Iraq were Saddam Hussein to develop nuclear weapons. Plainly speaking, given Saddam's record, he cannot be *trusted*. In short, within a pluralistic security community trust turns peaceful change into a self-fulfilling prophecy and thus into a self-perpetuating phenomenon.

THE PLURALISTIC SECURITY COMMUNITY OF WEST EUROPEAN STATES

Since World War II the countries of Western Europe have gradually constituted themselves into a pluralistic security community. Discovering that the welfare state is not viable if maintained by purely national means,[49] many of these states have created supranational economic institutions while retaining their internationalized sovereignty in security affairs. In this way, West European states have extricated themselves from the cycle of war and generally do not suspect fellow community members of aggressive intentions. In Western Europe,

> Security problems are minimal, even without U.S. protection. Among West European nations, common democratic values inhibit the use of force in their relations; the ideologies of democratic nations do not conflict, and it would be difficult for a European democracy to legitimate an act of war against another democracy. Entrenched democracies help protect minorities against human rights abuses. . . . Western Europe has a highly developed human rights regime. Economic growth, stability, and integration managed by the EC help prevent economic competition from spilling over into military conflict. . . . Economic interdependence among European nations has led to the spread of "liberal nationalism," and liberal values undermine dangerous nationalist impulses which can lead to conflict.[50]

This commonality of central values and institutions is accompanied by a high degree of mutual responsiveness or "we-feeling," which has been enhanced by increasingly open borders that permit the free flow of people, goods, and ideas, and by the increasing interpenetration of West European civil societies by means of a variety of economic, social, cultural, and scientific interactions.

The EC is the security community's core; the other countries composing the community belong to the European Free Trade Association (EFTA). In 1954 some of the EC countries created the West European Union (WEU), a security organization that lay dormant until recently but has shown new signs of life after the recent dramatic changes in Europe. Most members of the security community belong to NATO, which, together with a strong nuclear deterrent, has helped maintain peace between East and West. All members of the security community belong to the CSCE. Thus, as community bonds and common practices became increasingly institutionalized, balance-of-power relations faded from importance in Western Europe, to be replaced by a league of peace of the kind foreseen by Kant.

Democracy, economic growth and interdependence, nuclear weapons, and a bipolar international system conditioned West European nations to a rational expectation of greater utility from peace than from war. Nevertheless, while nuclear weapons partly explain why West and East were deterred from open hostilities during the cold war, they cannot explain the almost complete absence of reciprocal threats between the two West European nuclear states, and why, even should the United States eventually leave the European stage, Germany has committed itself not to develop nuclear weapons. While it is true that bipolarity was a necessary background condition for the birth of the pluralistic security community, it cannot explain why the community bonds and the practice of internationalized sovereignty were actually developed, maintained, and strengthened.*

Indeed no other factor has been more important than European integration in conditioning the learning and socialization processes involved in building a security community. Even when economic integration seemed to have come to a standstill, as in the 1970s, the bonds that "create the common purposes and knowledge that lead to collective identity" continued to grow.[51] The common identity that was created through processes of economic integration may not have been enough to sustain political amalgamation—although in the last years amalgamating bonds appear to have been strengthened[52]—but it was enough to change the meaning of sovereignty and to produce a common identification with the community, which has become a source of security and well-being for all of its members.

THE TRANSATLANTIC PLURALISTIC SECURITY COMMUNITY

On 18 June 1991, in a speech that the press characterized as "potentially the most important American policy statement since the Cold War began,"[53] U.S. Secretary of State James Baker said that North America and Western Europe had become a value community based on Enlightenment ideas of universal applicability: "These values are based upon the concept of individual political rights and economic liberty [and] are the foundation for a Euro-Atlantic community already reaching beyond Berlin to the East."[54] Pointing to

---

*Structural change toward multipolarity may not lead to instability and war after all, at least not in Western Europe, because stability there is no longer maintained by a system of power balances, but by community bonds that sustain dependable expectations of peaceful change.

common organizations such as NATO, the EC, the CSCE, and the G-7, as well as to the extensive informal and private relations among the democracies, Baker added that "Euro-Atlantic integration has made it literally inconceivable that localized disputes could become a source of serious conflict among these states."[55]

In principle, Mr. Baker is right to argue that a transatlantic pluralistic security community is already a reality. But while it is safe to argue that the members of the transatlantic community share dependable expectations of peaceful change, their common identity would have to be strengthened still further before the community is firmly established. Part of the problem has been that throughout its history, the United States could not make up its mind whether it was a European power. Moreover, many of its elites have held the view that the United States has merely been a force with significant influence on the equilibrium of Europe and have therefore associated the special security relationship with the continent exclusively with NATO.[56] Still weak, then, is the realization that the future of American and European security is intimately linked by common values and expectations to a pluralistic security community, with or without NATO.

This realization, however, must also take place in Europe, and most importantly among EC political elites. Sharing the perception of many Americans that the United States is merely a military partner, some EC members and their elites have been arguing that with the passing of the common military threat, the security ways of Europe and the United States must part. In this spirit they have called for the creation of a European security organization.[57] We will be able to say that mutual responsiveness and common identity at the transatlantic level have been firmly established only when Europeans, referring to a European security organization or system, take for granted that it also includes North Americans.

FROM SAN DIEGO TO VLADIVOSTOK: A PLURALISTIC SECURITY COMMUNITY

In the long run—within a decade or two—a pluralistic security community stretching from San Diego to Vladivostok may be encouraged by the increasing unattractiveness and implausibility of interstate war in that region and by the increasing penetration of the basic political and economic values of the West into Central and Eastern Europe. For the United States, such a community may offer the best way to maintain a foothold in Europe and preserve its security interests there.

Secretary of State Baker recently recognized this point of view when he said that the U.S. objective "is both a Europe whole and free, and a Euro-Atlantic community that extends from Vancouver to Vladivostok." Adding that "the door to the Euro-Atlantic community is open" and that "only the Soviets can decide to step over the threshold," Baker said that "the time has come to set new goals, which go beyond the concept of balance, and begin to establish the basis for a real cooperative security."[58]

The enlarged pluralistic security community would constitute itself as an extension of that already existing in Western Europe and North America. The separate units would retain their sovereignty and the power to enforce law and order at home and could have independent foreign policies. But their economies would become increasingly integrated; people, money, and goods and services would flow freely among them. (The economic integration of Eastern Europe into the West would have to take place very gradually, however, to prevent the collapse of the entire structure.)

The EC and its institutions will probably be the nucleus of the security community for quite some time. Germany, instead of becoming another power in a multipolar balance-of-power system, will be the keystone of this nucleus. The United States will remain the world's military superpower for the foreseeable future and the shield against military threats stemming from outside the community. But it is the EC that, like a magnet, is now attracting non-aligned European nations such as Austria and Sweden and an increasing number of East European states eager to fashion some sort of bond with this strong core.

An enlarged pluralistic security community cannot be constituted before four conditions are met. First, the EC must not constitute itself into a United States of Europe; instead, it should maintain its pluralistic political nature while at the same time committing itself to gradually integrating the economies of East European countries that have adopted liberal political and economic regimes and made some economic progress. The reason is simple. An amalgamated EC state would pull the rug out from under the idea of a Euro-Atlantic community of *sovereign* states. Amalgamation might discourage East European countries from seeking integration with the EC on a pluralistic basis; the latter would then lose its function as a core of strength. A United States of Europe might also give rise to fears that Europe is pursuing power-oriented goals; this could slow down or even halt the community-building process.

Second, because a security community cannot be imposed from above but grows from below, no attempt should be made at present to create a collective security system based on the CSCE. Only when the members of the CSCE have constituted themselves into a security community will a CSCE collective security system make sense.

Third, Eastern Europe and the former Soviet Union should be encouraged to finish the processes they have begun. There will be no CSCE security community without the successful completion of democratization and liberalization in the East. Fourth, the United States must lend political support to the idea and practice of a CSCE pluralistic security community.

If the goal is a Euro-Atlantic pluralistic security community order, our classical ideas of national security and of security institutions are no longer particularly useful.[59] Since the seventeenth century, individuals have identified their own security with that of their sovereign states and have taken the balance of power as a necessary condition for dissuading other states from challenging their own sovereignty, or, for that matter, the sovereignty principle itself.

Within a pluralistic security community, however, national identity is expressed through the merging of efforts in a larger entity.[60] The institutional context for the exercise of power changes;[61] the right to use force shifts from the units to the collectivity of sovereign states and becomes legitimate only against external threats or against community members that return to their old illiberal and undemocratic ways. Power balances, nuclear deterrence, and threats of retaliation retain meaningful and functional roles, but only in thought about the community as a whole, vis-à-vis other political units. In case of an external threat or attack, the Euro-Atlantic community might have to respond as an integrated military defense organization. In its present form, however, the

CSCE is not, and may never become, such an organization. On the other hand, NATO—by all means an integrated military defense organization—will for the foreseeable future continue to guarantee the security of only part of the Euro-Atlantic region. Hence the task of providing a collective deterrent and shield against external threats to the enlarged community would have to be redefined and given to a reconstituted or even entirely new type of security structure.

This structure would nevertheless be neither an alliance nor a collective security system in any classic sense. On the one hand, its *raison d'être* would be defending the security community on a permanent basis, whenever defense is required and as long as the community exists, rather than merely bringing together the forces of autonomous states on a temporary basis to face a common short-term threat. On the other hand—since in our case security should be understood neither in narrow terms of the nation-state nor in universalist terms of the whole world, but rather in terms of a regional community of sovereign states—collective security would then mean not only dealing collectively with security threats within the community, but also dealing collectively with outside threats.

It follows, however, that a pluralistic security community must also organize itself to face potential conflicts and threats arising from within the community. Here is where the institutional context for the exercise of power really breaks new ground because power imbalances become less meaningful and the community, when dealing with security problems from within, must turn into a collective security system that *would not use force*. For example, border disputes, ethnic conflicts within multinational states, human rights abuses, non-democratic practices, deterioration of civilian control of the military, terrorist activities, immigration, and economic and environmental crises would require institutions and practices involving a complex network of political, economic, and social relations among states, ethnic groups, dislocated peoples, old and new immigrants, etc. that go beyond classic Westphalian military security measures.[62]

These institutions and practices may involve Confidence-Building Measures (CBMs), mechanisms for the peaceful resolution of ethnic disputes, non-offensive military cooperation, weapons reduction zones, nuclear-weapons-free zones, the use of collective and binding economic sanctions as punitive responses, and collective peace-keeping forces to separate combatants.[63] Most important, they would have to enhance security by helping create a commonality of values and by strengthening mutual responsiveness.

Can NATO become such an institution? Weber says it should.[64] I disagree. During the transition from the old order to the new, NATO—together with the remnants of military balance and nuclear deterrence—should continue to play its classic historical security role. This is because the constituent republics of the former Soviet Union may still end up as praetorian states and therefore never join the Euro-Atlantic pluralistic security community.[65] But if and when they change their spots, power balances would lose even more of their classic meaning, and weapons, including nuclear weapons, would have to be aimed at new targets. At this point, NATO would have reached its day of reckoning. It would either turn into the external arm of a security community stretching from San Diego to Vladivostok or be faced with extinction, making room for other institutions more appropriate to the new situation.

Furthermore, NATO is powerless to deal with threats and conflicts arising within the community involving ethnic, human rights, economic, and environmental issues. We need not go far to prove this point. Events in the last couple of years have shown that "there is little that NATO . . . can do about civil war in Yugoslavia, Soviet intervention in the Baltic states, or conflict between Romania and Hungary."[66]

This brings us back to the transition period. Weber believes that NATO is best suited to help convert East European countries and the former Soviet Union to democratic and liberal values because it can (1) offer these countries some pointers about how to restructure their military forces; (2) squeeze them with economic conditionality; and (3) if nothing else works, threaten them with direct intervention.[67] From a security community perspective, these measures do not make sense, however. Plainly speaking, there must be better ways to create "we-feeling" among peoples.

One such way might be to build institutions that link the development of peaceful means of conflict-resolution and CBMs to common human rights, economic, scientific, and cultural activities. The Helsinki process and the CSCE have evolved into this kind of institution and become "the one group that brings together all the countries of Europe and North America on the basis of a common commitment to human rights and democratic principles."[68] NATO would still have a role to play in the building of a Euro-Atlantic pluralistic security community: providing a protective atmosphere for the CSCE processes. Likewise, the EC would also have a role to play in community building: bringing East European countries and the former Soviet Union into Europe.

CREATING A SECURITY COMMUNITY FROM SCRATCH: THE CSCE

The CSCE is the institutional embryo of a pluralistic security community stretching from San Diego to Vladivostok. In the words of Victor Ghebali,

It was never the aim of the Helsinki process to ensure, let alone guarantee, security in Europe, and the Charter of Paris [CSCE, 1990] has done nothing to alter this fundamental fact. Its concern is not collective security, but . . . security considered in terms of the interdependence of its economic, ecological, and humanitarian, as well as its political and military, dimensions.[69]

Unlike other international institutions in the world arena and with almost no formal organization, the CSCE institutionalized, at the international level, the tacit agreement of its members to practice liberal democratic values and peaceful change. In other words, the CSCE's business has been to establish and diffuse a collective liberal conscience in civil societies and their states, with the result that solutions are increasingly framed collectively in terms of human rights, basic human freedoms, and the free exchange of goods, persons, and ideas. Furthermore, the CSCE's ongoing processes and procedures have come to resemble a clearing house for ideas and a means for solving problems through conferences and diplomacy, turning it into a laboratory for novel practices of peaceful change.

Defining areas of common interest, the CSCE selects appropriate institutional channels (not necessarily those of the CSCE) for translating broad agreement about values and expectations into specific multilateral cooperative measures. The basic idea is for the

CSCE to spread its influence to the entire community of nations and their institutions, providing legitimacy and moral force to the activities of international organizations such as NATO, the Organization for Economic Cooperation and Development (OECD), and the Council of Europe.[70]

The CSCE was constituted in August 1975 by the Helsinki Final Act, which was signed by all European states (except Albania), Canada, and the United States.[71] This act, as subsequently supplemented over the years by a series of follow-up conferences and expert meetings, provides a normative framework for its member states based on adherence to multi-party democracy, free elections, human rights, and liberal economic systems.

The Helsinki Final Act created three broad areas of activity, known as "baskets." Basket One contains the ten basic principles of the CSCE, as well as the guidelines for a common security system based on CBMs, disarmament, and mechanisms for the peaceful resolution of disputes. Through the years it has added injunctions concerning human rights and international terrorism.[72] Basket Two created the framework for cooperation in the economic, scientific, and environmental realms, stressing the elimination of restrictions to trade, industrial cooperation, and technology transfer. In Basket Three, dealing with the "human dimension," members committed themselves "to facilitate family reunification and meetings, marriage between citizens of different countries, an expansion of contacts and travel, especially in tourism, business, sports, and among young people."[73]

The effectiveness of the CSCE processes has depended on the way in which these baskets were tied together in negotiation processes[74]—for example, linking human rights with military security and territorial guarantees, or linking economic with environmental issues, environmental issues with human rights, and security with the flow of goods, persons, and ideas.

CSCE decisions are taken by unanimous vote (which explains the length of the negotiations)—a liability by all means. But once an agreement has been reached, its political legitimacy is paramount. For fifteen years the CSCE lacked formal organization. The process derived some structure and continuity from the follow-up conferences and expert meetings, at which the CSCE continuously reviewed, updated, and monitored compliance with its basic principles. The

Belgrade follow-up meeting (1977–78), held in the shadow of rising superpower tensions, could do no more than provide continuity to the process. The second follow-up conference, in Madrid (1980–83), was more successful because it prepared the ground for the 1986 Stockholm CBMs agreements. The third follow-up conference, in Vienna (1986–89), further expanded human rights commitments and called for the protection of minorities. It also instituted annual reviews.[75]

The Vienna conference also played an important role in the security field by providing a pan-European-American institutional roof for negotiations between NATO and the Warsaw Treaty Organization (WTO) on conventional arms control. At Vienna the CSCE also created the Conference on the Human Dimension, which met in Paris (1989), Copenhagen (1990), and Moscow (1991). Regarding Basket Two, a meeting on the environment was held in Sofia in 1989; a conference on economic cooperation in Europe, the second of its kind, met in Bonn in 1990.[76]

On 19–21 November 1990, the CSCE adopted the "Charter of Paris for a New Europe." Stressing the historical moment that Europe and the world were experiencing, the charter not only reaffirmed the values on which the CSCE was based, but also set higher expectations, which amount to a vision of a CSCE pluralistic security community. For example, the member states pledged to undertake mutual cooperation and support measures to "make the democratic gains irreversible."[77] The charter also made a procedural change by dividing the three baskets into seven sections: the human dimension, security, economic cooperation, the environment, culture, immigrant workers, and the Mediterranean.

The Paris meeting went further, however, and created formal institutions. First, it arranged for regular political consultations at three levels: (1) heads of state; (2) foreign ministers, meeting once a year as a Council of Ministers; and (3) senior officials, meeting twice a year as a Committee of Senior Officials. Second, it created a permanent secretariat (Prague), a Conflict Prevention Center (Vienna), and an Office for Free Elections (Warsaw). In June 1991, it was agreed that any CSCE member, with the support of twelve other member states, may convene an emergency meeting of the Committee of Senior Officials to deal with unrest in another member state. Emergency meetings will take place within two days of the request—providing a new mechanism for peaceful resolution of conflicts.[78]

This short description of the CSCE's structures and processes points to its many advantages. First, it is a comprehensive process which transcends East-West conflicts and mindsets, placing neutral and/or small states on an equal footing with the superpowers.[79] Second, the CSCE is a continuous cooperative process, always correcting itself, changing course if necessary, and adding new ideas and institutions to its baskets. Third, it defines security in nonmilitary terms, extending the concept to the area of ethnic strife, immigration, economics, human rights, and the environment. It is therefore attuned to Europe's new security threats. Fourth, its approach is pragmatic and in many ways functional. Fifth, it amounts to an intermediate solution for European integration—short of amalgamation but beyond state independence. Sixth, the CSCE complements rather than substitutes for the work of other institutions. Redundancy is not a problem, however, because of the way in which the CSCE and other institutions have divided their labor. Seventh, the CSCE legitimates the return of East European countries and the former Soviet Union to Europe. Finally, through the CSCE, the United States continues to be involved in European security affairs without at the same time having to play old-style European balance-of-power games.

The revolutions of 1989 that transformed East European countries into multi-party democracies and more open economies, the evolution of the Soviet Union toward political pluralism and economic openness, and the development in these countries of human rights regimes—the most extensive these countries have ever known*—are, in the words of a recent U.S. report on CSCE activities, "a credit to the CSCE process, the standards of state behavior

---

*Today, for example, Polish pluralism is "rampant," and after free parliamentary elections in 1990 Hungary is "close to being a full-fledged democracy with a civil society." Bulgaria's new independent national assembly has passed laws that are in full accordance with CSCE principles, allowing Bulgarians to gain many of their basic freedoms. Czechoslovakia, led by a former prisoner of conscience, Vaclav Havel, has established a republican government. And even Romania, whose leadership is suspected of having "hijacked" the revolution, has declared its adherence to the Vienna concluding documents and taken steps to establish a pluralistic regime (U.S. Department of State, report on Helsinki Final Act, 1989–90 [note 72 below], pp. 5, 18, 21).

it set, the mutual confidence it built, the openness to change it encouraged, and the respect for human rights it demanded."[80] Thus, this report concluded, "Now, for the first time, the values long promulgated by CSCE are universally recognized as valid throughout the CSCE community of states, if not yet fully practiced."[81]

CSCE injunctions were not imposed on East European countries and the Soviet Union, but functioned as signposts in their democratization and liberalization, defining the direction they should take for transitional governments, newly elected democratic governments, and many independent citizen groups.[82] For example, in the early 1980s, the CSCE was already offering Poland's Solidarity movement "a goal which it viewed as effectively realizing some of its own European ideals."[83] The fact that the Soviets did not take military action against Poland in 1981 may have had something to do with CSCE principles, adherence to which the Soviets saw as being in their own interest.[84] In the paragraphs that follow I shall describe in more detail the progress within the framework of the CSCE's three baskets.

BASKET ONE

CSCE processes were not inconsequential for the progress achieved on human rights in Eastern Europe and the former Soviet Union. First, the CSCE provided the West with a way to link human rights to common security and economic issues on which the East placed preeminent value. Second, at CSCE forums member states not only exchanged opinions, but they also bargained about the meaning of human rights. By the end of the Vienna follow-up meeting, the parties had more or less reached a consensus on the nature of human rights. Third, the CSCE became a legitimating force that empowered Eastern grass-roots and opposition groups to strive for human rights. As soon as the CSCE established its human rights principles, with Western encouragement, human rights, opposition, and minority groups used these principles against the state establishments that were not living up to their commitments on human rights.

Although much remains to be done in the area of human rights, basic human rights are now being respected in Eastern Europe and the former Soviet Union. In Hungary, Poland, and Czechoslovakia most human rights are guaranteed by law. People are free to engage in political activities and may exercise their right of public assembly. Freedom of speech, religion, conscience, and organization are also guaranteed. In elections held in Bulgaria in 1990, the Movement for Rights and Freedom (whose base is in the districts inhabited by ethnic Turks) gained 23 of the 400 seats in the Grand National Assembly. In the Soviet Union, since the end of 1988 there had been no known political or religious prisoners, and no cases of new long-term hospitalization of dissidents have been reported. Citizens could express their opinion about their government and its policies more or less freely, and the limits on Jewish emigration stemmed from Western restrictions and absorption difficulties in Israel. A cloud of suspicion still hangs over Romania's new leaders for not having prosecuted members of the old regime's secret police, the Securitate. Nonetheless, basic freedoms in Romania are more or less unrestricted.[85] All of the above countries have also stopped jamming foreign radio transmissions.

This progress led the Council of Europe to grant Hungary, Poland, Czechoslovakia, Yugoslavia, and the Soviet Union special guest status. Hungary has already become a full member, and the other countries are expecting to join soon. East European countries also expect to adhere to the European Convention on Human Rights.[86]

If the changes reported above have improved European security by increasing mutual responsiveness and trust—due to the new-found legitimacy of East European countries and the former Soviet Union in Western eyes—the common security measures approved under the aegis of the CSCE have provided for military transparency, reduced risk of escalation, and, after the signature of the CFE conventional arms control agreement in November 1990, a greatly diminished threat to Western Europe of Soviet surprise attack. The CSCE's greatest achievement in the security realm, however, has been the development of a set of practices and methods for building mutual confidence and for settling disputes peacefully.

It is in this context that we should understand the importance of the 1986 Stockholm CBMs agreement.[87] Prior notification of military activities down to a certain level of forces, mandatory invitations to all members to observe military exercises above a certain size, exchange of annual forecasts of military activities, and the right of on-site ground or airborne ("challenge") inspection are functional security measures as well as ways to increase human contacts and the exchange of information among military establishments. Thus they create mutual trust and responsiveness. For example, challenge inspections have become almost a routine element in military cooperation and "the observation programs for military exercises are also a natural way for an ever-growing network of experts to keep in touch."[88]

In Vienna new CBMs were added to the list, such as the reporting of "hazardous" incidents of a military nature and the promotion of military-to-military contacts between senior representatives.[89] For example, in January–February 1990, a Military Doctrine Seminar brought together some of the highest ranking officers of both alliances, as well as many experts, to discuss defense budgets and training and military doctrine.[90]

The signature of the CFE agreement was a major arms control achievement because, within the territory between the Atlantic and the Urals, conventional weapons parity was instituted at much lower levels than before: 20,000 tanks, 30,000 armored combat vehicles, 20,000 artillery pieces, 6,800 combat aircraft, and 2,000 attack helicopters.[91]

The CSCE also became directly involved in the development of emergency mechanisms for the peaceful settlement of disputes. One of these mechanisms, the emergency meeting of the Council of Senior Officials, was first tested in 1991, when Croatia and Slovenia declared their independence from the Yugoslav federation. Soon after the commencement of hostilities, a CSCE emergency meeting was convened; it called for the peaceful resolution of the crisis and, more important, empowered two EC delegations—one for mediation, the other to monitor a cease-fire—to make sure that the CSCE resolutions were implemented. The CSCE's unanimous decision helped frame the nature of the solution in a collective way, carried diplomatic weight, and legitimated the practical steps taken by EC ministers. Going beyond the immediate crisis, it set a precedent and created a new practice for dealing peacefully with ethnic strife within the boundaries of the CSCE states.

BASKET TWO

According to the most recent U.S. report on CSCE activities, by the end of March 1990, "every country of Eastern Europe was governed by a regime committed to implementing market-based reform in its economy."[92] The CSCE contributed to this situation by providing various mechanisms for economic cooperation between Western and Eastern Europe. CSCE conferences also became a forum where practical solutions were first raised and discussed. In addition, East European countries began to understand that *the road to the EC runs through the CSCE* and its principles.

The response of Western countries to the sudden economic freedom in the former Eastern bloc countries has been to establish normal levels of East-West trade, finance the process of Eastern Europe's transition to capitalism (here the new European Bank for Reconstruction and Development [EBRD] will play a significant role), facilitate privatization processes, and bring these countries into the Bretton Woods institutions. Significant economic assistance has already been extended to some countries and is being considered for others. Among the commitments being coordinated by the EC are $15 billion in aid pledged to Hungary and Poland through 1992. The World Bank plans to increase its loans to Eastern Europe from $540 million in fiscal 1988/89 and $1.8 billion in fiscal 1989/90 to $7.5 billion over the next three fiscal years.[93]

Following the EC proposal to sign special "European Agreements" with Poland, Czechoslovakia, and Hungary, East European countries have begun to expect to join the EC sooner rather than later. In accordance with the special agreements, the EC will eliminate the remaining quotas on imports from the East and will gradually draw the associated countries into its free trade regime. Reciprocity will be forfeited to allow East European countries to catch up. In Hungary the removal of subsidies, the liberalization of import controls, moves toward convertibility, and the adoption of Western-style banking systems and accounting norms have been implemented with one eye on economic efficiency and the other on eventual EC membership. In Poland the government appointed a plenipotentiary for Polish-European integration, with the task of ensuring that Polish standards and economic regulations are adapted to EC norms.[94] Thus the EC has begun to fulfill its role as the community's core of strength.

There has also been a clear trend to balance trade between East and West, which means reorienting Eastern trade toward the West. For example, during 1990 Czechoslovakia's trade with the Soviet

Union fell between 14 and 15 percent, while trade with the West increased. The same trend was evident in Hungary, where in the course of 1990 the proportion of total exports going to Eastern Europe fell from 41 to 29 percent, while the share of imports from Eastern Europe decreased from 40 to 32 percent. Poland actually had a $3.8 billion trade surplus in 1990, and the trend of its trade shifted toward the West.[95]

The foreign investment picture complements that of trade. At the end of 1990 East European countries had as many as 10,000 joint ventures with foreign participation. In Hungary alone new foreign capital investment in joint ventures surpassed $1 billion between January 1990 and March 1991.[96] In Hungary, Czechoslovakia, Poland, Romania, and Bulgaria the framework for privatization has been established by law. This framework includes large state-owned companies as well as small business. Restitution of properties confiscated by the Communist regimes has already begun. For example, last February the Czech government passed a law on the restitution of 70,000 properties confiscated under the old regime.[97] Poland has devised a creative privatization plan under which over 27 million adults will receive majority ownership of 400 state-owned factories, representing 25 percent of the country's industrial sales.[98] In the Soviet Union new legislation set no limit to foreign exposure, profit, and participation, and there were strong pressures for privatization.[99]

Environmental protection has been one of the most important values adopted by the CSCE and a symbol of Europe's new common security problems and solutions. CSCE processes and institutions, by supporting nongovernmental environmental groups and civic associations, have been a means for strengthening Eastern Europe's fragile civil societies, while at the same time helping to build a measure of mutual responsiveness between them. "Green" movements played an important role in the liberalization of East European societies from communism, especially in Hungary and Bulgaria. Ecological protests by Soviet intellectuals and later by a broader stratum of the population marked an early stage of the reform movement in the Soviet Union.[100] With the passage of time, some environmental civic associations became parties, special ministries for the environment were set up, and the declassification of environmental data led to a new wave of environmentalist activity throughout the region.

In March 1989 the first CSCE-sponsored environmental conference met in Sofia. Romania objected to some resolutions and unanimity was not achieved. Later, however, Romania withdrew its
opposition. In 1990 the Danube Charter of Sustainable Development
was signed by some twenty organizations from Austria and Czechoslovakia. A group of countries including Austria, Czechoslovakia,
Hungary, and Italy has been working to foster regional cooperation
on environmental management and data systems, waste management, and nuclear safety. The EC has so far pledged $65 million for
environmental programs in Poland and Hungary and has plans to
extend its loan programs to Bulgaria, Czechoslovakia, and Romania.
Most, if not all, of the countries of the former Eastern bloc are
candidates for admission to the European Environmental Agency,
whose primary task will be to collect uniform, continent-wide data
on the environment. There has also been some pressure to create
an environmental office and lending program within the EBRD.[101]
Bilateral and multilateral environmental relations are developing
steadily within the region. For example, the United States has
contributed funds to create the Regional Environmental Center for
Central and Eastern Europe, based in Hungary. The EC has also
contributed funds for this project.[102]

BASKET THREE

The CSCE's Basket Three helps build the infrastructure of
human relations that is a necessary condition for generating mutual
responsiveness. Because it deals with the mobilizing forces of mass
tourism; the universalist tendencies of the mass media, culture,
science, and education; and the economic incentives to supranational cooperation, it has helped not only to strengthen civic associations, grass-roots groups, sports clubs, scientific associations,
churches, and trade unions,[103] but also to create bridges among the
civil societies themselves.

As a result of the liberal reforms in Eastern Europe and the
Soviet Union, travel regulations have largely been abandoned. For
example, in Romania alone half a million passports were issued in
the first months of 1990. The Soviet Union no longer restricted its
citizens' contacts with foreigners. Between October 1989 and April

1990, the U.S. embassy issued almost 40,000 visas to private Soviet visitors. In the same period, the U.S. embassy in Poland issued more than 75,000 visas to private Polish visitors. During the same period, only 7 Soviet nuclear families remained separated by national borders (and none in East European countries). In a comparable six-month period (October 1984-April 1985), the number of nuclear families that remained separated was much larger (108 [Soviet Union], 82 [Romania], 187 [Poland], 10 [Bulgaria], 2 [Hungary], and 1 [Czechoslovakia]).[104]

Cultural ties between East and West are also being built by the free flow of information through newspapers, radio, television, and the like. It has been estimated that more than 300,000 Hungarian homes receive Western satellite TV broadcasts. The Polish media now compare favorably with their counterparts in Western Europe.[105] Furthermore, the CSCE has directly tried to influence the creation of mutual identity by bringing together thousands of intellectuals, writers, and artists to discuss the role of art and culture in European society.[106]

INTEGRATION OR DISINTEGRATION? YES

In a recent article, John L. Gaddis has argued that the post–cold war order will be characterized by both integrative and disintegrative forces.[107] Here I have dealt mainly with the former: collective security, economic and ecological interdependence, diffusion and integration of ideas, and peace. But Gaddis is right. The increase of integrative forces has been and will continue to be accompanied by the dividing forces of nationalism, ethnic strife, economic protectionism, religion, and racism. This phenomenon is by no means new; Europe has experienced a dialectical conflict between integration and disintegration since at least the fall of the Roman Empire. Elsewhere, John Ruggie and I have described world order as an accommodation of opposites, constituted by different mutually exclusive aspects of reality that nevertheless add to our understanding of the phenomenon as a whole. Integration and disintegration are therefore different aspects of the same international reality. In a dialectical fashion, gains for integration trigger disintegrative forces, and vice versa.[108]

I have argued here that of the different kinds of international organization and integration, a pluralistic security community seems to be the best for reconciling the need for international governance with the still strong desire to cling to national and regional identities. The balance between unity and fragmentation would have to be tipped in favor of the former, however, before a pluralistic security community from San Diego to Vladivostok could become part and parcel of international reality.

The EC has been and remains reluctant to integrate additional states into its successful experiment, partly because of the desire of many of its members for some kind of political amalgamation. Moreover, many EC countries fear that "broadening" may come at the expense of "deepening." There is the real fear—"If it ain't broke, don't fix it"—that the broadening process could dismantle some of the gains already achieved.

Regarding the CSCE itself, many of its institutions and practices are still in their infancy, and some may never take off. In spite of the gains reported above, Eastern Europe and the former Soviet Union still have much ground to cover before they develop the kind of "we-feeling" that already exists among the nations of Western Europe and North America.

Ethnic strife probably poses the greatest danger and the toughest challenge to the constitution of a pluralistic security community from San Diego to Vladivostok. The most imminent threat seems to come from the potential fragmentation of Central and East European states, and especially the former Soviet Union, into their ethnic/national components. Everywhere in the East, minorities are demanding territorial and political changes; what is happening in Yugoslavia today may turn out to be child's play compared with what can happen in the former Soviet Union.

Lately, however, the ghosts of old disintegrative ethnic forces have been roaming free in some West European states (Belgium, France, Spain), a fact that has affected the position of these states regarding Croatian and Slovenian independence. And on the other side of the Atlantic, the U.S. government still has not made up its mind whether to continue playing the role of world policeman or to practice what it preaches, at least in the Northern Hemisphere, and actively strive for the institutionalization of a pluralistic security community stretching from San Diego to Vladivostok. The various disintegrative forces in the East, however, may persuade the U.S. government that the community's hour has not yet arrived. U.S. inaction, in turn, may prove a self-fulfilling prophecy that dooms the constitution of the enlarged security community.

We are in no position to predict the ultimate balance between integrative and disintegrative forces. The outcome will depend on many future choices and decisions made by at least thirty-five nation-states in the next decade or so. Whatever the outcome, it will never be final. It is always discouraging to be reminded of the fact that while cooperation and common identity efforts usually take years to build, they can be destroyed almost overnight by forces of disintegration. In addition, regional conflicts, involving Third World countries that have mastered the technological secrets of mass destruction, may become more than a sideshow for a league of peace attempting to live up to its democratic values.

On the other hand, as a matter of interest and practice, peaceful change in the area between San Diego and Vladivostok has never been closer to achievement. Institutional innovation, in the shape of CSCE processes, has promoted pluralistic integration and given rise to an international learning process about pluralistic integration while at the same time attempting to control tribal instincts and pressures in a peaceful manner. New measures, some of which are starting to be discussed, may further help control nationalist passions and strengthen community bonds. I have in mind (1) new types of confederative arrangements in which sovereignty is shared between the center and its constitutive parts; (2) the development of CSCE international regimes, such as dealing with the transfer of dual-purpose technologies and arms to politically and militarily sensitive areas outside the community; (3) the creation of nuclear-weapons-free zones, not necessarily involving all CSCE states; (4) the development of common energy policies and measures to deal with energy crises; and (5) the creation of collective CSCE mechanisms for humanitarian and relief efforts wherever they are needed, inside or outside the community.

The CSCE's ultimate goal, then, is not to eliminate national and ethnic sentiments; that is impossible. What can and must be done, so long as states benefit from pluralistic integration, is to keep them underground. During the cold war, a bipolar structure helped to "bury" national and ethnic sentiments in a wide area of Eastern and Western Europe. The CSCE should try to bury them again, this time under a structure of common values, understandings, and practices. If CSCE processes succeed, eventually, the resulting league of peace will still be at the mercy of the now more or less permanent dialectical conflict between integration and disintegration. Contrary to Kant's predictions, for the foreseeable future we should expect only a *non-perpetual* peace.

NOTES

I wish to thank Beverly Crawford and Avi Segal for their useful comments and Anat Toder for research assistance. I am also indebted to the Leonard Davis Institute for International Relations, the Hebrew University of Jerusalem, for financial support.

1. Karl W. Deutsch et al., *Political Community and the North Atlantic Area* (Princeton: Princeton University Press, 1957). The concept of "security community" was first introduced by Richard W. Van Wagenen, *Research in the International Organization Field: Some Notes on a Possible Focus* (Princeton: Princeton University, Center for Research on World Political Institutions, 1952). The classic study on peaceful change is Edward H. Carr, *The Twenty Years' Crisis 1919–1939: An Introduction to the Study of International Relations* (London: Macmillan, 1951). During the 1930s, an International Studies Conference on Peaceful Change (and collective security) produced a large number of studies. For an introductory report on the conference, see Blanch W. Cook, Sandi E. Cooper, and Charles Chatfield, eds., *Peaceful Change: Procedures, Raw Materials, Colonies*, vol. 1 of Proceedings of the Tenth International Studies Conference, Paris, 28 June–3 July 1937 (New York: Garland, 1972). For a detailed bibliography of the conference studies, see Fergus Chalmers Wright, *Peaceful Change: Population and Peace: A Survey of International Opinion on Claims for Relief from Population Pressure*, International Studies Conference vol. 2 (New York: Garland, 1972). See also Esko Antola: "Theories of Peaceful Change: An Excursion to the Study of Change in International Relations in the 1930s," *Cooperation and Conflict* 19 (1989): 235–50, and "Peaceful Change as a Model for Europe," *Current Research on Peace and Violence* 7 (1984): 229–46.

2. Immanuel Kant, *Perpetual Peace and Other Essays*, tr. Ted Humphrey (Indianpolis: Hackett, 1983), p. 117. The Latin term *foedus* may be translated as league, covenant, or treaty. Kant also used terms such as association, union, or federation. As F. H. Hinsley has said, "Because of his use of such phrases most people firmly believe that he advocated international federation in our modern sense of the term. . . . This is not the case" (*Power and the Pursuit of Peace* [Cambridge: Cambridge University Press, 1967], p. 66).

3. Kant, *Perpetual Peace* (note 2), p. 117.

4. Andrew Hurrell, "Kant and the Kantian Paradigm in International Relations," *Review of International Studies* 16 (1990): 183. See also Hinsley (note 2).

5. As quoted in Hinsley (note 2), p. 63. The translation of the passage from Kant is from C. F. Friedrich, *Inevitable Peace* (1948), appendix, p. 257.

6. Kant, *Perpetual Peace* (note 2), p. 117.

7. Hurrell (note 4), p. 193.

8. Hinsley (note 2), p. 66.

9. Immanuel Kant, "Idea for a Universal History with a Cosmopolitan Purpose," in Kant, *Perpetual Peace* (note 2), pp. 29–40.

10. See, for example, Hedley Bull, *The Anarchical Society* (New York: Columbia University Press, 1977), and Martin Wight, "An Anatomy of International Thought," *Review of International Studies* 13 (July 1987).

11. When "bashing" Kantian thought, realists found it more convenient to stress Kant's cosmopolitan and deterministic optimistic tendencies rather than the idea that a separate peace is possible among sovereign states. See Kenneth N. Waltz, "Kant, Liberalism, and War," *American Political Science Review* 56 (June 1962).

12. For example, see Stephen Krasner, ed., *International Regimes* (Ithaca: Cornell University Press, 1983), and Robert O. Keohane, *After Hegemony* (Princeton: Princeton University Press, 1984). For a study of this nature dealing with Europe, see Jack Snyder, "Averting Anarchy in the New Europe," *International Security* 14 (Spring 1990): 5–41. An exception is Alexander Wendt, "Sovereignty and the Social Construction of Power Politics," unpublished draft (November 1990).

13. Michael W. Doyle, "Kant, Liberal Legacies, and Foreign Affairs," *Philosophy and Public Affairs* 12 (Spring 1983): 226. "There have been alliances and ententes aplenty in the last 400 years of European history. There has been nothing like the European Community as it exists today, to say nothing of the community of the future that is now being planned and constructed" (James Goodby, "Commonwealth and Concert: Organizing Principles of Post-Containment Order in Europe," *Washington Quarterly* 14 [Summer 1991]: 76–77).

14. Hurrell (note 4), p. 205.

15. Doyle (note 13); Zeev Maoz and Nasrin Abdolali, "Regime Types and International Conflict, 1816–1976," *Journal of Conflict Resolution* 33 (March 1983): 3–35; R. Rummel, "Libertarian Propositions on Violence between and within Nations," *Journal of Conflict Resolution* 29 (1985): 419–55. See also John Mueller, *Retreat From Doomsday: The Obsolescence of Major War* (New York: Basic Books, 1988); Robert L. Rothstein, "Democracy, Conflict and Development in the Third World," *Washington Quarterly* 14 (Spring 1991): pp. 43–63; and Mark W. Zacher, "The Decaying Pillars of the Westphalian Temple: Implications for International Order and Governance," in *Government without Government*, ed. James Rosenau (Cambridge: Cambridge University Press—forthcoming).

16. Robert Gilpin, *War and Change in World Politics* (Cambridge: Cambridge University Press, 1981).

17. Kenneth N. Waltz, *Theory of International Politics* (Reading, Mass: Addison-Wesley, 1979), and John Mearsheimer, "Back to the Future: Instability in Europe after the Cold War," *International Security* 15 (Summer 1990): 5–56.

18. Robert Jervis, *The Meaning of the Nuclear Revolution* (Ithaca: Cornell University Press, 1989), and John L. Gaddis, *The Long Peace* (New York: Oxford University Press, 1987).

19. Mueller (note 15); Robert O. Keohane and Joseph S. Nye, Jr., *Power and Interdependence* (Boston: Little Brown, 1977); Emanuel Adler, "Seasons of Peace," in *Progress in Postwar International Relations*, ed. Emanuel Adler and Beverly Crawford (New York: Columbia University Press, 1991), pp. 128–73; Wendt (note 12).

20. Hedley Bull, "The Theory of International Politics, 1919–1969," in *The Aberystwyth Papers: International Politics, 1919–1969*, ed. Brian Porter (London: Oxford University Press, 1972), pp. 42–43.

21. Gregory Flinn and David S. Schiffer, "Limited Collective Security," *Foreign Policy* 80 (Fall 1990): 83.

22. Deutsch et al. (note 1), p. 5. For some of the best work on the subject by Deutsch's students, see Bruce M. Russett, *Community and Contention: Britain and America in the Twentieth Century* (Cambridge, Mass.: MIT Press, 1963); Donald J. Puchala, *European Integration: Progress and Prospects* (New Haven: Yale University, Political Science Research Library, 1965); Richard L. Merritt, *Symbols of American Community: 1735–1775* (New Haven: Yale University Press, 1966); Peter J. Katzenstein, *Disjoined Partners: Austria and Germany since 1815* (Berkeley: University of California Press, 1976). The subject of communication has been studied formally by Hayward R. Alker, Jr.; see, for example, "From Political Cybernetics to Global Modeling," in *From National Development to Global Community: Essays in Honor of Karl W. Deutsch*, ed. Richard L. Merritt and Bruce M. Russett (London: George Allen and Unwin, 1981), pp. 353–78.

23. Deutsch et al. (note 1), p. 6.

24. Lynn Miller, *Global Order: Values and Power in International Politics*, 2d ed. (Boulder: Westview Press, 1990), p. 93.

25. Deutsch et al. (note 1), pp. 36; 125–33. Among the successful cases of pluralistic security communities cited by Deutsch et al. are Norway-Sweden (since 1907); United States-Canada (since the 1870s); United States-Mexico (since the 1930s); United Kingdom-Netherlands (since perhaps 1815); United States-United Kingdom (as early as 1871); and Denmark-Sweden (since the late nineteenth or early twentieth century (*ibid.*, p. 29).

26. *Ibid.*, pp. 29–35.

27. *Ibid.*, p. 163.

28. *Ibid.*, pp. 28, 38.

29. *Ibid.*, p. 115.

30. "The pluralistic security community among the Scandinavian countries was prepared for and strengthened by the cultural and political movement of Scandinavianism and the network of actual inter-Scandinavian communications, transactions, and institutions in social, cultural, and scientific fields which developed during the nineteenth century and became even stronger thereafter" (*ibid.*, p. 116).

31. *Ibid.*, p. 189. See also Ernst B. Haas, *The Uniting of Europe* (London: Stevens and Sons, 1958), and Leon N. Lindberg and Stuart A. Scheingold, *Europe's Would-Be Polity: Patterns of Change in the European Community* (Englewood Cliffs, N.J.: Prentice Hall, 1970).

32. Deutsch et al. (note 1), pp. 163, 191.

33. Donald J. Puchala, "Integration Theory and the Study of International Relations," in Merritt and Russett, eds. (note 22), p. 157.

34. Haas, *The Uniting of Europe* (note 31), p. 7.

35. Robert J. Lieber, *Theory and World Politics* (London: George Allen and Unwin, 1973), p. 58.

36. Joseph S. Nye, "Comparative Regional Integration: Concept and Measurement," *International Organization* 22 (Fall 1968): 873.

37. Arend Lijphart, "Karl W. Deutsch and the New Paradigm in International Relations," in Merritt and Russett, eds. (note 22), pp. 233–51. Deutsch's integration paradigm was put to an empirical test by William E. Fisher, "An Analysis of the Deutsch Sociocausal Paradigm of Political Integration," *International Organization* 23 (Spring 1969): 254–90.

38. For a recent article on counterfactuals, see James D. Fearon, "Counterfactuals and Hypothesis Testing in Political Science," *World Politics* 43 (January 1991): 169–95.

39. Haas, *The Uniting of Europe* (note 31), p. 7.

40. Steve Weber, "Does NATO Have a Future?," in this volume.

41. Krasner, ed. (note 12).

42. For the propensity to do so, see, for example, Morten Kelstrup, "The Process of Europeanization: On the Theoretical Interpretation of Present Changes in the European Regional Political System," *Cooperation and Conflict* 25 (1990): 21–40; Volker Rittberger, Manfred Eifinger, and Martin Mendler, "Toward an East-West Security Regime: The Case of Confidence- and Security-Building Measures," *Journal of Peace Research* 27 (1990): 55–74.

43. For various approaches about and causes of regimes, see Krasner, ed. (note 12).

44. John G. Ruggie, "Continuity and Transformation in the World Polity: Toward a Neorealist Synthesis," *World Politics* 35 (1983): 261–85.

45. Stanley Hoffmann, "The Case for Leadership," *Foreign Policy* 81 (Winter 1990–91): 37.

46. R. Duvall and A. Wendt, "The International Capital Regime and the Internationalization of the State"; paper presented at the 1987 German-American Workshop on International Relations Theory, Bad Homburg, 1987; R. B. J. Walker, "Security, Sovereignty, and the Challenge of World Politics," *Alternatives* 15 (Winter 1990): 3–27.

47. Wendt (note 12), p. 46.

48. Ronald Inglehart, *Culture Shift in Advanced Industrial Societies* (Princeton: Princeton University Press, 1990), pp. 396–97. See also Diego Gambetta, ed., *Trust: Making and Breaking Cooperative Relations* (New York: Blackwell, 1988).

49. Ernst B. Haas, "The Limits of Liberal Nationalism in Western Europe," in *The New Europe Asserts Itself: A Changing Role in International Relations*, ed. Beverly Crawford and Peter W. Schulze (Berkeley: International and Area Studies, 1990), p. 333.

50. Beverly Crawford, "The Impact of Europe's Transformation on International Relations," in Crawford and Schulze, eds. (note 49), p. 403.

51. Wendt (note 12), p. 35.

52. Haas ("Limits of Liberal Nationalism"—note 49) takes the former view, Inglehart (note 48), the latter.

53. William Pfaff, "Baker's Commonwealth of Democracies," *International Herald Tribune*, 26 June 1991, p. 8.

54. U.S. Information Agency, "Euro-Atlantic Link from Vancouver to Vladivostok," *The Wireless File* (text: Baker address to Aspen Institute), pp. 7–10. (Cited hereafter as U.S. Information Agency, Baker address.)

55. *Ibid.*

56. Goodby, "Commonwealth and Concert" (note 13), p. 76.

57. See, for example, Malcolm Chalmers, "Beyond the Alliance System," *World Policy Journal* 7 (Spring 1990): 215–50.

58. U.S. Information Agency, Baker address (note 54), p. 11. According to Richard Merritt (note 22), security communities constitute themselves following "formative events." The main formative events leading to a pluralistic security community stretching from San Diego to Vladivostok would be the revolutions in Eastern Europe, the liberalizing changes in the Soviet Union, the reunification of Germany, and the end of the cold war.

59. National security has been described as an essentially contested concept. Barry Buzan, *People, States, and Fear: The National Security Problem in International Relations* (Chapel Hill: University of North Carolina Press, 1983), p. 6.

60. Robert E. Hunter, "The Future of European Security," *Washington Quarterly* 13 (Autumn 1990): 59.

61. John G. Ruggie, "International Structure and International Transformation: Space, Time, and Method," in *Global Changes and Theoretical Challenges*, ed. Ernst Otto Czempiel and James N. Rosenau (Lexington, Mass: Lexington Books, 1989), p. 28.

62. Max Jakobson, "CSCE Summit: Collective Security Is More than Arms Control," *International Herald Tribune,* 17–18 November 1990, p. 10; Hunter (note 60).

63. Daniel N. Nelson, "Europe's Unstable East," *Foreign Policy* 82 (Spring 1991): 157.

64. Weber (note 40).

65. Snyder (note 12). For a balanced study on the prospects of stability and peace in Europe, see Stephen Van Evera, "Primed for Peace: Europe after the Cold War," *International Security* 15 (Winter 1990/91): 7–57.

66. Pierre Hassner, "Europe Beyond Partition and Unity: Disintegration or Reconstruction?," *International Affairs* 66 (1990): 467.

67. Weber (note 40).

68. U.S. Information Agency, Baker address (note 54), p. 10.

69. Victor-Yves Ghebali, "The CSCE in the Post Cold War Europe," *NATO Review* 39 (April 1991): 10.

70. *Ibid.,* p. 8.

71. When Germany was reunited in 1990, the number of member states went down to thirty-four; it went up again to thirty-five when Albania joined the ranks in 1991. For some general works on the CSCE, see Karl E. Birnbaum and Inge Peters, "The CSCE: A Reassessment of Its Role in the 1980s," *Review of International Studies* 16 (1990): 305–19; Geoffrey Edwards, "The Conference on Security and Co-Operation in Europe after Ten Years," *International Relations* 8 (November 1985): 397–406; Mathias Jopp et al., *Ten Years of the CSCE Process: Appraisals of, and Prospects for, all European Detente and Cooperation* (Frankfurt: Peace Research Institute Frankfurt, 1985); Michael Lucas, "The Conference on Security and Cooperation in Europe and the Future of U.S. Foreign Policy," in Crawford and Schulze, eds. (note 49), pp. 45–83; John Maresca, *To Helsinki: The Conference on Security and Cooperation in Europe, 1973–1975* (Durham: Duke University Press, 1985); Vojtech Mastny, *Helsinki, Human Rights, and European Security* (Durham: Duke University Press, 1986); and U.S. Department of State, *The Conference on Security and Cooperation in Europe: Public Statements and Documents, 1954–1986* (Washington, D.C.: GPO, 1986).

72. The ten principles are (1) respect for the rights inherent in sovereignty; (2) refraining from the threat or use of force; (3) inviolability of frontiers; (4) territorial integrity of states; (5) peaceful settlement of disputes; (6) non-intervention in internal affairs; (7) respect for human rights and fundamental freedoms; (8) equal rights and self-determination of peoples; (9) cooperation among states; and (10) fulfillment in good faith of obligations under international law. U.S. Department of State, Bureau of Public Affairs, "Implementation of the Helsinki Final Act: Twenty-Eighth Semiannual Report. October 1, 1989–March 31, 1990"; Special Report No. 184 (Washington, D.C.: GPO, 1990), p. 9. (Cited hereafter as U.S. Department of State, report on Helsinki Final Act, 1989–90.)

73. *Ibid.,* p. 44.

74. Lucas (note 71), pp. 47–50.

75. U.S. Department of State, report on Helsinki Final Act, 1989–90 (note 72). See also Davis Memorial Institute of International Studies, "From Helsinki to Belgrade: Report of the Helsinki Review Group," n.d.; J. Sizoo and R. Th. Jurrjens, *CSCE Decision-Making: The Madrid Experience* (The Hague: Martinus Nijhoff, 1984); U.S. Information Agency, "Concluding Document of the Vienna Meeting 1986–1989" (Washington, D.C., 1989).

76. U.S. Information Agency, "Concluding Document" (note 75); Uffe Ellemann-Jensen, "The Copenhagen Meeting on the Human Dimension of the CSCE," *NATO Review* 38 (August 1990): 9–15; Lucas (note 71). On 19 January 1989, Soviet Foreign Minister Eduard Shevardnadze said, "The Vienna meeting has shaken up the Iron Curtain, weakened its rusty supports, made new breaches in it, and sped up its corrosion" (quoted in William Friis Moller, "Reducing the Impact of Europe's Borders: The CSCE Follow-up Meeting," *NATO Review* 37 [April 1989]: 3).

77. "Charter of Paris for a New Europe," as reprinted in *NATO Review* 38 (December 1990): 27–31. For an early assessment of the charter, see W. R. Smyser, "Vienna, Versailles, and Now Paris: Third Time Lucky?," *Washington Quarterly* 14 (Summer 1991): 61–70.

78. Marc Fisher, "Security Talks Settle on a Compromise," *International Herald Tribune*, 21 June 1991, p. 1.

79. I build on Ghebali (note 69) and Birnbaum and Peters (note 71). The CSCE can also be seen as a model to be applied to other regions. See, for example, Hans Henrich Wrede, "The Applicability of the CSCE Experience to the Middle East Conflict Area"; paper presented to the conference "If New Order Comes, Can Chaos Be Far Behind? Europe and the Middle East after the Gulf War," Leonard Davis Institute for International Relations, Hebrew University of Jerusalem, 11–13 June 1991.

80. U.S. Department of State, report on Helsinki Final Act, 1989–90 (note 72), p. 2.

81. *Ibid.* For a balanced account of the development of democracy in Eastern Europe, see Valerie Bunce, "The Struggle for Liberal Democracy in Eastern Europe," *World Policy Journal* 7 (Summer 1990): 397–430. For a more pessimistic view, see Nelson (note 63).

82. U.S. Department of State, report on Helsinki Final Act, 1989–90 (note 72), p. 5.

83. Markku Reimaa, "The Significance of the CSCE Yesterday and Now," *Yearbook of Finnish Foreign Policy, 1990* (Finnish Institute of International Affairs, 1990), p. 20.

84. Lucas (note 71), p. 54.

85. Vladimir Vikusin, "The Elections Compared and Assessed," *Report on Eastern Europe*, no. 28 (13 July 1990): 44, and U.S. Department of State, report on Helsinki Final Act, 1989–90 (note 72), pp. 10–26.

86. Richard Weitz, "The Expanding Role of the Council of Europe," *Report on Eastern Europe*, no. 34 (24 August 1990): 50–51; Judith Pataki, "Major Political Changes and Economic Stagnation," *Report on Eastern Europe*, no. 1 (4 January 1991): 23.

87. John Borawski, Stan Weeks, and Charlotte E. Thompson, "The Stockholm Agreement of September 1986," *Orbis* 30 (Winter 1987): 463–662; James Goodby, "The Stockholm Conference: Negotiating a Cooperative Security System for Europe," in *U.S.-Soviet Security Cooperation: Achievements, Failures, Lessons*, ed. Alexander George, Philip Farley, and Alexander Dallin (Oxford: Oxford University Press, 1988), pp. 144–72; Rittberger et al. (note 42); Birnbaum and Peters (note 71).

88. Reimaa (note 83), p. 23.

89. Bruce George, "The Negotiations on Confidence- and Security-Building Measures: The Vienna Agreement and Beyond," *NATO Review* 39 (February 1991): 16–17; Vieri Traxler, "The CSBM Negotiations in Vienna: Background and Prospects," *NATO Review* 37 (October 1989): 5–10.

90. U.S. Department of State, report on Helsinki Final Act, 1989–90 (note 72), p. 8.

91. Scott Sullivan, "Hailing a Brave New World," *Newsweek*, 26 November 1990, p. 24.

92. U.S. Department of State, report on Helsinki Final Act, 1989–90 (note 72), p. 36.

93. *Ibid.*, p. 36; Marvin Jackson, "The International Economic Situation and Eastern Europe," *Report on Eastern Europe*, no. 52 (28 December 1990): 39; Reuters, 20 November 1990 and 23 September 1990, in *ibid.*

94. Vlad Sobell, "East European Integration: The Disbanding of the CMEA," *The Economist Intelligence Unit European Trends*, no. 1 (1991): 78–79; *The Economist Intelligence Unit Country Report—Hungary*, no. 2 (1991): 23; *The Economist Intelligence Unit Country Report—Poland*, no. 1 (1991): 20.

95. *The Economist Intelligence Unit Country Report—Hungary*, no. 2 (1991): 22; *The Economist Intelligence Unit Country Report—Czechoslovakia*, no. 1 (1991): 19; *The Economist Intelligence Unit Country Report—Poland*, no. 1 (1991): 18.

96. Marvin Jackson, "The Privatization Scorecard for Eastern Europe," *Report on Eastern Europe*, no. 50 (14 December 1990): 30; Hungarian Telegraph Agency in English, 0024 gmt, 26 April 1991, in BBC Monitoring Summary of World Broadcasts, *Weekly Economic Report, Eastern Europe*, Part 2 (Caversham Park, Reading, Great Britain), 9 May 1991, p. A/1.

97. *The Economist Intelligence Unit Country Report—Czechoslovakia*, no. 2 (1991): 10.

98. "Poland, Capitalist Genius," *International Herald Tribune*, 9 July 1991, p. 6.

99. Jeffrey M. Hertzfeld, "Joint Venture: Saving the Soviets from Perestroika," *Harvard Business Review* 69 (January–February 1991): 84.

100. Eugen Gabiwitsch, "The Ecological Situation in Estonia in the Time of the 'Singing Revolution,'" *Environmental Policy Review* 4 (July 1990): 27.

101. Hilary F. French, "Green Revolutions: Environmental Reconstruction in Eastern Europe and the Soviet Union," *Environmental Policy Review* 5 (January 1991): 3–4.

102. Stanley J. Kabala, "The Environment: Adjustments to a New Reality," *Report on Eastern Europe*, no. 2 (11 January 1991): 15.

103. Lucas (note 71), pp. 52–53.

104. U.S. Department of State, report on Helsinki Final Act, 1989–90 (note 72), pp. 44–48; U.S. Department of State, Bureau of Public Affairs, "Implementation of the Helsinki Final Act, Eighteenth Semiannual Report. October 1, 1984–April 1, 1985"; Special Report No. 130 (Washington, D.C.: GPO, 1990), p. 23.

105. U.S. Department of State, report on Helsinki Final Act, 1989–90 (note 72), p. 54.

106. Lucas (note 71), p. 65.

107. John Lewis Gaddis, "Toward the Post–Cold War World," *Foreign Affairs* 70 (Spring 1991): 102–22.

108. John G. Ruggie, "Changing Frameworks of International Collective Behavior: On the Complementarity of Contradictory Tendencies," in *Forecasting in International Relations*, ed. Nazli Choucri and Thomas W. Robinson (San Francisco: W. H. Freeman, 1978), pp. 399, 402; Emanuel Adler, "Cognitive Evolution: A Dynamic Approach for the Study of International Relations and Their Progress," in Adler and Crawford, eds. (note 19), p. 76.

COMPETING FOR EUROPEAN SECURITY: THE CSCE, NATO, AND THE EUROPEAN COMMUNITY IN A CHANGING INTERNATIONAL ENVIRONMENT

Peter W. Schulze

A NEW BEGINNING FOR EUROPEAN HISTORY

In 1989 and 1990 Europe reemerged as a subject of history. One could argue that the stage for all sorts of fundamental changes was prepared with the signing of the Single European Act, outlining the vision of a single European market by 1992. Ever since the European Community (EC) began to discuss security and foreign policy objectives, a sentiment of dynamism and expectations was created which did not go unnoticed in the East. Conversely, from the moment the West started to realize and to accept the irreversibility of Mikhail Gorbachev's political and economic reforms, it became clear that the single European market of 1992 and the project of Soviet reforms created the necessary synergy which finally would end the division of Europe. The chain of events unleashed by the revolutionary processes in Eastern Europe created a "relief map" of the Old Continent in 1989 (Brandt 1991). It gave rise to hopes that the era of division and military alliances which flattened the cultural diversity of part of the continent was over for good. The incredible speed with which revolutionary events advanced in the Eastern half of the continent indicated how anachronistic the systems of rule had been.

The political overthrow of the old regimes was the first step for reconnecting Eastern Europe to the West European discourse on the future economic, political, and social shape of Europe. But of equal importance, and probably more painful in social terms, are the post-revolutionary tasks of introducing market mechanisms and building democratic political and social institutions from scratch. In addition, these societies have to overcome the legacy of ancient regimes: social immobilism, a culture of dependency, and the lack of professional groups with sufficient knowledge and international experience to guide them through the stages of transformation. It maybe well be that these tasks could lead to cataclysmic experiences which could destroy the social and political cohesion of their countries and result in the alienation of people from political life. Such a situation could even nourish sentiments amenable to authoritarian solutions and cause a range of new conflicts throughout Europe. However, Eastern Europe's new democratic societies have no alternative but to continue on the path of systemic changes.

Although the demise of the anachronistic and repressive systems of "Realsocialism" seems final, the West has not yet started to come to terms with challenges stemming from the new situation. Yet these have already affected and will continue to influence all aspects of Western societies, devaluating former perceptions of threats and creating demands for economic, technological, social, and political aid which in some cases may overburden Western institutions.

SHIFTS IN THE INTERNATIONAL ENVIRONMENT

Politically we have just set foot in the post-Yalta, post–cold war era, into which we set foot economically in the mid-1970s. In this sense one may recall the 1970s as the economic watershed. The cold war order ceased to predominate in international relations, and the United States lost its ability to dominate international trade and capital flows.

Preeminent among the many reasons for the decline of superpower influence is the failure to solve the emerging and accumulating asymmetries between the superpowers' domestic and international economic needs and their global security policies. The increasingly interdependent and internationalized world economic system contradicted the realm of politics, where political, ideological, and security issues were dictated by national actors and resulted in arcane security structures. In other words, a gap widened between an international political domain still dominated by national actors (the bipolar world of both superpowers) and an internationalized economic-technological structure which required more multilateral agreements.

The implications of structural changes in the global economy did not hit the political, ideological, and security institutions of the cold war system until the mid-1980s. Only under the impact of political reforms in Eastern Europe and West European integration did the core institutions and doctrines of the militaristic cold war security order begin to crumble.

Until the mid-1970s, the global equation of power rested on the congruence of economic and military dominance and found its most extreme ideological expression in the Pax Americana. The basis of U.S. hegemony in the global system was enshrined in the country's leadership in productivity and technology after 1945. Since the 1970s the United States declined in competitiveness in crucial sectors. The penetration of domestic markets by foreign competitors, huge trade deficits, and the cumulative effect of public debt were indicative of a weakened economy. The asymmetry between foreign policy goals and U.S. economic interests increased, helping foreign competitors, especially Japan and the EC, to advance their economic position in the world economy. While there was initial hope that the Bush administration would address the issue, its policy during and in the aftermath of the Gulf War has resembled a replay of the Pax Americana à la Nixon. It was pure Kissinger, although dressed in more fashionable designer clothes of the "New World Order," at the top of which was the United States, guiding the world in military, political, and technological matters. On the next level, with some degree of regional independence, were the reborn middle powers of Japan, the EC, and Germany, which provided the financial and economic foundations for the U.S. leadership.

In comparison, the USSR was locked throughout the cold war in an economically vulnerable position. There were constant tensions between its global political interests and national security objectives, on the one side, and the need to provide economic and social goods for its people. But it was only during the later part of the Brezhnev era that the problem developed to acute dimensions. A good deal of evidence points to the fact that the USSR lost economic control over some COMECON countries during the 1970s. With the Polish crisis in full blossom, the region became an economic burden for the USSR, aggravating its enormous domestic problems.

Obsessed with security issues and engaged in a global arms race, both superpowers allowed their allies among the former European and Asian middle powers to gain economic ground. The United States's European and Asian allies pledged the required political and security allegiance and accepted the protection of U.S. bloc leadership. And the grateful United States turned a blind eye to their growing economic and political strength. In fact, the economies of the middle powers flourished best when they ceded this security allegiance whereby they abided by conditions of "limited sovereignty."

In the early 1980s it became obvious that both bloc leaders suffered from similar syndromes: global political designs and military overcommitment had siphoned off economic wealth and political attention from domestic problems. Symptoms of social decay and political decline appeared in both societies.

IMMOBILISM AND DECLINE IN THE EAST: THE DECONSTRUCTION OF THE SOVIET EMPIRE

The Soviet Union was never well integrated into the world economy. Still, the shifts in the international economy and the advent of the information revolution in production and communication technologies affected the Soviet economy as well. The USSR proved incapable of stimulating its outdated production system using the old methods of political control and economic planning. In short, the Soviet model of stimulating economic growth by the extensive use of physical and human capital and applying repressive and patronizing means for social integration proved to be incapable of enhancing the social and material well-being of Soviet citizens. Since the beginning of the 1980s the Soviet society has experienced, as Gorbachev put it, a grave and serious systemic crisis.

It was not until 1985 that the Soviet leadership fully recognized its bleak economic and social circumstances and tried in a more coherent manner to develop programs to reduce military expenditures and revitalize the economy. Gorbachev's "new thinking" in security matters, including the negotiated withdrawal from Afghanistan and the cleansing of the international climate of irrational distortions with the United States, established a platform from which he could address domestic and global issues. Both *glasnost* and *perestroika* propelled the USSR into a "deconstructionist" overhaul of its social, political, and economic system, allowing it to eliminate the bureaucratic, oppressive, and immobilizing forces of the Stalinist past.

Reassessing national security. For the USSR to prioritize domestic policies required a radical review of the country's foreign and security policies, including a fundamental critique of the militarization of security and foreign policy. In supporting the "Common European Home" concept, the Soviet leadership accepted the new diversity in economic and political power relations among Western Europe, the United States, and Japan for the first time in postwar history. The revision in Soviet foreign and security thinking concentrated on the role of Eastern Europe in Soviet defense strategies and the "German question." While respecting the underlying rationale and focus on containing Germany as set down in the Yalta agreement, the Warsaw Pact had a more limited function of providing a tighter version of a *cordon sanitaire* for Soviet national security. The questions Soviet policy-makers confronted at the end of the 1970s were:

– How could the cold war be ended, and implicitly the arms race, in order to free scarce resources for the economic and technological modernization of Soviet society?

– What were the benefits of keeping the East European security glacis, with its mounting economic costs and decreasing security benefits, if the climate between the superpowers improved?

These questions reflected a growing awareness among groups of the Soviet elite of the contradictory and strained relationship between foreign policy objectives and economic performance. While the Soviet Union had achieved parity with the United States in strategic deterrence, it had squandered, as Gorbachev put it, nearly a quarter of its GNP to achieve that goal and keep the Warsaw Pact intact. Gorbachev's confession that military expenditure had ruined the country came as a late victory for Pentagon cold warriors. Their brutal rationale for the arms race was finally proved correct. But achieving parity in strategic weapons reduced the validity of military doctrines based on conventional warfare assumptions. As a consequence, and contrary to former scenarios, Eastern Europe lost its important function as a buffer zone against an attack from NATO. Faced with the strains on its economy, the Soviet leadership came to the conclusion that ending the arms race was the precondition for reforming Soviet policy.

Ending the arms race required a policy to end the cold war on its home turf—in Europe. The first and crucial step Gorbachev took in July 1989 was to repudiate the Brezhnev doctrine of "limited sovereignty." From there it was merely a question of time, as opposition groups in Eastern Europe gained confidence that the Soviet military would not repeat the traumatic events of Prague in 1968. The litmus test was passed in summer 1989, when the Hungarians opened the border for East German refugees, allowing them to pass through to Austria and on to West Germany. In the wake of the following transformations, the Red Army lost its *raison d'être* as a guarantor for the political stability and ideological survival of client regimes in Eastern Europe. And given the shifts in Soviet military doctrine, the region lost its relevance for safeguarding Soviet security.

When the German question came up, the USSR was faced with a choice between two evils: to block unification or to endorse it. The Soviet leadership's decision not to block German unification cannot be traced to one single reason. There were always at least two conflicting lines of Soviet thinking on Germany and Europe, according to Professor V. I. Daschitschev (1990), head of the former Institute for Socialist World Economy (now the Institute for International Economic and Political Studies). One line was hostile to unification, considering Europe's and Germany's division as the keystone of Soviet security policies since 1945. (This position was predominant in the Politburo.) The second linked the cold war status quo in Europe to the arms race, which in turn depleted the Soviet economy of resources and human capital. Confronted with the dire economic and sociopolitical situation, the anti-status quo school triumphed.

Once the unification issue was settled, the remaining question—whether Germany should stay inside or outside NATO—seemed to have caused limited conflict among the USSR's political elites. In retrospect, West Germany seemed to have passed the litmus test of credibility in security terms when the conservative-liberal German government elected in 1982 continued the detente policy, despite the intensification of cold war activities under Reagan.

In light of twenty years of detente one could well argue that both the present coalition government in Bonn and the USSR leadership cashed in on a detente dividend which was put in effect in the early 1970s. Economic and political experts close to the Soviet leadership shared the view that a united Germany, deprived of offensive weapons systems and anchored in NATO, could well function as a bridge to the USSR. Given Germany's central position in Europe, this would amount to Gorbachev's last move in making necessary economic progress toward a market economy with the help of the powerful economic German engine.

It is not a coincidence that the first international act of the newly unified country in October 1990 was the signing of the Soviet-German treaty on mutual economic cooperation and nonaggression. The treaty aimed to link Germany's interests in the stability of its eastern border with the Soviet Union's interest in economic modernization and in playing an active part in future collective European peace and agreements. In this sense, German unification may serve as a double insurance policy for Soviet reform and security needs. Again, Gorbachev's decision seemed to be vindicated during the recent G-7 summit in London in July 1991, when the German chancellor supported the Soviet demand for concerted assistance from the West.

Socialist resurrection terminated. The project of glasnost/perestroika was intended to break the petrified layers of Soviet bureaucracy and to implement participatory, decentralized, and more indirect forms of political government and control. As John Lloyd (1990) argued, perestroika originally had two aims: to ensure that the USSR reached the third millennium as a superpower, and to ensure the survival and renaissance of socialism in the USSR and within its orbit of economic, political, and security interests. Neither objective will be achieved. The USSR did not reach the end of the 1980s as a superpower, nor did it survive as a unitary nation.

Three years into perestroika and glasnost, all Soviet efforts to find a "third way" between state socialism and capitalism have collapsed. For the time being, there seems to be no viable systemic alternative to Western liberalism (Fukuyama 1990). This indeed brings to an end the era which started in 1917.

At the beginning of the new decade we stand at the end of the first chapter of the Soviet reform program; its title is "socialist resurrection ended." This leaves ample room for discussing scenarios for the end of the Soviet empire. With socialist resurrection over, Gorbachev is now understanding the logic of his own reform initiatives. While he rejected the proposals of Stanislav Shatalin in 1990, he now seems to endorse the new joint initiative of Grigory Yavlinski and Graham Allison. The "Grand Bargain Plan" is equally clear and frank about its objectives: the introduction of unequivocal market rules, including private ownership.

The second pillar of the "Window of Opportunity Plan" explicitly calls for Western economic interference, through advice, cooperation, capital investments, and credits to stabilize the transformation period. It is this second element which could become the albatross around Gorbachev's neck. If the West does not rally to deliver huge amounts of capital (up to $35 billion over six years), synchronized with a step-by-step implementation of economic and democratic reforms, the Soviet leader could be exposed by the left and right opposition as a pro-Western fool who has gambled away the Soviet empire. Soviet politics arrived at a crossroads in July/August 1991, when a coup by the old nomenklatura tried to stop the transformation of the Soviet Union into a commonwealth of independent republics organized along federal principles. The coup failed, and as a consequence the historical process accelerated, bringing about the fragmentation of the USSR into fifteen sovereign states, and the downfall of Gorbachev.

EUROPE'S REEMERGENCE

It is generally agreed that the resurgence of Western Europe as an important economic and political international actor stemmed from the rapidity by which economic, political, and social integration was pursued after 1985. After nearly twenty-five years of some petty squabbles in the shadows of superpower policies, the vision of an integrated single market by 1992 stimulated a debate which reached well beyond questions of capital flows and market inte-gration. In addition to the thorny issue of political union (which was put on the agenda in December 1990 and was decided along "federalist" lines in Maastricht at the end of 1991), the EC generates aspects of a European domestic policy. The EC now touches upon matters such as the harmonization of industrial relations, a more balanced regional development throughout Europe, enhanced par-ticipatory rights of workers to strengthen industrial democracy, and the necessity to unify policies on mergers and acquisitions, as well as on regulations for transnational European companies. Such trends—even the controversy over an Economic and Monetary Union (EMU) and a single European currency as a keystone for a future European central bank—add to the gradual shift of policy-making authority from national states to EC institutions. The next logical decisions that need to be made are how to integrate the Community politically, and which foreign and security policies it should adopt.

Contrary to the hopes of a few member states that German unification would hamper the progress toward the EMU and Euro-pean political union, the intra-EC debate does not support such opinion. Instead the debate has been further enhanced by the need to provide some security assurance to Eastern Europe and the complexities stemming from the fragmentation of the former Soviet Union into fifteen independent states which are only partly inte-grated into a feeble union called the Commonwealth of Independent States (CIS). Taken together, the debate since autumn 1990 over a common foreign and security position of the Community has fo-cused on merging the West European Union (WEU) with the EC. This indeed would provide the EC with a genuine foreign policy institution, somewhat independent of NATO and the United States. Contrary to the hopes of the more Atlanticist-minded members of the European defense community, the Gulf War provoked more initiatives on behalf of a European defense identity. Finally, the erupting Yugoslav crisis contributed to a strong tendency in the EC and among the European members of the CSCE to treat this conflict as a genuine European matter.

REASSESSING NEUTRALITY: EUROPE'S NONALIGNED COUNTRIES AND THE EC

One year before the completion of the single market, the slip-stream of 1992 appears noticeable in requests from EFTA and former COMECON countries for membership in the EC or close links of association. For them the alternative is clear: either join the economic bandwagon and enter the orbit of EC policies, or remain as non-aligned countries on the sidelines of the new dynamism in European policies. Time and timing are crucial factors for the EFTA countries. They have to take into consideration the ongoing debate in the EC over establishing a European defense identity. The longer they post-pone the decision to join, the less they can influence its future shape. To join an EC with a fully developed foreign and security dimension by the mid-1990s could cause severe political problems in their societies. However, to stay outside of the EC has repercussions and could possibly undermine the social fabric and cohesion of their societies. Therefore—of course with considerable variations—a very strange paradox appears to dominate the attitudes of the EFTA countries toward EC concepts on security and foreign policy. In order to preserve a clean sheet on neutrality, the EFTA countries would prefer to join the EC and see it committed to not exploring the political and security aspects of European integration. In this respect neutrals would be more willing to favor a strong role for NATO and a distinct separation of economic and military issues by the two organizations.

The neutrals, mainly organized in EFTA, have tried to circum-vent the dilemma by entering negotiations with the EC to create a European-wide free trade zone, the European Economic Area (EEA). However, the single European market and divisive disagreements among the EFTA countries over the timetable, scope, and obliga-tions to the EEA have convinced some countries to pursue a dou-ble-track policy. They have remained part of the EC-EFTA dialogue and they have separately aspired to membership in the EC. Put in this context, the EEA can be described as a useful but transitional tool until the real issues of membership can be addressed.

Austria was first, applying for EC membership in 1990. The Swedish government declared its intention to join the EC in July 1991, while Finland, out of domestic sensitivities arising from its long border with Russia, is still hesitant to move. Because of its geopolitical situation, the country has always been a latecomer to European institutions. For Sweden the argument for joining the EC is mainly economic. Until October 1991 its government emphasized the traditional commitment to neutrality as an immovable obstacle for membership, one which prevented the country from joining the EC in the first place in the early 1960s and again in 1971–72. But with the collapse of the East-West divide in Europe it became clear that the concept of neutrality, which was never enshrined in the country's constitution, would give way to a very pragmatic recognition and evaluation of the Swedish position in the new Europe. Hence neutrality became a flexible instrument, and pressured by economic factors, it was assessed as compatible with membership in the EC.

Most surprising of all the decisions was that of the Swiss. It was generally assumed that the country's strong stand on neutrality and its attitude of nonengagement in collective institutions emanated from enshrined beliefs in neutrality that were integral to the Swiss national character. The speed by which public opinion in Switzerland changed conceded that neutrality was merely a policy option, instrumental and dependent on external political circumstances.

Although reasons for neutrality differ historically in the Swedish, Swiss, and Austrian cases, one may argue that after 1955 neutrality was coupled with cold war antagonism. As long as the East-West conflict continued unabated, Europe's neutrals assumed a role of "bridges" and negotiators, first to contain the danger of open war, and second to prepare a platform for trans-bloc negotiations. In the latter sense they reached their zenith of influence during the CSCE process. Paradoxically this very CSCE process, in presenting an outline for pan-European security, undermined the role neutral countries could play in the future Europe. The demise of the cold war nourished notions for a more collective or common security order in Europe. The surge of such notions intensified in the aftermath of the Gulf War. To build a European defense identity threw the neutral states into a tight political squeeze between economic pressures to find an arrangement with the EC and its potential threatening transformation into a regional security and defense organization. Having successfully rebuffed Western pressures for joining NATO throughout the cold war era, such ideas run counter to the neutral states' objections to regional security and military alliances. In essence, these alliances threaten the very foundation of their neutrality and sovereignty.

It is predictable that negotiations for membership in the EC will begin with Austria, Sweden, and Switzerland early in 1993, and they could be successfully concluded by the mid-1990s. By the end of the 1990s, the EC membership could include close to twenty European countries. This raises a fundamental question of the future shape and strategy of the European Community: should it prioritize widening or deepening its structures? While there are convincing arguments on either side, the debate itself seems to be strangely detached from the fast-moving reality in Europe. Apart from such thorny issues of transport and fishing rights, economic negotiations with wealthy Scandinavian countries and with Switzerland and Austria will not pose difficulties. Discord will raise political questions—e.g., whether to strengthen the European Parliament or to allow the transfer of national sovereignty to Brussels. For most East European countries the issues at stake have an existential dimension and escape rational terms of negotiation.

As in the case of German unification, a situation may arise in which the EC may find itself in no position whatsoever to steer and control the pace of requests for social and economic assistance and/or to reestablish political order in the countries. Still, there is an understandable tendency among some EC countries, motivated by particular economic and social interests, to pursue a closed shop policy vis-à-vis new applications.

In November 1990 Czechoslovakia was the first former COMECON country to apply for membership. Applications from Hungary and Poland followed. Under public pressure from some member states, the EC Commission conceded that all three countries would be given associated status, allowing them to ease the problems of economic, monetary, and social convergence as a precondition for membership. Provided the three East European countries meet the hurdles of convergence, their membership is foreseen at the end of the 1990s.

In the case of East European countries the question is not of fast entry, but rather what kind of transitional phases could be designed to cushion the social and material costs of transforming and modernizing those societies. In the case of the fragile new democracies of Eastern Europe, the EC may be obliged to assist, faced with the threat of mass migration to the West, as already seems to be the case with Poland and Germany. There is no limit to worst-case scenarios. It is not unthinkable that the new East European democracies may give way to populist authoritarian governments if they cannot deliver the promises of democracy and market economy. In any such event the people of the East would know where to go: West. With the decline of the USSR, the EC has become the only organization which can deliver a promising future for European countries. (This is probably better understood in Eastern Europe than in some corners of the EC itself.)

A NEW, EXTENDED DEFINITION OF EUROPEAN SECURITY

The rapid political transformation of Eastern Europe and Germany's unification have thrown open fundamental questions about the future security and peace of Europe as a whole. By now the whole of Europe is engaged for the first time since 1945 in a truly European debate over its own future. The former superpowers are invited to participate, but are in no capacity to act as hegemonic bloc leaders or to direct the outcome of the inter- or pan-European dialogue.

The collapse of the GDR stripped the inner German border of its function as the divide between two antagonistic social systems. The sudden downfall of the GDR not only shifted the border east, but the whole center of political gravity in Europe has moved to the east as well. At the same time, the downfall of the GDR suspended in mid-air two gigantic military machines, NATO and the Warsaw Pact—both deprived of their respective rationales to counter external threats. The age of deterrence, of mutually assured destruction (MAD), had come to an end.

There was a sudden realization on the part of European political elites that the vacuum created by the withdrawal of hegemonic bloc powers must not be filled from the outside again. However, without any counterpart in the eastern half of the continent, Western institutions are running the danger of becoming overburdened by the problems they face. First, European political elites in the EC have to sustain the momentum for political, economic, monetary, and social union in the EC. Second, they have to develop economic, political, and security links between Eastern and Western Europe. Third, they are involved in quite a delicate and complex balancing act—namely, to provide new functions and objectives for Western institutions bypassed by the events of 1989. Fourth, in a constantly changing environment of pressures from Eastern Europe and from within, they have to steer a flexible but coherent course between those who want to enlarge the Community and those who want to strengthen the EC by deepening it.

Although European states must still organize their security needs, it is generally assumed that the threats they have to face will differ immensely from those of the cold war. In fact, potential new threats will emanate from the transformation of Eastern Europe and the former USSR, causing social and economic imbalances (Ramsbotham 1991). The potential dangers are that national rivalries among the successor states of the former Soviet Union or ethnic and religious conflicts elsewhere in Eastern Europe will lead to the demise of multi-racial and multi-ethnic states. The consequence would be the uprooting of millions of people who simply would move westward toward the promised lands of democracy and socioeconomic stability. The bloody incidents following the declaration of independence by the breakaway republics of Slovenia and Croatia from the federal structure of Yugoslavia illustrate such dangers. Balkanization and disintegration, civil war and revolution may be confined to one part of the continent (Hassner 1990: 461). But there is the real danger that the Hegelian theme of "reconciling unity and virtue with modern freedom and peace" will instead end with Western Europe becoming "East Europeanized, Third Worldized or simply thrown back to its own heroic and barbaric past, complete with new religions and new cars, new prophets and new Caesars" (Hassner 1990: 462).

There is no Iron Curtain any more which could prevent waves of migrant workers and uprooted refugees from entering Western societies. Measures short of outright repression would not prevent migrants from crossing the borders. Their arrival in Western societies would deal a deadly blow to the networks of social and political cohesion. If one starts with an understanding of the present degree of xenophobia, racism, and the potential for neo-authoritarian and fascist tendencies in Western regions bordering the East, it is easy to foresee that political systems would simply crumble under the polarizing pressure from those groups. The rapid reaction of the EC and CSCE in the Yugoslav crisis is a good indicator of how alarmed both institutions became by the course of events, their constraints on acting decisively notwithstanding.

However, the search for the building blocks of a new European security order involves more than the redesign or enlargement of old institutions. Those of the East are gone. The EC and even the CSCE do not offer an adequate programmatic and institutional foundation for dealing effectively with the expected perils. Their ability to deal with crisis phenomena emanating from the East European transformation process would increase considerably if these institutions would find a joint platform for policy formation.

One year after the fall of the Berlin Wall a strange paradox appeared: the East-West conflict did not simply end, but rather became transformed and lives on in a new configuration. Stripped of the military doomsday dimension, a new division of Europe was brought to light. The contours of the regional, economic, social, and cultural East-West divide, which were always there but overshadowed by ideological and military matters, became visible again. While the Iron Curtain was dismantled, a new divide in Europe became apparent, one further east, separating a prosperous, wealthy EC from an impoverished East. In some ways the new divide resembles the border between the United States and Mexico. To prevent the Oder-Neisse border from becoming the European Rio Grande, no single country, but rather the EC must address the problem of economic and political security in the whole of Europe.

NATO refused to allow the former member states of the Warsaw Pact to join the alliance because of recognized Soviet security claims, implying that Eastern Europe would have to live in some sort of a security vacuum for some time. The region has to achieve stability by its own means. Some countries are exploring initiatives to either enter bilateral agreements or pursue strategies for a collective Central European Peace and Security Order. In light of the Yugoslav crisis, however, the question remains whether these countries are capable of securing peace in their region if they are unable to settle their own ethnic and social struggles.

The specter of national disintegration is not exclusive to the USSR. Similar bleak scenarios could evolve in other parts of

Eastern Europe, as the present crisis in Yugoslavia demonstrates. The real and future challenges for Europe stem from the dynamism of the East European revolution itself. After decades of political repression and denial of cultural, ethnic identities, there is the severe danger that the newly emancipated nations could embrace the phony temptations of nationalism, the nation state, and national sovereignty. To open a Pandora's box of fundamentalist nationalism—kept shut since 1945—could ignite latent ethnic, social, and religious conflicts and destroy the fruits of the revolution of 1989. If nationalism develops into a fundamentalist mass movement, destabilization and Balkanization of the region will follow. Bloody ethnic and zealously fought religious conflicts, massacres, and constant territorial struggles may spill over and drag Western Europe into action. Dreadful as such developments would be, there is a danger that the breakup of the Soviet empire could allow terrorists and separatists to gain possession of chemical, biological, and even nuclear weapons.

If the new democracies fail to deliver the social and material improvements the people fought for in the first place and East European societies plunge even deeper into economic and social misery as the costs of restructuring their economies rise and living conditions worsen, it very well may mobilize hundreds of thousands of refugees to move to Western Europe. A foretaste of such disaster was revealed to the people of West Berlin when hundreds of thousands of Poles crossed the new border every week during summer 1990 to use the city as a base for consumer goods.

Again, the possible collapse of the new democracies under the pressure of social and economic demands would only accelerate processes of further political radicalization and polarization. As a result, a potentially explosive situation could arise and push Eastern Europe again into the tentacles of populist and authoritarian dictatorships. Two years into the transformation process, it is too soon for a final assessment of the combined economic and political reform programs, but evidence based on recent developments in Poland, Hungary, Czechoslovakia, and East Germany suggests that their societies are plagued with similar and enormous social faults. Noncompetitive and run-down industries, gigantic costs for cleaning up the environment, loss of markets, and absence of infrastructure make free market conditions perilous. High unemployment, short-time work, halving of incomes, reduction of GNP, and high inflation rates are some of the consequences.

NATO IN SEARCH OF A NEW ROLE: SAFEGUARDING THE TRANSITION

It seems plausible that the West's remaining, predominantly military alliance, NATO, is in no position to deal with such potential developments. And given the changes in East-West relations, the nuclear assurances which were at the core of NATO's security role will lose their structuring function in East-West and in West-West relations (Hassner 1990: 465). They will retain a role but fade into the background, assisting NATO's new role as an insurance policy.

While the alliance will continue to serve important interests of its member states, the organization as such is too rigid and not adequately equipped to deal with possible confrontations emanating from the destabilization of Eastern Europe. Such conflicts would bring the new, expanded set of security issues (migration, ecological issues, ethnic and national strife) into the open and demand policies and solutions beyond the narrow scope of military objectives. Even in the case of East European interstate conflicts, NATO would not be the instrument to deal with such problems because the alliance does not command policies and instruments for regulating and solving conflicts of a regional nature or within states. That does not imply the end of NATO in the search for a security architecture for the new Europe, but a different structure and security role for it. The search for a new role for NATO was highlighted in the London Declaration of 5–6 July 1990, emphasizing the concept of common defense and partnership "with all nations of Europe."

NATO has recognized the challenges and acted surprisingly quickly to undertake a complete organizational shakeup for the mid-1990s. Prospects for the new military structure were agreed to during the 28 May 1991 meeting of ministers in Brussels. Forces will be reduced by more than 20 percent over the next years and will be reshuffled into multilateral/mixed formations. There will be deep cuts in British and U.S. troops stationed in Central Europe. It is expected that the U.S. army alone is to be reduced from over 200,000 to about 70,000. The current figure of over 55,000 British troops in Germany will be halved. The three armored divisions of the British Army of the Rhine will be consolidated, serving as an important element in a future Rapid Reaction Force under British command.

The review of the future requirements for European security has moved beyond the confinements of defense on NATO terms. Indeed there are now three interlocking forums of debate: the EC's intergovernmental conference, the WEU, and the NATO strategy review. There is talk in NATO circles of a division of labor between the two European actors, the EC and the WEU, on the one side, and NATO on the other, to counterbalance the challenges flowing from the East European transition. According to one scenario, the EC would focus on environmental and economic issues, while NATO's responsibilities would predominantly lie in directing East-West relations (Shea 1990: 134).

At the heart of the matter are two interconnected questions. First, how will a stronger European role in collective defense affect NATO? Second, what will become of the "community of interests" between the European and North American members if trends toward European self-assertiveness in political and security matters continue and trade-related conflicts between the two regional powers intensify?

There is no other military and defense organization in Europe which offers an integrated defense structure, which borders on a globally integrated strategy, and which is either trusted or respected by Europeans and Americans alike (Hurd 1991). In addition to introducing stability to Europe, NATO's main achievement, on which the prolonged relevance of the alliance rests, lies precisely in the collective security aspect of its integrated military command structure, which so far has prevented a relapse into the "renationalization" of European security. Without another collective security structure on the horizon there is no alternative to NATO, and the alliance will continue to play an important interim role—but only if it succeeds in redefining its military and political functions, presently under review, to post–cold war conditions. However, the task of changing NATO's doctrine and strategy has become more complicated with the advent of new players on the security field.

The challenge is twofold: On the one hand, NATO has to find an answer to the shift in superpower relations from confrontational to cooperative politics. On the other, the search for a new security doctrine and strategy is coupled with an internal reorganization of NATO. For better or worse, the thorny question of a "European defense identity" is on the agenda and cannot be reduced to simply a European pillar within the alliance. In addition, further complications arise from the advent of competing actors—the EC and the WEU, which could offer concepts of common and collective security as well.

Regardless and possibly because of uncertainties about the fate of the Soviet society, NATO has to offer genuine cooperation on questions of common security. But in light of such uncertainties and despite the dissolution of the Warsaw Pact, the former Soviet Union will remain Europe's most powerful military actor. Accordingly NATO is challenged to revise its threat perception. Addressing most probable "residual risks" rather than threats, it is seeking a defense posture which strives for maximum deterrence with a minimum of weapons.

There are radically different assessments of the uncertainties of the final political and territorial shape of the CIS and the external effects of the convulsive reform process in those countries. Even though there are legitimate fears that the "dual" character (Woerner 1991: 63) of NATO's relationship to the successor states of the former USSR may be too complex to be handled by the alliance, there appears to be a solid consensus among NATO members not to attempt to lock these states out from the economic, political, and security debates in Europe.

In an era of mutual force reductions and conventional disarmament, a "Europeanized" NATO, a reorganized alliance in which decisions will be more strongly influenced by European allies, could provide "security assurance" even without relying on the presence of numerous U.S. troops and weapons in Europe. The shrinking of the East's military might will make it easier for some European member states to either trust in independent nuclear forces or give up the illusion of cover from the U.S. nuclear umbrella (always a myth). In this respect, it is hoped that NATO will gradually but decisively undergo a metamorphosis of its own, to shift from a predominantly military to a political organization, and from a security provider to an active actor in the peace structures of Europe. The concept of a North Atlantic cooperation council reaching out to the CIS is already an important step forward to extend some stabilizing influence for the East.

If the alliance could restore in its relations with the successor states of the USSR some degree of "normality," NATO could function as a building block for the European security structure in a dual way. As we have stated, it remains the only powerful military alliance which can implement the objective of Yalta—namely, the containment of Germany (Mortimer 1990). Acting in this capacity, it will survive as long as no other security order is in sight or operation. In this sense, NATO functions to satisfy the needs of Germany's neighbors, including the USSR. In implementing this task, it might create enough stability and time for the preparation of a new European security order outside NATO which would be pan-European in scope. Apart from such limited contributions to the European security structure, NATO's role and objectives preserve traditional functions, such as maintaining the European-American link, discouraging external threats, and coordinating security and defense policies between the United States and Western Europe. In the course of implementing these functions, NATO will transform itself and may become the "Atlantic balcony" of the European peace and security order.

To assist the transition and manage the reorganization of European security is not without problems. The second challenge NATO is now facing is of a relatively new and different quality and probably more difficult to overcome in the long run: the end of bipolarity and the cold war has brought competitors to the fore which dispute NATO's monopoly on defense in Europe. Since the emergence of the CSCE as an institution of European security and the intergovernmental debate in the EC on coordinating foreign and security policies in the wake of Europe's disastrous dithering in the Gulf War, the scene has become more complicated. An inter-West European security dimension has been added to the East-West axis, undermining NATO's monopoly on security and defense in the region.

This new development has had a divisive effect on the defense and security community in Europe, splitting political parties into warring pro- and anti-European defense identity factions. British and Dutch circles argue that European security is impossible or too costly to achieve without American military guarantees. Douglas Hurd, the British foreign minister who opposes a more independent role of European institutions to formulate security and foreign policy objectives, dislikes the fact that defense is being dragged into the discussions about the European union. Hurd scorns the "creeping belief that the debate on a common foreign and security policy is empty unless it extends to include defense" (Hurd 1991). Hurd, like others, would not oppose the notion of a stronger "European defense identity" if it simply implied Europe's recognition of new threats (like mass immigration, terrorism, and the struggle for the control of resources) and rapidly changing, unpredictable threats which lie well beyond NATO's perimeter. But to allow other institutions to manage defense would create competing organizations and eventually undermine NATO. The position of the present British government on this matter is clear and echoed by the Dutch and by other conservative voices in Germany and NATO:

> We agree that the construction of an integrated Europe must include security and defense. But European defense without the United States does not make sense. The common foreign and security policy should include some broad security issues (Conference on Security and Cooperation in Europe, arms control and non-proliferation) but it should not compete with the military tasks of NATO (Hurd 1991).

Opponents of a genuine European defense identity argue that Europe cannot deliver a defense on its own. The costs would be too high and it would lack deterrent credibility. The argument about costs deflects from the core concern that an EC-dominated defense would alienate the United States from Europe. In some circles there is still the widespread belief that "European security is made in the United States." Arguments against a European defense identity based on financial concerns ultimately make no sense. As we know, defense budgets will fall as a result of arms control agreements and fundamental alterations in threat perceptions. Military diversification is already on the European agenda. Even if one assumes that potential and unpredictable "out-of-area" events cannot be calculated, the forces needed to impede and cope with such possible developments will be of a different calibre, and less costly, than the former defense deterrent.

The heart of the matter is not costs, but the future nature of U.S.-European relations. Unlike in the early 1980s there is no movement or party of any significance in Europe which questions NATO's existence or would like to drive the United States out of Europe. The question which arises is whether an eventual shift in security and defense authority from NATO to EC-related institutions will conflict with a U.S. presence in Europe. Given the British concerns of Washington bypassing London during the unfolding European events of 1989–90—which may have influenced the country's quick response to follow U.S. policies in the Gulf in order to re-cement the "special relationship"—it is quite understandable that this issue is of greater concern in the UK, in NATO headquarters, and among other staunch Atlanticist supporters than in France and Germany. For the time being, the British position is to link NATO via the WEU to the EC. In Britain's view, this ranking order would be reflected in the future chain of command. In agreement with the United States, Britain would block every move toward a European defense identity if it would trespass across boundaries complementary to already existing NATO responsibilities. A compromise for the time being was reached at the last WEU conference, just before Maastricht in December 1991. While welcoming the development of the "European security and defense identity" and setting the "role of the WEU as the defense component of the European Union," the view was taken that this should only be a means to "strengthen the European pillar of the Atlantic alliance" (European Council 1991).

CSCE: THE SOFTWARE FOR THE EUROPEAN SECURITY AND PEACE ORDER

As argued above, NATO's integrated military structure has contributed, although with varying degrees among member states, to the denationalization of defense and security concepts in Europe. In addition, forty years of NATO have created a highly integrated, consensus-driven military and political security elite in Western Europe. Both factors could be of considerable importance for the rethinking of Europe's security.

From the scope of the debate on the CSCE, involving countries from NATO and the now defunct Warsaw Pact, as well as neutral states which are on the edge of joining the EC, it seems inconceivable that European security will be limited to national, regional, or subregional force constellations. Nor will it develop narrowly in the cast of traditional military alliances or national concepts of security. Europe has been offered the opportunity to build a new security structure which does not depend on the individual nation-state. Instead, it is expected that multilateral, cooperative, collective, and integrated security structures linked to transnational political institutions will emerge.

With the breakup of the old military bloc system, awareness has grown that European security is indivisible and that it requires a new and extended definition. In accordance with the altered threat scenario, the core body of the new security equation will be defined predominantly in economic, social, and political terms. But there is still widespread uncertainty as to what that requires. The picture becomes even more complicated when one considers that the "domestic" European debate over security is overshadowed by external demands by the United Nations and the United States (for instance) in out-of-area conflicts.

It is likely that a future security order will arise from the CSCE, which since 1975 has resolved conflicts and established general principles for human rights in Europe. From its beginning, the CSCE has resembled a step-by-step approach to a European peace order by nonmilitary means, involving all European countries (with the exception of Albania), plus the United States and Canada. The common principles of the CSCE seem to have influenced the present security debate considerably—in particular the politicization of the security debate. The two main objectives of the CSCE—to establish security with decreasing levels of offensive weapons systems and to link such efforts with cooperative, multilateral regimes of verification—are currently the only adequate approach to conflicts in Europe. But it is interesting to note, as Senghaas (1991) has pointed out, that before the fall of the Berlin Wall, the CSCE never seriously contemplated the idea of building a regional system of collective security based on the principles of peaceful conflict-resolution and collective security. Only with the end of the East-West confrontation did the idea move to the agenda of a "new CSCE" during the 1991 conference in Valetta. Yet even now in the post–cold war era many European states hesitate to accept the legitimacy of a supranational institution. Senghaas is correct in postulating the need for such institutions—especially instruments for peaceful conflict-resolution in Europe—if bilateral conflicts or interstate conflicts are to be stripped of their escalating potential. Organizations pursuing peaceful conflict-resolution are the precondition for collective security.

The CSCE has defined principles of political behavior, based on accepting the territorial status quo in Europe. Further principles include collective, non-offensive military structures; institutions to verify and monitor military operations and the process of disarmament and arms conversion; and organizations specifically designed for the prevention of conflicts. Despite the weakness of the CSCE in handling the present crisis in Yugoslavia, the very dangers involved in the crisis serve as a catalyst for accelerating the creation of integrated force structures which would involve the whole of the continent. Another body of CSCE objectives focuses on social, ecological, cultural, economic, and human rights conditions.

In both military and political capacities the CSCE is the institution equipped to deal with the likely threats to the security and peace of Western Europe. The crucial question, however, remains: How can it bring about such a collective security system? The question points to whether other actors are willing to transfer authority from nation-states or subregional political, economic, and security alliances to CSCE institutions.

So far the CSCE has developed as an alternative to a strictly confined military security structure, which in the end was too inflexible to adapt to the rapid changes in Europe. Now, after the demise of the Soviet threat, the CSCE has to unfold outside and in competition with already existing structures which contain similar functions. Already a difference of opinion is quite noticeable among the now thirty-five (including Albania) signatory states in regard to the future function and capacity of the CSCE. The CIS thinks of it as a necessary and helpful instrument to link its special security and socioeconomic interests with the rest of the continent so as to avoid political marginalization. The former Warsaw Pact states are using the CSCE as the natural framework from which the new European collective security system ought to emerge. Such a notion points to the historic function of the CSCE in locking NATO and the Warsaw Pact into a decade-long negotiation process which delivered, in the final Paris meeting of November 1990, asymmetric reductions in conventional offensive weapons systems.

There is little doubt that in the absence of a security system for Eastern Europe the new CSCE will acquire security-relevant functions. Given the former hostility of NATO to the CSCE, and despite all other differences, the two organizations share a very peculiar affinity, which may even grow into symbiosis: both are interim institutions born under conditions of bipolarity which no longer exist. This means there is the danger that both NATO and the CSCE may have to relinquish their place in delivering peace, security, and stability to Europe.

The redefinition of security in Europe, the shift to different threat scenarios, has highlighted the domestic sources of conflict. While it is generally understood that the CSCE would be better equipped to deal with such conflicts, and might even develop institutions for conflict prevention, the CSCE cannot offer the necessary economic and social assistance to conflict areas. This can only be achieved in the framework of the EC. The pressing needs in the East are focused less on external security and new alliances and more on the troublesome and urgent task of converting their economies and societies. In this regard the CSCE cannot offer much assurance.

During an emergency meeting of the thirty-five member states (including Albania) on 4–5 July 1991 in Prague, it became clear that the CSCE's new flexible instruments of conflict prevention and conflict management were of little influence in the continuing conflict in Yugoslavia. CSCE initiatives—such as a "good offices" mission to facilitate a political dialogue between Belgrade and the Slovenian and Croatian governments—were either rejected by Belgrade or watered down, due to disagreement among CSCE member states with ethnic or religious problems similar to those of Yugoslavia. The way the CSCE dealt with the crisis is indicative of its strengths and weaknesses. The proposals adopted at the Prague meeting reflected the concern of countries such as the former USSR that the Yugoslav case would serve as a pretext for interventionism in other regions.

As the crisis in Yugoslavia demonstrates, the CSCE must come to terms with clashing principles. In order to reduce the threat of open warfare resulting from a mix of ethnic, economic, and cultural conflicts, a regional security institution will be forced at some stage to weigh the principle of nonintervention in domestic affairs against the fact that the causes of war are generated by domestic conditions. Without discarding nonintervention as a governing principle of the nation-state, any regional or international security institution will have to consider intervention by economic sanctions and political means. It can only be hoped that one outcome of the Yugoslav crisis will be the CSCE's ability to draw this fine line.

Unable to break the deadlock in negotiations with the Yugoslav government, the CSCE authorized the EC to act on its behalf. Only then were its proposals taken seriously. The CSCE and the EC demanded a cease-fire and the return of federal troops to their barracks. They further called for the restoration of constitutional rule in the rotation of the Yugoslav presidency and—most important of all—for the suspension of the declarations of independence of the Slovenian and Croatian republics for three months. The disengagement of troops and the implementation of the cease-fire would be monitored by civil and unarmed military observers from CSCE countries.

During the crisis a salient shift of political initiatives and activity toward the EC became manifest. Surprisingly, and perhaps because there were no rules, the EC acted quickly to attempt to defuse the conflict. This is even more astounding if one considers the deep differences among EC member states over the response to the independence problem. Initially countries like the UK, France, Spain, and Holland favored a federal solution which would allow the survival of a unitary Yugoslav state. The German government was split on the issue, while Hungary and Austria openly supported Slovenian and Croatian independence. However, as laudable as the swift intervention of the EC was, the objectives of the intervention were less clear. In supporting the concept of a unitary Yugoslav state, the EC arrived at a compromise position but took sides against the principle of self-determination of the peoples of Europe. In sending its "troika" of foreign ministers repeatedly to Yugoslavia and using its most powerful weapon, economic sanctions, the EC attempted to decrease the threat of an all-out civil war.

The Yugoslav crisis has offered the EC an ideal case scenario to put its embryonic efforts toward a more cohesive foreign and security policy into practice. Demonstrating political will and adopting an assertive role on a core European issue, the EC acted as though it had a mandate for securing peace in Europe. The absence of the

United States and the USSR in proposing solutions for the Yugoslav crisis was quite remarkable. It seems that apart from relations with the USSR, the United States has adopted a hands-off policy on all matters concerning Eastern Europe. This event highlights the EC's challenge to NATO in European security matters.

A EUROPEAN DEFENSE IDENTITY: THE EC AS A NUCLEUS FOR A EUROPEAN PEACE ORDER?

The forces unleashed by West European economic, social, and monetary integration have already accumulated such a critical mass of institutions, treaties, economic ties, social legislation, and R & D cooperation that the step toward more active political and security cooperation is long overdue. In this respect the Gulf War, as well as the present conflict in Yugoslavia, have served as catalysts to bring forth the hidden potential for political and security integration.

in light of the Yugoslav crisis, two factors indicate that the future peace and security of Europe will be either decided within the EC framework or at least strongly influenced by Community initiatives. First, the geopolitical and economic position of the unified Germany in Central Europe will exert pressure on neighboring countries to accelerate the process of European political unity. Neither NATO nor the CSCE can anchor Germany in the Western orbit, unnecessary as that may seem. Only the EC can accomplish such a task. Second, Germany is rapidly approaching a debate on its future foreign and security role in Europe, not unlike the one which paved the way for the country's economic and defense integration into the Western community of nations during the 1950s. Viewed from the outside, its neighbors already describe this trend as Germany's return to a "normal" state. Nevertheless, it is too early to say whether the outside notion of "normality" will match the outcome of the domestic German debate. Third, the decline of the USSR as a superpower and the breakup of COMECON and the Warsaw Pact have left the EC as the only coherent transnational and collective organization in Europe. It has everything that the CSCE lacks and longs for: a strong organization, political coherence, a strong economic basis, and a political and social vision.

In this respect, the outcome of the intergovernmental conference of EC heads in December 1990 may be interpreted as interlocking the economic, monetary, and political aspects of integration. In the arcane world of EC bureaucracies such an achievement opened the floodgates for hectic intergovernmental activities and initiatives in all three areas.

Even if national objections to transfers of sovereignty are finally overcome, the process will proceed in small steps and most likely not produce tangible and palpable results before the mid-1990s. Nevertheless, the present debate, initiated in February 1991 by Hans-Dietrich Genscher and Roland Dumas with a memorandum on "Security Policy Cooperation within the Framework of the Common Foreign and Security Policy of the Political Union" (CFSP), produced an avalanche of counter- and seconding proposals from other member states. The document reflects the gloomy mood of European politicians after the Gulf events—specifically the realization that neither Europe's economic power nor the harmonization of foreign and security policies will allow Europe to play a more active role in international affairs. On a more optimistic note, both foreign secretaries seem determined to tailor European security and defense needs to the fundamental changes the continent has experienced since 1989. Soviet troops will have left Eastern Europe and Germany by the end of 1994, and there will be no direct border between NATO and enemy territory. All activities in Europe would be "out-of-area" for NATO.

The coordination of European foreign and security policies is further complicated by the fact that the membership of the existing organizations does not overlap. Ireland, Greece, and Denmark are not in the WEU. In addition, Ireland is the only neutral country in the EC, but not in NATO. To further complicate matters, East European countries and EFTA members are knocking at the EC door for membership. Political union is too much for some to warm up to, while the prospect of joining the EC with its fully developed security and defense policies would burden domestic debates within the aspiring countries.

After listing general foreign policy objectives, the Genscher/Dumas document discusses the implications of a common European security policy. It refers to important NATO tasks and asserts that "a continuing military presence of the United States in Europe remains indispensable for European security and stability" (CFSP, p. 1). Within the framework of the CFSP, political union should develop a common security policy "with the objective of establishing eventually a Common European Defence, without which the construction of the European union would remain incomplete" (CFSP, p. 2). In anticipating British objections, the initiative stresses the aim of strengthening the Atlantic alliance by giving "added responsibility" to the Europeans in the context of security and defense policy. It takes pains to acquiesce to British fears by noting that any upgrading of competing defense organizations would undermine NATO and push the United States out of Europe. In this capacity the WEU could become a bird of passage between the European and the Atlantic/U.S. orbit:

> The WEU should become the channel through which the Political Union and NATO would cooperate with a view to ensure the mutual reinforcements of the European and transatlantic security structures. As the common European security policy evolves, the formal link established by the WEU Treaty with the alliance should be adapted accordingly.

The proposal specifies a catalogue of topics (CFSP, p. 3) which are either already dominated by coordinated European efforts or could easily be integrated into the CFSP, such as the following: disarmament and arms control, security issues, including peacekeeping measures within the UN framework; nuclear nonproliferation; and economic aspects of security, export controls of armaments, including dual-use goods such as chemical and biological weapons materials. Genscher and Dumas propose that the European Council should be given the power to decide which security topics should become matters for the common policy. The work of the WEU should be organized so that an "organic relationship" can develop between the Political Union and the WEU (CFSP, p. 4).

In order to bring the WEU closer to the Political Union, cooperation will be sought through the following measures: a) the decisions of the European Council on the principles and orientation of the CFSP should also serve as a guide for cooperation under the Brussels Treaty; b) the sequence and duration of the presidencies of the WEU and Political Union shall be harmonized as much as possible; and c) dates and venues of meetings of the council and the WEU shall be synchronized, the flow of information eased, and links between the European Parliament and the WEU assembly established. Finally, to strengthen links between NATO and the WEU, and between the EC and the WEU, the WEU's organs shall be transferred to Brussels.

There is already agreement among member states, including Britain, as to the desirability of a link between the WEU and the EC directed under the umbrella of the European Council. While it is generally recognized that the WEU could form an effective bridge between the Community and NATO, the question remains as to whether this would be an interim solution until the Community directly addressed security and defense issues. In other words, to what extent would a new European defense community be separate from NATO? Jacques Delors, in delivering the Alastair Buchan lecture to the International Institute for Strategic Affairs in London, left no doubt as to the final destination of the voyage. He concluded that it was about time for the Community to "allow for common defence issues to be dealt with by the European Council and by the joint council of foreign and defence ministers."

In the light of these developments it was hardly surprising that the intergovernmental conference at Maastricht incorporated the WEU as an "integral" part of the EC. The WEU should function as a "defense bridge" with NATO. But even more interesting is the attempt of the European union to move into the broader fields of foreign and security policies. The EC acknowledges the relevance of NATO but indicates further efforts to harmonize policies in order to achieve a "common" foreign and security policy, "including the eventual framework of a common defense policy which might in time lead to a common defense" (Political Union 1991).

PERSPECTIVE: REGIONAL SECURITY STRUCTURES

With the collapse of the USSR as a superpower, the United States is without any serious international checks on its military and short-term national interests—probably for the first time in postwar history. Yet this does not imply that the United States will dominate international activities. It will play a prominent role, but it "will have to cope with unprecedented problems of interdependence that no great power can solve by itself" (Nye 1990: 520). The pretense that Russia as the largest successor state of the Soviet Union is still a superpower can no longer be maintained, even if there is enough unfinished business in coming START and CFE II talks. Consequently the United States will be an important international actor, but one among seven, as the negotiations and talks during the London G-7 summit of July 1991 demonstrated. "The superpowers are dancing their last tango" (Lichfield 1991).

Hence we cannot characterize the post–cold war system of international relations as either "unipolar" or truly "multipolar." There is a diffusion of power among various economic-political centers, as well as global conflicts and challenges which transcend military scenarios. With the emergence of "extended nonmilitary threats," the rigidity of the former arms race axis is rapidly fading into the background. It gives way to a more diversified gallery of international relations emphasizing competition in economic, ecological, political, and cultural matters. It is precisely on these nonmilitary grounds that other regional centers can bring their competitive advantages to full fruition.

This suggests a possible framework of a new system of international relations, one based on regulated cooperation and strongly influenced by regional components. Hence reducing the structural "security dilemma" of military force and counterforce deployments would contribute to demilitarizing international politics and allow for a more even distribution of political power.

Regional conferences on security and cooperation modeled on the CSCE process could open the agenda by addressing ecological, social, economic, and human rights issues. This does not imply an ahistoric transfer of the European CSCE model to other global regions. More important is the transfer of its procedures. The mix of methods and instruments has to respect the political-cultural context of each region. Given the lack of ideological divisions, such regionalized systems of confidence-building and cooperation could exert an even higher degree of restraint on superpower behavior—through binding norms and codes of conduct—than the former arms race and policy of mutually assured destruction were ever capable of delivering.

Regional collective security structures could then replace unilateral and subregional alliances, as well as maintain an international dimension, organized by the United Nations. In the wake of such transformations, military factors will become less relevant than policies to strengthen economic and social cohesion and to eliminate the causes of war and conflict within regions. In this narrow sense we would accept Fukuyama's (1991) description of a changed world in which "economics has become vastly more important as the basis for great power status, and democratic legitimacy has proven crucial to political power."

REFERENCES

Brandt, Willy. 1991. "Eine Friedensordhung für den Nahen Osten." *Europa Archiv* 5 (10 March).

CFSP: Genscher, Hans-Dietrich; and Dumas, Roland. 1991. "Security Policy Cooperation within the Framework of the Common Foreign and Security Policy of the Political Union." Bonn: Foreign Office, Germany. February.

Daschitschev, V. I. 1990. Interview in *Die Tageszeitung*, 5 November.

Declaration of the Member States of the Western European Union. 1991. Issued on the Occasion of the Forty-Sixth European Council Meeting, 9 and 10 December, Maastricht. In European Council, Maastricht, 9 and 10 December 1991, Presidential Conclusions.

Fukuyama, Francis. 1989. "The End of History." *The National Interest*, Summer 1989, pp. 3–4.

————. 1991. "Changed Days for Ruritania's Dictator." *The Guardian*, 8 April.

Hassner, Pierre. 1990. "Europe Beyond Partition and Unity: Disintegration or Reconstitution?" *International Affairs* 66, 3.

Hurd, Douglas. 1991. "No European Defence Identity without NATO." *Financial Times*, 15 April.

Lichfield, John. 1991. "Last Tango of the Superpower Era." *The Independent*, 14 July.

Lloyd, John. 1990. In *Financial Times*, 17 September.

Mortimer, Edward. 1990. "Solution in Search of a Problem." *Financial Times*, 9 October.

Nye, Joseph. 1990. "American Strategy after Bipolarity." *International Affairs* 66, 3.

Political Union. 1991. "Protocol on Economic and Social Cohesion, Annex 1," SN 252/1/1991, 11 December; and "Common Provisions," SN/1/1991. Maastricht.

Ramsbotham, Oliver. 1991. "Britain, Germany and the New European Security Debate." IPPR, *Defense and Security*, Paper No. 1. London.

Shea, Jamie. 1990. *NATO 2000: A Political Agenda for a Political Alliance.* Brussels: Brassey's. Atlantic Commentaries No. 3.

Senghass, Dieter. 1991. "Friedliche Streitbeilegung im neuen Europa." *Europa Archiv* 10 (25 May).

Woerner, Manfred. 1991. "Die Atlantische Allianz in den neunziger Jahren." *Europa Archiv* 3 (10 February).

DOES NATO HAVE A FUTURE?

Steve Weber

INTRODUCTION

Historians will quarrel over a date for the "end" of the cold war. I prefer 6 July 1990, the day on which representatives of the sixteen NATO governments signed the "London Declaration on a Transformed North Atlantic Alliance." This document pledged NATO, the alliance whose principal purpose was deterring Soviet aggression in Western Europe, to the following goals:

1. Revising its forward defense strategy;
2. Reducing greatly its reliance on nuclear weapons, to something approximating no early first use;
3. Acting as an "agent of change" and setting "new standards for the establishment and preservation of free societies."[1]

Others may not agree with my choice of dates, but they should recognize the significance of what was finally decided and put down on paper in London. The basic characteristics of the security problem in Europe were no longer what they had been for forty-odd years. As Beverly Crawford nicely pointed out, Europe's postwar security system was history.

What do we do now? For forty years, NATO was the principal answer to almost any question about security in Europe, no matter which side of the Atlantic posed it. With the end of the cold war, governments in Europe are now looking curiously at a number of alternative fora for discussing security. Americans tend to be less eclectic in their tastes, asking questions like "Should we keep NATO or get rid of it and create something else?" I would like to rephrase the question. "Something else" is already in place—in fact, many institutions with some claim to a role in European security exist— and the survival of NATO need not be an all-or-nothing proposition.

The right questions are these: What is the appropriate "division of labor" among institutions, and how can that division of labor be worked out? Does NATO have any role to play within it?

Other contributors to this volume will probably answer no to the last question. The argument against NATO is not just that it is irrelevant to security in Europe; it is that NATO may actually harm European security and more parochial American interests as well. From the American perspective, NATO costs Washington money, and it ensures a level of American military presence on the continent that some find distasteful. From a European perspective, NATO lost its legitimacy with the end of the cold war. NATO perpetuates an anachronistic militarist view of security, which the Soviet bloc has managed to transcend. And it perpetuates an image of American predominance that is at best unjustified and at worst damaging to the prospects for a "new Europe" or a "common European home." The sooner NATO joins the Warsaw Pact in the history books, the better.

Each of these arguments has some merit. Like any institution, NATO has significant costs. But those costs are minimal compared to the important role NATO still has to play in Europe. I agree with Crawford that peace and security in Europe over the next decade are not guaranteed and that the institutional choices made over the next few years can affect the prospects greatly. The problem is that our theories of peace and war, of security and insecurity, are neither sufficiently precise nor proven to guide that choice with any precision.

Given the character and the level of uncertainty, I will argue that the best strategy is one that is robust across the foreseeable possibilities. Maximizing the leverage that the West (i.e., Western Europe and the United States) has over the character and direction of the economic, political, and social transitions that are taking place in Eastern Europe is the right strategy. By leverage over the transition, I mean using in the most vigorous way possible the various sources of power that states have to influence the direction of social and political evolution within the domestic systems of East European states, as well as their international alignments. NATO is the right institution to provide that kind of leverage.

In this chapter I start by distinguishing between an alliance and a security community and link each to a school of thought about the causes of peace. Since we do not yet know which of these causes could be decisive in Europe, I justify the argument that leverage over transitions—a strategy that is relatively robust across those causes—is the best means for improving the prospects of peace and security. I then explore some of the peculiar features of NATO as an institution that make it a decent tool of leverage. I describe in more detail what NATO could do on that score and compare this to what NATO is actually now doing and what NATO thinkers foresee as their future. I explain why other institutions—which no doubt have places of their own in the division of labor—cannot do what NATO can. Finally, I lay out some objections to my argument and consider what NATO could do to overcome them.

ALLIANCE, SECURITY COMMUNITY, OR SOMETHING ELSE?

In the introduction above Beverly Crawford notes that "our beliefs about the causes of war and conditions for peace shape the kinds of security arrangements we prefer." In a broad sense and without specifying to whom "our" and "we" refer, that is probably correct. "Beliefs" is also a tricky term; it appropriately replaces the word "theory." Political scientists do not yet have a comprehensive undertanding of the causes of war and conditions of peace, but only a jumble of arguments, hypotheses, and generally underspecified, partial theories, many of which are not close to being tested. Right now, the major split in those arguments seems to rest on the fault line between what Kenneth Waltz long ago called the third and second images of international relations. Wars are the "result" either of certain parametric conditions in the international system, or of the kinds of states that populate that system.[2]* While the debate continues, statesmen and the states they represent will continue to choose strategies and design institutions based on some (frequently implicit) beliefs about which of these arguments is right.

What kinds of choices do states actually make? We expect, combining Waltz and Stephen Walt, that states will ally to increase

---

*I use the term "result" carefully here because I do not want to fully engage epistemological and other questions about proximate versus underlying or profound causes, necessary versus sufficient causes, etc. The theories that I am characterizing here are not always themselves clear on that score. I do not think it necessary to settle the question here in order to proceed.

their security against perceived threats.[3] In any particular balance-of-power system, there are usually groups of states that share to some extent an assessment of those threats. The decision to ally does not, however, erase anarchy. Groups of states face two kinds of threats. The first is usually the reason they join forces in the first place—an external threat from a potential aggressor who is not part of the group. The second is more insidious but often just as danger-ous—an internal threat from a member of the group itself which chooses to betray its friends and use force against them. A group of states can create an institutional structure that is optimized to lessen one or the other threat, but it is hard to lessen both at the same time.

Figure 1 illustrates the logic of the dilemma. I distinguish between two polar ideal types, the alliance and the security com-munity. In an alliance, states join together to defend against a common external enemy (or—much less frequently—to attack a common external target). This requires that states make promises to each other that an attack on one is an attack on all; an individual state must promise that it will use force to defend its allies even when its own security is not immediately threatened. Such a prom-ise is difficult to make credible: in an international system without central enforcement, the incentives to defect are frequently high. Democracies may find it particularly difficult to make a credible promise to use force in defense of another state's security. Even states that have no overt intention to defect or free-ride on alliance commitments must still take some steps to enhance the credibility of their promise, to bind themselves away from "involuntary defec-tion" and to reassure their allies that they are in fact so bound.

There are many different ways to enhance the credibility of an alliance promise.[4] Creating an institutional structure for the alliance can be an important contributing factor, so long as it is constructed in the proper way. The best institutional arrangement for an alliance would be one with an authoritative or at least a hierarchical decision structure. There should be a unified military command with as much coordination among national armed forces as is practicable. States should agree to joint training, exercises, and procurement. The aim would be to maximize integration of command, deployment, and operation of armed forces so that when the external threat chal-lenged, states would have no real choice but to proceed with the plans of the alliance and fight in defense of their allies.

Figure 1

ALLIANCE VERSUS SECURITY COMMUNITY

	Alliance	Security Community
Purpose	States join to defend against common external enemy	States join to increase common welfare by enhancing interdependence
What kind of promise?	An attack on one is an attack on all: "I *will* use force to defend my allies even when my own security is not threatened."	Disputes between states are settled peaceably: "I will *not* use force against any other member of the security community."
What kinds of institutions add credibility to the promise?	Authoritative or hierarchical decision structure Unified military command Maximum integration of armed forces	Egalitarian decision structure Peaceful dispute-settlement procedures Other means for enhancing transparency, sharing information, building "confidence"

The goals of a security community are different and in some sense broader. States in a security community engage each other in high levels of economic, social, and political interdependence. Their willingness to do so rests on a set of promises that they will not use force among themselves, that no member of the security community will attack another as a means of settling disputes. The logic of credibility in this strategic situation is different from that in an alliance. The challenge is to make a credible promise *not* to use force against other states. Democracies probably are better suited to this game than to the alliance game, although the theoretical arguments here (often associated with Michael Doyle) are widely contested.[5] Karl Deutsch's argument that security communities rest on politically relevant strata of the participant states having compatible values is probably more generalizable. In any case, domestic institutions and shared values are rarely enough to make the promise credible.

Security communities can have international institutions of their own that help. Since authority and coercion go against the notion of formally equal states that recognize each other's legitimate sovereignty, the institutions of a security community will be different from those of an alliance. Instead of stressing hierarchy, these institutions will stress equivalence. Decisions will be taken by consensus and implemented voluntarily. International institutions will exist principally to enhance transparency and to facilitate the transfer of information among states that have every reason to want to share it. This may include confidence-building measures and procedures for peaceful settlement of disputes, but the least constraining institutions will generally be seen as best.*

The logic of these ideal types links closely to theories about the causes of peace and war in post–cold war Europe, which I cartooned above as dividing between the third and second image. John Mearsheimer, cartooner of the third, sees anarchy as a continuing cause of insecurity. Unless they are able to protect themselves with independent nuclear arsenals, the smaller states of Europe had best form an alliance to safeguard collectively their autonomy against an ascendent Germany. Francis Fukuyama, cartooner of the second, sees ideological convergence as a cause of security. States that share his triumphant set of ideas about how to organize society and polity may disagree over technicalities but will hardly threaten each other's existence; they ought to join in a security community and consummate their interdependence.

I do not know who is right, but I am certain that no responsible decision-maker relishes the idea of betting on one or the other. I am more comfortable with a middle-of-the-road approach which presumes that a less harsh ideological divide will probably be a cause of peace, while the continuing independence of nations will be a

---

*A security community might later extend itself toward a confederal or even a federal structure among the states that were a part of it, but at that point it is no longer a security community per se because it is no longer a group of sovereign states. I need to limit the definition in this way because I want to apply these ideal types to Eastern Europe, as will become clear below. Whatever happens to Eastern Europe in the next decade or so, it is not likely to become part of a confederal or federal Europe. If the EC does continue in this direction, it will have gone beyond a security community as I define it here.

permanent cause of war. Given our uncertainty about the magnitude of each of these causes and others as well, the best course is probably not to bet on either but to devise a strategy that promises to be robust across the divide. In terms of institutional structures, this means avoiding the choice between alliance and security community for as long as states can afford to pay the costs of compromise.

NATO through most of its history has been a peculiar mixture of alliance and security community.* The principle alliance goal—to defend NATO territory against external invasion from the Soviet Union—was balanced against the security community goal—to prevent the use of force among the NATO members, and particularly to solve the Franco-German security dilemma. NATO's institutional structure reflects a compromise between the logical demands of these goals. It includes unprecedented elements of supra-sovereign authority over the armed forces of states; at the same time it constrains that authority in ways that severely complicated the problem of actually mounting an effective defense. The compromise was frequently awkward. It was at once a source of frustration for military thinkers and a source of comfort for political analysts, who were able to assume away the challenge of deterrence and proclaim that NATO was first and foremost a "political alliance"—by which they meant something approximating my ideal-type security community. Like most compromises, NATO did something to promote each of its tasks, but it did so in ways that were generally nonoptimal, sometimes clumsy, and often expensive.

With a waning cold war, NATO's peculiar institutional structure can be criticized easily as a historical anachronism. It can also be seen as a lucky coincidence. Quirky evolutionary processes sometimes produce structures that are well adapted to a changed environment. There is no intentionality or teleology to the fit, but NATO is in fact decently suited to support the strategy that I propose: to maximize and capitalize on the leverage that the West has over East European transitions.

The logic behind this strategy is, to repeat, its robustness across schools of thought about the causes of peace and war. The goal of the strategy would be to nudge and cajole the "new" East European states in particular directions of social and economic development;

---

*I will expand on the story of NATO's quirky evolution below, to show how it got that way.

to try to create a specific kind of state in Eastern Europe. The modal state would fit the general consensus expressed in the November 1990 Joint Declaration of Twenty-Two States and the Charter of Paris for a New Europe.[6] These documents reaffirm the 1975 Helsinki Final Act provisions and add something very important: that states should aim for democratic governance ("open" democratic societies with pluralistic political systems in which leaders are selected in free elections) and "free market" economies. A group of such states in Europe could fulfill many of the conditions of peace that derive from both second and third image theories at the same time.

Consider the second image. I think it is unfortunate that we do not yet have a theoretically sophisticated answer to the general question of how alike states have to be in order to cooperate. In the context of modern Europe, however, we have good reason to believe that what *The Economist* calls "RRE states"—those sharing broad political ideals from the Renaissance, Reformation, and Enlightenment—will find it easier to cooperate or at least to live in peace with one another. I do not say this with only a blind faith in Doyle's conclusions. RRE states are less likely to suffer nationalist conflict or economic turmoil; when they do, there are channels of legitimate action that subnational groups can access before they turn to violence. For much the same reason, RRE states are also less vulnerable to the "praetorian" politics that worry Jack Snyder.[7] And for those who fear that isolated small states in the middle of Europe would present too tempting a target for Russian or German expansionists, the emergence of states that share a set of norms and values should at least diminish the possibility of isolation.

Leverage is also meaningful for third image arguments because the character of domestic politics in East European regimes will matter for the international alignments and responsibilities of these states. Within Europe, there is a great deal of interest in expanding old institutions and creating new ones that would foster interdependence in economics and politics. If the East Europeans are to participate, they will have to be able to make credible promises to those institutions. They will face the same problems of credibility that all states face, but they have fewer advantages to work with. New, small, and weak states have neither power nor reputation nor long-standing legal systems to enhance the credibility of promises that they want to make. For them, the most hopeful means to attain credibility is to create a domestic political system that ensures transparency to outsiders.[8] If other states can "look inside" a state's polity and decision making system, they can understand the state's interests and how those interests get translated into policy. In that case, the state can make a credible promise that it will fulfill contracts with international institutions because others can see that the contract accords with the state's interests. Given that East European states will probably have fractured polities with conflicting sets of preferences for some time to come, open democratic governments with established and internationally known decision-making procedures will maximize the degree to which transparency works in their favor. That will be important regardless of whether the institutions East European states want to join are those of a security community or an alliance.

There is a broad consensus in Europe today about the way that states should try to organize politics and economics. Without a declaration of world government or the end of history, there are both second and third image reasons to think that a group of such states could in fact live peaceably together on the European continent for some time to come. But the kinds of states that will emerge from the transitions in Eastern Europe may not quite fit the mold. The West has a profound interest in trying to steer these transitions in the desired direction. The limits to the strategy I propose are obvious but need to be mentioned. I do not mean imposing Western political systems or values on states that are not interested. I mean creating signposts with carrots and sticks for states and societies whose future directions are uncertain. Without being arrogant, the West has considerable resources to steer change in particular directions. We should be thinking about institutions that could facilitate a strategy aimed at making maximum use of those resources.

LEVERAGE AND NATO

Why institutions? The answer to this question is that some of the methods of leverage I will propose are not readily available to individual states. Persuasion and the force of example are exceptions—both are available to individual states and are currently being used.* Conditionality, however, is a more demanding approach. States can offer aid, financial and otherwise, in steps attached to general or specific conditions that East European states must fulfill along the way. Because conditionality must be carefully coordinated among offering states in order to have any force, institutions play a large role.† Finally, there is the possibility of direct imposition. Although the place for this approach is strictly limited, when it is used it will require a predominance of power on the side of the imposing states. Institutions would play an important part in cementing and maintaining the power for that purpose.

In the course of its evolution as a mixture of alliance and security community, NATO developed an institutional structure with elements that make it decently suited for all three approaches.[9] NATO is not, of course, a supranational organization and does not take decisions *formally* by rules other than unanimity and consent.[10] When member countries "assign" forces to NATO, they agree to relinquish some aspects of operational command during wartime but do not compromise the principle that "full command over all aspects of the military operations and administration of those forces . . . remain under national command in peace time."[11] When it comes to a function like armaments standardization, which should be central to my ideal-type alliance, NATO's formal role is strictly limited to "advice and coordination."[12] Politically NATO does just about what a "functional regime" ought to be expected to do: it facilitates communication through a network of permanent and intermittently meeting bodies as well as ad-hoc groups set up at the request of member states.[13]** The constraints on NATO's authority

*International institutions can support and coordinate these efforts and make them more efficient, but the institution is not critical. The EC, for example, has organized a series of "talking shops" and "expert exchanges" that expand upon and coordinate individual states' initiatives.

†This might not be the case if power were as unevenly distributed as it was in 1945. However, we no longer have the benefits of hegemony. If conditionality is not coordinated, the target state can play the offering states off against each other in ways that dilute the force of conditionality.

**Political consultation within NATO can and has ranged widely, to include discussion of "matters significantly affecting the alliance so long as they are not of a purely domestic character." States sometimes turn to NATO as a forum simply because of its convenience: the political committee of the alliance meets at least once a week in Brussels, and the North Atlantic Council deputies (who vis-à-vis sovereign states are not particularly surprising, although they have often been terribly frustrating to military and even political leaders charged with the responsibility of mounting a credible defense of Europe, particularly in the 1950s. The costs in terms of military efficiency have been high.

Yet NATO does have facets of supranational power that are remarkable in the context of modern international institutions. Some are informal or a result of precedent. On the political side, there are well-established norms of consultation and cooperation that date back to the 1956 Committee on Non-Military Cooperation (a.k.a. Committee of Three, or more frequently Three Wise Men). The recommendations of this committee, approved by the North Atlantic Council shortly after the Suez crisis, tie member states to the norm that they should not "without adequate advance consultation, adopt firm policies or make major political pronouncements on matters which significantly affect the Alliance or any of its members." States and the NATO secretary general have the right to raise for discussion in the council *any* subject of common interest so long as it is not purely domestic in its implications. If the members reach a consensus, governments are obligated to abide by it or to explain to the Council why national reasons make compliance impossible. Finally, if a dispute of any kind arises among member governments and that dispute cannot be settled directly, the states are expected to submit to "good offices procedures within the NATO framework, before resorting to any other international agency."[14] These norms have been in place for over thirty-five years and have a strong claim on expectations among the member states.

More formal and probably more important are sources of supranational power that reside in NATO's military organization, part of the legacy of NATO's quirky history as an alliance. These sources of power were *not* present in NATO at its birth. Nothing in the North Atlantic Treaty of April 1949 gave the United States, any other member, or the NATO secretariat a privileged position vis-à-vis sovereign states within the military or political structures of the alliance. The first four-year defense plan for NATO, which came into force a year later, preserved the principle of national command

---

represent their governments at the ambassadorial level) can be called into session in as little as two hours if necessary.

for military forces and did not broach the notion of an integrated military command. The United States, in fact, declined to participate in defense planning groups with responsibility for alliance regions outside of the North Atlantic Ocean and North America.[15] For the moment, NATO was far from the ideal-type alliance that member states might have felt constrained to accept had the external threat from the Soviet Union been perceived as immediate and military in character. Because the Red Army seemed satisfied with its occupations in Eastern Europe, even NATO's military organization looked more like the seeds of a security community among the West Europeans than an alliance per se.

Perceptions changed after the invasion of Korea in late June 1950.[16] In late July, the North Atlantic Council Deputies (who meet in continuous session as a kind of secretariat for the North Atlantic Council) elected Charles M. Spofford, an American, to be their permanent chairman. When the Council itself gathered in New York in September, it adopted the principle of "forward defense" for Europe. This principle—that alliance territory would be defended as far to the east as possible—demanded a fundamental reorganization of NATO's military structure. The forces and the level of coordination among them that would be needed to turn forward defense into a reality meant that NATO would have to adopt some of the institutional features of my ideal-type alliance. In that spirit, the Council instructed its Defense Committee to develop plans for "the establishment at the earliest possible date of an integrated force under centralized command and control composed of forces made available by governments," with a "supreme commander" to be appointed by NATO.[17] Those plans were finalized and approved in December 1950, with quite broad terms of reference for the new SACEUR, General Dwight Eisenhower. SACEUR's authority would stem from the principle that forces made available by member states, while remaining under national control in peacetime, had to be organized, equipped, trained, and ready to implement the agreed defense plans of the alliance should an emergency arise. In 1951, SACEUR gained a supreme headquarters (SHAPE) and an international military staff which has since grown to over four hundred people. The next year, NATO established two additional integrated commands (SACLANT—based in Norfolk, Virginia, and the commander always an American; and

CINCHAN—based at Portsmouth, UK, and the commander always a Briton) to complete its military structure.

These commands have extensive authority over the assigned forces that come under their jurisdiction. In wartime, SACEUR would control all land, sea, and air operations in Europe apart from internal defense and coastal water defense. Although NATO armies remain formally under national command in peacetime, SACEUR is responsible for planning training and exercises, and has considerable influence over decisions about deployment. The NATO commanders also play a pivotal role in the force planning process of the alliance and by implication in the defense plans of member states. Every second year, the NATO machinery generates a set of force goals for the alliance according to guidance from the defense ministers and the Military Committee. The NATO commanders elaborate these goals into force proposals for their own area; these set out *for each member state* the level and type of contribution as well as specific improvements that NATO desires. Member states submit their own plans to NATO headquarters, where they are analyzed by the international military staff and compared to the alliance plan so as to bring them into line. At the end of each year, the North Atlantic Council reviews the results of the bargain and its implementation.* Anyone vaguely familiar with NATO's history knows that member states have rarely lived up to the expectations of the unified command in this regard, but the process itself is significant. It has led to a systematic, continuous, and detailed exchange of data among governments on military programs that is unprecedented in peace or in war.†

---

*The NATO Military Committee consists of the Chiefs of Staff of member countries. The Council adopts as well a five-year defense plan each December, but this document has less practical significance. Although member states are asked to accept the five-year plan in a general sense, they make a firm commitment only to the first year's force and financial requirements. The procedure I describe here was adopted in 1966. (*NATO: Facts and Figures*, p. 222.)

†A similar process exists for NATO infrastructure. NATO commanders propose infrastructure needs for their forces based on the agreed long-term force proposals. The Council approves certain projects as "NATO Common Infrastructure"; installations that are so designated are financed collectively according to a cost-sharing formula set up to compensate "host countries" that would otherwise bear an inordinate share of the responsibility. The common infrastructure program is not insignificant: it includes 230 airfields, 50,000 km. of com-

There is another important facet of supranational power in NATO's military organization which derives from Germany's special position within the alliance. The Federal Republic regained most of its sovereignty with the signing of the Paris Agreements in October 1954, but the Bundeswehr was constrained in significant ways. In a protocol to the Brussels Pact that was also signed in 1954, the FRG accepted numerical limits on its forces of twelve divisions and half a million military personnel.[18] More important was the arrangement under which the FRG would be invited to join NATO and contribute a national army "to be integrated into the forces of the Alliance."[19] What this meant in practice was that Germany would no longer have a national military command structure at the highest levels. The German general staff, which was believed by many to have been a source of militarism, anti-democratic sentiment, and aggressive state behavior, would not be reconstituted. The functions of a general staff were transferred to NATO's integrated military command and have remained there since. Apart from some small "territorial defense units" that belong to the Lander and are nearly analogous to the U.S. National Guard, all of Germany's regular armed forces were placed under SACEUR and all high level planning and command functions were delegated to NATO. Thirty-five years later, the Treaty on the Final Settlement with Respect to Germany (Two-plus-Four Agreement) reinforced that arrangement with its provision prohibiting the stationing of NATO forces in what used to be East Germany until 1994.[20] I know of no one who has expressed any serious interest in overturning this arrangement in order to establish a new German national command structure. It is a powerful precedent with potential value for attaining leverage over transitions in Eastern Europe. I will come back to this point below.

NATO'S FUTURE TASKS

First I shall discuss the easier task that NATO will have to face in the 1990s—to dismantle the armaments legacy of the cold war while maintaining security against the residual or a reconstituted

---

munications lines, 11,000 km. of fuel pipelines linked to 3 million cubic meters of storage capacity, extensive radar warning installations, etc.

Soviet threat. NATO propaganda stresses the latter by reminding anyone who will listen that the former Soviet Union remains by far the largest military power on the continent. The goal of the alliance at this point, according to Jamie Shea, is not "minimum deterrrence" per se but "maximal deterrence with minimal weapons."[21] That seems to me a reasonable philosophy. Maintaining a prudent insurance policy against an unlikely but dangerous contingency makes sense, and states are going to do it in one way or another. If they do it within NATO, the results are likely to be more organized, less expensive, and less worrisome to the former Soviet states than otherwise. NATO has great experience in planning against the Soviet threat, and although the character of that threat has certainly changed, the expertise is not obsolete. Part of that expertise lies in NATO's ability to rationalize and coordinate member states' obligations in the area of arms control. If the CFE process continues, it will bite hard into individual states' force planning. It is far more practical for NATO (with its coordinated force planning process) to apportion arms control cuts within the alliance than for the Western states to negotiate against the former Soviet states *and* against each other in Vienna. NATO has also played an important role in coordinating member states' positions at the CSCE since the first exploratory contacts in 1970.[22] I do not mean to say that these tasks will be easy, but they fall with relative comfort inside NATO's traditional mandate.

The more interesting challenge comes in extending NATO's reach to East European transitions. NATO could do several things to enhance Western leverage over that process, and some with unique competence. The realm where NATO has the most well-developed institutional capabilities (and where there is a precedent from the German case) is in the organization of military forces. That is something that governments in Eastern Europe, still basking in one or another version of a velvet revolution, have chosen in the public arena to ignore or downplay for the moment.[23] I suspect they are not ignoring it in private, or at least will not be doing so for very much longer. These countries are too small, too exposed, and too vulnerable to unsettled neighbors to imagine that they can exist forever without determined efforts at defense.[24] Czechoslovakia, Poland, and Hungary in their more sober moments recognize that they will not be dismantling their military forces but rather de-Sovietizing them—

i.e., reformulating defense postures, capabilities, and doctrines for military forces which had been dominated by Soviet plans and planners for forty years. These countries will no longer have militaries optimized for supporting a Soviet thrust into Western Europe. What will they have instead?

In the short term, reform will probably be limited to the reduction of numbers and adjustments in deployment. Under the logic of the Soviet plan, East European forces used to be arrayed mainly near the western borders of Warsaw Pact territory. Now downsized units are being shifted eastward.[25] The problem is that neither change modifies the basic character of these armies. Their weapons, training, and doctrine are still set up for rapid invasion of territory. There is certainly talk about more substantial reform—replacing current forces with smaller, professionalized armies carrying modern and smaller weapons—but with the low budget priority for military spending in Eastern Europe it will probably remain just talk. Keep in mind also that these forces are directed by senior officers trained for the most part in Soviet military academies and schooled in the virtues of "offensive doctrines."* While the military is currently under the control of civilian defense ministers in Czechloslovakia and Hungary and probably soon will be in Poland as well, these civilians will lack the institutional base and experience to exert much influence over military decision-making for some time.

This adds up to offense-oriented forces in small countries with powerful military leaderships schooled in offensive doctrines, facing each other across sometimes unsettled borders in a part of the world subject to ethnic, racial, and economic tensions that will probably generate considerable domestic instability. It is a recipe for trouble, or at least for a severe version of the security dilemma that could poison hopes for reducing military tensions on the continent.† Even if East European leaders recognize this possibility now and understand what it could do to their visions of "successful" transitions to democracy, there may be little they can do *on their*

---

*I understand from conversations that there has been some discrediting of the military leadership, but that few of the top individuals have actually been "purged."

†It will then, obviously, become much harder to maintain reductions in military expenditures.

own to avoid it. NATO, however, could make an important contribution.

A few years after the end of World War II, NATO took command of and reorganized the military forces of a state that was formerly an enemy of the West. That has left both precedents and institutional structures that could be extended to Eastern Europe. This would require a pro-active as opposed to a reactive stance for NATO, but the logic of the argument seems compelling. SHAPE has the machinery and the knowlege to take over effectively the task of reorganizing East European militaries and training their officers in less provocative doctrines. NATO could even replace Soviet-supplied weaponry with smaller, more defensively oriented systems.* East European armies could be included in NATO's annual force planning process, which would involve them as well in detailed data exchanges with their neighbors. None of these things would guarantee the maintenance of peace in Eastern Europe, but as a package they would probably diminish what could be a significant source of tension. As a form of leverage on the transition it may be indirect, but it is potentially very important.

A more direct means of leverage comes in the form of conditionality, with which the West is now experimenting across economic and political domains. While I doubt that NATO will be a major player in economics per se, there are natural linkages between economic and military issues on which the West can capitalize. Private investors will not be anxious to send money to Soviet or East European economies which spend inordinate portions of GNP on the military. Government aid or official assistance for private investors can be explicitly tied to a set of politically motivated conditions: reductions in military spending, conversion or closing of arms production facilities, constraints on sales of weapons and weapons technology to the Third World. This is already a significant issue in Czechoslovakia, where Vaclav Havel's valiant pledge to curtail sharply his nation's role in the international arms trade is

---

*Some of these weapons might come from NATO's own stocks demobilized under CFE agreements; we might also have to pay for some new weapons. That may seem troubling until we think about how much money and potentially lucrative investment oppotunities we stand to lose in Eastern Europe should there be even a small war between states struggling with the transition to democracy.

crumbling barely a year later.* The West has a profound interest in seeing that Czechoslovakia and others not take the easy way out, and we have resources that can be used to modify substantially the calculus of interests for governments faced with similar dilemmas. The problem lies in enforcing conditionality. If Western governments try to do it on their own, they will likely undercut each other's terms and encourage target states to bargain for the best deal. The force of the sanction, as well as part of its legitimacy, will be lost.

NATO, however, has an institutional structure with the potential to implement conditionality as a means of leverage. It is the only institution with a specific mandate in the area of military affairs that combines the major Western players, including the United States. It gives the United States a de facto privileged position in decision making, nearly a condition of success for states trying to coordinate conditionality.[26] NATO also puts the United States in a better position to offer concessions, or carrots to accompany the sticks, without incurring too much wrath among domestic political constituencies. Acting by and through international institutions has become a source of policy legitimacy for the Bush administration, and it might become particularly important should the United States soften its stand on aid to the former Soviet Union. Conciliatory decisions taken at NATO headquarters will be less odious to many in the American right wing than similar decisions taken at the CSCE.[27]

A final, less happy possibility lies in the realm of direct imposition. Military tensions could rise inadvertently between East European states as a result of an exacerbated security dilemma that

---

*Mr. Havel is certainly in a quandary. Apart from the fact that his country's economy overall has been heavily dependent on arms exports for CMEA trade and for hard currency, some of the largest arms factories—including the ZTS Martin plant that makes T-72 tanks—are located in Slovakia, where over 80,000 people work in arms production. The Czechoslovak leadership was persuaded to allow new exports in order to avoid a sharp rise in Slovak unemployment, which was seen as a boost to separatists there. The potential customers include Iran, which is reportedly negotiating a weapons-for-oil barter deal worth nearly $3 billion, and Syria, which will probably buy around 300 T-72 tanks ("Prague and Iran Plan Oil-for-Arms Deal," *Financial Times*, 12 March 1991, p. 4; "Hard-Pressed Czechs Retain Arms Trade," *New York Times*, 3 May 1991, p. A3).

I mentioned above, but tensions could also rise because of actual and severe conflicts of interest. There seems to be a consensus among Western analysts (not always shared by East Europeans) that the most likely near-term source of such conflicts of interest is ethnic/racial problems. If large minorities fall victim to serious human rights abuses and civil violence erupts, it seems doubtful that the violence could be contained within the borders of any single small country in Eastern Europe. Demands for intervention that would inevitably arise would be satisfied first through diplomacy and economic sanctions. If those failed, the question might quickly change from whether or not to use military forces, to whose military forces should be used. The worst outcome would be to have East European armies confront each other, even if they did so primarily for defensive purposes or to insulate their own countries from instability next door. Almost as bad would be to have individual West European states intervene on their own. I admit that there is little open sentiment today in Western Europe (and particularly among the Germans) for even thinking along these lines, but we should not lose sight of geography, history, or power. If there is no alternative mechanism for dealing with this latent problem, states will sooner or later develop their own capabilities in anticipation or in response.

NATO is a less bad alternative. The integrated military command is a logical place to coordinate and train Western armies assigned to the alliance for possible small-scale interventions in the East. Better still would be for NATO to rely on multinational forces that belong entirely to the alliance and not to individual states. Four such forces already exist: 3 are naval, and one is a rapid deployment brigade of 5,000 men drawn from several alliance countries including Germany. These forces are under the exclusive control of SACEUR and are the closest thing to a real military force under the sole authority of an international institution.[28] If expanded and trained for the most likely contingencies, NATO's multinational army could be a serious option for intervention in Eastern Europe. This again requires that NATO be pro-active. The need for military intervention may never arise, but having a viable capability ready under NATO command may slow or even stop the efforts of individual states to prepare themselves for such an eventuality. That dampening effect is likely to be most pronounced in states where domestic politics predispose against such action—most importantly Germany.

Would any of these responsibilities that I envision for NATO inhibit individual states' or international institutions' efforts at persuasion, the least intrusive method of attaining leverage? I do not think so. In fact, NATO can play a meaningful role in persuasion as well. NATO is not "first and foremost a political alliance," but it does have very important political components. The norm that member states can and should discuss any subject not purely of domestic interest that affects the alliance within NATO councils and use NATO as the first court of appeal for internecine disagreements is a powerful one and has been operating (sometimes under difficult circumstances) for forty some years. The NATO role in Greece and Turkey's extended quarrel over Cyprus is a good example. When Greek Cypriots of the Cyprus National Guard with the support of the junta in Athens overthrew Archbishop Makarios in July 1974 and seized control of the island, the North Atlantic Council met immediately and called on Greece and Turkey to "exercise the greatest restraint."[29] When Turkish forces invaded Cyprus on 20 July, an emergency Council meeting was convened within two hours, with both Greece and Turkey present.[30] After several more meetings, in which a cease-fire plan was discussed, amended, and finally agreed upon, the specter of full-scale war between Greece and Turkey, which had been quite real, began to fade. U.S. Secretary of State Henry Kissinger, while acknowledging that the cease-fire plan came essentially from Washington, credited "diplomatic efforts within the North Atlantic Treaty Organization" and the "complete unanimity" he had found there as critical factors in preventing war.[31] NATO in this crisis played at least the role of functional regime, facilitating emergency negotiations and smoothing the way toward a peace conference that met in Geneva for two sessions that summer.

NATO also facilitated the exercise of U.S. power over preferences that Washington would have found it awkward to articulate outside of an international institution. The United States was in an extremely delicate position, disapproving of the Greek military junta and its assertive behavior in Cyprus, but at the same time needy of bases on the Greek mainland for supporting the Sixth Fleet in the Mediterranean and keeping supply lines to the Middle

East open. While Washington proclaimed publicly its support for an independent Cyprus and the peaceful resolution of disputes, the North Atlantic Council could go further. On 17 July, the Council declared "broad support for the elected regime of President Makarios" and "general support" for the British demand to Athens that the Greek officers currently holding power in Cyprus be replaced.[32] The junta stepped down on 23 July, and on the same day Nikos Giorgiades Sampson, self-proclaimed president of Cyprus for about a week, yielded his office to Glafkos Clerides, president of the House of Representatives and a well-respected figure on the island.[33] U.S. endorsement of these changes again came in the form of declarations of support for NATO's role in consultations deemed critical in containing the crisis. While conceding damage to NATO's military strength on the southern flank, American officials argued that the crisis had actually strengthened the alliance in political terms by showing that it could mediate if not resolve a grave conflict of interest between two of its more belligerent members.[34]

NATO may have done more over the longer term, to the extent that the preservation of the institution itself remained a valued end for most of the allies. That end would for the others reassert itself powerfully in 1980, as the world began to look much less secure from Athens's perspective than it had in 1974. It is true that Greece withdrew from NATO's military structure in August 1974, following the allies' unwillingness to pressure Turkey to pull completely out of Cyprus. But the Greeks retained their political ties to NATO (on the French model) and moved to rejoin the integrated military command in 1980, with Turkish acquiescence.[35] Both states needed the alliance to bolster their security in the face of the Iranian revolution, the Soviet intervention in Afghanistan, the uncertain status of Yugoslavia after Tito, and the Iran-Iraq war. Turkey in particular sought U.S. and West European support for renewed efforts at domestic economic and political reform. The alliance, for its part, needed Greece and Turkey. More than fifteen years after the crisis erupted, Cyprus remains divided by the "Green Line," with an anomalous Turkish Republic of North Cyprus recognized only by Turkey. Ankara and Athens still disagree over the ultimate disposition of the island and how to manage relations between its Greek and Turkish inhabitants. But the two states have never gone to war over the issue, and they remain for all intents and purposes allies, if wary ones. NATO seems part of the explanation.

NATO has also acted as an autonomous source of ideas about security and defense matters for member states. The International Military Staff is empowered to initiate research and recommend policy on matters referred to it by any member government or NATO authority, including military commanders and other agencies. Although staff work in the past sometimes closely followed the logic of that year's Pentagon fashion, on some occasions the International Military Staff has generated important studies that acted as a source of new ideas, a source lying outside national boundaries.[36] The same is generally true of the NATO Political Affairs Division. Because ideas that evolve in this way would not be attached to any individual government, they would likely have a head start in gaining legitimacy among East European "targets." I do not mean to say that NATO can match the CSCE on this score. But when it comes to certain issues that fall within NATO's special competence—particularly matters of military doctrine and strategy—NATO's status can in fact be a source of legitimacy for ideas. That, in turn, contributes persuasive power to the alliance and to individual governments as well.

What I am proposing here is NATO as a major organ in a concert system, an ambitious concert that goes beyond what Castlereagh and Metternich managed to engineer. There will be other organs—the CSCE, the WEU, the EC, and even the EBRD have roles to play. It is a fair question whether these other organs could be expanded to do the tasks I assign to NATO, or if an institution "perfectly" adapted to those tasks could be created de novo. I think the answer is no.

WHY THE ALTERNATIVES WILL NOT WORK

Consider first the CSCE. With an institutional structure quite close to my ideal-type security community, the CSCE would be an excellent way to facilitate cooperation among states that already look alike and share a common set of interests. It can enhance the credibility of states' promises not to use force in their dealings with each other. But it cannot exert much leverage over states that are not yet ready for a security community.* To enforce conditionality or to venture into the realm of direct imposition, the CSCE would need a European Security Commission or a Security Council like that of the United Nations that could supersede the requirement for unanimity among all thrity-five members. Who would be on such a council and how would it take decisions? The answer to the first question would logically include the former Soviet states. The answer to the second would logically include unit veto by the major powers, even if a qualified majority voting rule were put into place.† Answer either of these questions differently and the "new" CSCE security organ starts to look very much like NATO. Why recreate what is already effectively in place?

The EC and WEU are more limited, "European" alternatives. If the problems and tasks I envision for security institutions were ten or twenty years in the future, both might be worth serious discussion. But it was only in March 1991 that Jacques Delors first dared to speak the phrases "common defense policy" and "amendments to the Treaty of Rome" in the same breath.[37] The furthest the EC seems likely to go in the foreseeable future is toward the French-German plan of February 1991, under which the European

---

*In case this point needs emphasizing, I cite the example of recent controversy over Soviet compliance with the CFE treaty. Moscow violated both the spirit and the letter of this agreement by moving nearly 20,000 tanks, 25,000 artillery pieces, and 15,000 armored vehicles east of the Urals prior to the signing of the treaty; after it was signed, the Soviets simply reclassified two divisions as naval infantry, exempting another 3,500 tanks, artillery, and armored vehicles from the agreement (Douglas Clarke, "Arms Control and Security: The Hope of A New Era after a Dramatic Year," Radio Free Europe\Radio Liberty, *Report on Eastern Europe*, 4 January 1991, p. 55.) The CSCE has done nothing substantial in response. It is the United States and NATO that pressed the complaint with Moscow. I do not mean to imply that these violations were militarily significant or that they signaled some kind of aggressive intent on the part of the Soviet Union; I do not think either is true. But the political impact on East-West relations and on the possibility of further arms control agreements is significant. It is essential for maintaining the West's willingness to cooperate with the East that we have some effective way to respond.

†As suggested by German Social Democrat Egon Bahr. In late June 1991, the CSCE adopted a new procedure whereby any thirteen member states can call an emergency meeting to discuss "major disruptions endangering peace, security, or stability," but unanimous consent is still required for any decisions to be taken. The Soviet Union was adamant that this procedure not be used to address "internal" or "domestic" issues.

Council would decide unanimously what areas of *foreign* policy should be made in common. It would then fall to foreign ministers to make that policy and implement it by majority vote. *Defense* and *security* policy could not be a part of the Community agenda at least until 1997, when the WEU is set to expire.*

The WEU itself gained some attention from its coordinating role among European naval forces in the recent Gulf War.† The French-German plan says that this kind of coordinating role should continue and that the WEU should move closer (both geographically and functionally) to the EC. The endpoint of this plan, date unspecified, is for the WEU to be absorbed into the Community as its defense and security arm. The British view of the WEU as an enhanced "Eurogroup," facilitating relations between the European members of NATO and the United States, is probably more realistic.** An important factor here may be lessons from the Gulf War that are usually spoken in hushed tones because of difficulties for the French. From political and military standpoints alike, Gaullism blew up in France's face.†† After some discreet probing of alternatives, President François

*I will not address the many sources of opposition to this plan; I simply mention it as the most ambitious proposal to date. I find it hard, in any event, to understand how states could delimit a common foreign policy from a defense and security policy since much of what will have to be done in foreign policy requires a credible threat to use force, if necessary, at some point in the process. It seems to me that the realm for common foreign policy-making would be so tightly delimited as to be nearly irrelevant.

†It has, of course, been in place ever since the Brussels Pact of 1947, when it was known as the Western Union. (The name changed when Germany joined in 1954.) Joseph Joffe describes it as a princess that has been kissed again and again by all sorts of suitors over the years but has never woken up.

**Britain presented its proposal a week after the French-German plan; see *Financial Times*, 28 February 1991. The British plan is to keep defense outside the Treaty of Rome and outside the Community, and to ensure the autonomy of the WEU so that it could act most effectively as a kind of coalition within NATO. Hence my reference to Eurogroup, formed of European NATO members in 1968 as a way of strengthening the bargaining hand of the European pillar. German Defense Minister Gerhard Stoltenberg endorsed this view in its essentials in a speech before the Elventh German-American Roundtable sponsored by the Konrad Adenauer Stiftung on 13 April 1991 in Washington, D.C.

††Some individuals in the French foreign ministry saw this coming for a long time. Others began to see it more clearly in spring 1990, when it was evident that the unification of Germany was only a few months away (see my "Security after 1989," in *The Future of Nuclear Weapons*, ed. Patrick Garrity [New York: Plenum Press, 1992]). France's experience in the Gulf War showed again the

Mitterrand in late spring 1991 moved back publicly to the traditional French line of opposition to America's privileged position in Europe. Yet given the right combination of face-saving devices (and the WEU might be one), some French move back toward NATO's military institutions looks increasingly plausible.

I do not mean to imply that other institutions have no role to play in European affairs or European security; quite the contrary. I argue only that NATO can do things that these other institutions cannot, and that some of those functions may be critical. I admit that NATO is not perfectly suited to any of these roles, and that it is in some sense a historical anachronism. But international institutions are rarely if ever the product of functional or utilitarian designs. An institution created de novo would not have the concentration of decision-making power within one state that NATO has. It would not have an integrated military command. It would not have the precedent of Germany's special status. And it might not have an effective nuclear deterrent that continues to provide a baseline confidence against the least likely but most dangerous contingencies of Eastern aggression. Sometimes, on closer examination, historical anachronisms start to look surprisingly valuable.

WHAT NATO THINKS ABOUT ALL THIS

NATO spent 1991 rethinking its own rationale, in a massive three-part study of future force structures and strategies.* There is some speculation and even more confusion about precisely what

---

less attractive side of Paris's independence and "freedom of action." French forces suffered operationally in the Gulf, particularly when it came to intelligence capabilities; the British and U.S. forces were better integrated as a result of working together in NATO (see "France Concedes Its Faults in War," *New York Times*, 8 May 1991). Even with access to allied intelligence, the aging French Jaguar underperformed the British Tornado and was put to shame by American military aircraft. From a political standpoint, France was not able to please or even appease its Arab friends, but it did manage to irritate the Western allies with its wavering, lukewarm support of the coalition. Finally, Paris's "freedom" to act autonomously and compete in selling arms and arms technology to Iraq-like states showed some of its uglier effects.

*The Council is carrying out part one, which focuses on broad political issues. Part two is a strategic review, tasked to formulate a new military strategy state-this study will produce, and much of what has appeared in public sources in the United States is simply the favored proposals of one or another think tank. It was not until the late spring that a few details about what was being thought and done in Brussels became available.

Stephen Hadley, U.S. Assistant Secretary of Defense for International Security Affairs, described in April 1991 an emerging consensus among the allies on four broad goals for the 1990s NATO. They are:

1. To deter a "residual" threat from the east, specifically from the former Soviet Union should failed reform there turn outwardly aggressive.
2. To preserve a long-term "balance of strategic power" in Europe. This means keeping in place mechanisms, infrastructures, and latent capabilities to reconstitute a substantial defense if Soviet power should recover.
3. To deter and defend NATO against "any other adversaries." Hadley offered in this context the specific example of Turkey's recent nervousness about Iraq.
4. To "create a security environment in Europe which . . . puts a resort to force between nations there off-limits."[38]

I was not surprised by Hadley's first and second goals, but the suggestion that the third and fourth were part of a consensus among the allies astounded me. I suspect there may be an accord on general language regarding these points, but I would be as surprised as anyone if those words turned out to reflect a deeper consensus on meaning. Still, in what we have since come to know about how NATO ministers intend to implement these general goals, there seems to be emerging what is indeed a surprising amount of agreement on some larger objectives.

The first details are in the area of force reduction. The Pentagon plans to prune U.S. deployments in Europe to two or three divisions and three tactical airwings by 1995 and to cut American forces in Europe overall by half toward the end of the decade. This is in line

ment consistent with the general goals outlined in the London Declaration (revamping "forward defense," no "early first use,"). Part three deals with specific military arrangements and is the responsibility of the military committee.

with NATO's plan for smaller but more mobile forces ready to mount a defense *of* the border instead of a defense *at* the border.[39] As part of this reorganization, the allies in April agreed on the need to create at least several multinational corps made up of three or four national divisions.* One multinational corps would be maintained at high readiness as a rapid deployment force that could be sent for action in NATO operations in a matter of days. Also in April, NATO's Military Committee agreed to recommend to the Council that this corps be set up as an expansion of NATO's current rapid deployment brigade—which, as noted, is under the exclusive control of the integrated military command and does not answer to individual governments.† I presume this is part of the apparatus designated for goals 3 and 4.

At the end of May, NATO defense ministers put their signatures to a reorganization scheme that went a good bit further. According to this plan, central front forces would be reduced to five corps, all of which would be multinational and manned partially by reserves.** A sixth corps under alternating German and Danish command would be placed astride the southern approaches to Denmark, while a fully German corps would be stationed on what used to be East German soil. The rapid deployment force proposed in April would be constituted as a multinational corps of between 50,000 and 70,000 troops deployed in Germany under British command.†† Washington agreed in principle that this rapid reaction force could be "double hatted,"—

---

*At this time, the proposal called for a total of four corps (only one or perhaps two of which would be multinational) to replace the eight allied corps that used to be lined up along the West German border (*The Economist*, 30 March 1991).

†The committee recommended expanding this brigade to a "corps-sized formation," between 70,000 and 100,000 troops. It would be headquartered in Germany, with a British commander. General Vigleik Eide of Norway, chairman of the committee, said (without naming names) that "most member countries had agreed to participate" ("NATO Agrees to Expand a Rapid Reaction Force," *New York Times*, 4 April 1991, sect. 1, p. 4). This plan was originally formulated by SACEUR, General John Galvin.

**Two corps would be commanded by Germany and one each by the United States, Holland, and Belgium. Each corps would be backed by "augmentation forces" kept in home countries ("A New Start," *The Economist*, 1 June 1991).

††This "rapid reaction force" would be ready for deployment in NATO area operations within 5–7 days. It would be spearheaded by a mobile brigade of about 5,000 troops ready to deploy in 72 hours.

i.e., a subset of it could eventually be made available to the WEU or some other European defense entity for use in out-of-area operations. At the same time, the United States successfully turned back French demands that the force be given its own intelligence and airlift facilities to make it potentially independent of NATO. Although the French did not agree to participate in the force and balked at several other features of the reorganization plan, Paris signed a NATO foreign ministers' communique in early June recognizing that "NATO [has] a particular position . . . and is the essential forum for consultation among the allies and the forum for agreement on policies bearing on the security and defense commitments of its members."[40] The final plan is scheduled to be approved by a meeting of the North Atlantic Council slated for November 1991 in Rome.

It may not make sense generally to develop force structures and strategies prior to solving basic political questions, but in this instance NATO appears to have successfully seized the initiative. Timing is significant in the U.S.-European security relationship. By announcing its radical reorganization plan in May and promising to pull together the details by November, NATO usurps primacy from the Community's discussions taking place within and around the intergovernmental conferences about a European defense identity. Now that debate will be framed in a NATO context. Throughout these discussions, the United States has made clear its interest that NATO retain an integrated military command, and despite some early talk of offering the post to some other national there is now explicit agreement among the allies that SACEUR should continue to be an American.[41] Regarding the sticky problem of how a new or revised "European defense identity" would relate operationally to SACEUR, Washington's official position remains that any European pillar institution attractive to the Europeans is acceptable to the United States so long as it is complementary to and does not detract from NATO.[42] That is also, roughly, the British position. The Germans are more relaxed about making allowances for the French, and it is in Paris where the crux of the problem lies. President Mitterrand at least has not yet budged in public from the Gaullist view that since the United States is in Europe for its own interests, the Europeans should make no concessions to keep it there. The solution may lie in constructing some sort of association between the WEU and NATO which would bring France into alliance military affairs de facto. The trick, of course, is to "find a way of giving the Europeans enough of a feeling that they can pursue security policies of their own without at the same time forming a European defense association that would drive the Americans away."[43] If there is in fact convergence around that goal and some shared understanding of what it means is developing (particularly between Paris and Washington), finding an acceptable arrangement to make it work will not be exceedingly hard.

Settling NATO's relationship to Eastern Europe may be a trickier problem. Czechoslovakia's aspirations to join NATO were confirmed when President Havel visited Brussels in March 1991, but his overtures met a cold shoulder. NATO has been equally aloof to flirtations from Hungary. The argument in Brussels and among the NATO governments is simple: while the East European states have reason to want to join the alliance and the alliance may have reason to want them, NATO must remain terribly wary of upsetting conservative elements in the former Soviet Union by absorbing Moscow's former allies. On 5 June 1991, NATO foreign ministers adopted a special statement on Eastern Europe which found a compromise: while not offering any promise of membership, NATO would increase significantly its military contacts with the East European states and move gradually to forge closer links with them. Where will this process end? In March, Havel told his hosts that "an alliance of countries united by the idea of freedom and democracy should not be forever closed to neighbouring countries that are pursuing the same goals."[44] Forever is a long time, and I suspect that Vaclav Havel's logic will prove compelling somewhat sooner than that.

CONCLUSION

There are many objections to what I propose in this paper. I leave it to others to discuss some of them—in particular, whether the NATO I prefer on the grounds of an "international relations argument" is or could be made consistent with the constraints of domestic politics in the most important states. Alternative institutional forms for pursuing security are available in Europe. Elsewhere, I have argued that NATO's institutional structure was not overdetermined in 1949, and that it is even less so today.[45] In the abstract, European security could become a game played by "clubs" of several states, bilateral alliances, or individual states protecting their borders with small arsenals of nuclear weapons. I believe that we would be heading in the wrong direction if one or more major players found the scheme I propose entirely illegitimate or deeply at odds with its conception of vital interests.

How likely is that? Germany and the main successor state of the Soviet Union, the RSFSR, seem the two candidate spoilers. I have yet to see much overt sympathy in Germany for a unilateral path to security. That may reflect the long-term impact of an international institution and an accompanying set of ideas that were put in place under American hegemony but sustained through forty years of changing power configurations through political and cognitive processes separate from power. NATO, on this logic, did some of the things that "reflectivists" claim international institutions can do.* Within NATO's peculiar mix of alliance and security community, security was linked to the domestic characteristics of states according to a set of propositions that fudged the distinction between second and third images of international relations. Security within NATO became joined to political standards of multiparty democracy, human rights, and economic freedoms—and to a broad mandate for peace management, social progress, and other kinds of positive cooperation between states. That linkage seems to have gained broad acceptance all over Europe, and in Germany most of all. There are aspects of NATO that irritate the Germans—e.g., a heavy military presence on its soil, substantial stockpiles of short-range nuclear weapons—but these can and will be mitigated by coming reforms. Unless the Germans are anxious to take on the East European problem and any potential Soviet problem on their own, NATO with its warts is still the best realistic alternative. I believe they are not currently anxious. And particularly if international institutions have had a lasting impact on conceptions of self-interest in security as elsewhere, there is no inexorable logic of international politics that will drive them to become so.

---

*Specifically, it changed the conceptions of self-interest among the vital actors, not just affecting the strategic context in which they interact with predetermined preferences (as the rationalists argue). Robert Keohane distinguishes between "rationalist" and "reflectivist" approaches in "International Institutions: Two Approaches," *International Studies Quarterly* 32 (December 1988): 379–96.

The case for Moscow's finding NATO legitimate has to be based on a more stark reckoning of interests. In 1989, the government of Mikhail Gorbachev seemed genuinely opposed to NATO and especially to the reunified Germany's membership in it, on the grounds that the end of the cold war made the alliance irrelevant. The Soviet government soon came to its senses and step by step removed any substantial conditions for the Two-plus-Four accord, leaving only a vague promise on the part of the West that it would work to create a new security system for all of Europe.[46] Thankfully, logic overcame what was left of ideology. The Soviet leaders (minus a few unreconstructed generals and their allies in the conservative factions) now recognize and acknowledge openly that NATO poses no threat to their vital security interests. In a future Europe, that threat could come realistically only from Germany, and it would have to be a nuclear Germany at that.* NATO is a barrier to both.[†] In the short term, the confederation replacing the Soviet Union will probably find it easier to negotiate arms control agreements with NATO than it would with three or four large and separate states. For these reasons, it is far better for Moscow to have NATO as its main interlocutor in European security than it would be to have an independent Germany, a German-dominated European coalition, or an uncoordinated set of powerful states. As is true for Germany, the things about NATO that irritate the Soviets can be made less irritating over time.** The counterargument, that efforts put into

*The independent republics of the former Soviet Union on the Western side would probably have a relationship to NATO similar to what I propose for Eastern Europe.

†A Germany secure within NATO is at the same time likely to be more (not less) conciliatory toward Moscow; the logic of the situation is not very different from Willy Brandt's *Ostpolitik* of the late 1960s. The new and more powerful Germany will be able to bring others along with it (or at least point them) toward more conciliatory positions as well. For example, the Germans have been the leading force among the Western allies ever since the Houston G-7 summit (summer 1990) on the question of emergency and long-term economic aid to the Soviet Union. The Germans were instrumental in pressing the EC to reinstate aid after it was suspended for about a month as a protest against the "occupation" of Lithuania in winter 1991. That story is likely to become a familiar one.

**The London Declaration takes some important first steps by calling for an end to forward defense and substantially reduced reliance on nuclear weapons. Subsequently, NATO extended invitations for the Soviet foreign minister to visit

NATO alienate and isolate the USSR and could incite a revanchist reaction there, is spurious and is brought forward to serve other purposes. The Soviet leadership understood and the Russian leadership understands that the threat to their country's security does not come from NATO.*

Finally, I do not want my argument confused with "narrow" definitions of "purely military ways of thinking about security" that have become a favorite intellectual target now that the cold war is over.† Security is also about preserving, enhancing, and even promoting a way of life. NATO cannot do that on its own, and that is why I see NATO as only one ingredient in a mixture of international institutions that will help states pursue security in the new Europe. I reject the idea that NATO's military demeanor must get in the way. It would indeed be hard to preserve what we see as a desirable way of life in an alliance that was drawing 20 percent of states' GNP into defense expenditures or otherwise deeply militarizing society. NATO never did that, and it never will.**

But certain "hard" components of security are necessary as a prerequisite for other, "softer" ones. They are even more necessary

---

Brussels; this could be extended at some point to a permanent liaison arrangement. American willingness to take the CSCE seriously also helps. Moscow has moved from seeing the CSCE as a political instrument of peaceful coexistence, to a collective security system in lieu of alliances, finally to a "process that should develop into an element that complements other institutions" (from translation of Jobst Echterling, "Soviet Views on the Future Design of European Security," *Bericht des Biost* 60 [1990]; given to me by George Breslauer).

*Early in the U.S. deployment in Saudi Arabia preparatory to the Gulf War, some Soviet generals expressed concern that U.S. or NATO forces might be tempted to intervene in a Soviet civil war. They were ridiculed and overruled by Gorbachev (see my "The United States, The Soviet Union, and Regional Conflicts"—note 4). It stretches the most florid imagination to conjure up a scenario under which NATO would consider such action, and there is much the alliance can and is doing in any case in the way of reassurance on this score.

†The target is in any event a caricature. I do not know any serious scholar who ever thought about security as just a conglomeration of bombs and rockets. Yet the concept of security, as Robert Powell points out eloquently, should not be broadened so much that it gets confused with the "national interest."

**Arguably, for much of the cold war period, NATO did precisely the opposite. Security in Western Europe was relatively cheap and unobtrusive for most of the member states relative to the magnitude of the threat they were facing from the East.

when the private sector is going to be responsible for most of the initiatives that promise to bring "soft" security to places that have not had it. Investment, economic development, and environmental programs do not take place naturally in regions that are territorially insecure. Will Western bankers and businessmen send money to Eastern Europe if those countries are vulnerable to political disruption from outside and from within? Will the United States and its allies share technology with states that could be part of an adversarial coalition a few years hence? Economic logic, theories of international politics, and history all say no. Yet it is easy to see how a failure to take such initiatives could contribute inadvertently to the outcomes we are all trying to avoid. NATO is not the perfect solution, but it can provide some of the prerequisites for moving forward with other parts of security-building. The fears that stand in the way of taking chances will not be removed by any international institution, but the NATO I propose will make the risks substantially smaller.

NOTES

I thank David Stuligross and Stephanie Gluckman for research assistance and valuable criticism, and Beverly Crawford and Felicia Wong for further criticisms of an earlier draft of this paper.

1. London Declaration on a Transformed North Atlantic Alliance, issued by Heads of State and Government participating in the meeting of the North Atlantic Council in London, 5–6 July 1990.

2. Kenneth Waltz, *Man, The State, and War* (New York: Columbia, 1954).

3. Kenneth Waltz, *Theory of International Politics* (Reading, Ma: Addison-Wesley, 1979); Stephen Walt, *The Origins of Alliance* (Ithaca: Cornell, 1987).

4. See my discussion of various strategies in "The United States, the Soviet Union, and Regional Conflicts after the Cold War," in *Beyond the Cold War: Conflict and Cooperation in the Third World*, ed. George W. Breslauer, Harry Kreisler, and Benjamin Ward (Berkeley: International and Area Studies, 1991).

5. See Michael W. Doyle: "Kant, Liberal Legacies, and Foreign Affairs," *Philosophy and Public Affairs* 12 (Summer 1983): 205–35, and "Kant, Liberal Legacies, and Foreign Affairs, Part II," *Philosophy and Public Affairs* 12 (Fall 1983): 322–53. There is good support for the more moderate claim that democracies find it

more difficult to decide to use military force than do other kinds of states. Given the particular character of state-society relations in many European democracies and in the United States at the end of the twentieth century, I would add that the reluctance of democracies to resort to force will tend to be most pronounced when motives are internationalist and not parochial to the state.

6. Accompanies the signing of the Conventional Forces in Europe (CFE) Treaty in Paris, 19–21 November 1990.

7. Jack Snyder, "Averting Anarchy in the New Europe," *International Security* 14 (Spring 1990): 5–41.

8. See Weber, "The United States, the Soviet Union, and Regional Conflicts" (note 4). Thanks to Peter Cowhey for making me think about the problem in this way.

9. I discuss the evolution of NATO as an institution in *Multilateralism in NATO: Shaping the Postwar Balance of Power 1949–1961* (Berkeley: International and Area Studies, 1991).

10. As NATO propaganda goes to great pains to point out. See, for example, *NATO: Facts and Figures* (Brussels: NATO Information Service, 1989), p. 321.

11. *Ibid.*, p. 351. With certain important exceptions which I will describe below.

12. *Ibid.*, p. 263.

13. On functional regimes, see Robert Keohane, *After Hegemony* (Princeton: Princeton University Press, 1984).

14. An exception is made for legal or economic disputes where there are other specialized international agencies with specific competencies in the area of the disagreement (*NATO: Facts and Figures*, p. 187).

15. As a slight concession to the French, the United States did agree to consult informally with regional planning groups for Western Europe, Northern Europe, and Southern Europe–Western Mediterranean. See Report of the Working Group on Organization of the North Atlantic Council, *Foreign Relations of the United States 1949*, vol. 4, pp. 322–36. Cited hereafter as *FRUS*.

16. Of course perceptions started to change among the Washington elite somewhat earlier; but the Korean War was the decisive event for American policy. Deborah Larson, *Origins of Containment: A Psychological Explanation* (Princeton: Princeton University Press, 1985), chronicles the change in perceptions among a few key individuals. I stress the importance of the spring 1948 Communist coup in Czechoslovakia in *Multilateralism in NATO*, pp. 25–29.

17. North Atlantic Council Resolution, 26 September 1950; in Acheson to Webb, *FRUS 1950*, vol. 3, p. 350.

18. *FRUS 1952–54*, vol. 5, pp. 1443–45. These numbers have of course been superseded by recent agreements.

19. *NATO: Facts and Figures*, p. 46. Note that in the Protocol to the North Atlantic Treaty on the Accession of the Federal Republic of Germany, 23 October 1954, there is a special statement to the effect that Germany will "refrain from any

action inconsistent with the strictly defensive character of the [North Atlantic] treaty." No other country merits such special attention. This constraint is reinforced strongly by tradition and weakly by provisions within the German Basic Law—although the precise legal and political implications of those provisions became controversial in the wake of the Gulf War.

20. See Article 5, which states that "only German territorial defense units which are not integrated into the alliance structures to which German armed forces in the rest of German territory are assigned will be stationed in that territory" (U.S. Department of State, *Foreign Policy Bulletin*, November/December 1990, p. 4).

21. Jamie Shea, *NATO 2000: A Political Agenda for a Political Alliance* (London: Brassey's, 1990), p. 51. Shea is Special Projects Officer, NATO Political Directorate, Brussels.

22. *NATO: Facts and Figures*, pp. 78, 85–87, 95, 191. In March 1988, the North Atlantic Council issued a declaration, "Conventional Arms Control: The Way Ahead," which was developed into a comprehensive "Statement on Conventional Arms Control" in December. This NATO document formed the basis of the mandate for the CFE talks and new Confidence and Security Building Measures negotiations, both of which began in March 1989 (*ibid.*, pp. 236–39).

23. *The Economist* quotes Czech Foreign Minister Jiri Dienstbier as laughing at the notion of "military doctrine. . . . It makes sense for the United States. But for Czechoslovakia?" (30 March 1991, p. 43). He may not be laughing for long.

24. Thomas Schelling raised this line of argument in discussions in January 1990.

25. *The Economist*, 30 March 1991.

26. For examples and explanation, see Lisa Martin, *Coercive Cooperation: Explaining Economic Sanctions* (forthcoming).

27. For a general discussion of "policy legitimacy," see Alexander L. George, "Domestic Constraints on Regime Change in U.S. Foreign Policy: The Need for Policy Legitimacy," in *Change in the International System*, ed. Ole Holsti, Randolph Siverson, and Alexander George (Boulder, Colo.: Westview, 1980).

28. *NATO: Facts and Figures*, pp. 351–52.

29. "NATO Meets on Cyprus Crisis: Backs an Appeal for Restraint," *New York Times*, 17 July 1974.

30. "NATO Urges Talks," *New York Times*, 21 July 1974.

31. Robert D. McFadden, "U.N. Reports Cyprus Cease-Fire," *New York Times*, 23 July 1974; "Soviet Challenges Kissinger," *New York Times*, 24 July 1974.

32. "NATO Meets on Cyprus Crisis" (note 29); "Showdown on Cyprus," *New York Times*, 18 July 1974. Greece, present at the NATO Council meeting that adopted this resolution, abstained.

33. "Government Who Deposed Makarios Is Replaced: Junta's Rule Ends," *New York Times*, 24 July 1974; "Cyprus Unity Bid: Sampson Turns Over His Presidency to Parliament Chief," *New York Times*, 24 July 1974.

34. "Soviet Challenges Kissinger" (note 31); "Now Some Good News," *New York Times*, 24 July 1974; "NATO's Cyprus Score," *New York Times*, 30 July 1974.

35. "Greece Rejoins the Military Wing of NATO after a Six-Year Absence," *New York Times*, 21 October 1980.

36. The several studies of NATO's requirement for an autonomous MRBM capability in the latter half of the 1950s are a prominent example. John Steinbruner, *The Cybernetic Theory of Decision* (Princeton: Princeton University Press, 1974), discusses these studies; I add a few details in *Multilateralism in NATO* (note 9).

37. Albeit in a visible forum—the Alastair Buchan lecture at IISS, reported in *Financial Times*, 8 March 1991, p. 1.

38. From comments delivered at the Eleventh German-American Roundtable, 13 April 1991.

39. This is the wording of Secretary of Defense Richard Cheney, who also spoke at the Eleventh German-American Roundtable in April 1991. He did not say precisely to which "border" he was referring.

40. *New York Times*, 8 June 1991, p. 6.

41. *The Economist*, 30 March 1991; confirmed by Cheney at the German-American Roundtable.

42. Reginald Bartholomew set out this position in a tersely worded letter to the European allies in February. Secretary of State James Baker reaffirmed it with equal vehemence in April.

43. *The Economist*, 30 March 1991.

44. *Europe*, April 1991, p. 22.

45. In *Multilateralism in NATO* (note 9). Multilateralism (as I define it in that piece) is not in any sense a necessary outcome of the changing security and power environment in Europe, then or now. For example, if Mearsheimer's logic is sound, we would expect to see states nervously guarding their autonomy and searching for more reliable ways to safeguard their security in this newly multipolar world.

46. See *New York Times*, 31 May 1990, p. A1; "Bush-Gorbachev Talks: A View to the Future," *Washington Post*, 3 June 1990, p. A 24.

INDEX

Abreu, Dilip, 91
Adenauer, Konrad, 224, 226, 241
Adler, Emanuel, 21, 27, 28, 35
Afghanistan, 232, 331
Aggression, 189–91
Agh, Attila, 55
Aid, 203–4, 312, 334, 390n
Airbus, 94, 95, 135
Air France, 94
Albania, 6, 55, 306, 349, 350, 351
Alliances, 8–9, 16, 34–37, 295, 363–68
Allison, Graham, 203n, 334
Alt, James, 90
Amalgamated security communities, 291, 295
Antall, Josef, 60, 69, 73, 273n, 280–81
Arbatov, Alexei B., 16–17, 20–21, 32
Argentina, 109, 132n
Armenia, 6, 198
Arms control: advances in, 153–54, 161, 251; under bipolarity/multipolarity, 8, 17; via CSCE, 35, 162–68, 307, 311, 350; via NATO, 36, 42–43, 257–58, 360, 374, 385–86; Soviet stance on, 331–32, 382. *See also* Nuclear arms/deterrence
Arms exports, 15, 67–69, 71–72, 376, 377n
Art, Robert, 3
Aslund, Anders, 203n
ASW, 167
Australia, 132n, 136
Austria, 58, 99, 196, 314; international memberships/alignments of, 10, 66, 283, 301, 336, 338; relations with Eastern Europe of, 71, 274, 352
Azerbaijan, 188, 202n

Bahr, Egon, 44, 382n
Bahrain, 69
Baker, James, 57, 202n, 257, 299–301
Baksay, Jozef, 69
Balcerowicz, Leszek, 272n

Balkan Pact, 9, 59
Ballistic missile defenses (BMD), 160
Baltic republics, 6, 156, 164, 252, 255
"Bandwagoning," 180
Basket One (CSCE), 306, 309–11
Basket Two (CSCE), 306, 307, 311–14
Basket Three (CSCE), 306, 314–15
Bates, Robert, 102
Belarus, 147. *See also* Belorussia
Belgium, 99, 131, 316, 386n
Belorussia, 66, 156, 164. *See also* Belarus
Berlin Wall, 226
Bernhardi, Friedrich von, 180
Bernheim, R. Douglas, 90–92
Bipolarity: effects of dissolution of, 1, 9, 11, 16; reinforcement of peace via, 8, 152, 170, 192, 298–99; in security system, 161, 250
Blackwill, Robert, 203n
Blagovolin, S., 51
BMD. *See* Ballistic missile defenses
Borrus, Michael, 13
Bosnia-Herzegovina, 196
Boundaries/borders: and conditionality, 200–201; contested/changing, 3, 5, 192, 196–97, 265, 375; ideological 5–6, 21–22, 171–72, 266; as threats to security, 1, 3–7, 27, 31
Bozo, Frédéric, 44, 47
Brandt, Willy, 390n
Bretton Woods system, 107
Brezhnev Doctrine, 332
Brunswick International Schoolbook Institute, 184
Brussels Treaty, 57, 383n
Bulgaria: arms/troop restructuring in, 24–25; and East-West relations, 61, 116; economic relations of, 98, 100, 102–3, 111–14, 313–14; ethnic minority problems of, 6, 157, 252; reforms in, 308, 310, 315
Bull, Hedley, 289
Bunce, Valerie, 28, 29

INSIGHTS IN INTERNATIONAL AFFAIRS SERIES

1. *Confrontation in the Gulf: University of California Professors Talk about the War.* Ed. Harry Kreisler. $7.95

2. *Refugees: A Multilateral Response to Humanitarian Crises.* Sadako Ogata. $5.95

3. *American Intervention after the Cold War.* Robert W. Tucker. $3.95

4. *Crisis in the Balkans.* Eugene A. Hammel, Irwin M. Wall, & Benjamin N. Ward. $6.95

CENTERS FOR SOUTH & SOUTHEAST ASIA STUDIES
MONOGRAPH SERIES

32. *Scavengers, Recyclers, & Solutions for Solid Waste Management in Indonesia.* Daniel T. Sicular. $16.50

33. *Indonesian Transmigrants and Adaptation: An Ecological Anthropological Perspective.* Oekan S. Abdoellah. $14.95

34. *Thai Music and Musicians in Contemporary Bangkok.* Pamela Myers-Moro. $22.50

35. *In the Shadow of Change: Images of Women in Indonesian Literature.* Tineke Hellwig. $22.00

OCCASIONAL PAPERS SERIES

15. *The Penis Inserts of Southeast Asia: An Annotated Bibliography with an Overview & Comparative Perspective.* Donald E. Brown, J. W. Edwards, & R. P. Moore. $6.00

16. *Patterns of Migration in Southeast Asia.* Ed. Robert R. Reed. $19.50

17. *Bridging Worlds: Studies on Women in South Asia.* Ed. Sally J. M. Sutherland. $17.50

18. *Essays on Southeast Asian Performing Arts: Local Manifestations and Cross-Cultural Implications.* Ed. Kathy Foley. $14.95

LANGUAGE TEACHING MATERIALS

Devavanipravesika: Introduction to the Sanskrit Language. Robert P. Goldman & Sally J. Sutherland. $23.50

Teaching Grammar of Thai. William Kuo. $23.50

Tamil for Beginners, 2 vols. Kausalya Hart. $12.50 ea.